Financial Crime in the 21st Century

Financial Crime in the 21st Century

Law and Policy

Nicholas Ryder

University of the West of England, UK

Edward Elgar
Cheltenham, UK • Northampton, MA, USA

Published by
Edward Elgar Publishing Limited
The Lypiatts
15 Lansdown Road
Cheltenham
Glos GL50 2JA
UK

Edward Elgar Publishing, Inc.
William Pratt House
9 Dewey Court
Northampton
Massachusetts 01060
USA

A catalogue record for this book
is available from the British Library

Library of Congress Control Number: 2010939194

ISBN 978 1 84844 324 2 (cased)

Typeset by Servis Filmsetting Ltd, Stockport, Cheshire
Printed and bound by MPG Books Group, UK

Contents

Contributors

Andrew H. Baker, Liverpool John Moores University
and
Dr Karen Harrison, University of Hull

Abbreviations

AML	anti-money laundering
ARA	Assets Recovery Agency
CFI	Court of First Instance
CTR	Currency Transaction Report
ECJ	European Court of Justice
EU	European Union
FATF	Financial Action Task Force
FBI	Federal Bureau of Investigation
FinCEN	Financial Crimes Enforcement Network
FIU	Financial Intelligence Unit
FSA	Financial Services Authority
IMF	International Monetary Fund
MLR	Money Laundering Regulations
OFAC	Office of Foreign Assets Control
SAR	Suspicious Activity Report
SEC	Securities and Exchange Commission
SFO	Serious Fraud Office
SOCA	Serious Organized Crime Agency
UN	United Nations

Preface

Financial crime has gained increased notoriety since the international community recognized the problems posed by money laundering in the 1980s. Since the introduction of the first anti-money laundering initiatives in the late 1980s, different types of financial crime have gained international recognition. For example, the terrorist attacks on 11 September 2001 resulted in the instigation of the 'financial war on terrorism' by President George Bush. Similarly, the collapse of Barings Bank, Enron and WorldCom and the threat posed by mortgage fraud during the financial crisis have propelled fraud to the top of many countries' financial crime policies. Insider trading has also become a significant problem to the global financial services sector. This work focuses on the financial crime policies adopted by the international community and how these have been implemented in the United Kingdom and the United States of America. Furthermore, it also considers the appropriateness of confiscation and forfeiture of the proceeds of crime. The work also focuses on the financial crime agencies in both jurisdictions and the effectiveness of their sentencing policies towards financial crime. The objective of this work is to recommend a 'model financial crime policy' based on a detailed analysis of the measures discussed in this book.

Acknowledgements

There are many people who I would like to thank who have helped me during the writing of this book. Firstly, I would like to thank the colleagues and friends who reviewed early draft chapters especially Clare Chambers, Karen Harrison, Miriam Goldby, Sabine Hassler, Lachmi Singh, Robert Stokes and Umut Turksen. The usual caveat applies for all errors and omissions. This book would not appear in its present form without the kind assistance and support of the Department of Law, University of the West of England. The final acknowledgement goes to my wife Ruth and son Ethan, without whose support, love and understanding this book would not have been possible and it is to them that I dedicate this book.

1. Introduction

1.1 FINANCIAL CRIME – IN CONTEXT

When President Richard Nixon declared 'war' on the illegal drug cartels in the 1970s by targeting their proceeds of crime, no one could have foreseen that four decades later the 'war' would become global and fought on many fronts. Financial crime has evolved into a multifaceted business or industry with a global reach and is commonly associated with the illegal drugs trade, human trafficking, organized criminals and terrorists. It has become a global problem that demands a global response. Financial crime gained notoriety in the 1980s when money laundering was propelled to the top of the international community's agenda by the United States of America (US) following its battle with the drugs trade. Resultantly, the United Nations (UN) introduced a series of legal instruments designed to tackle the problems associated with money laundering. Additionally, the Financial Action Task Force (FATF) was established with the purpose of making a series of recommendations aimed at tackling money laundering. The terrorist attacks on 11 September 2001 transformed the way in which the international community tackled financial crime and efforts moved from money laundering to terrorist financing after President George Bush instigated the 'financial war on terror'. The terrorist attacks resulted in the introduction of several UN Security Council Resolutions and the enactment of a plethora of statutory measures by nation states. Fraud has recently emerged from the shadow of money laundering and terrorist financing following several high profile instances of fraudulent activities involving multinational corporations.[1] The impact and scale of these scandals are overshadowed by a new threat to the financial markets in the US and the United Kingdom (UK) – mortgage fraud.[2] Furthermore, insider dealing materialized in the

---

[1]   This includes for example the Bank of Credit and Commerce International, Barings Bank, Enron and WorldCom.
[2]   Ryder, Nicholas and Chambers, Clare (2010), 'The credit crunch and mortgage fraud – too little too late? A comparative analysis of the policies adopted in the United States of America and the United Kingdom' in S. Kis and I. Balogh (eds), *Housing, housing costs and mortgages: trends, impact and prediction*, Nova Science, New York, pp. 1–22.

US in the 1970s following the Ivan Boesky affair,[3] yet although its existence in the UK was documented in the 1950s and 1960s,[4] it was not until 1980 that insider dealing was criminalized in the UK.[5]

1.2   WHAT IS FINANCIAL CRIME?

According to the International Monetary Fund (IMF), 'there is no internationally accepted definition of financial crime' and it 'interprets financial crime in a broad sense, as any non-violent crime resulting in a financial loss'.[6] However, they did admit that 'while there seems to be broad agreement on the meaning of such concepts as money laundering, corruption, and tax evasion, the terms financial abuse and financial crime are far less precise'.[7] It has been suggested that in its broadest context financial crime has been 'used to refer to any type of illegal activity that results in a pecuniary loss. This would include violent crimes against the person or property such as armed robbery or vandalism'.[8] Conversely, 'the term has been used in a more narrow sense to refer only to those instances where a nonviolent crime resulting in a pecuniary loss crime also involves a financial institution'.[9] Financial crime has also been referred to as 'white collar crime'; a term first used by Professor Edwin Sutherland which has since 'become synonymous with the full range of frauds committed by business and government professionals'.[10] More recently the Department of Treasury and HM Treasury have referred to financial

---

[3]   For a more detailed discussion see Hatch, J. (1987), 'Logical inconsistencies in the SEC's enforcement of insider trading: guidelines for a definition', *Washington and Lee Law Review*, **44**, 935–954.

[4]   Financial Services Authority (2007d), 'Insider dealing in the city', Speech by Margaret Cole at the London School of Economics, 17 March 2007, available at http://www.fsa.gov.uk/pages/Library/Communication/Speeches/2007/0317_mc.shtml (accessed 10 June 2009).

[5]   Companies Act 1980, ss. 69–73.

[6]   International Monetary Fund *Financial system abuse, financial crime and money laundering – background paper* (International Monetary Fund: Washington, DC, 2001) at p. 5.

[7]   *Ibid.*, at 3.

[8]   International Monetary Fund above, n 6 at 20.

[9]   *Ibid.*, at 20.

[10]   Federal Bureau of Investigation (n/d), 'White collar crime', available at http://www.fbi.gov/whitecollarcrime.htm (accessed 1 March 2009). For a more detailed discussion see Sutherland, Edwin (1949), *White Collar Crime*, The Dryden Press, New York, Hanning, P. (1993), 'Testing the limits of investigating and prosecuting white collar crime: how far will the courts allow prosecutors to go?',

crime as 'illicit finance'.[11] Within the UK, a useful starting point is the Financial Services and Markets Act 2000 (FSMA 2000), which states that financial crime includes 'any offence involving fraud or dishonesty; misconduct in, or misuse of information relating to, a financial market; or handling the proceeds of crime'.[12] Fleming noted that 'financial crime as defined by the FSMA relates to a broad and potentially indistinct range of offences'.[13] Financial crime has been referred to as a 'victimless crime' and sometimes it is impossible to identify who or what has suffered a financial loss.[14] If this statement is to be believed, why do so many governments dedicate resources and time to limit financial crime? The answer to this question is found in the following quote from the FATF, 'criminal proceeds have the power to corrupt and ultimately destabilise communities or whole national economies'.[15] Furthermore, financial crime is attributed to organized criminals who seek to maximize their profits so that they can enjoy a so-called 'champagne lifestyle',[16] and it can erode the integrity of a nation's financial institutions.[17] Vaithilingam and Nair stated that 'financial-related crimes have significant economic and social consequences for nations worldwide. It weakens the financial systems which are the main players for global financial transactions'.[18] It is also a threat to national security because terrorists need money and resources to carry out their illegal activities.[19] Although much of the finance for terrorism comes

---

University of Pittsburgh Law Review, **54**, 405–476 and Strader, J. (1999), 'The judicial politics of white collar crime', *Hastings Law Journal*, **50**, 1199–1273.

[11] Department of Treasury (n/d), 'Fighting illicit finance', available at http://www.ustreas.gov/topics/law-enforcement/index.shtml (accessed 16 April 2010) and HM Treasury (n/d), 'Counter illicit finance', available at http://www.hm-treasury.gov.uk/fin_money_index.htm (accessed 16 April 2010).

[12] Financial Services and Markets Act 2000, s. 6(3).

[13] Fleming, M. *FSA's Scale & Impact of Financial Crime Project (Phase One): Critical Analysis Occasional Paper Series 37* (Financial Services Authority: London, 2009) at p. 2.

[14] For a more detailed commentary see Hansen, L. (2009), 'Corporate financial crime: social diagnosis and treatment', *Journal of Financial Crime*, **16**(1), 28–40.

[15] Financial Action Task Force *Report on Money Laundering and Terrorist Financing Typologies 2003–2004* (Financial Action Task Force: Paris, 2004).

[16] National Audit Office *The Assets Recovery Agency – Report by the Comptroller and Auditor General* (National Audit Office: London, 2007) at p. 4.

[17] International Monetary Fund above, n 6 at 8.

[18] Vaithilingam, S. and Nair, M. (2007), 'Factors affecting money laundering: lesson for developing countries', *Journal of Money Laundering Control*, **10**(3), 352–366, at 353.

[19] See Ryder, N. (2007a), 'A False Sense of Security? An Analysis of Legislative Approaches Towards the Prevention of Terrorist Finance in the United States and the United Kingdom', *Journal of Business Law*, 821–850.

from legitimate sources a large percentage stems from criminal activities; a good example of this is the terrorist attacks in September 2001 where some of the finances were obtained from credit card fraud and identity theft.[20]

What is the extent of financial crime? It is important to note that despite the best efforts of such agencies as the UN, the FATF and nation states, it is impossible to accurately state the extent of financial crime. It is simply fraught with too many methodological difficulties. However, it is possible to refer to official documentation that offers an intriguing insight into the estimated levels of different types of financial crime. For example, the FATF, citing the IMF, stated that between 2 and 5 per cent of the world's gross domestic product (GDP) is associated with money laundering, which equates to $590bn and $1.5tn.[21] According to the Treasury Department, the estimated amount of money laundered in the US is approximately $600bn per year,[22] while Mitchell claimed that the figure is nearer $300bn.[23] Therefore, it has been estimated that 99.9 per cent of the proceeds of crime is successfully laundered.[24] According to HM Treasury 'organised crime generates over £20bn of social and economic harm in the UK each year'.[25] In 2004, the Home Office stated that organized crime 'reaches into every community, ruining lives, driving other crime and instilling fear'.[26] According to the FATF:

---

[20]   The 9/11 Commission *The 9/11 Commission Report – Final Report of the National Commission on Terrorist Attacks upon the United States* (Norton & Company: London, 2004) at p. 170.

[21]   Financial Action Task Force (n/d), 'Money laundering FAQ', available at http://www.fatf-gafi.org/document/29/0,3343,en_32250379_32235720_33659613_1_1_1_1,00.html (accessed 13 January 2010).

[22]   Weller, P. and Roth von Szepesbela, K. (2004), 'Silence is golden – or is it? FINTRAC and the suspicious transaction reporting requirements for lawyers', *Asper Review of International Business and Trade Law*, **4**, 85–130, at 86.

[23]   Mitchell, D. (2003), 'US Government agencies confirm that low-tax jurisdictions are not money laundering havens', *Journal of Financial Crime*, **11**(2), 127–133, at 128.

[24]   Baker, R. (1999), 'Money Laundering and Flight Capital: The Impact on Private Banking', testimony before the Permanent Subcommittee on Investigations, Committee on Governmental Affairs, US Senate, 10th November, 1999, available at http://www.brookings.edu/testimony/1999/1110financialservices_baker.aspx (accessed 2 August 2010).

[25]   HM Treasury *The financial challenge to crime and terrorism* (HM Treasury: London, 2007) at p. 6.

[26]   Home Office *One Step Ahead – A 21st Century Strategy to Defeat Organised Crime* (Home Office: London, 2004b) at p. 1.

UK law enforcement estimates the economic and social costs of serious organised crime, including the costs of combating it, at upwards of £20bn a year. It is estimated that the total quantified organised crime market in the UK is worth about £15bn per year as follows: drugs (50%); excise fraud (25%); fraud (12%); counterfeiting (7%); organised immigration crime (6%).[27]

Financial crime has an adverse impact on the economies of countries. For example, Scanlan noted the economic impact of terrorism and stated that 'the disruption to the transport system in London caused by the bomb attacks of 7 and 21 July 2005 alone have been estimated to have cost the nation in excess of £3bn'.[28] Similarly, the Bishopsgate bomb in London in 1993 caused damage to property in excess of £1bn.[29]

1.3 RATIONALE

The aim of the book is to provide a detailed commentary and analytical review of the financial crime policies adopted by the international community and how these have been implemented in the UK and the US. A question that needs to be addressed is why this book concentrates on the US and the UK. The US was one of the first countries to tackle and criminalize different types of financial crime, and it is an integral player in the development and implementation of the international community's financial crime policies. The book illustrates the role of the US in the implementation of a number of international legal instruments designed to tackle money laundering and terrorist financing. Furthermore, through the Department of Treasury, the US has played a key role in the creation of the FATF. Another reason why the US is utilized is the importance of its financial services and banking sector and the threat posed to it by financial crime. There are approximately 1800 chartered commercial banks with $6tn assets, over 900 state chartered banks with $1.3tn assets, over 5200 commercial and savings banks with $2tn assets in addition to a large number of savings associations and over 8500 credit unions. The same

---

[27] Financial Action Task Force *Summary of third mutual evaluation report: anti-money laundering and combating the financing of terrorism – United Kingdom of Great Britain and Northern Ireland* (Financial Action Task Force: Paris, 2007) at pp. 1–2.

[28] Scanlan, G. (2006), 'The enterprise of crime and terror – the implications for good business. Looking to the future – old and new threats', *Journal of Financial Crime*, **13**(2), 164–176, at 164.

[29] HM Treasury *Combating the financing of terrorism* (HM Treasury: London, 2002) at p. 11.

can also be said about the US securities sector which has \$5.4tn in assets and \$256bn in capital.[30] During his eight-year tenure, President George Bush's administration was forced to tackle a large number of corporate frauds and terrorist financing which led to the introduction of a plethora of legislative provisions, the creation of numerous fraud task forces and the instigation of the financial war on terror. Therefore, important comparisons are sought with the policies adopted by President Barak Obama toward financial crime and those implemented by President George Bush.

The UK has adopted a robust stance toward financial crime and it shares the lead role with the US in the global fight against financial crime. The UK has fully implemented its international money laundering, terrorist financing, fraud and insider dealing obligations and acted as the president of the FATF in 2007. There have also been significant developments in the UK policies towards money laundering, fraud and terrorist financing including the creation of the Serious Organized Crime Agency (SOCA), the impact of the decision of the Supreme Court in *A v HM Treasury*[31] on its terrorist financing policy and the fraud policy implemented by the former government following the recommendations of the Fraud Review. The proposed creation of a 'super economic crime agency' by the coalition government also makes this a timely review of the UK's financial crime strategies. The most significant factor for using the UK is the importance of its financial services and banking sector to its economy. The economic functions of the financial services sector can be divided into three broad categories – matching savers, borrowers and investment through the investment chain; risk pooling and management; and facilitating payments.[32] From an historical perspective, London's importance as the centre of the global financial services sector can be traced to the twelfth century.[33] Blair took the view that 'the process of internationalisation received an important boost in London's "big bang" in the mid 1980s . . . which led to enormous inward investment'.[34] Furthermore, there are more companies listed on the London Stock Exchange than the Tokyo or

---

[30]   Financial Action Task Force *Third mutual evaluation report anti-money laundering and combating the financing of terrorism – United States of America* (Financial Action Task Force: Paris, 2006) at p. 10.

[31]   UKSC 2.

[32]   HM Treasury *The UK financial services sector: rising to the challenges and opportunities of globalisation* (HM Treasury: London, 2005) at p. 5.

[33]   For a general discussion see Davies, Glyn (2002), *A history of money from ancient times to the present day*, University of Wales Press, Cardiff; Ferguson, Niall (2008), *The ascent of money*, Allen Lane, London.

[34]   Blair, W. (1998), 'The reform of financial regulation in the UK', *Journal of International Banking Law*, **13**(2), 43–49, at 43.

New York stock exchanges.[35] HM Treasury reported that 'the UK financial services sector also contributes directly to output, employment, trade and productivity in the UK. It accounts for over 5 per cent of UK gross value added, one million jobs and a trade surplus of 1.6 per cent of GDP. Moreover, there is evidence that it is a source of higher-than-average productivity within the UK, and that productivity within the sector is growing faster than in the economy as a whole'.[36] The British Bankers Association reported that 'the UK's financial industry has grown faster than any other business sector over the past ten years'.[37] Its Chief Executive stated that 'financial services are the powerhouse of the UK economy: a massive contributor to the Exchequer through tax, an employer of more than a million people directly and one of the UK's last acknowledged world-leading industries'.[38] The UK has a long history of financial scandals that have plagued the overall effectiveness of its financial crime strategy and important comparisons can be made between the policy approaches adopted in the UK and the US.

1.4   CONTENTS OVERVIEW

The book concentrates on four types of financial crime: money laundering, terrorist financing, fraud and insider dealing. The second chapter critically reviews the anti-money laundering policies in both the US and the UK in light of the measures introduced by the international community. It is the author's contention that the US anti-money laundering strategies can be divided into two parts – the criminalization of money laundering and reporting identifiable or suspected money laundering transactions to the relevant authorities. The UK's policy can be divided into three parts: the criminalization of money laundering; regulated financial institutions being compelled to put in place systems to preclude and identify money laundering; and reporting identifiable or suspected money laundering transactions to the relevant authorities. Chapter 3 deals with terrorist financing and it is the author's contention that the US and the UK terrorist financing policy can be divided into three parts – the criminalization of terrorist financing; the ability to freeze the assets of known

---

[35]   HM Treasury above, n 32 at 9.
[36]   *Ibid.*, at 18.
[37]   British Bankers Association (2008), 'Financial services sector tops UK growth tables', Press Release 18 January 2008, available at http://www.bba.org.uk/bba/jsp/polopoly.jsp?d=1569&a=12022 (accessed 9 June 2009).
[38]   *Ibid.*

or suspected terrorists; and the reporting of suspicious transactions. There is a link between terrorist financing and fraud. Several commentators have suggested that terrorists use this type of financial crime to fund their activities.[39] Furthermore, fraud is the 'crime of choice for organised criminals',[40] and it must be taken seriously. Therefore, the fourth chapter investigates the anti-fraud policies adopted in the US and the UK. The development of a global anti-fraud policy is difficult to determine because unlike money laundering and terrorist financing, there is no international instrument from either the UN or the EU that targets fraud. Both have concentrated their efforts on fraudulent activities on their own finances. The international community has had no impact on the US anti-fraud policy and only a minimal impact on the UK's strategy. The chapter concludes that the US and the UK anti-fraud policy can be divided into three parts – criminalization of fraudulent activities; regulatory agencies; and anti-fraud reporting requirements.

The fifth chapter of this book deals with insider dealing and market abuse. This chapter concentrates on the link between the misuse of insider information. In particular, it discusses the provisions designed to ensure the integrity of securities markets and the legislation aimed at tackling insider dealing and market manipulation in the financial services sector. Although a long-standing part of US law this is a relatively new arena for UK lawmakers and regulators. The chapter also looks at the market abuse regime created by the FSMA 2000 and regulated by the FSA and outlines the influence of the EU Market Abuse Directive. An integral part of the global financial crime strategy is the ability of law enforcement agencies to deprive organized criminals, drug cartels and terrorists of their illegal earnings, which is the focus of Chapter 6. The international measures that allow the confiscation of illicit profits are extensive and have been implemented in the US and the UK. The ability to confiscate the proceeds of crime has become an integral part of the financial crime policies in the US and the UK. The seventh chapter identifies the regulatory and law enforcement agencies that have been created to tackle the different types of financial crime referred to in this text. This chapter identifies the agencies at a global, regional and national level and places the agencies in the US and the UK into three distinctive categories – primary, secondary and tertiary. The penultimate chapter deals with the sentencing policies adopted in the

---

[39]   Ryder above, n 19 at p. 825.

[40]   Wright, R. (2007), 'Developing effective tools to manage the risk of damage caused by economically motivated crime fraud', *Journal of Financial Crime*, **14**(1), 17–27, at 18.

US and the UK towards people who have been convicted of committing the types of financial crime outlined in previous chapters. In particular this chapter discusses the aims of sentencing offenders of financial crime and what options are available to the courts.

2.   Money laundering

Globalisation has increased the scope and extent of money laundering. With lightning speed, money can be wired from Yemen to terrorists in Florida for the destruction of buildings in New York and Washington. Business corruption, drug trafficking, arms smuggling and terrorism are sustained by the loopholes in the financial structure that allow illegal funds to slip through the system undetected.[1]

2.1   INTRODUCTION

The goal of a large number of criminal acts is to generate a profit for the individuals or groups that carry out the acts. Money laundering is the process by which organized criminals and drug cartels disguise their proceeds of crime. It is of critical importance to them, as it enables them to enjoy the profits without jeopardizing their source. Money laundering is a criminal activity that involves the practice of concealing assets to avoid any discovery of the unlawful activity that fashioned them. The historical development of money laundering is largely contained in the myth that the term was first used by Al Capone.[2] In its early origins, organized criminals laundered their proceeds of crime through cash intensive businesses such as casinos.[3] By the 1950s it was already a complicated and cleverly planned system of financial management.[4] The first reported sighting of the term 'money laundering' in a legal context was in the case of *US v $4,255,625.39*.[5] Money laundering was criminalized in both the United

---

[1]   Lacey, K. and George, N. (2003), 'Crackdown on money laundering: a comparative analysis of the feasibility and effectiveness of domestic and multilateral policy reforms', *Northwestern Journal of International Law and Business*, Winter, **23**, 263–351, at 350–351.

[2]   Robinson, Jeffrey (1995), *The Laundrymen*, Pocket Books, London, at p. 4.

[3]   Gallant, Michelle (2005), *Money Laundering and the Proceeds of Crime*, Edward Elgar, Cheltenham, at p. 11.

[4]   Gill, M. and Taylor, G. (2004), 'Preventing money laundering or obstructing business? Financial companies' perspectives on "know your customer" procedures', *British Journal of Criminology*, **44**(4), 582–594, at 582.

[5]   (1982) 551 F Supp.314. For a more detailed discussion of the significance of this case see Buchanan, B. (2004), 'Money laundering – a global obstacle', *Research in International Business and Finance*, **18**, 120–122.

States of America (US) and the United Kingdom (UK) in 1986 by virtue of the Money Laundering Control Act (MLCA)[6] and the Drug Trafficking Offences Act (DTOA).[7] Money laundering has since received worldwide regulatory attention as a result of the US-led war on drugs and the establishment of the Financial Action Task Force (FATF).[8] Money laundering has been described as the 'secretive phenomenon',[9] and it has been claimed that it is the world's third largest industry.[10] The United Nations (UN) has estimated that the annual amount of money laundering is $500bn,[11] which according to the International Monetary Fund (IMF) is between 2 and 5 per cent of the world's gross domestic product.[12] Morais took the view that 'because of the clandestine nature of money laundering, it is very difficult to determine the precise magnitude of the money laundered globally on an annual basis'.[13] The calculation of its extent is also hampered because there is no visible data on the amount of money laundered. This has been referred to as the 'shadow economy', or a nation's unrecorded financial

---

[6]   The Money Laundering Control Act 1986 was a direct response to the case of *US v. Anzalone* (766 F.2d 676 (1st Cir. 1985). For a more detailed commentary on this case see Schwartz, J. (1987), 'Liability for structured transactions under the Currency and Foreign Transactions Reporting Act: a prelude to the Money Laundering Control Act of 1986', *Annual Review of Banking Law*, **6**, 315–340.

[7]   The Drug Trafficking Offences Act 1986 was introduced as a result of the decision of the House of Lords in *R v Cuthbertson* (1981) AC 470, and it criminalized drug money laundering with the 'all' money laundering offence being introduced by the Criminal Justice Act 1993.

[8]   Gill and Taylor above, n 4 at 583. For a more detailed discussion on the links between money laundering and drugs see Levi, M. (2002a), 'Money laundering and its regulation', *The Annals of the American Academy of Political and Social Science*, **582**(1), 181–194, at 182.

[9]   Unger, Brigitte (2007), *The scale and impacts of money laundering*, Edward Elgar, Cheltenham, at p. 21.

[10]   Robinson above, n 2.

[11]   Solomon, P. (1994), 'Are money launderers all washed up in the western hemisphere? The OAS model regulations', *Hastings International and Comparative Law Review*, Winter, **17**, 433–455, at 434.

[12]   International Monetary Fund (1998), 'Michael Camdessus, Address to the FATF at the Plenary Meeting of the Financial Action Task Force on Money Laundering, 10 February 1998', available at www.imf.org/external/np/speeches/1998/021098.htm (accessed 6 September 2009).

[13]   Morais, H. (2005), 'Fighting international crime and its financing: the importance of following a coherent global strategy based on the rule of law', *Villanova Law Review*, **50**, 583–644, at 591. For similar comments see Alexander, K. (2001), 'The international anti–money laundering regime: the role of the Financial Action Task Force', *Journal of Money Laundering Control*, **4**(3), 231–248, at 232.

activity.[14] It has been argued that any 'economic analysis of money laundering is an area fraught with difficulty . . . [and] in the absence of hard statistical data; studies to date have had to employ indirect methods of estimation'.[15] According to the Department of Treasury, the estimated amount of money laundered in the US is approximately $600bn per year,[16] while Mitchell claimed that the figure is nearer $300bn.[17] Conversely, the amount of money laundered annually in the UK is lower and estimates vary from £19bn to £48bn.[18]

In spite of its mysterious nature, money laundering has three recognizable stages – placement, layering and integration.[19] In the first stage, the money launderer introduces the illegal profits of crime into, for example, the financial system.[20] This is sometimes achieved by separating larger sums of money into smaller amounts that can be deposited into several bank accounts which can easily avoid any money laundering reporting requirements.[21] At the second step, the launderer enters into several transactions to distance the illegal money from its original source. The final

---

[14]   Collins, R. (2005), 'The unknown unknowns – risks to the banking sector from the dark side of the shadow economy', *The Company Lawyer*, **26**(3), 84–87, at 84.

[15]   There are traditionally two approaches towards calculating the extent of money laundering. The first is largely based upon assumption from macroeconomic data and the second on the financial information made available by antimoney laundering agencies. See Harvey, J. (2004), 'Compliance and reporting issues arising for financial institutions from money laundering regulations: a preliminary cost benefit study', *Journal of Money Laundering Control*, **7**(4), 333–346, at 333.

[16]   Weller, P. and Roth von Szepesbela, K. (2004), 'Silence is golden – or is it? FINTRAC and the suspicious transaction reporting requirements for lawyers', *Asper Review of International Business and Trade Law*, **4**, 85–130, at 86.

[17]   Mitchell, D. (2003), 'US Government agencies confirm that low-tax jurisdictions are not money laundering havens', *Journal of Financial Crime*, **11**(2), 127–133 at 128.

[18]   Harvey, J. (2005), 'An evaluation of money laundering policies', *Journal of Money Laundering Control*, **8**(4), 339–345, at 340.

[19]   Robinson categorizes these stages of money laundering as immersion, layering and spin dry. See Robinson above, n 2 at 12.

[20]   For an excellent commentary on how organized criminals will seek to hide their proceeds of crime at the placement stage of the layering process see Simser, J. (2008), 'Money laundering and asset cloaking techniques', *Journal of Money Laundering Control*, **11**(1), 15–24.

[21]   This process is commonly referred to as smurfing where criminals will deposit money in a financial institution in amounts that are lower than the level at which the financial institution must complete a suspicious activity report. For a more detailed and fascinating discussion about smurfing and money laundering see Welling, S. (1989), 'Smurfs, money laundering, and the federal criminal law: the crime of structuring transactions', *Florida Law Review*, **41**, 287–339.

stage is referred to as integration, and it is at this phase of the money laundering cycle that the monies re-enter the economy. Money laundering has become a multinational occurrence where extremely disciplined and well-funded organized criminals manipulate national anti-money laundering (AML) rules to move and disguise their proceeds of crime.[22] HM Treasury took the view that money laundering 'frequently involves routing transactions through many countries to disguise the illegal origin of the money'.[23] Money launderers are even utilizing more complicated techniques through a larger number of financial transactions and shell corporations in order to legitimize the proceeds of crime.[24] Therefore, it can be postulated that an immeasurable number of mechanisms exist which could be exploited by organized criminals to launder money undetected.[25] This means that virtually *any* financial transaction could involve money laundering.[26]

2.2 THE DEVELOPMENT OF A GLOBAL ANTI-MONEY LAUNDERING STRATEGY

The IMF and World Bank, 'several internationals and task forces are involved in efforts to counter money laundering'.[27] Tsingou took the view that the global AML regime is developing on two fronts, prevention and enforcement, and at three levels: national, regional and international.[28] Money laundering is an international crime that demands an effective international response.[29] Therefore, it is necessary to identify the

---

[22]   Alexander above, n 13 at 231.

[23]   HM Treasury *Anti-Money Laundering Strategy* (HM Treasury: London, 2004) at p. 12.

[24]   Financial Services Authority *Consultation Paper 46 Money Laundering – The FSA's new role* (Financial Services Authority: London, 2000) at para. 3.2.

[25]   Alldridge, Peter (2003), *Money Laundering Law*, Hart, Oxford, at p. 3.

[26]   *Ibid.*, at 2–3.

[27]   International Monetary Fund and World Bank *Enhancing contributions to combating money laundering: policy paper* (International Monetary Fund and World Bank: Washington, DC, 2001) at p. 10. For a more detailed commentary of the role of the International Monetary Fund in relation to money laundering see Holder, W. (2003), 'The International Monetary Fund's involvement in combating money laundering and the financing of terrorism', *Journal of Money Laundering Control*, 6(4), 383–387.

[28]   Tsingou, E. (2005), *Global governance and transnational financial crime opportunities and tensions in the global anti-money laundering regime* (CSGR Working Paper No. 161/05) at p. 4.

[29]   Stessens, Guy (2000), *Money laundering – a new international law enforcement model*, Cambridge University Press, at p. 18.

international community's AML policy, which can be found by highlighting and investigating the measures introduced by the UN, the FATF and the European Union (EU).

2.2.1   The United Nations

The birth of the international community's AML efforts can be found in the UN's policy towards narcotic substances.[30] This is illustrated by the fact that 'the United Nations' efforts to combat money laundering are coordinated by the United Nations Office on Drugs and Crime, by way of its Global Program against Money Laundering'.[31] Of particular relevance is the 1939 Convention for the Suppression of the Illicit Traffic in Dangerous Drugs, which imposed the first obligation to confiscate the proceeds of drug-related sales.[32] The most significant international AML instrument is the UN Convention against Illicit Traffic in Narcotic Drugs and Psychotropic Substances, or as it is more commonly referred to, the Vienna Convention.[33] This was implemented due to the inadequacies of the Single Convention on Narcotic Drugs (1961) and the Convention on Psychotropic Substances (1971).[34] The Vienna Convention provided that signatories must, *inter alia*, criminalize the laundering of drug proceeds,[35] take measures to establish their jurisdiction over the offence of money laundering,[36] permit the confiscation of the proceeds of the sale of illegal

---

[30]   For example, the International Opium Convention (1912) and the Convention Limiting the Manufacture and Regulating the Distribution of Narcotic Drugs (1931). For a more detailed commentary of these international measures see Thomas, C. (2003), 'Disciplining globalization: international law, illegal trade, and the case of narcotics', *Michigan Journal of International Law*, **24**, 549–574.

[31]   Morais above, n 13 at 593.

[32]   Convention for Suppression of the Illicit Traffic in Dangerous Drugs (1939), Article 10.

[33]   United Nations Convention against Illicit Traffic in Narcotic Drugs and Psychotropic Substances (1988). Bosworth-Davies took the view that 'this document has passed into money laundering history as the Vienna Convention'. Bosworth-Davies, R. (2006), 'Money laundering: towards an alternative interpretation – chapter two', *Journal of Money Laundering Control*, **9**(4), 346–364, at 356.

[34]   Alford, D. (1994), 'Anti-money laundering regulations: a burden on financial institutions', *The North Carolina Journal of International Law and Commercial Regulation*, **19**, 437–468, at 441–442. For an excellent commentary of the international efforts to tackle the illegal drugs trade see Bassiouni, M. (1989), 'Critical reflections on international and national control of drugs', *Denver Journal of International Law and Policy*, **18**(3), 311–337.

[35]   Above, n 33 article 3.

[36]   *Ibid.*, article 4.

drugs and/or materials used in their manufacturing,[37] provide mechanisms to facilitate extradition matters[38] and take measures to improve mutual legal assistance.[39] Of particular relevance to this chapter is Article 3, which criminalizes money laundering. It prohibits:

> i) The conversion or transfer of property, knowing that such property is derived from any offence or offences established in accordance with subparagraph *a)* of this paragraph, or from an act of participation in such offence or offences, for the purpose of concealing or disguising the illicit origin of the property or of assisting any person who is involved in the commission of such an offence or offences to evade the legal consequences of his actions;
> ii) The concealment or disguise of the true nature, source, location, disposition, movement, rights with respect to, or ownership of property, knowing that such property is derived from an offence or offences established in accordance with subparagraph *a)* of this paragraph or from an act of participation in such an offence or offences.

Png noted that 'the new requirements added teeth to earlier developments by calling for countries to prosecute persons who launder drug proceeds'.[40] Similarly, Bosworth-Davies noted that the Convention 'did more to provide, at least in theory, a sound basis upon which global money laundering efforts to combat the effects of narcotic trafficking would be achieved, than any other initiative has realized either before or since'.[41] However, the scope of the Vienna Convention was limited to the laundering of the proceeds of crime from the manufacturing and sale of narcotics.[42] The scope of the Vienna Convention was extended by the

---

[37] Above, n 33 article 5.

[38] *Ibid.*, article 6.

[39] Above, n 33 article 7. For a more detailed examination of these obligations see Zagaris, B. (1989), 'Developments in international judicial assistance and related matters', *Denver Journal of International Law and Policy*, **18**(3), 339–386, Defeo, M. (1989), 'Depriving international narcotics traffickers and other organised criminals of illegal proceeds and combating money laundering', *Denver Journal of International Law and Policy*, **18**(3), 405–415 and Stewart, D. (1989), 'Internationalizing the war on drugs: the UN Convention Against Illicit Traffic in Narcotic Drugs and Psychotropic Substances', *Denver Journal of International Law and Policy*, **18**(3), 387–404.

[40] Png, Cheong-Ann (2008a), 'International legal sources I – the United Nations Conventions', in W. Blair and R. Brent (eds), *Banks and financial crime – the international law of tainted money*, Oxford University Press, Oxford, 41–59, at 41.

[41] Bosworth-Davies above, n 33 at 356. The Vienna Convention was implemented in the UK in 1990 by the Criminal Justice (International Co-operation) Act.

[42] Unger above, n 9 at 16. For an excellent commentary on the money laundering provisions of the Vienna Convention see Gilmore, William (2004) *Dirty money – the evaluation of international measures to counter money laundering and the financing of terrorism*, Council of Europe, Brussels, 53–61.

Palermo Convention, which in relation to money laundering included 'all serious offences', not just those relating to the sale or the manufacture of narcotics.[43] Signatories to the latter Convention were required to criminalize participation in an organized criminal group, money laundering, corruption and the obstruction of justice.[44] Therefore, an integral part of the international community's policy towards money laundering is its criminalization.[45] Other noteworthy measures introduced by the UN to combat money laundering included the 'Global Programme against Money Laundering, Proceeds of Crime and Terrorist Financing' and the 'Political Declaration and Action Plan against Money Laundering'.

2.2.2 Financial Action Task Force

The next step in the development of a global AML policy was the establishment of the FATF. This organization was created in 1989 following 'the General Assembly of the UN's adoption in 1988 of a universal pledge to put a halt to money laundering'.[46] The FATF is an inter-governmental body whose function is to development and promote AML policies; it consists of 34 countries, two international bodies and several regional organizations.[47] The FATF issued a set of 40 Recommendations in 1990 (the Recommendations),[48] which according to Johnson 'provide a complete set of anti-money laundering procedures which covers the relevant laws and their enforcement, the activities and regulation of the financial system and matters relating to international co-operation'.[49] The Recommendations are divided into four parts – the criminalization and the confiscation of

---

[43]   United Nations Convention against Transnational Organized Crime (2000).

[44]   *Ibid.*, article 6.

[45]   For an earlier commentary of this suggestion see Zagaris, B. and Castilla, S. (1993), 'Constructing an international financial enforcement sub regime: the implementation of anti-money laundering policy', *Brooklyn Journal of International Law*, **18**, 871–965, at 908–909.

[46]   Johnson, J. (2008), 'Is the global financial system AML/CTF prepared?', *Journal of Financial Crime*, **15**(1), 7–21, at 8.

[47]   *Ibid.*, at 9–10. The standards have been approved by 180 countries and both the International Monetary Fund and World Bank. See Financial Action Task Force *Financial Action Task Force Annual Report 2007–2008* (Financial Action Task Force: Paris, 2008) at p. 2.

[48]   It is important to note that the 40 Recommendations have been amended in 1996 and 2003 and were extended to include nine Special Recommendations on terrorist financing following the terrorist attacks in the US in September 2001.

[49]   Johnson above, n 46 at 11. Also see Hulsse, R. and Kerwer, D. (2007), 'Global standards in action: insights from anti-money laundering regulation', *Organization*, **14**(5), 625–642, at 628.

property laundered;[50] measures to be taken by financial institutions to prevent money laundering and terrorist financing;[51] institutional and other measures necessary to combat money laundering;[52] and terrorist financing and international co-operation.[53] The importance of the Recommendations is illustrated by UN Security Council Resolution 1617 which strongly urges 'all Member States to implement the comprehensive, international standards embodied in the FATF Forty Recommendations on Money Laundering'.[54] Members of the FATF are clearly committed to implementing the Recommendations and have agreed to be subject to multilateral surveillance, peer review and the publication of the Non-cooperative Countries and Territories list. All member countries have their implementation of the Recommendations monitored through a two-pronged approach: an annual self-assessment exercise and a more mutual evaluation process. The FATF also carries out cross-country reviews of measures taken to implement particular Recommendations. In order to encourage compliance the FATF was initially reliant upon a system of coercion.[55] This was illustrated by the publication of the Non-cooperative Countries and Territories list in 2000. Doyle described the list as 'disturbing and [it] suggests a policy redolent of extraterritorial bullying'.[56] It was deemed controversial and condemned by both the IMF and World Bank,

---

[50] The first four recommendations define the scope of the criminal offence for money laundering and the confiscation of the proceeds of crime.

[51] The second set of recommendations, 5–25, deals with customer due diligence, record keeping, the reporting of suspicious transactions and regulation.

[52] The third set of recommendations, 26–34, concentrate upon competent authorities and transparency of legal persons.

[53] The final recommendations specifically deal with mutual legal assistance and extradition.

[54] United Nations Security Council Resolution 1617 (2005) S/RES/1617 (2005), adopted by the Security Council at its 5244th meeting on 29 July 2005. Also see Resolution 60/288 of the UN General Assembly (20 September 2006) which provides 'to encourage states to implement the comprehensive international standards embodied in the Forty Recommendations on Money Laundering and the Nine Special Recommendations on Terrorist Financing of the Financial Action Task Force'. It is important to note that this was a US-sponsored resolution. For a more detailed discussion see US Government Accountability Office *International Financial Crime – Treasury's roles and responsibilities relating to selected provisions of the USA Patriot Act 2001* (US Government Accountability Office: Washington, DC, 2006).

[55] Hulsse, R. (2007), 'Creating demand for global governance: the making of a global money-laundering problem', *Global Society*, **21**(2), 155–178, at 167.

[56] Doyle, T. (2002), 'Cleaning up anti-money laundering strategies: current FATF tactics needlessly violate international law', *Houston Journal of International Law*, **24**, 279–313, at 282.

which resulted in the FATF changing its policy to merely persuasion.[57] It has even been argued that it abandoned the publication of this list largely because it feared losing its authority as the global AML agency.[58]

The Recommendations have clearly influenced the AML policies in the US and the UK. For example, Recommendation 1 requires countries to 'criminalise money laundering on the basis of the United Nations Convention against Illicit Traffic in Narcotic Drugs and Psychotropic Substances, 1988 and United Nations Convention against Transnational Organized Crime, 2000'. Furthermore, Recommendations 4 to 12 are aimed at financial institutions and other professions to prevent money laundering.[59] Recommendations 13–16 require financial institutions to report any suspicious transactions.

2.2.3 The European Union

Between 1977 and 1980 the Council of Europe's European Committee on Crime Problems created a Select Committee to investigate the illegal transfer of the proceeds of crime between Member States. The Select Committee made a formal recommendation which concentrated upon the importance of thwarting money laundering through prevention and the role that central banks could play.[60] Furthermore, it stipulated that banks should ensure that identity checks are undertaken on all clients when an account is opened or money deposited.[61] However, the recommendation was not implemented. More importantly, the EU has implemented three Money Laundering Directives. The First Money Laundering Directive,

---

[57] Hulsse above, n 55 at 167.

[58] Alldridge, P. (2008), 'Money laundering and globalisation', *Journal of Law and Society*, **35**(4), 437–463, at 444. For a more detailed discussion see Hulsse, R. (2008). 'Even clubs can't do without legitimacy: Why the anti-money laundering blacklist was suspended', *Regulation & Governance*, **2**(4), 459–479.

[59] Under these recommendations financial institutions are expected to undertake customer due diligence and record-keeping, which includes verifying the customer's identity and determining the nature of the business relationship.

[60] This recommendation contained a series of initiatives that aimed to create a far-reaching anti-money laundering regime. See Council of Europe, Committee of Ministers *Measures against the transfer and the safekeeping of funds of criminal origin – recommendation no. R (80) 10*. This was adopted by the Committee of Ministers of the Council of Europe on 27 June 1980.

[61] Alexander, K. (2000), 'Multi-national efforts to combat financial crime and the Financial Action Task Force', *Journal of International Financial Markets*, **2**(5), 178–192, at 182.

introduced in 1991,[62] was implemented in the UK in 1993.[63] Its important features were the need to ensure client identification, the examination and reporting of suspicious transactions, indemnities to be given for good faith reporting of suspicious transactions, identification records to be kept for five years after the client relationship has ended, co-operation with the authorities and adequate internal procedures and training programmes to be adopted.[64] However, by the end of the 1990s there was a consensus of opinion amongst commentators and legislators that the Directive was ineffective.[65] The Second Money Laundering Directive contained two important themes. Firstly, it lengthened the list of predicate offences for which the suspicious transaction reports were compulsory from just drug trafficking offences to all serious criminal offences. Secondly, it also extended the scope of the Directive to a number of professions and non-financial activities.[66] The UK implemented the Second Directive via the Money Laundering Regulations 2003.[67] In 2004, the European Commission decided to merge the existing Directives and published proposals for a Third Directive.[68] An agreement was reached in June 2005 and Member States were given until 15 December 2007 to fully implement the Directive. The modifications were to extend the scope of predicate offences and provide more guidance to improve customer identification procedures. The Directive requires Member States to 'expand their anti-money laundering regimes to combat the proceeds of all serious crime'.[69] The Third Money Laundering Directive was implemented in the UK via the Money Laundering Regulations 2007 (MLR).[70]

---

[62]   European Council, *Directive on the Prevention of the Use of the Financial System to Launder Money* 91/308, 1993 O.J. (L 166).

[63]   This Directive was implemented by Money Laundering Regulations 1993, S.I. 1993/1933.

[64]   These are referred to as preventative measures based upon the 40 recommendations of the FATF. See Mitsilegas, V. and Gimlore, B. (2007), 'The EU legislative framework against money laundering and terrorist finance: a critical analysis in light of evolving global standards', *International and Comparative Law Quarterly*, **56**(1), 119–140, at 120.

[65]   *Ibid.*, at 122.

[66]   This includes, for example, lawyers, notaries, accountants, estate agents, art dealers, jewellers, auctioneers and casinos.

[67]   S.I. 2003/3075.

[68]   Directive 2005/60/EEC.

[69]   Fisher, J. (2002), 'Recent international developments in the fight against money laundering', *Journal of International Banking Law*, **17**(3), 67–72, at 67.

[70]   S.I. 2007/2157.

2.3 THE UNITED STATES OF AMERICA

The origins of the US AML policy can be found in the 1960s when it 'became increasingly concerned about the use of secret "offshore" bank accounts by Americans engaged in illegal activity'.[71] The policy was initially linked with the illegal sale of narcotics and the war on drugs in the 1980s. This was a point raised by Burnett who noted 'one of the most pervasive problems affecting our Nation and its people is the increasing use of illegal narcotics and drugs and the concomitant money laundering activities associated with rising drug-trafficking'.[72] However, Provost took the view that the money laundering policy is now broader than its original scope in the 1980s: 'though anti-money laundering efforts were initially aimed at thwarting the proceeds of illegal narcotics trafficking, today, a range of profitable criminal activities are targeted including the illegal sales of weapons, human trafficking, fraud, political corruption, and the financing of terrorism'.[73] The General Accounting Office stated that 'federal law enforcement officials estimate that between $100 billion and $300 billion is laundered [in the US] each year'.[74]

Therefore, an effective AML policy in the US is essential as it has been estimated that over half of the money laundered globally is conveyed through the US banking sector.[75] The US policy predates the international measures outlined above, which began with the enactment of the Bank Secrecy Act in 1970 (BSA).[76] Despite its introduction, it wasn't until the 1980s that money laundering became an item of political debate and conjecture. As will be outlined below, a number of financial scandals resultant from the inherent weaknesses of the BSA finally led to the criminalization of money laundering by the MLCA. Despite this, and several amending

---

[71]   Doyle above, n 56 at 287.

[72]   Burnett, A. (1986), 'Money laundering – recent judicial decisions and legislative developments', *Federal Bar News Journal*, **33**, 372.

[73]   Provost, M. (2009), 'Money laundering', *American Criminal Law Review*, **46**, 837–861, at 838.

[74]   General Accounting Office *Money laundering – needed improvements for reporting suspicious transactions are planned* (General Accounting Office: Washington, DC, 1995) at p. 2.

[75]   Takats, E. *A theory of 'crying wolf': the economics of money laundering enforcement – IMF Working Paper* (International Monetary Fund: Washington, DC, 2007) at p. 7.

[76]   Levi, M. and Reuter, P. (2006), 'Money laundering', *Crime & Justice*, **34**, 289–368, at 296. The Bank Secrecy Act 1970 was formerly referred to as the Financial Reporting and Currency and Foreign Transaction Reporting Act (1970) 31 U.S.C. § 5311.

statutes in the 1990s it wasn't until the implementation of the Money Laundering and Financial Crimes Act 1998 or the 'Strategy Act', which required the issuance of an annual National Money Laundering Strategy that the US had a codified AML policy. The aim of the Act was to 'better coordinate the efforts of law enforcement agencies and financial regulators in combating money laundering'.[77] The Strategy Act provides that the US Money Laundering Strategy should include five objectives – reducing the extent of money laundering; developing a coordinated response to money laundering;[78] the implementation of mechanisms to improve the discovery and prosecution of money laundering; improving links between financial institutions and law enforcement agencies; and the enrichment of links between federal and state authorities.[79] According to Lacey and George, there are three reasons why this Act was introduced.[80] Firstly, Congress needed to comprehend that money laundering is linked with other crimes including drugs and bribery. Secondly, it is important to tackle money laundering and its association with bribery. Thirdly, the legislation was necessary to ensure that the integrity of the US financial services sector was protected. Under the Act, the Department of Treasury and the Justice Department were required to produce five reports, which have resulted in the publication of several National Money Laundering Strategies.[81] The first was published in 1999 and it aimed to strengthen the domestic enforcement mechanisms to disrupt the flow of illicit money; to enhance the regulatory and public–private efforts to prevent money laundering; to strengthen partnerships to fight money laundering; and to reinforce international cooperation.[82] The second Strategy document stated that law enforcement efforts should concentrate upon the prosecution of major money laundering organizations; attempts should be made to measure the effectiveness of AML efforts; money laundering should be prevented through joint public–private measures; state and local governments should

---

[77] General Accounting Office *Combating money laundering – opportunities exist to improve the national strategy* (General Accounting Office: Washington, DC, 2003) at p. 1.

[78] It must be noted that despite this particular objective, federal law enforcement agencies have experienced coordination problems. See General Accounting Office *Investigating money laundering and terrorist financing – federal law enforcement agencies face continuing challenges* (General Accounting Office: Washington, DC, 2004).

[79] General Accounting Office above, n 77 at 54.

[80] Lacey and George above, n 1 at 298.

[81] 31 U.S.C. § 5341(a)(1) & (2).

[82] Department of Treasury *The National Money Laundering Strategy 1999* (Department of Treasury: Washington, DC, 1999).

work together to disrupt money laundering and measures should be introduced to strengthen the international co-operation to combat it.[83] The third Money Laundering Strategy represented a fundamental change in the US money laundering policy as it included the financing of terrorism.[84] This document stated that the focus of law enforcement and regulatory resources would be on identifying, disrupting, and dismantling terrorist financing networks in addition to the reiterated objectives outlined in the second strategy document above. The most recent Money Laundering Strategy was published in 2007.[85] It was a direct result of the publication of the US Money Laundering Threat Assessment in 2005 and it reverted exclusively to tackling money laundering.[86]

The US money laundering policy is administered by several federal agencies, but it is largely implemented by offices within the Department of Treasury. This includes for example the Office of Terrorism and Financial Intelligence (which is responsible for the Office of Foreign Assets Control, Treasury Executive Office for Asset Forfeiture and Financial Crimes Enforcement Network (FinCEN)), the Office of Terrorist Financing and Financial Crime and the Office of Intelligence and Analysis. Furthermore, the Justice Department is responsible for overseeing the investigation and prosecution of money laundering offences. Within the Justice Department, the Asset Forfeiture and Money Laundering Section, Criminal Division, Counterterrorism Section, Criminal Division, the National Drug Intelligence Center and the Office of International Affairs, Criminal Division all play a role in tackling money laundering. Within the State Department, support is provided by the Bureau of Economic and Business Affairs, Bureau of International Narcotics and Law Enforcement Affairs and the Office of the Coordinator for Counterterrorism. In addition to these government departments, a number of law enforcement agencies also play an important role in the US money laundering policy. This includes, for example, the Federal Bureau of Investigation, the Drug

---

[83]   Department of Treasury *The National Money Laundering Strategy 2000* (Department of Treasury: Washington, DC, 2000).

[84]   Department of Treasury *The National Money Laundering Strategy 2002* (Department of Treasury: Washington, DC, 2002). For an excellent discussion of the merger between money laundering and terrorist financing strategies see Zagaris, B. (2004), 'International money laundering: from Latin America to Asia, who pays? The merging of anti-money laundering and counter-terrorism financial regimes after September 11, 2001', *Berkeley Journal of International Law*, **2**, 123–157.

[85]   Department of Treasury *The National Money Laundering Strategy 2007* (Department of Treasury: Washington, DC, 2007).

[86]   Department of Treasury *US Money Laundering Threat Assessment* (Department of Treasury: Washington, DC, 2005a).

Enforcement Administration, the Department of Homeland Security, Immigration and Customs Enforcement, Customs and Border Protection, Internal Revenue Service Criminal Investigation and the Postal Inspection Service. Additionally, there are a large number of regulators including the Board of Governors of the Federal Reserve System and Securities and Exchange Commission.[87] One could argue that there are too many agencies attempting to tackle money laundering. However, this appears to be of little concern to the FATF who concluded that 'the US has designated law enforcement authorities that have responsibility for ensuring that ML offenses are properly investigated. These authorities have adequate powers, are producing good results and seem to be working effectively'.[88] The US stance towards money laundering has been described as including 'federal anti-money laundering effort involves the implementation of various statutes, collection and analysis of currency transaction data, financial industry supervision and criminal enforcement'.[89] According to the FATF the US AML strategy focuses on achieving three goals. Firstly, to more effectively cut off access to the international financial system by money launderers and terrorist financiers. Secondly, to enhance the federal government's ability to target major terrorist financing and money laundering organizations and systems. Thirdly, to strengthen and refine the AML/combating the financing of terrorism (CFT) regime for financial services providers to improve the effectiveness of compliance and enforcement efforts and to prevent and deter abuses.[90] For the purposes of this chapter, the US AML policy can be broadly divided into two areas – criminalization and financial intelligence.

2.3.1 The Criminalization of Money Laundering

Money laundering was criminalized because of a nature of non-compliance with the BSA, the use of structured payments to avoid the financial reporting thresholds, the acceleration of the drug trade and the large amount of money associated with it.[91] The MLCA criminalized money laundering

---

[87] Financial Action Task Force *Third mutual evaluation report on anti-money laundering and combating the financing of terrorism – United States of America* (Financial Action Task Force: Paris, 2006) at 15–24.

[88] *Ibid.*

[89] General Accounting Office *Money laundering – the US government is responding to the problem* (General Accounting Office: Washington, DC, 1991) at p. 2.

[90] Financial Action Task Force above, n 87 at 14.

[91] Sultzer, S. (1995), 'Money laundering: the scope of the problem and attempts to combat it', *Tennessee Law Review*, **63**, 143–237, at 158.

and imposed a maximum sentence of 20 years' imprisonment and hefty fines if convicted.[92] The Act separated money laundering into four distinctive groups: 'transaction money laundering, transportation money laundering, sting operations and spending of laundered property'.[93] The 1986 Act criminalized money laundering,[94] the crime of monetary transactions,[95] and it also criminalized structured or prepared financial transactions that seek to avoid the reporting requirements of the BSA.[96] The first offence created under the MLCA 1986 is divided into three parts and relates to domestic money laundering,[97] international money laundering[98] and the use of sting operations by federal agencies to expose illegal activities.[99] In order to achieve a conviction the prosecution has to prove that the illegal funds were derived from a specified unlawful activity and the accused must have participated in such an activity.[100] In order for a person to be convicted of international money laundering, the defendant must have knowledge that the proceeds derive from an illegal activity.[101] Provost took the view that the Act 'created liability for any individual who conducts a monetary transaction knowing that the funds were derived through unlawful activity'.[102] Weaver took the view that the MLCA 'is a more direct attempt to combat money laundering. It criminalizes the act

---

[92]   Title 18 U.S.C. §§ 1956 and 1957, Money Laundering Control Act of 1986, Pub. L. 99–570. The Act also introduced civil and criminal forfeiture for violations of the Bank Secrecy Act and instructed banks to create and maintain procedures to ensure compliance with the reporting requirements under the BSA 1970. Levi and Reuter stated that the Act was 'explicitly a component of the federal war on drugs, stimulated in part by the findings of a high-profile undercover investigation in the centre of the drug trade, southern Florida. Operation Greenback found numerous instances of couriers for drug dealers carrying cash into banks in quantities just under $10,000 in order to evade the formal requirements of the BSA'. See Levi and Reuter above, n 76 at 296.

[93]   Amann, D. (2000), 'Spotting money launderers: a better way to fight organised crime?', *Syracuse Journal of International Law and Commerce*, **27**, 199–231, at 210.

[94]   18 U.S.C. § 1956.

[95]   18 U.S.C. § 1957.

[96]   Alford took the view that the structured payments system 'has severely hampered the implementation of Congressional policy to detect suspected money laundering transactions'. See Alford above, n 34 at 458.

[97]   18 U.S.C. § 1956(a)(1) (2006).

[98]   18 U.S.C. § 1956(a)(2) (2006).

[99]   18 U.S.C. § 1956(a)(3).

[100]   18 U.S.C. § 1956(a)(1)(A)(I). For a list of examples of specified unlawful activities see § 1956(c)(7) (1994).

[101]   18 U.S.C. § 1956(a)(3).

[102]   Provost above, n 73 at 838.

of money laundering itself, as well as assistance thereof by any financial institution'.[103] The 1986 Act became an important tool in the armoury of federal prosecutors. Sultzer asserted that there was only one conviction in 1987, yet by 1993 857 defendants were convicted.[104] More recently, the FATF reported that in 2005 at a federal level 1075 people were convicted under the MLCA 1986.[105]

In addition to criminalizing money laundering, the Anti-Money Laundering Act 1992 was introduced as a direct result of the collapse of the Bank of Credit and Commerce International.[106] The Act reinforced the penalties for breaching the BSA, introduced the requirement for suspicious activity reports (SARs), extended the scope of AML obligations to wire transfers and created the Bank Secrecy Act Advisory Group.[107] More importantly, the Anti-Money Laundering Act provides federal authorities with the ability to revoke the charter of any US bank if it is guilty of money laundering. Alford stated if a US bank 'is convicted of money laundering, the appropriate domestic bank regulator must hold a hearing to determine if the bank should lose its charter or deposit insurance. Thus, these "death penalty provisions" – loss of a bank charter or loss of deposit insurance – discourage banks from inadvertently becoming involved in money laundering'.[108] Sultzer took the view that these powers could be used and can result in 'the termination of a bank's charter, its insurance, or its licence to conduct business in the United States if it is convicted of money laundering'.[109] These powers, in addition to the penalties for breaching the reporting obligations under the BSA, represent an important deterrent to banks and other financial institutions that have previously adopted an apathetic stance towards combating money laundering.

---

[103] Weaver, S. (2005), 'Modern day money laundering: does the solution exist in an expansive system of monitoring and record keeping regulations?', *Annual Review of Banking and Financial Law*, **24**, 443–465, at 446.

[104] Sultzer above, n 91 at 177.

[105] Financial Action Task Force above, n 87 at 37.

[106] This Act became known as the Annunzio-Wylie Anti-Money Laundering Act and was introduced as part of the Housing and Community Development Act of 1992. For a more detailed commentary of this Act see Morgan, M. (1997), 'Money laundering: the American law and its global influence', *NAFTA: Law & Business Review of the Americas*, **3**, 24–52, at 40–47. For a more detailed commentary on the collapse of BCCI see Arora, A. (2006), 'The statutory system of the bank supervision and the failure of BCCI', *Journal of Business Law*, August, 487–510.

[107] The Treasury Department introduced 31 C.F.R. § 103.18 and the OCC, 12 C.F.R. § 21.11.

[108] Alford above, n 34 at 460. See 12 U.S.C. § 93(d)(1) (1994).

[109] Sultzer above, n 91 at 214. See 12 U.S.C. §§ 93, 1818, 3105 (1994).

It is likely that these measures, in addition to the criminalization of money laundering, have had the desired effect and improved compliance with the obligations outlined above.

As will be outlined in Chapter 4 of this book, prior to the terrorist attacks on 11 September 2001 (9/11) the US attempts to legislate against financial crime were directed at money laundering and fraud.[110] The terrorist attacks altered the US policy towards money laundering due to a process called 'reverse money' laundering. Reverse money laundering takes place *before* the commission of an illegal act; it is not the product of the illegal act. It has been asserted by a number of commentators that al-Qaeda utilized this method of money laundering to fund several terrorist attacks, including those in 2001.[111] Cassella highlighted the threat of reverse money laundering and stated that it 'is the new modality, and merits the attention of all'.[112] Therefore, President George Bush signed the Uniting and Strengthening America by Providing Appropriate Tools to Restrict, Intercept and Obstruct Terrorism Act of 2001 (USA Patriot Act 2001).[113] Of relevance to the US policy on money laundering was the International Money Laundering Abatement and Financial Anti-Terrorism Act of 2001,[114] the purpose of which was 'to prevent, detect and prosecute international money laundering and terrorist financing'.[115] In addition to criminalizing terrorist financing, the USA Patriot Act 2001 introduced new measures to improve customer identification measures,[116] banned financial institutions from conducting businesses with overseas shell banks,[117] compelled financial institutions to adopt due dili-

---

[110]   For a more detailed discussion on the US policy toward fraud see Chapter 4.

[111]   See Cassella, S. (2003), 'Reverse money laundering', *Journal of Money Laundering Control*, **7**(1), 92–94, at 92.

[112]   *Ibid.*, at 94.

[113]   Pub. L. No. 107–56, § 302(a)(1), 115 Stat. 272 (2001). It is worth noting that prior to the Terrorist attacks in 2001, the Treasury Department attempted to introduce three pieces of legislation to tackle money laundering that were not enacted. This included the Money Laundering Deterrence and Anti-Corruption Act, the Money Laundering Control Act and the International Counter-Money Laundering Act. Lacey and George took the view that these statutes were not implemented due to pressure from the US banking lobby. Lacey and George above, n 1 at 290–291.

[114]   Pub. L. No. 107–56, 115 Stat 272, Title III.

[115]   KPMG *Global Anti-Money Laundering Survey 2007 – How banks are facing up to the challenge* (KPMG, 2008) at p. 57.

[116]   Pub. L. No. 107–56, § 326.

[117]   Pub. L. No. 107–56, § 313.

gence procedures,[118] introduced measures to strengthen the exchange of information between financial institutions and the government,[119] increased the scope for AML requirements to all financial institutions,[120] increased the penalties for money laundering,[121] obliged the Department of Treasury with the power to impose 'special measures' on countries, transactions and institutions that are categorized as a primary money laundering concern.[122] As a result of the Act, KPMG noted that US banks are required to create an AML compliance programme that contains four integral parts, 'the development of internal policies, procedures and controls, the designation of a compliance officer, an ongoing employee training program and an independent audit function to test the regime'.[123] These measures are heavily reliant upon the support of the financial services sector, which means that the industry plays a central part in the US AML policy.[124] The Act introduced a number of measures that permit US authorities to impose sanctions on foreign jurisdictions that fail to co-operate with its AML policy.[125] It also extended the definition of money laundering to include its commission over the Internet and it permitted the seizure of the assets of non-US banks and broadened the interpretation of a financial institution.[126] Bosworth-Davies noted that the USA Patriot Act 2001 'has changed the face of the global approach towards anti-money laundering, and its provisions contain some of the most draconian

---

[118]   Pub. L. No. 107–56, § 312.

[119]   Pub. L. No. 107–56, § 314.

[120]   Pub. L. No. 107–56, § 321.

[121]   Pub. L. No. 107–56, § 329.

[122]   Pub. L. No. 107–56, § 311. Furthermore, as a result of the scope of the provisions of the USA Patriot Act 2001, the BSA's interpretation of 'within the United States of America' has been extended to include the 'Commonwealth of Puerto Rico, the Virgin Islands, Guam, the Northern Mariana Islands, American Samoa, the Trust Territory of the Pacific Islands, a territory or possession of the United States, or a military or diplomatic establishment'. See *United States v Wray*, No. CR.2002–53, 2002 WL 31628435 (D.V.I., 2002) as cited in Shetterly, D. (2006), 'Starving the terrorists of funding: how the United States Treasury is fighting the war on terror', *Regent University Law Review*, **18**, 327–348, at 334.

[123]   KPMG above, n 115.

[124]   Gallant above, n 3 at 81.

[125]   USA Patriot Act 2001, s. 311. Hutman *et al.* noted that 'FINCEN has used section 311 in several cases as a more independent extraterritorial enforcement tool, proposing to designate the Commercial bank of Syria, Infobank of Belarus, and First Merchant Bank OSH Limited of Turkish-controlled Cyprus, as financial institutions or primary money laundering concerns'. See Hutman, A., Herrington, M. and Krauland, E. (2005), 'Money laundering enforcement and policy', *The International Lawyer*, **39**(2), 649–661, at 655.

[126]   Weaver above, n 103 at 447–448.

penalties ever devised, even in war time'.[127] The legislative powers outlined above clearly represent a robust and formidable approach towards money laundering. The 'death penalty' measures introduced by the Anti-Money Laundering Act of 1992 act as a deterrent and will go some way to ensure that financial institutions comply with their money laundering obligations. It is clear that the financial services institutions play a fundamentally important role in the US money laundering policy, a point further illustrated by the second part of its policy, financial intelligence.

2.3.2 Financial Intelligence

The final part of the US money laundering policy is heavily reliant upon the information provided by Currency Transaction Reports (CTRs) and SARs. The first piece of legislation introduced to tackle money laundering was the BSA 1970.[128] The Act demanded a joined-up approach between the Department of Treasury and banks who were to become 'compatriots in the fight against money launderers'.[129] The initial purpose of the Act was to prevent overseas financial institutions from laundering the illegal proceeds of crime to avoid US taxes.[130] Conversely, Meltzer took the view that the BSA was introduced to 'prevent money laundering of profits resulting from drug sales'.[131] However, it must be noted that this Act was not specifically an AML law: 'it focuses on financial institutions rather than on the individuals who use them and it requires reports even of legally obtained cash. Yet it aims to help regulate money laundering by creating a paper trail through which launderers might be traced'.[132] The American Bankers Association took the view that 'the Bank Secrecy Act was originally passed in 1970 with the requirement that banks file currency transaction reports and maintain other BSA-related records, with the goal of making financial information more readily available to law enforcement

---

[127]   Bosworth-Davies, R. (2007a), 'Money laundering – chapter four', *Journal of Money Laundering Control*, **10**(1), 66–90, at 68.

[128]   Public Law 91–508, 84 Stat, 1114.

[129]   Lyons, G. (1990), 'Taking money launderers to the cleaners: a problem solving analysis of current legislation', *Annual Review of Banking Law*, **9**, 635–675, at 639.

[130]   Villa, J. (1988), 'A Critical View of Bank Secrecy Act Enforcement and the Money Laundering Statutes', *Catholic University Law Review*, **37**, Winter, 489–509, at 491.

[131]   Meltzer, P. (1991), 'Keeping drug money from reaching the wash cycle: a guide to the Bank Secrecy Act', *The Banking Law Journal*, **108**(3), 230–255, at 230.

[132]   Amann above, n 93 at 208–209.

without generating undue burden'.[133] Despite this uncertainty over the initial purpose of the BSA, it became a central tenant of the AML policy. By virtue of Title II of the Act, the Department of Treasury was authorized to implement reporting requirements so that it could retain financial information that could be used in the event of a criminal trial.[134] The Act, in addition to specific regulations from the Department of Treasury,[135] created a reporting requirement that was prompted by transactions (including exchanges, withdrawals and deposits) in excess of $10000.[136] More specifically, banks are required to complete a CTR. However, it must be noted that the obligation to file CTRs was first introduced in a small number of criminal instances by the Trading with the Enemy Act 1958.[137] Other reports that are to be filed are a CTR by Casinos, the Report of International Transportation of Currency or Monetary Instruments, and the Report of Foreign Bank and Financial Accounts.[138] In addition to these obligations, Department of Treasury has implemented rules that necessitate all businesses that wire money internationally to register with the government, to supply the names of all parties involved in the wire transfer, to report all suspicious transactions and to file a report for all wire transfers over $750.[139] Therefore, in its simplest terms, the Act seeks to detect money laundering by creating a 'paper trail'.

The effectiveness of the reporting obligations imposed by the BSA has been questioned. For example, Sultzer took the view that 'the BSA has minimal impact on money laundering throughout the 1970s and 1980s'.[140] Sultzer added that 'banks of that period rarely complied with CTR reporting requirements and bank regulators often did not catch reporting irregularities. Consequently, the most cost effective method for placing large amounts of cash into the financial system in anticipation of layering continued to be walking into the lobbies of banks across the country and depositing garbage bags and suitcases full of cash, with few

---

[133] American Bankers Association *A new framework for partnership – Recommendations for Bank Secrecy Act/Anti-money laundering reform* (American Bankers Association: Washington, DC, 2007) at p. 1.

[134] Rusch, J. (1988), 'Hue and cry in the counting-house: some observations on the Bank Secrecy Act', *Catholic University Law Review*, **37**, 465–488, at 467. The authority of the Treasury Department under Title II of the Bank Secrecy Act has been delegated to the Director of the Financial Crimes Enforcement Network.

[135] Title 31, section 5313 of the United States Code.

[136] Meltzer above, n 131 at 230.

[137] 50 U.S.C. App. § 5(b) (1958).

[138] Rusch above, n 134 at 467–468.

[139] 31 C.F.R. § 103 (2008).

[140] Sultzer above, n 91 at 177.

questions asked'.[141] Furthermore, the $10000 threshold was extremely ineffective due to the process of structured payments, or smurfing. As discussed above, Congress recognized the problems and criminalized structured payments by virtue of the MLCA. The usefulness of CTRs was also questioned by Benning who took the view that although they 'produced a large quantity of reports, it produced little useful information'.[142] Similarly, the US Government Accountability Office took the view that 'because there is no overall control or coordination of the reports, there is no way of ensuring that the information is being used to its full potential'.[143] Despite its laudable aims, the effectiveness of the reporting system has been questioned. For example, it has been argued that such reporting obligations are limited because they are the most 'least useful for providing intelligence information on possible criminal activity'.[144] Furthermore, the Government Accountability Office took the view that the 'use of information received by law enforcement at federal and state levels is limited and inconsistent'.[145] The Anti-Money Laundering Act 1992 introduced a very important amendment to the BSA and introduced the use of SARs and it also specified that financial institutions were required to develop and implement internal money laundering controls.[146] A factor that has limited the effectiveness of these reporting requirements is the definition of the term 'suspicious'. According to the US Code of Federal Regulations, a transaction is to be reported if the financial institution 'knows, suspects, or has reason to suspect' it involves or is an attempt to disguise proceeds from illegal activity; is designed to evade the requirements of the BSA; or it appears to have no business or apparent lawful purpose'.[147] The Government Accountability Office took

---

[141] *Ibid.*

[142] Benning, J. (2002), 'Following dirty money: does bank reporting of suspicious activity pose a threat to drug dealers?', *Criminal Justice Policy Review*, **13**(4), 337–355, at 337–338.

[143] General Accounting Office above, n 77 at p. 2. It is worth noting that similar concerns have been raised in the United Kingdom by KPMG *Money Laundering: Review of the Reporting System* (KPMG: London, 2003) and Serious Organized Crime Agency *Review of the Suspicious Activity Reports Regime* (Serious Organized Crime Agency: London, 2006).

[144] *Ibid.*, p. 4.

[145] General Accounting Office above, n 77 at p. 26.

[146] Annunzio-Wylie Anti-Money Laundering Act § 1517. For an interesting commentary on the policy reasons for the introduction of suspicious activity reports in the US see Hall, M. (1995–96), 'An emerging duty to report criminal conduct: banks, money laundering, and the suspicious activity report', *Kentucky Law Journal*, **84**, 643–683.

[147] 31 C.F.R. § 103.21(a)(2) (1995).

the view that a 'specific criteria for determining whether a transaction is suspicious has never been developed'.[148] It has been argued 'one cannot use a single criterion that will definitively indicate a connection between a financial transaction and an illegal activity'.[149] It must be noted that the problems associated with the interpretation of the term are not exclusive to the US.

Another weakness of the reporting requirements imposed by the BSA is the escalating compliance costs. Lacey and George took the view that 'since the initial adoption of the BSA, financial institutions have consistently complained that compliance with the reporting requirements of the BSA is expensive and administratively burdensome'.[150] According to a survey conducted in 1990 by the American Bankers Association, as cited by Byrne, 'small banks estimated their cost of compliance under the Bank Secrecy Act to be \$120 million'.[151] Similarly, Tsingou, citing the American Bankers Association, stated that the reporting obligations imposed on banks by the BSA and the MLCA are 'first in the ranking of compliance costs faced by banks'.[152] More recently, KPMG stated that 'North American banks have seen the highest percentage rise in expenditure of any region in the survey over the past three years by 71%'.[153] In 2007, the American Bankers Association reported that AML compliance costs have increased between 2001 and 2004 by 66 per cent.[154] Similarly, Alford took the view that the legislation introduced in the US 'has placed a heavier regulatory burden on banks in order to detect and prevent money laundering. The question arises whether the cost of the new regulations and the resulting changes in bank operations are worth the improved prevention of money laundering and drug trafficking. The answer is not clear. These new laws and regulations require banks to bear an investigatory burden that they are not equipped to handle'.[155] However, it is important to note that there are very few AML schemes which are cost effective.[156]

---

[148] General Accounting Office above, n 77 at 12.
[149] Rusch above, n 134 at 467–468. For some judicial guidance on the interpretation of this phrase see *United States v Tobon-Builes*, 706 F.2d 1092, 1094–95 (11th Cir. 1983).
[150] Lacey and George above, n 1 at 304.
[151] Byrne, J., Densmore, D. and Sharp, J. (1995), 'Examining the increase in federal regulatory requirements and penalties: is banking facing another troubled decade?', *Capital University Law Review*, **24**, 1–66, at 52.
[152] Tsingou above, n 28 at 14.
[153] KPMG above, n 115 at 56.
[154] American Bankers Association above, n 133 at 1.
[155] Alford above, n 34 at 466.
[156] Rhan R. (2003), 'Follow the money: confusion at Treasury', 5 February

Several important amendments have been made to the reporting provisions of the BSA.[157] The most important amendment was the creation of FinCEN by the Department of Treasury in 1990.[158] Its mission is 'to enhance US national security, deter and detect criminal activity, and safeguard financial systems from abuse by promoting transparency in the US and international financial systems'.[159] Therefore, FinCEN plays a lead role in the collection of financial intelligence. This is to be achieved by four mechanisms – administering the BSA; supporting law enforcement agencies via the analysis of financial intelligence; seeking global co-operation with other financial intelligence units; and networking.[160] The purpose of FinCEN was to collate financial information which would then be analysed and circulated to US and overseas law enforcement agencies.[161] It is important to note that due to amendments introduced by the USA Patriot Act 2001, the function of FinCEN has been broadened beyond the BSA and in 2004 it became part of the Department's Office of Terrorism and Financial Intelligence. FinCEN plays a very important role in the US

2003, The Cato Institute, available at http://www.cato.org/pub_display.php?pub_id=2980 (accessed 11 November 2001).

[157]   See, for example, the Anti-Drug Abuse Act 1988 which extended the scope of the Currency Transaction Reporting requirements to such enterprises as car dealerships and real estate closing employees. Furthermore, the Act required the confirmation of the identity of clients who purchased money instruments over $3000. For a more detailed discussion of these issues and the Anti-Drug Abuse Act 1988 see Hernandez, B. (1993), 'RIP to IRP – money laundering and the drug trafficking controls score a knockout victory over bank secrecy', *North Carolina Journal of International Law and Commercial Regulation*, **18**, Winter, 235–304. The Intelligence Reform and Terrorism Prevention Act 2004 (Pub. L. No. 108–458, § 1011, 118 Stat. 3638 (2004)) altered the BSA to compel the Secretary of the Treasury to introduce regulations that require some financial institutions to report cross-border electronic fund transfers if it is deemed necessary to prevent money laundering and the financing of terrorism. For a more detailed discussion of this Act see Bay, N. (2005), 'Executive power and the war on terror', *Denver University Law Review*, **83**, 335–386.

[158]   Organization, Functions, and Authority Delegations, 55 Fed. Reg. 18,433 (1990).

[159]   Financial Crimes Enforcement Network (n/d), 'Mission', available at http://www.fincen.gov/about_fincen/wwd/mission.html (accessed 12 November 2009).

[160]   For a more detailed discussion about how FinCEN aims to achieve these goals see FinCEN *Strategic Plan Financial Crimes Enforcement Network Fiscal Years 2008–2012* (FinCEN: Washington, DC, 2007).

[161]   Organization, Functions, and Authority Delegations, 55 Fed. Reg. 18,433 (1990). For an excellent commentary on the creation of FinCEN and the initial concerns about the right to privacy in the US see Kleiman, M. (1992), 'The right to financial privacy versus computerised law enforcement: a new fight in an old battle', *Northwestern University Law Review*, **86**, 1169–1228.

AML policy for two reasons. Firstly, it utilizes money laundering legislation to compel a broad range of institutions to adopt reporting mechanisms and the maintaining of records, but also to report any suspicious transactions so that a paper trail of evidence can be utilized by law enforcement agencies. Secondly, the agency seeks to provide intelligence and analytical support to law enforcement agencies. FinCEN clearly meets the requirements as contained in Recommendation 26.[162] Nonetheless, the FATF noted a 'few issues that should be addressed to improve its effectiveness and strengthen its role in the AML/CFT chain'.[163] In particular, a problem identified by the FATF is that FinCEN will receive approximately 14 million reports on an annual basis. Therefore, it is 'not able to perform a comprehensive analysis of each SAR, but instead devotes its analytical resources to those SARs considered most valuable to law enforcement, in accordance with the following parameters'.[164] The fundamental flaw with this approach was graphically illustrated in 2000 when one of the al-Qaeda terrorists involved in the attacks of 9/11 was the subject of a SAR, yet no further action was deemed necessary.

2.4   THE UNITED KINGDOM

The UK's money laundering policy has been led by HM Treasury, a point illustrated by the publication of its 'Anti-money laundering strategy' in 2004.[165] It must be noted that there are other actors who play an equally important role in the UK's policy. This includes the Financial Services Authority (FSA), the Joint Money Laundering Steering Group (JMLSG) and the Serious Organized Crime Agency (SOCA). In its policy document, HM Treasury stated that its strategy was based upon three objectives – effectiveness, proportionality and engagement.[166] In terms

---

[162]   Recommendation 26 provides that 'Countries should establish a Financial Intelligence Unit (FIU) that serves as a national centre for the receiving (and, as permitted, requesting), analysis and dissemination of STR and other information regarding potential money laundering or terrorist financing. The FIU should have access, directly or indirectly, on a timely basis to the financial, administrative and law enforcement information that it requires to properly undertake its functions, including the analysis of STR'.

[163]   Financial Action Task Force *Summary of third mutual evaluation report on anti-money laundering and combating the financing of terrorism* (Financial Action Task Force: Paris, 2006) at p. 3.

[164]   *Ibid.*

[165]   HM Treasury above, n 23.

[166]   *Ibid.*, at p. 12.

of the first objective, HM Treasury took the view that the UK would continue to ensure that it preserves an effective AML scheme so that it achieves its international obligations.[167] This is achieved by a series of domestic measures including the Proceeds of Crime Act 2002 (PCA 2002), the MLR 2007, professional guidance issued by the JMLSG and specific AML rules issued by the FSA. These measures also seek to achieve the international standards set by the 40 Recommendations of the FATF, the obligations imposed on the UK by the Third Money Laundering Directive and those contained in the Vienna and Palermo Conventions. The second objective, proportionality, means that the government will continue to adopt a risk-based approach toward money laundering. This seeks to ensure that its AML measures are cost effective so that firms can adopt a flexible approach towards meeting their obligations.[168] The final objective, engagement, provides that the authorities will continue to work with firms to ensure that the consultation process is fully utilized and that the levels of feedback regarding the performance of the regulated sector are communicated to them.[169] HM Treasury outlined how it aims to achieve these objectives: 'the existing regime consists of measures ranging from provisions in the *criminal law* [author's emphasis] to punish money launderers and to deprive them of their proceeds, to the obligation on the *financial services industry* [author's emphasis] and certain other sectors and professions to identify their customers and to report *suspicious activities* [author's emphasis] when necessary'.[170] Therefore, for the purpose of this chapter, the UK's AML policy can be divided into three parts – the criminalization of money laundering; regulated financial institutions being compelled to put in place systems to preclude and identify money laundering; and the use of reporting identifiable or suspected money laundering transactions to the relevant authorities. The next part of the chapter seeks to critically comment on the success and appropriateness of the UK's AML policy as outlined above.

---

[167]   HM Treasury above, n 23 at 7.
[168]   It is important to note that other countries within the European Union have adopted a risk-based approach towards money laundering regulation. See Geiger, H. and Wuensch, O. (2007), 'The fight against money laundering: an economic analysis of a cost–benefit paradoxon', *Journal of Money Laundering Control*, **10**(1), 91–105.
[169]   HM Treasury above, n 23 at 7.
[170]   *Ibid.*, at 11. For a similar view see Leong, A. (2007a), 'Chasing dirty money: domestic and international measures against money laundering', *Journal of Money Laundering Control*, **10**(2), 140–156, at 141–142.

2.4.1 The Criminalization of Money Laundering

The primary money laundering legislation is contained in Part 7 of the PCA 2002.[171] The PCA 2002 received Royal Assent on 24 July 2002 and applies 'where money laundering activities took place on or after 23 February 2003'.[172] The three principal money laundering offences created by the PCA 2002 are concealing, disguising, converting or transferring criminal property or removing it from the jurisdiction;[173] entering into or becoming concerned in an arrangement knowing or suspecting it to facilitate the acquisition, retention, use or control of criminal property by or on behalf of another person;[174] and acquiring, using or possessing criminal property.[175] These offences may be committed by any person, irrespective of whether they work within the 'regulated sector' or undertake a 'relevant business'.[176] Other offences created by the PCA 2002 include failing to disclose by the regulated sector,[177] failure to disclose by nominated officers in the regulated sector,[178] failure to disclose by other nominated officers,[179] tipping off,[180] and prejudicing an investigation.[181] A person commits an offence under s. 327 if they conceal criminal property, disguise criminal property, convert criminal property, transfer criminal property or remove criminal property from England and Wales or from Scotland or from Northern Ireland.[182] All of these offences apply to property which is criminal property if '(a) it constitutes a person's benefit from criminal conduct or it represents such a benefit (in whole or part and whether directly or indirectly), and (b) the alleged offender knows or suspects that it

---

[171] It is important to note that drug money laundering was initially criminalized by the Drug Trafficking Offences Act 1986, while money laundering was criminalized by virtue of the Criminal Justice Act 1993.

[172] Forston, Rudi (2008), 'Money laundering offences under POCA 2002', in W. Blair and R. Brent (eds), *Banks and Financial Crime – The International Law of Tainted Money*, Oxford University Press, Oxford, 155–202, at 157.

[173] Proceeds of Crime Act 2002, s. 327.

[174] Proceeds of Crime Act 2002, s. 328.

[175] Proceeds of Crime Act 2002, s. 329.

[176] For a definition of these terms see Forston above, n 172 at 160–161.

[177] Proceeds of Crime Act 2002, s. 330.

[178] Proceeds of Crime Act 2002, s. 331.

[179] Proceeds of Crime Act 2002, s. 332.

[180] Proceeds of Crime Act 2002, s. 333A.

[181] Proceeds of Crime Act 2002, s. 342.

[182] Proceeds of Crime Act 2002, s. 327(1). The interpretation of criminal property is broad because it includes property anywhere in the world, Proceeds of Crime Act 2002, s. 340(9).

constitutes or represents such a benefit'.[183] The scope of this offence is wide and it is possible for *any* person to have made a 'gain', not just the person who committed the offence. There are three important points to note. Firstly, the Act goes as far as stating that it is of no consequence 'who carried out the conduct' or 'who benefited from it' or 'whether the conduct occurred before or after the passing of this Act'.[184] Secondly, while the gain must 'flow from that criminal activity', this doesn't necessarily mean a financial gain and it could include improvements in someone's standard of living or profits derived from the criminal activity.[185] Thirdly, also that it 'represents such a benefit'.[186] A person breaches s. 327 if they know or suspect that it constitutes or represents such a benefit.[187] Section 340(3) of the PCA 2002 offers a definition of criminal property, which enables the prosecution to argue that the offender has committed an offence under s. 327. Criminal property is defined as '(a) it constitutes a person's benefit from criminal conduct or it represents such a benefit (in whole or part and whether directly or indirectly), and (b) the alleged offender knows or suspects that it constitutes or represents such a benefit'.[188] It is a defence for a person to make an authorized disclosure via a suspicious activity report; this is referred to as an authorized disclosure.[189] A person does not commit an offence if he makes an authorized disclosure,[190] he has a reasonable excuse for not making a disclosure,[191] and the action he does is in accordance with undertaking a function that relates to the enforcement of a provision under the PCA 2002.[192]

The second criminal offence created by the PCA 2002 provides that a person commits an offence if they enter or become concerned in an arrangement that they know or suspect facilitates 'the acquisition, retention, use or control of criminal property by or on behalf of another person'.[193] To establish a conviction, the prosecution must prove that a person became

---

[183]   Proceeds of Crime Act 2002, s. 340(1). For a critical discussion of the interpretation of this phrase see Bentley, D. and Fisher, R. (2009), 'Criminal property under POCA 2002 – time to clean up the law?', *Archbold News*, **2**, 7–9.

[184]   Proceeds of Crime Act 2002, s. 340(3)(a).

[185]   Hudson, Alistair (2009), *The Law of Finance*, Sweet and Maxwell, London, at p. 345.

[186]   *Ibid.*, at 344.

[187]   Proceeds of Crime Act 2002, s. 340(3)(b).

[188]   Proceeds of Crime Act 2002, s. 340(3)(a).

[189]   Proceeds of Crime Act 2002, s. 338.

[190]   Proceeds of Crime Act 2002, s. 338(1)(a).

[191]   Proceeds of Crime Act 2002, s. 338(1)(b).

[192]   Proceeds of Crime Act 2002, s. 327(2).

[193]   Proceeds of Crime Act 2002, s. 328(1).

concerned in an arrangement which they knew or suspected would make it simpler for another person to acquire, retain, use or control criminal property. Furthermore, that the person concerned also knew or suspected that the property constituted or represented benefit from criminal conduct.[194] In order for a person to be guilty of the offence under this section the definition of criminal property is again of central importance. The interpretation of several phrases under s. 328 has caused uncertainty and anxiety amongst professionals. The important phrases under s. 328 are 'becomes concerned in', 'arrangement' and 'facilitates'. The first test of s. 328 was the infamous judgment of Dame Butler-Sloss in *P v P*.[195] Here, the High Court held that where a solicitor suspects their client will become involved in an arrangement, an authorized disclosure must be made and consent from the National Criminal Intelligence Service (NCIS) is required for the solicitor to continue. The legal profession were concerned with the potential conflict between their duty of confidentiality and the duty to disclose suspicions. The High Court decided that the amount or value of the criminal property is immaterial; a disclosure must be made.[196] As a result of this decision, the legal profession, if acting for a client in divorce proceedings, would be required to investigate the financial affairs of both parties in some detail, and that any irregularity would require the solicitor to stop proceedings while they made their disclosure to the NCIS and awaited guidance. In *Bowman v Fels*,[197] the Court of Appeal overturned the High Court decision. The court made it clear that s. 328 was not intended to cover or affect the ordinary conduct of litigation and that it reached its decision by interpreting the phrase 'being concerned in an arrangement'. Brooke LJ stated that there was a 'strong argument for a restricted understanding of the concept of being concerned in an arrangement in s. 328', extending to say 'as a matter of ordinary language, our impression on reading s. 328 was and remains that, whatever Parliament may have had in mind by the phrase "entering into or becomes concerned in an arrangement which . . . facilitates" it is most unlikely that it was thinking of legal proceedings'.[198] The same defence of an authorized disclosure is available under this section

---

[194] This section amends and updates section 50 of the Drug Trafficking Act 1994, section 93A of the Criminal Justice Act 1988, section 38 of the Criminal Law (Consolidation) (Scotland) Act 1995 and Article 46 of the Proceeds of Crime (Northern Ireland) Order 1996.

[195] [2004] Fam 1.

[196] *Ibid.*, at para 56.

[197] [2005] EWCA Civ 226.

[198] *Ibid.*, at para 64.

of the Act, as discussed under s. 327.[199] The final offence provides that a person commits an offence if they acquire criminal property, use criminal property or have possession of criminal property.[200] This offence is not committed if a person makes an authorized disclosure,[201] planned to make such a disclosure but had a reasonable excuse for not doing so,[202] acquired or used or had possession of the property for adequate consideration,[203] or undertook a function relating to the enforcement of any provision of the PCA 2002 or other relevant enactment,[204] that the conduct occurs overseas and is lawful in that particular jurisdiction,[205] and that the act is done by a deposit-taking body.[206] In order for a person to be convicted of an offence, it has to be proven that the property handled is 'criminal property' and that it comprises a benefit. Furthermore, it has to be proven that the defendant knows or suspects that the property is obtained from criminal conduct.

It is important to note that terrorist property is not covered by the PCA 2002, but dealt with in the Terrorism Act 2000.[207] The laundering of terrorist property is governed by Part III of the Terrorism Act 2000.[208] Terrorist property is defined as 'money or other property which is likely to be used for the purposes of terrorism',[209] 'proceeds of the commission of acts of terrorism',[210] and 'proceeds of acts carried out for the purposes of terrorism'.[211] Section 15 of the Act created three offences – for a person to solicit,[212] or to receive,[213] money or property on behalf of terrorists, or to provide money or property if the person knows or has reasonable cause to suspect that such money may be used for the purpose of terrorism.[214] Alexander stated 'the first two

---

[199] Proceeds of Crime Act 2002, s. 327(2).
[200] Proceeds of Crime Act 2002, s. 329(1).
[201] Proceeds of Crime Act 2002, s. 329(1)(a).
[202] Proceeds of Crime Act 2002, s. 329(1)(b).
[203] Proceeds of Crime Act 2002, s. 329(1)(c).
[204] Proceeds of Crime Act 2002, s. 329(1)(d).
[205] Proceeds of Crime Act 2002, s. 329(2A), (2B).
[206] Proceeds of Crime Act 2002, s. 329(2C).
[207] For an interesting debate on the merger of the two offences of money laundering and terrorist financing see Alexander, R. (2009b), 'Money laundering and terrorist financing: time for a combined offence', *Company Lawyer*, *30*(7), 200–204.
[208] The foundations of the offences created by the Terrorism Act 2000 are to be found in Home Office *Legislation Against Terrorism – A consultation paper* (Home Office: London, 1998b).
[209] Terrorism Act 2000, s. 14(1)(a).
[210] Terrorism Act 2000, s. 14(1)(b).
[211] Terrorism Act 2000, s. 14(1)(c).
[212] Terrorism Act 2000, s. 15(1).
[213] Terrorism Act 2000, s. 15(2).
[214] Terrorism Act 2000, s. 15(3).

offences cover those who pass round the tins (or undertake the larger-scale operations), the third those who donate'.[215] Section 16 creates the offence of use or possession of money for terrorist purposes.[216] The next offence adopts the concept of the knowingly concerned person in creating an offence for a person who enters into or becomes concerned in an arrangement in which money or property is made available to another and the person knows or has cause to suspect that it may be used for terrorism.[217] Under section 18, a person commits an offence if they enter or become concerned in an arrangement that 'facilitates the retention or control by or on behalf of another person of terrorist property' either by concealment,[218] by removal from the jurisdiction,[219] by transfer to nominees,[220] or in any other way.[221] It is a defence for the defendant 'to prove that he did not know and had no reasonable cause to suspect that the arrangement related to terrorist property'.[222] Section 19 also creates the offence of failure to disclose belief or suspicion that an offence has been committed under sections 15 to 18. The 2000 Act makes it a criminal offence for people who conduct relevant business in the regulated sector not to make known their suspicion or knowledge that a person is engaged in money laundering.[223] The Act provides the identical defence for disclosure of any suspicious activities involving terrorist property to SOCA as provided by PCA 2002.[224]

2.4.2 Regulated Financial Institutions

The second part of the UK's AML policy is reliant upon the regulations imposed by the FSA who are under a statutory duty to reduce financial crime. Financial crime has been defined as any offence including fraud or dishonesty,[225] misconduct in, or misuse of information relating to, a financial market;[226] or handling the proceeds of crime.[227] The FSA, like

---

[215] Alexander, Richard (2007), *Insider dealing and money laundering in the EU: Law and Regulation*, Ashgate, Aldershot, at p. 175.

[216] Terrorism Act 2000, s. 16(1).

[217] Terrorism Act 2000, s. 17.

[218] Terrorism Act 2000, s. 18(1)(a).

[219] Terrorism Act 2000, s. 18(1)(b).

[220] Terrorism Act 2000, s. 18(1)(c).

[221] Terrorism Act 2000, s. 18(1)(d).

[222] Terrorism Act 2000, s. 18(2).

[223] Terrorism Act 2000, s. 21A.

[224] Terrorism Act 2000, s. 20.

[225] Financial Services and Markets Act 2000, s. 6(3)(a).

[226] Financial Services and Markets Act 2000, s. 6(3)(b).

[227] Financial Services and Markets Act 2000, s. 6(3)(c).

other institutions, has adopted a risk-based approach towards money laundering. This means that firms are able to allocate their resources in a cost effective and proportionate manner so that they can focus on the most relevant risks from money laundering. The FSA has adopted a two-stage policy. Firstly, it has devised a list of services and products that categorize risk status and, secondly, it has put in place a set of procedures to ensure that firms verify the identity of a client.[228] The risk-based approach between the FSA and firms will vary between the 'highest' and 'lowest' at-risk firms. The highest-risk firms will benefit from 'continuous relationship', while the lower-risk firms will have a 'remote relationship' with the FSA.[229] The FSA has extensive rule-making powers to impose regulations upon the regulated sector.[230] Until 2006, the obligations imposed were contained in the Money Laundering Sourcebook (ML).[231] Each member of the sector was required to have in place a money laundering reporting officer,[232] procedures to ensure the accurate identification of a client,[233] internal money laundering reporting requirements,[234] the use of national and international findings on material deficiencies in AML regimes,[235] and procedures to ensure that members of staff were trained to detect money laundering.[236] In addition there was a series of unique provisions for sole traders and professional firms.[237] In January 2006 the FSA announced that it was streamlining ML,[238] and it became obsolete in August 2006. ML was replaced with a principles-based approach in the Senior Management Arrangements, Systems and Controls, or SYSC, part of the Handbook. Part 3 provides that firms must have in place systems and controls which are appropriate for the firm to conduct its business.[239] In particular, a

---

[228]   Gill, M. and Taylor, G. (2003), 'The risk-based approach to tackling money laundering: matching risk to products', *Company Lawyer*, **24**(7), 210–213, at 212.

[229]   Sergeant, C. (2002), 'Risk-based regulation in the Financial Services Authority', *Journal of Financial Regulation and Compliance*, **10**(4), 329–335, at 333.

[230]   Financial Services and Markets Act 2000, s. 146.

[231]   Financial Services Authority *Money Laundering Handbook* (Financial Services Authority: London, 2006). The FSA adopted the MLR 1993 via the Financial Services and Markets Act 2000 Regulations (Relating to Money Laundering Regulations) 2001, S.I. 2001/1819.

[232]   *Ibid.*, s. 2.

[233]   *Ibid.*, s. 3.

[234]   *Ibid.*, s. 4.

[235]   *Ibid.*, s. 5.

[236]   *Ibid.*, s. 6.

[237]   *Ibid.*, s. 8.

[238]   *Ibid.*

[239]   Financial Services Authority *FSA Handbook* (Financial Services Authority: London, 2006), at SYSC 3.1.1.

firm is required to 'take reasonable care to establish and maintain effective systems and controls for compliance with applicable requirements and standards under the regulatory system and for countering the risk that the firm might be used to further financial crime'.[240] Therefore, firms are required to carry out regular assessments of the adequacy of the AML systems they have in place to prevent themselves from being used to further financial crime,[241] allocate a director or senior manager with overall responsibility for establishing and maintaining the AML system and to appoint a money laundering reporting officer.[242] The FSA has extensive investigative and enforcement powers. For example, it has the ability to require information from firms,[243] to appoint investigators,[244] to obtain the assistance of overseas financial regulators[245] and provide appointed investigators with additional powers.[246] Furthermore, it has become a prosecuting authority for certain money laundering offences.[247] The FSA also has the power to impose a financial penalty where it establishes that there has been a contravention by an authorized person of its rules.[248] The FSA has imposed a series of fines on firms who have breached ML even where there was no evidence of money laundering.[249] More recently, it has fined a firm's money laundering reporting officer.[250]

The FSA also implements the 2007 MLR, the purpose of which is to

---

[240]   *Ibid.*, at SYSC 3.2.6 R.

[241]   See n 239 above, at SYSC 3.2.6 C.

[242]   *Ibid.*, at SYSC 3.2.6 H and I.

[243]   Financial Services and Markets Act 2000, ss. 165–166.

[244]   Financial Services and Markets Act 2000, ss. 167–168.

[245]   Financial Services and Markets Act 2000, s. 169.

[246]   Financial Services and Markets Act 2000, s. 172.

[247]   Financial Services and Markets Act 2000, s. 402(1)(a). The scope of the FSA's prosecutorial powers were approved by the Court of Appeal in *R. v Rollins (Neil)* [2009] EWCA Crim 1941 and confirmed by the Supreme Court in *R v Rollins* [2010] UKSC 39.

[248]   Financial Services and Markets Act 2000, s. 206(1).

[249]   The FSA has fined Royal Bank of Scotland £750000, Northern Bank £1.25m and the Abbey National £2.2m for breaches of its Handbook. See Ryder, N. (2008b), 'The Financial Services Authority and money laundering: a game of cat and mouse', *Cambridge Law Journal*, 67(3), 635–653.

[250]   See, for example, Financial Services Authority (2008c), 'FSA fines firm and MLRO for money laundering controls failings', 29 October 2008, available at http://www.fsa.gov.uk/pages/Library/Communication/PR/2008/125.shtml (accessed 29 October 2008) and Financial Services Authority (2010a), 'FSA fines Alpari and its former money laundering reporting officer, Sudipto Chattopadhyay for anti-money laundering failings,' 5 May 2010, available at http://www.fsa.gov.uk/pages/Library/Communication/PR/2010/077.shtml (accessed 6 May 2010).

prevent businesses based in the UK from being abused by criminals and terrorists for the purposes of money laundering. This is further illustrated by the following quote from Hudson who noted that the 2007 Regulations 'are concerned generally with the general regulatory objectives of promoting market confidence and public awareness, and of protecting consumers and reducing financial crime',[251] each of which is a statutory objective of the FSA under FSMA 2000. The first Regulations were introduced in 1993 and amended by the 2001 Money Laundering Regulations, and then revoked by the 2003 Money Laundering Regulations, which broadened their scope to include a wider range of businesses including notaries, estate agents, auditors, money transmission providers, dealers in high value goods and casinos. The most recent set of regulations came into force on 15 December 2007,[252] and were implemented in a response to the Third Money Laundering Directive.[253] The 2007 Regulations apply to credit institutions,[254] financial institutions,[255] auditors,[256] insolvency practitioners,[257] external accountants[258] and tax advisers,[259] independent legal professionals,[260] trust or company service providers,[261] estate

---

[251]   Hudson above, n 185 at 360.

[252]   Money Laundering Regulations 2007, S.I. 2007/2157.

[253]   Council Directive (EC) 2005/60 of 26 October 2005, [2005] OJ L309/15.

[254]   As defined in Article 4(1)(a) of the Banking Consolidation Directive 2000/12/EC of the European Parliament and of the Council of 20 March 2000 relating to the taking up and pursuit of the business of credit institutions.

[255]   This is defined as an undertaking, including a money service business, when it carries out one or more of the activities listed in points 2 to 12 and 14 of Annex 1 to the Banking Consolidation Directive.

[256]   An auditor is defined as 'any firm or individual who is a statutory auditor within the meaning of Companies Act 2006'.

[257]   Any person who acts as an insolvency practitioner within the meaning of Insolvency Act 1986, s. 388 as amended by Insolvency Act 2000, s. 3.

[258]   This is a firm or sole practitioner who by way of business provides accountancy services to other persons, when providing such services. Money Laundering Regulations 2007, regulation 3(7).

[259]   This is defined as a firm or sole practitioner who by way of business provides advice about the tax affairs of other persons, when providing such services. Money Laundering Regulations 2007, regulation 3(8).

[260]   An independent legal professional is a firm or sole practitioner who provides services of a legal nature concerning the sale and acquisition of real property, the administration of client money and other related activities. Money Laundering Regulations 2007, regulation 3(9).

[261]   A trust or company service provider is defined as a firm or sole practitioner who provides business services relating to the formation of legal entities or acts as an agent for another party to operate as a director or in another relevant position within a company. Money Laundering Regulations 2007, regulation 3(10).

agents,[262] high value dealers[263] and casinos.[264] The 2007 Regulations impose a variety of more detailed obligations on the financial services sector and other persons to prevent money laundering and terrorist funding. For example, under regulation 7 a firm is required to apply due diligence, as defined by Regulation 5, measures where they suspect the transaction concerns money laundering or terrorist financing or where they distrust a customer's identification. This means that the firm is required to authenticate the identity of the customer and monitor their business relationships.[265] Casinos are under an individual obligation to determine the identity of customers by virtue of Regulation 10. The 2007 Regulations also impose obligations relating to record keeping,[266] policies and procedures[267] and staff training.[268] The Regulations also contain provisions and obligations relating to supervision and registration,[269] creating enforcement powers for supervisors,[270] provisions for the recovery of penalties and charges[271] and impose an obligation on some public authorities to report suspicions of money laundering or terrorist financing.[272]

2.4.3 Financial Intelligence

The third part of the UK's policy is the use of SARs to gather financial intelligence, which was initially introduced by the DTOA 1986, which has since been codified by the PCA 2002 and the MLR 2007.[273] The PCA 2002 provides that SARs should be submitted if they 'suspect'[274] or have 'reasonable grounds for suspecting' that an offence has been committed.[275]

---

[262] As defined by the Estate Agents Act 1979, s. 1.
[263] A high value dealer is a business or sole trader that deals in goods where the payment/s is at least 15000 Euros in total. Money Laundering Regulations 2007, regulation 3(12).
[264] A casino holds an operating licence by virtue of the Gambling Act 2005, s. 65(2).
[265] Money Laundering Regulations 2007, regulation 8.
[266] Money Laundering Regulations, regulation 19.
[267] Money Laundering Regulations, regulation 20.
[268] Money Laundering Regulations, regulation 21.
[269] Money Laundering Regulations, regulations 23–36.
[270] Money Laundering Regulations, regulations 37–47.
[271] Money Laundering Regulations, regulation 48.
[272] Money Laundering Regulations, regulation 49.
[273] It is important to note that the reporting obligations imposed by the Proceeds of Crime Act 2002 have been severely criticized by the Court of Appeal in *UMBS Online Ltd* [2007] EWCA Civ 406.
[274] Proceeds of Crime Act 2002, s. 328(1), s. 330(2)(a) and s. 331(2)(a).
[275] Proceeds of Crime Act 2002, s. 330(2)(b) and s. 331(2)(b).

Brown and Evans concluded 'it is worthy of note that the test to be applied where the section refers to "suspect" is a subjective test, whereas where there is reference to "reasonable grounds to suspect", an objective test should be applied with the result under the objective test that a defendant's "neglect" to properly comply with the obligations in POCA could result in a criminal conviction'.[276] If a firm has 'reasonable suspicion'[277] or any possibility provided that it is more than 'fanciful' that it is being used for the purposes of money laundering, it is required to notify its money laundering reporting officer who will complete a SAR and send it to the UK's Financial Intelligence Unit, or SOCA, who will then determine if further action is to be taken.[278] Wadsley contended that disclosure is required 'not just in clear-cut cases where there is knowledge of money laundering, but also where there is merely suspicion'.[279] The interpretation of the term 'suspicion' has been contemplated by courts in England and Wales on many occasions, and is seen by many commentators as limiting the effectiveness of money laundering reporting requirements.[280] Longmore LJ in *R v Da Silva* took the view that:

> It seems to us that the essential element of the word suspect and its affiliates, in this context, is that the defendant must think that there is a possibility, which is more than fanciful, that the relevant facts exist. A vague feeling of unease would not suffice.[281]

The Court of Appeal added:

> The essential element in the word 'suspect' and its affiliates, in this context, is that the defendant must think that there is a possibility, which is more than

---

[276] Brown, G. and Evans, T. (2008), 'The impact: the breadth and depth of the anti-money laundering provisions requiring reporting of suspicious activities', *Journal of International Banking Law and Regulation*, **23**(5), 274–277, at 276.

[277] It is important to note that the Court of Appeal in *R v Da Silva* [2006] EWCA Crim. 1654 rejected the argument by Da Silva that the court 'could not imply a word such as "reasonable" into the relevant statutory provision'. *Ibid.*, at 275.

[278] *K Ltd v National Westminster Bank plc* [2007] 1 WLR 311.

[279] Wadsley, J. (2008), 'Painful perceptions and fundamental rights – anti-money laundering regulation and lawyers', *Company Lawyer*, **29**(3), 65–75, at 67.

[280] Other guidance for the definition of suspicion is offered by Joint Money Laundering Steering Group *Prevention of money laundering/combating terrorist financing guidance for the UK financial sector Part 1* (Joint Money Laundering Steering Group: London, 2007b) Guidance 6.9.

[281] [2006] EWCA Crim. 1654. This case related to the interpretation of the phrase under the Criminal Justice Act 1988.

fanciful, that the relevant facts exist. A vague feeling of unease would not suffice. But the statute does not require the suspicion to be 'clear' or 'firmly grounded and targeted on specific facts', or based upon 'reasonable grounds'.[282]

According to the Court of Appeal in *K v National Westminster Bank, HMRC, SOCA*,[283] the interpretation of 'suspicion' is the same in civil law as it is in criminal law.[284] Brown and Evans took the view that 'in most cases, the statement by those making a SAR that they have a suspicion will be enough. It will be exceptional for the courts to require those that report a suspicion to provide justification for having a suspicion. In reality, it will be for those challenging the making of a SAR to prove that no suspicion existed'.[285] However, it is important to consider the decision of the Court of Appeal in *Shah v HSBC Private Bank (UK) Ltd*.[286] Here, Longmore LJ took the view that 'I cannot see why, rather than submit to summary judgment dismissing the claim, Mr Shah cannot require the bank to prove its case that it had the relevant suspicion and be entitled to pursue the case to trial so that the bank can make good its contention in this respect'.[287] As a result of the Court of Appeal's decision Stanton took the view that 'a simple assertion that a professional person suspected the client to be money laundering does not suffice: evidence needs to be produced to prove the existence of the suspicion'.[288]

The overall effectiveness of the SARs regime has been questioned by several recent studies. For instance, KPMG identified a number of deficiencies within the reporting requirements.[289] The deficiencies were the ineffective SARs database, the monitoring of enforcement outcomes, inadequate training and the lack of government support for the scheme. The report also made a series of recommendations aimed at improving the monitoring of law enforcement outcomes and the provision of

---

[282]   *Ibid.*
[283]   [2006] EWCA Civ 1039.
[284]   Forston above, n 172 at 163.
[285]   Brown and Evans above, n 276 at 275. For a more detailed discussion see *K Limited v National Westminster Bank* [2006] EWCA Civ 1039.
[286]   [2010] EWCA Civ 31; [2010] Lloyd's Rep F.C. 276 (CA (Civ Div)). For an analysis of the impact of this case see Marshall, P. (2010), 'Does Shah v HSBC Private Bank Ltd make the anti-money laundering consent regime unworkable?', *Butterworths Journal of International Banking & Financial Law*, **25**(5), 287–290.
[287]   *Ibid.*, at 22.
[288]   Stanton, K. (2010), 'Money laundering: a limited remedy for clients', *Professional Negligence*, **26**(1), 56–59, at 58.
[289]   KPMG *Money Laundering: Review of the Reporting System* (KPMG: London, 2003), at p. 14.

training in relation to SARs.[290] Another critical report was published in 2005 and stated that SARs were under-used by law enforcement agencies.[291] Another criticism according to the 2005 report was that law enforcement agencies continue to have poor management information on how SARs are utilized.[292] A review of the SARs regime undertaken by Sir Stephen Lander noted several weaknesses of the regime including a lack of overall management and responsibility of the scheme, inconsistent reporting by the regulated sector and inappropriate training.[293] A common criticism of the reporting requirements imposed in the UK, as illustrated above in the US, is that reporting requirements have created a 'fear factor' which has resulted in a significant increase in the number of SARs submitted.[294] KPMG noted that the number of SARs submitted between 1995 and 2002 increased from 5000 to 60 000.[295] In 2009, SOCA reported that it had received 228 834 SARs between October 2008 and September 2009.[296]

This represents an increase of approximately 200 000 reports during a period of 13 years. The increase is associated to the threat of sanctions by the FSA, and it has led to the regulated sector adopting a tactic that has been referred to as 'defensive' or 'preventative' reporting.[297] The banking sector has raised concerns about the SARs regime,[298] and it has been suggested that the requirements should be abandoned and that the resources should be redirected elsewhere. The British Bankers Association claims that its members spend £250m each year to comply with the regulations.[299] Conversely, KPMG estimated that annually the costs are

---

[290]   *Ibid.*, at 17–20.
[291]   Fleming, M., *UK Law Enforcement Agency Use and Management of Suspicious Activity Reports: Towards Determining the Value of the Regime* (University College London: London, 2005) at p. 48.
[292]   *Ibid.*
[293]   Serious Organized Crime Agency *Review of the Suspicious Activity Reports Regime* (Serious Organized Crime Agency: London, 2006) at pp. 16–17.
[294]   Sarker, R. (2006), 'Anti-money laundering requirements: too much pain for too little gain', *Company Lawyer*, **27**(8), 250–251, at 251.
[295]   KPMG above, n 289 at 14.
[296]   Serious Organized Crime Agency *The Suspicious Activity Reports Regime Annual Report 2008* (Serious Organized Crime Agency: London, 2009) at p. 14.
[297]   Leong above, n 170 at 142.
[298]   Home Office *Report on the Operation in 2004 of the Terrorism Act 2000* (Home Office: London, 2004c) at pp. 19–20.
[299]   *Ibid.* Alexander claims that the annual costs of the AML to banks in the UK are £650m. See Alexander above, n 215 at 119.

nearer £90m.[300] Research has suggested that the AML costs in the UK are higher than in other countries including Germany, France and Italy.[301]

2.5 CONCLUSIONS

Since the implementation of the Vienna Convention and the creation of the FATF, both the US and the UK have introduced specific AML policies that have criminalized money laundering and utilized financial intelligence gathered from reports filed with their financial intelligence units by a wide range of financial institutions. Of the two countries reviewed in this chapter, it is appropriate to provide an overall conclusion on the US policy first.

2.5.1 The United States of America

The US has undertaken a lead role in the development and at times the implementation of a global AML policy as a member of both the UN and the FATF. Importantly, its AML policy predates any initiative introduced by either of these international organizations. The US policy is largely administered and implemented by several government agencies, law enforcement bodies and a plethora of other organizations. It was during the 1980s that money laundering became a criminal offence by virtue of the MLCA and the reporting requirements introduced by the BSA 1970 were re-examined by successive governments. However, it wasn't until President Bill Clinton signed the 'Strategy Act' in 1998 that the US actually had a codified AML policy. Uniquely, this Act required the Treasury and Justice Departments to write and implement a Money Laundering Strategy. As outlined above, the terrorist attacks of 11 September saw a fundamental change in the US AML policy and it was merged with terrorist financing largely by the response of President George Bush and the introduction of the USA Patriot Act in 2001. The criminal offences created by the MLCA 1986 have become a very important weapon for

---

[300] KPMG above, n 289 at 46–47. For an excellent commentary of the difficulties in calculating the costs of the SARs regime see Sproat, P. (2007), 'The new policing of assets and the new assets of policing: a tentative financial cost–benefit analysis of the UK's anti-money laundering and asset recovery regime', *Journal of Money Laundering Control*, **10**(3), 277–299, at 278–288.

[301] Yeandle, M., Mainelli, M., Berendt, A. and Healy, B. *Anti-money laundering requirements: costs, benefits and perceptions* (Corporation of London: London, 2005) at p. 24.

federal prosecutors. Nonetheless, the FATF concluded that 'while there are a few deficiencies in the criminalization of money laundering, particularly in relation to the coverage of foreign predicate offences, this record demonstrates that the system is working effectively overall'.[302] The AML policy adopted by the US can be described as robust yet its fixation with imposing more obligations on an ever increasing number of financial institutions must be questioned. The continuation of this policy is sadly fundamentally flawed as organized criminals and terrorists are utilizing new and even more sophisticated methods to either launder the proceeds of crime or to fund acts of terrorism without even entering the US banking system. This was a point raised by one commentator who stated that 'the future challenge of regulators and law enforcement authorities is to combat money laundering in those traditionally unregulated entities and to tailor money laundering regulations applicable to commercial banks to ensure that the increased regulatory burden and associated costs produce an effective decrease in money laundering and drug trafficking, not in bank profitability'.[303] Bosworth-Davies, writing in 2007, supported this view and stated that money launderers would 'look elsewhere for business offerings which provide the line of least resistance'.[304] Since the introduction of the BSA 1970, the banking sector has complained that the measures are intrusive, they undermine the unique relationship between banks and their clients, and they are too expensive and burdensome to comply with. These complaints have largely been ignored and successive administrations have imposed more and more burdens upon the financial services sector. In its most recent Mutual Evaluation Report on the US policy towards money laundering and terrorist financing, the FATF noted that the US has 'significantly strengthened its overall AML/CFT measures since its last mutual evaluation, implementing a very large number of statutory amendments and structural changes'.[305] The report concluded:

> The US authorities are committed to identifying, disrupting, and dismantling money laundering and terrorist financing networks. They seek to combat money laundering and terrorist financing on all fronts, including by aggressively pursuing financial investigations. These efforts have produced impressive results in terms of prosecutions, convictions, seizures, asset freezing, confiscation and regulatory enforcement actions. Overall, the US has implemented an

---

[302]   Financial Action Task Force above, n 163 at 2.
[303]   Alford above, n 34 at 468.
[304]   Bosworth-Davies, R. (2007b), 'Money laundering – chapter five: the implications of global money laundering laws', *Journal of Money Laundering Control*, **10**(2), 189–208, at 190.
[305]   Financial Action Task Force above, n 163 at 2.

effective AML/CFT system, although there are remaining concerns in relation to some of the specific requirements for undertaking customer due diligence, the availability of corporate ownership information, and the requirements applicable to certain designated non-financial businesses and professions.[306]

2.5.2 The United Kingdom

The UK has fully complied with its international obligations under the Vienna and Palermo Conventions and its requirements under the Money Laundering Directives. In fact, the UK's measures go beyond its international obligations. The criminalization of money laundering occurred in 1986, since when the legislative framework has been updated and codified by the PCA 2002. The involvement of the FSA is an innovative attempt to reduce the impact of money laundering. It is the first time that a financial regulatory body in the UK has been given such a specific role, a position that can be contrasted with the US. The FSA has implemented a costly and at times unnecessarily complicated regime, yet it has at least attempted to lessen the AML obligations by implementing SYSC. The scheme introduced by the FSA will, in the main, do little to discourage well-organized criminals from laundering money in the UK. The SARs reporting requirements have imposed significant administrative burdens on financial institutions. They have led to an increased level of record-keeping, report filing, and internal policing requirements. The imposition of even more mandatory reporting requirements was inevitable given the government's tough stance towards money laundering. It is questionable, however, whether the filing of a SAR will make any difference given the difficulties in securing prosecutions in money laundering offences. It is also possible to argue that the reporting requirements have created a 'needle-in-the-haystack' problem, especially given the large number of SARs annually submitted. In its 2004 policy document, HM Treasury referred to the 2003 IMF review of the UK's AML legislative framework and policy. The review concluded that 'the UK has a comprehensive legal, institutional and supervisory regime for AML'.[307] Similarly, Harvey noted that 'the UK is particularly assiduous in the application of its anti-money laundering systems and procedures and has been identified as the greatest devotee of anti-money laundering provisions within the European Union'.[308] However, the UK's AML approach can be criticized because of its ambit and the burden imposed on the sectors that are forced to comply

---

[306] *Ibid.*
[307] HM Treasury above, n 223 at 7.
[308] Harvey above, n 18 at 341.

with it.[309] The effectiveness of imposing more AML regulations has been questioned by Harvey who took the view that 'there remains little evidence to suggest that the policy of imposing greater regulatory burden on both society and the financial institutions in particular is likely to have the desired impact of reducing money-laundering activity'.[310] Maylam noted that despite the best efforts of the UK, the fight against money laundering 'can only be effective if conducted on a global basis with a spirit of co-operation and legal compatibility'.[311] Harvey concluded that despite the best efforts of the UK AML authorities 'it remains on the list of identified money laundering countries'.[312]

---

[309]   Rhodes, R. and Palastrand, S. (2004), 'A guide to money laundering legislation', *Journal of Money Laundering Control*, **8**(1), 9–18, at 17.

[310]   Harvey above, n 18 at 308.

[311]   Maylam, S. (2002), 'Prosecution for money laundering in the UK', *Journal of Financial Crime*, **10**(2), 157–158, at 157–158.

[312]   Harvey above, n 18 at 339.

3. Terrorist financing

> The 'fog of war' has long befuddled military and political leaders. Of all the battlefronts in today's war on terrorism, few are as 'foggy' as efforts to combat terrorist financing. Even to those in the midst of the campaign, uncertainty often colours the most fundamental question: are we winning or losing the battle?[1]

3.1   INTRODUCTION

Prior to the terrorist attacks in September 2001 (9/11), terrorist financing could be described as the 'sleeping giant' of the international community's financial crime policies. The United Nations (UN), the Financial Action Task Force (FATF) and the European Union (EU) responded by implementing rules and recommendations aimed at tackling terrorist financing. On 24 September 2001 President George Bush proclaimed that 'we will starve terrorists of funding',[2] thus instigating the 'financial war on terrorism'. The then Secretary to the Department of Treasury stated 'we will succeed in starving the terrorists of funding and shutting down the institutions that support or facilitate terrorism'.[3] However, the 'financial war on terrorism' was originally instigated by President Bill Clinton in 1998, who acknowledged that attacking the financial assets of al-Qaeda was essential if they were to be punished, after they were found to be responsible for the bombings of the US embassies in Kenya and Tanzania.[4] The objective of this chapter is to identify and provide a critique of the anti-terrorist financing policies of the international community, the United

---

[1]   Greenberg, M., Wechsler, W. and Wolosky, L. (2002) *Terrorist financing*, Council on Foreign Relations, New York, at p. v. Hereafter Greenberg *et al.*

[2]   The White House *Fact sheet on terrorist financing executive order* (White House: Washington, DC, 2001b) at 1.

[3]   The White House (2001c), 'President freezes terrorists' assets', Remarks by the President, Secretary of the Treasury O'Neill and Secretary of State Powell on Executive Order, Office of the Press Secretary, 24 September 2001, available at http://www.fas.org/terrorism/at/docs/2001/Bush-9-24-01.htm (accessed 11 October 2009).

[4]   A reaction to these attacks was the issuing of Executive Order 13 129 which prevented access to property and outlawed dealings with the Taliban. See Exec. Order No. 13 224, 3 C.F.R. 786 (2001), reprinted in 50 U.S.C.S. 1701 (2001).

States of America (US) and the United Kingdom (UK). The chapter begins by highlighting the financial mechanisms available to terrorists and discusses 'cheap terrorism'. The next part considers the impact of 9/11 and the legislative response of the international community, which has resulted in the US and UK adopting a three-pronged terrorist financing policy: (i) the criminalization of terrorist financing; (ii) the ability to freeze terrorist assets; and (iii) the imposition of reporting requirements on financial and deposit-taking institutions.

3.2   SOURCES OF TERRORIST FINANCING

Terrorists have traditionally relied on two sources of funding: state and private sponsors.[5] State sponsorship is where a government provides logistical and financial support to terrorist organizations.[6] A large percentage of terrorists during the 1970s and 1980s were backed by sympathetic governments and it was during this time that the US released its first state sponsors of terrorism list.[7] The Secretary of State has the authority to declare a country a state sponsor of terrorism by virtue of the Foreign Assistance Act 1961 and the Export Administration Act 1979. Four countries are designated as state sponsors of terrorism: the Sudan,[8] Syria,[9] Iran[10] and

---

[5]   Bantekas, I. (2003), 'The international law of terrorist financing', *American Journal of International Law*, **97**, 315–333, at 316.

[6]   Chase, A. (2004), 'Legal mechanisms of the international community and the United States concerning the state sponsorship of terrorism', *Virginia Journal of International Law*, **45**, 41–137, at 49.

[7]   Richard, A. (2005) *Fighting terrorist financing: transatlantic cooperation and international institutions*, Center for Transatlantic Relations, Washington, DC, at p. 6.

[8]   Sudan was added to the state sponsors of terrorism list on 12 August 1993.

[9]   Syria was added to the state sponsors of terrorism list on 29 December 1979.

[10]   Iran was added to the state sponsors of terrorism list on 19 January 1984. It is important to note that one of the first terrorist financing measures introduced by President Barak Obama was the Comprehensive Iran Sanctions, Accountability, and Divestment Act of 2010 (H.R. 2194). Tim Geithner, the Treasury Secretary, stated that 'the law provides Treasury with powerful new authorities to impose mandatory sanctions against foreign banks that knowingly provide financial services related to such conduct by Iran, or to the IRGC and its affiliates. These authorities strengthen Treasury's ongoing efforts to protect the international financial system from abuse'. Department of Treasury (2010a), 'Statement of Secretary Geithner on the Signing of the Iran Sanctions Act' 1 July 2010, available at http://www.treas.gov/press/releases/tg767.htm (accessed 10 July 2010).

Cuba.[11] Since the end of the 'Cold War' state-sponsored terrorism has declined and terrorists receive more funding from private sponsors. There are two reasons for this decline.[12] Firstly, there are fewer states involved in supporting terrorists.[13] Secondly, terrorists are no longer reliant on state sponsorship.[14] This decline has forced terrorists to diversify their funding activities and become self-sufficient.[15] Nonetheless, there are still an abundant number of sources of funding available,[16] which means that terrorists are able to 'manipulate an expanding array of tools to shield their wealth'.[17] For example, it has been argued that 'al-Qaeda's global fundraising network is built upon a foundation of charities, nongovernmental organisations, mosques, websites, intermediaries, facilitators, and banks and other financial institutions'.[18] The Department of Treasury stated that terrorist 'funds can be moved among corporate entities and financial institutions in many countries in the blink of an eye through wire fund transfers, making the untangling more and more difficult'.[19] Terrorists also use misapplied charitable donations and financing from legitimate operations, including membership fees, speaking tours, cultural and social events,

---

[11] Cuba has been on the state sponsors of terrorism list since 1 March 1982. For a more detailed discussion on the state sponsors of terrorism see State Department *Country Reports on Terrorism 2008* (United States State Department: Washington, DC, 2009) at pp. 181–186.

[12] See Richard above, n 7 at 5.

[13] *Ibid.*

[14] See Richard above, n 7 at 6.

[15] The self-sufficiency of terrorist cells was also recognized by the official report on the terrorist attacks on London on 7 July 2005. See House of Commons *Report of the Official Account of the Bombings in London on 7th July 2005* (House of Commons: London, 2005) at p. 23.

[16] Lowe, P. (2006), 'Counterfeiting: links to organised crime and terrorist funding', (2006) *Journal of Financial Crime*, **13**(2), 255–257.

[17] Alexander, K. (2001), 'The international anti-money laundering regime: the role of the Financial Action Task Force', *Journal of Money Laundering Control*, **4**(3), 231–248, at 231. This is a view supported by Rider, B. (2003), 'Thinking outside the Box', *Journal of Financial Crime*, **10**(2), 198.

[18] See Greenberg *et al* above, n 1 at 1.

[19] Department of Treasury *Contributions by the Department of the Treasury to the Financial War on Terrorism* (Department of Treasury: Washington, DC, 2002). Terrorists are also utilizing new electronic technologies to transfer money over the internet to conceal their true origin. See also Ping, H. (2004), 'New trends in money laundering – from the real world to cyberspace', *Journal of Money Laundering Control*, **8**(1), 48–55 and Baldwin, F. (2004), 'The financing of terror in the age of the internet: wilful blindness, greed or a political statement?', *Journal of Money Laundering Control*, **8**(2), 127–158.

appeals to wealthy members of the community and donations.[20] Terrorists also acquire funding through criminal activities such as fraud, the sale of counterfeit goods and drug trafficking.[21]

As a result of 9/11, the international community targeted alternative or non-remittance banking systems. Underground banking has been used to describe informal banking systems which take place outside the regulated financial sector.[22] One such method is the hawala system.[23] This system is based on trust which means that transferred funds are difficult to detect, and it has led to accusations that this system has been used for illegal purposes.[24] Indeed, after 9/11 hawala was declared a 'financial tool of terrorism',[25] a misleading categorization because it is a legitimate banking system in many jurisdictions. Conversely, it has been argued that al-Qaeda use the hawala system to support terrorist operations. This is a view supported by the *Washington Post* who reported that al-Qaeda abused this system to partly fund the African embassy bombings.[26] However, there is no conclusive evidence that al-Qaeda used this system to fund the attacks in 2001.[27] Indeed, the 9/11 Commission reported that the funds used in these attacks were transferred into the bank accounts of the terrorists

---

[20] General Accounting Office *Terrorist Financing – US Agencies should systematically assess terrorists' use of alternative financing mechanisms* (General Accounting Office: Washington, DC, 2003b).

[21] Linn, C. (2005), 'How terrorists exploit gaps in US anti-money laundering laws to secrete plunder', *Journal of Money Laundering Control*, **8**(3), 200–214, at 200.

[22] For a more in-depth discussion of the operation of underground banking systems see Trehan, J. (2002), 'Underground and parallel banking systems', *Journal of Financial Crime*, **10**(1), 76–84.

[23] Pathak, R. (2004), 'The obstacles to regulating the hawala: a cultural norm or a terrorist hotbed?', *Fordham International Law Journal*, **27**, 2007–2061, at 2008.

[24] Waszak, D. (2004), 'The obstacles to suppressing radical Islamic terrorist financing', *Case Western Reserve Journal of International Law*, **35**, 673–710.

[25] Jamwal, N. (2000), 'Hawala – the invisible financing system of terrorism', *Strategic Analysis*, **26**(2), 181–198. Passas took the view that 'the main problem is that [US] law enforcement did not focus very much on these types of transaction, network and ethnic group involved before 9/11'. See Passas, N. (2004), 'Law enforcement challenges in hawala-related investigations', *Journal of Financial Crime*, **12**(2), 112–119, at 112.

[26] Farah, D. (2002), 'Al-Qaeda's road paved with gold', *Washington Post*, 17 February 2002, available at http://www.washingtonpost.com/ac2/wp-dyn/A22303-2002Feb16?language=printer (accessed 7 July 2009).

[27] Maimbo and Passas took the view, however, that 'all evidence points to the use of banks, wire services, credit card accounts and other regulated remitters'. See Maimbo, S. and Passas, N. (2004), 'The regulation and supervision of informal remittance systems', *Small Enterprise Development*, **15**(1), 53–61, at 59.

through the US banking system, not the hawala system.[28] Furthermore, it must be noted that the terrorists received money via a series of wire transfers from the United Arab Emirates and they brought approximately $40 000 in cash that was declared to customs officials.[29] The hawala system is difficult to regulate, and previous attempts have been ineffective.[30] Rider argues that one of the main reasons for this is that 'law and enforcement policies which have been fashioned to address money laundering through conventional banking systems are of little practical relevance in the case of such underground systems'.[31] Several countries have even attempted to regulate and even ban this money transmission system.

The problem of terrorist financing is worsened because of the small amounts of money involved. This has been referred to as 'cheap terrorism', a concept, which makes it impossible to prevent terrorist financing. According to the Commonwealth Secretariat the 'Bishopsgate bomb in the City of London . . . is estimated to have cost only £3000'.[32] Similarly, the approximate costs of the bombing of the World Trade Center in 1993 were $3500.[33] This attack resulted in the death of six people and local businesses lost between $330m and $692m.[34] Indeed, the Commonwealth Secretariat concluded that 'detecting the transmission of such relatively

---

[28]   9/11 Commission *The 9/11 Commission Report – Final Report of the National Commission on Terrorist Attacks upon the United States* (Norton & Company: London, 2004) at 170–171.

[29]   McHugh, G. (2007), 'Terrorist Finance Tracking Program: illegality by the President or the Press?' *Quinnipiac Law Review*, **26**, 213–256, at 213. It has also been suggested that money was transferred to the terrorists from Germany to a SunTrust bank in Florida. See Santolli, J. (2008), 'The terrorist finance tracking program: illuminating the shortcomings of the European Union's antiquated data privacy directive', *George Washington International Law Review*, **40**, 553–582, at 556.

[30]   Navias, M. (2002), 'Financial warfare as a response to international terrorism', *The Political Quarterly*, 73(1), 57–79, at 61.

[31]   Rider, R. (2002), 'The weapons of war: the use of anti-money laundering laws against terrorist and criminal enterprises: pt. I', *Journal of International Banking Regulation*, **4**(1), 13–31, at 25.

[32]   Commonwealth Secretariat *Combating money laundering and terrorist financing – a model of best practice for the financial sector, the professions and other designated businesses* (Commonwealth Secretariat: London, 2006) at p. 13.

[33]   Bowman, S. (1994) *When the Eagle Screams: America's Vulnerability to Terrorism*, Carol Publishing Corporation, Secaucus, NJ, at pp. 66–67, as cited in Crona, S. and Richardson, N. (1996), 'Justice for war criminals of invisible armies: a new legal and military approach to terrorism', *Oklahoma City University Law Review*, **21**, 349–407.

[34]   Bublick, E. (2008), 'Upside down? Terrorists, proprietors, and civil responsibility for crime prevention in the post-9/11 tort reform world', *Loyola of Los Angeles Law Review*, **31**, 1483–1543, at 1492–1493.

small sums as they move through the financial system is challenging'.[35] An example of cheap terrorism was the terrorist attacks in London in July 2005, which cost approximately £8000.[36] HM Treasury stated that 'the sums required for an operation vary: the attacks in New York and Washington . . . are estimated to have cost $500000; the 7/7 London attacks and the Madrid train bombings cost less (£8000 and $10000 respectively); and an improvised explosive device in Iraq costs about $100'.[37] Similarly, Richard warned that 'discovering or tracking terrorist financing, however, has grown more difficult . . . smaller, dispersed terrorist groups also need smaller amounts of funds and assets that are harder for investigators to detect'.[38] Therefore, the international community has introduced a range of measures aimed at tackling terrorist financing with the aim of disrupting the financial infrastructures and limiting the sources of financing. The next part of the chapter examines these initiatives.

3.3   INTERNATIONAL LEGISLATIVE RESPONSE

The international community were not prepared to tackle terrorist financing.[39] The terrorist attacks of 9/11 set in motion an inventive legislative policy towards terrorist funding, and they had an instantaneous effect.

3.3.1   The United Nations

The international response to terrorist financing has been influenced by the US, but led by the UN, which is 'in the best position to lead the

---

[35]   Commonwealth Secretariat above, n 32 at 13. This is a view supported by Donohue, L. (2008), *The cost of counterterrorism – power, politics and liberty*, Cambridge University Press, Cambridge, at p. 154.

[36]   See House of Commons Report, above n 15, at 23.

[37]   HM Treasury *Public consultation: draft terrorist asset-freezing bill* (HM Treasury: London, 2010) at p. 5.

[38]   See Richard above, n 7 at 5. Similarly, HM Treasury noted that 'while individual attacks can yield great damage at low financial cost, a significant financial infrastructure is required to sustain international terrorist networks and promote their goals', HM Treasury *The Financial Challenge to Crime and Terrorism* (HM Treasury: London, 2007) at p. 11. For an interesting discussion of the terrorist financing see Tupman, W. (2009), 'Ten myths about terrorist financing', *Journal of Money Laundering Control*, **12**(2), 189–205.

[39]   Binning, P. (2002), 'In safe hands? Striking the balance between privacy and security – anti-terrorist finance measures', *European Human Rights Law Review*, **6**, 737–749, at 737.

international coalition against terrorism'.[40] The term terrorist financing was initially adopted by the UN in its Declaration to Eliminate International Terrorism (1994).[41] The Declaration stated that members should 'reaffirm that acts, methods and practices of terrorism are contrary to the purposes and principles of the UN; they declare that knowingly financing, planning and inciting terrorist acts are also contrary to the purposes and principles of the UN'.[42] In 1999, the UN instigated the International Convention for the Suppression of the Financing of Terrorism.[43] This provided that member states must criminalize terrorist financing, and take the necessary steps for the identification, detection and freezing of any funds used for the purposes of supporting terrorism.[44] The Convention resulted in 'an agreed global network within which the international community can collaborate more effectively'.[45] Prior to 9/11 the Convention had not received the minimum number of ratifications needed to become a Treaty, yet following the attacks 167 members of the UN have ratified it. The US incorporated the Convention by the Suppression of the Financing of Terrorism Convention Implementation Act of 2001 and it was implemented in the UK by the Al-Qa'ida and Taliban (United Nations Measures) (Overseas Territories) (Amendment) Order 2002.[46]

The UN implemented Security Council Resolution 1267,[47] which required members to impose sanctions against al-Qaeda, Osama bin Laden, the Taliban and other known or suspected associates.[48] This Resolution established the Security Council Sanctions Committee whose objective was to freeze the funds owned by or used for the benefit of the

---

40   Hardister, A. (2003), 'Can we buy peace on earth?: The price of freezing terrorist assets in a post-September 11 world', *North Carolina Journal of International Law and Commercial Regulation*, **28**, 606–661, at 624.

41   United Nations A/RES/49/60 84th plenary meeting, Measures to eliminate international terrorism, 9 December 1994.

42   *Ibid.*

43   Adopted by the General Assembly of the United Nations in resolution 54/109 of 9 December 1999.

44   Article 8. It also necessitates that signatories direct financial institutions and other relevant professions to introduce and implement the so-called 'know your customer' obligations, which include measures to determine the identification of clients and the use of suspicious transactions reports. *Ibid.*, Article 18.

45   Gilmore, William (2004) *Dirty money – the evolution of international measures to counter money laundering and the financing of terrorism*, Council of Europe, Strasbourg, at pp. 73–74.

46   S.I. 2002/266.

47   S.C. Res. 1267, U.N. SCOR, 4051st Mtg.

48   *Ibid.*, Article 4(b).

Taliban. A person or company is listed by the Committee on the request of a member; once listed the only recourse is for them to apply for de-listing. This Resolution 'established a new precedent . . . and called on States to take a number of steps to enhance international cooperation in the fight against terrorism'.[49] Of greater significance is Resolution 1373, the cornerstone of the international community's policy towards terrorist financing.[50] This imposes four obligations on members of the UN.[51] Firstly, it requires states to thwart and control the financing of terrorism.[52] Secondly, it criminalizes the collection of terrorist funds in their territories.[53] Thirdly, it freezes funds, financial assets and economic resources of people who commit or try to commit acts of terrorism.[54] Finally, it prevents any nationals from within their territories providing funds, financial assets and economic resources to people who seek to commit acts of terrorism.[55] The obligation on member states to freeze assets is absolute and compels collective application.[56] The Department of Treasury took the view that UN Security Resolution 1373 'has been critical in winning support for our campaign, and they have been essential tools for building the international coalition against terror financing'.[57] However, the interpretation of key terms such as 'terrorist' is still problematic.[58] In September 2003, the US government reported that all 191 UN members have submitted reports to the Security Council Counter-Terrorism Committee on the actions they have taken to suppress international terrorism; this includes blocking ter-

---

[49]　Flynn, E. (2007), 'The Security Council's Counter-terrorism Committee and human rights', *Human Rights Law Review*, **7**, 371–384, at 373.

[50]　Binning above, n 39. For a more detailed commentary on these measures see Gurule, J. (2009), 'The demise of the UN economic sanctions regime to deprive terrorists of funding', *Case Western Reserve Journal of International Law*, **41**, 19–63.

[51]　See Cabinet Office *The UK and the Campaign against International Terrorism – Progress Report* (Cabinet Office: London, 2002) p. 24.

[52]　S.C. Res. 1373, U.N. SCOR, 56th Sess., 4385th Mtg. Article 1(a).

[53]　S.C. Res. 1373, U.N. SCOR, 56th Sess., 4385th Mtg. Article 1(b).

[54]　S.C. Res. 1373, U.N. SCOR, 56th Sess., 4385th Mtg. Article 1(c).

[55]　S.C. Res. 1373, U.N. SCOR, 56th Sess., 4385th Mtg. Article 1(e).

[56]　See Kruse, A. (2005), 'Financial and economic sanctions – from a perspective of international law and human rights', *Journal of Financial Crime*, 12(3), 217–220, at 218.

[57]　Department of Treasury above, n 19 at 5.

[58]　For a more detailed commentary see Acharya, U. (2009), 'The war on terror and its implications for international law and policy – war on terror or terror wars: the problem in defining terrorism', *Denver Journal of International Law and Policy*, **37**, 653–679.

rorist finances as required by Resolution 1373.[59] Notwithstanding the high level of support for the UN stance on terrorist financing, the implementation of UN Resolution 1373 is not universal.[60] As a result of Resolution 1373 'we are left with a patchwork of domestic, bilateral, and regional efforts that at best work in parallel but not complementary fashion, and at worst work at cross-purposes'.[61]

3.3.2 Financial Action Task Force

> Prior to the events of 11 September 2001, the issue of terrorist financing had not assumed the position of any prominence in the activities of the Financial Action Task Force.[62]

Following 9/11, the FATF broadened its remit to include terrorist financing.[63] In October 2001 it produced a set of international principles, which are more commonly known as the 'Special Recommendations'.[64] There are nine Special Recommendations. Firstly, members should ratify and implement UN instruments.[65] Secondly, countries are expected to criminalize

---

[59] The White House *Progress Report on the Global War on Terrorism* (The White House: Washington, DC, 2003) at p. 6.

[60] See for example the initial response of Saudi Arabia as discussed in Roth, J., Greenburg, D. and Wille, S. (2004) *Monograph on terrorist financing: staff report to the Commission*, National Commission on Terrorist Attacks against the United States of America, Washington, DC, at p. 6. Hereafter Roth *et al*. However, 9/11 Commission concluded that there was no direct evidence that Saudi Arabia was involved in the funding of the attacks. See 9/11 Commission above, n 28 and Congressional Research Service *Saudi Arabia: Terrorist Financing Issues* (Congressional Research Service: Washington, DC, 2005), p. 5. These allegations have been refuted by Saudi Arabia. See Royal Embassy of the Kingdom of Saudi Arabia, Press Release, 'Response to CFR Report', 17 October 2002 and Royal Embassy of the Kingdom of Saudi Arabia, Press Release, 'Saudi Arabia blasts CFR task force report', 15 June 2004. For further information, see Greenberg *et al* above, n 1 at 1.

[61] Levitt, M. (2003), 'Stemming the flow of terrorist financing: practical and conceptual challenges', *The Fletcher Forum of World Affairs*, **27**(1), 59–70, at 62.

[62] Gilmore above, n 45.

[63] This decision was taken at an extraordinary plenary meeting on the financing of terrorism in October 2001. See Financial Action Task Force (2001), 'FATF cracks down on terrorist financing', Press Release, 31 October 2001, available at http://www.fatf-gafi.org/dataoecd/45/48/34269864.pdf (accessed 3 January 2009).

[64] Financial Action Task Force (n/d), '9 Special Recommendations (SR) on Terrorist Financing (TF)', available at http://www.fatf-gafi.org/document/9/0,3343,en_32250379_32236920_34032073_1_1_1_1,00.html (accessed 3 August 2010).

[65] This includes the International Convention for the Suppression of the Financing of Terrorism and UN Resolution 1373.

the financing of terrorism, terrorist acts and terrorist organizations.[66] The third Special Recommendation requires countries to introduce measures that allow the seizure of terrorist-related funds or assets.[67] The fourth Special Recommendation is to report suspicious transactions linked to terrorism. The next Recommendation encourages countries to provide the widest possible range of assistance to other countries who are conducting terrorist financing investigations. The sixth Special Recommendation deals with the imposition of anti-money laundering requirements on alternative remittance systems.[68] The seventh seeks to inhibit the ability of money launderers and terrorists from abusing the wire transfer system to move monies around the globe.[69] The penultimate Special Recommendation concerns non-profit entities such as charities and its objective is to ensure that they are not abused by terrorist organizations.[70] The final Recommendation provides that countries should have measures in place

---

[66] Countries are expected to criminalize the financing of terrorism, terrorist acts and terrorist organizations and to ensure that such criminal offences are designated as money laundering predicate offences. According to the Interpretative guidance note this Special Recommendation had two objectives. Firstly, to guarantee that countries have the capability to initiate criminal proceedings and enforce criminal sanctions against people who provide financial support for terrorists. Secondly, to stress the connection between necessitating countries to incorporate terrorist financing offences as predicate offences for money laundering. See Financial Action Task Force *Interpretative Note to Special Recommendation II: Criminalising the financing of terrorism and associated money laundering* (Financial Action Task Force: Paris, 2001) at p. 1.

[67] *Ibid.*

[68] The primary objective of this Special Recommendation is to encourage and strengthen the level of transparency of financial transactions by guaranteeing that countries implement and enforce constant anti-money laundering and anti-terrorist financing measures on alternative remittance systems. According to the FATF, this Recommendation contains three central elements. Firstly, countries should seek providers of alternative remittance systems to obtain a licence to conduct their financial transactions or register with an appropriate financial regulatory agency. Secondly, jurisdictions should require alternative remittance systems to comply with the Forty Recommendations and its Special Recommendations. Thirdly, if alternative remittance systems function without an appropriate licence or registration, sanctions should be imposed upon them.

[69] This Recommendation seeks to guarantee that the important information on the instigator of the wire transfer is instantaneously made available to any relevant law enforcement agencies, financial intelligence units and beneficiary financial institutions that are linked to the suspicious transaction report.

[70] For a brief discussion of the links between charities and terrorist financing in the United Kingdom see Ryder, N. (2007b), 'Danger money', *New Law Journal*, **157**(7300), (Charities Appeals Supplement) 6, 8, and Ryder, N. (2008a), 'Hidden money', *New Law Journal*, **158**(7348), (Charities Appeal Supplement), 36–37.

to detect the physical cross-border transportation of currency and bearer negotiable instruments. Gilmore stated 'the underlying philosophy was that these measures, when combined with the Forty Recommendations, would provide an appropriate framework for the prevention, detection and suppression of the financing of terrorism and terrorist acts'.[71]

3.3.3 The European Union

The policy adopted by the EU towards terrorist financing emerged following the events in 2001. In June 2002, the Council of Europe approved a framework decision on fighting terrorism.[72] Brent notes that this framework decision, combined with the Council Common Position[73] and the 2001 Council Regulation[74] 'constituted the Community's principal legislative response to the 11 September 2001 terrorist attacks . . . [and] it also partly implements the Community's obligation deriving from UN Security Council Resolution 1373'.[75] One of the most controversial aspects of the EU's policy towards terrorist financing is its terrorist sanctions regime. Council Regulation 2580/2001 'requires the freezing of funds, other financial assets, and economic resources belonging to, owned or held by individuals, groups or entities'.[76] This means that 'financial institutions are prohibited under the Regulation from providing financial services to those included on the blacklist'.[77] Furthermore, Council Regulation 881/2002 is very similar to Regulation 2580/2001, yet its blacklist is the same as that utilized by the UN Sanctions Committee. Controversially, the EU has no power to review the contents of the list.[78] These measures have been challenged on the grounds of illegality.[79] In *Ahmed Ali Yusuf and Al Barakaat International Foundation v Commission*[80] and *Yassin Adbullah Kadi v*

---

[71]   Gilmore above, n 45 at 124.
[72]   [2002] OJ L164/3.
[73]   [2001] OJ L344/93.
[74]   (EC) 2580/2001.
[75]   Brent, Richard (2008), 'International legal sources IV – the European Union and the Council of Europe', in W. Blair and R. Brent (eds), *Banks and financial crime – the international law of tainted money*, Oxford University Press, Oxford, 101–150, at 123.
[76]   *Ibid.*
[77]   Council Regulation (EC) 2580/2007, Art. 2(2).
[78]   Brent above, n 75.
[79]   See for example Case T-47/03 *Sison v Council*, unreported judgment of 11 July 2007; Case T-228/02 *Organisation des Modjahedines du Peuple d' Iran (OMP) v Council*, judgment of 12 December 2006.
[80]   Case T-306/01.

Council and Commission[81] the applicants argued that Council Regulation (No. 881/2002) should be annulled. The claim failed on several grounds. Firstly, the Court of First Instance (CFI) ruled that the European Council is competent to freeze the funds of individuals in connection with the fight against terrorism. Secondly, that the EU is bound to follow any obligations from the UN Charter, as are its members. Thirdly, the freezing of the applicant's funds did not infringe the fundamental rights and the applicants had not been arbitrarily deprived of their right to property.

In 2009, the European Court of Justice (ECJ) reversed these decisions on two grounds.[82] Firstly, it held that the EU was capable of executing the Security Council Resolution as a Regulation.[83] Secondly, the Court 'rejected the CFI's analysis and emphasised that the EC Regulation implementing that Resolution was subject to scrutiny in the light of EC law fundamental rights standards'.[84] Johnston concluded the 'ECJ's analysis of the EC's competence to adopt such EC measures, however, leaves rather more to be desired. The Council's response to the judgment is still awaited: its implications for the future operation of the legal regimes for terrorist asset freezing at EC, international and national levels will be substantial'.[85] Ziegler remarked 'for the applicants, however, the appeal from the Court of First Instance's judgments in *Kadi* and *Yusuf and Al Barakaat* amounted to a Pyrrhic victory'.[86] Cardwell *et al* noted that 'the approach of the ECJ is ultimately premised upon three key understandings, namely the autonomy of the EU legal system, the constitutionality of the EU legal system and the centrality of fundamental rights to the operation of that legal system'.[87]

3.3.4 Conclusion

The international community were totally unprepared to tackle terrorist financing prior to 9/11 and can only dream of the situation where

---

[81] Case T-315/01.

[82] *Kadi v Council of the European Union* (C-402/05 P) [2008] E.C.R. I-6351.

[83] Johnston, A. (2009), 'Frozen in time? The ECJ finally rules on the Kadi appeal', *Cambridge Law Journal*, **68**(1) 1–4, at 1.

[84] *Ibid.*

[85] Johnston above, n 83 at 4.

[86] Ziegler, K. (2009), 'Strengthening the rule of law, but fragmenting international law: the Kadi decision of the ECJ from the perspective of human rights', *Human Rights Law Review*, **9**(2), 288–305, at 288.

[87] Cardwell, P., French, D. and White, N. (2009), 'Kadi v Council of the European Union (C-402/05 P) (Case Comment)', *International Comparative Legal Quarterly*, **58**(1), 229–240, at 233.

'dismantled terrorist networks and zero terrorist attacks would mark true success in the fight against terrorist financing'.[88] This controversial regime has influenced the policies adopted in the US and the UK. However, 'in the US – unlike the UK, where September 11 accelerated a trend already under way – there was an abrupt change of course in respect of terrorist finance'.[89] Indeed, it has been argued that in the US 'terrorist financing was not a priority and there was little interagency strategic planning or coordination . . . most fundamentally, the domestic strategy for combating terrorist financing within the US never had any sense of urgency'.[90] If the objective of these measures is to disrupt the financial infrastructure of terrorists, then their effectiveness must be questioned. However, if the objective is to provide a benchmark for nation states to adhere to then they have been successful. What is clear from this discussion is that there are several common elements in the instruments outlined; this includes, for example, the criminalization of terrorist financing, the freezing of assets and the use of financial intelligence. The next part of the chapter discusses how the international measures have been implemented in the US and the UK.

3.4   THE UNITED STATES OF AMERICA

US government agencies participate in a number of interdependent efforts to address the transnational challenges posed by terrorist financing, including terrorist designations, intelligence and law enforcement, international standard setting, and training and technical assistance.[91]

The origins of the US policy can be found in the Trading with the Enemy Act (1917), the International Emergency Economic Powers Act (1977)[92] and the Anti-terrorism and Effective Death Penalty Act (1996).[93] There were two other mechanisms that tackled terrorist financing: the Financial Crimes Enforcement Network's (FinCEN) administration of the reporting obligations and the Office of Foreign Assets Control's (OFAC) management of economic sanctions against designated countries and

---

88   See Richard above, n 7 at 57.
89   Donohue above, n 35 at 147.
90   Roth *et al* above, n 59 at 4.
91   Government Accountability Office *Better Strategic Planning Needed to Coordinate U.S. Efforts to Deliver Counter-Terrorism Financing Training and Technical Assistance Abroad* (Government Accountability Office: Washington, DC, 2005) at p. 7.
92   P.L. 95-223, 91 Stat. 1626.
93   P.L. 104-132, 110 Stat. 1214. Donohue above, n 35 at 147–148.

groups.[94] The Trading with the Enemy Act was introduced to limit trade between countries who were unfriendly or aggressive to the US. Under the Act, the President is given the power to supervise and manage all trade between the US and her adversaries during times of war.[95] The International Emergency Powers Act is important because 'once the President declares a national emergency in regard to the specific threat, a broad range of powers goes into effect'.[96] Under the Act, the President is permitted to

> investigate, block during the pendency of an investigation, regulate, direct and compel, nullify, void, prevent or prohibit, any acquisition, holding, withholding, use, transfer, withdrawal, transportation, importation or exportation of, or dealing in, or exercising any right, power, or privilege with respect to, or transactions involving, any property in which any foreign country or a national thereof has any interest by any person, or with respect to any property, subject to the jurisdiction of the United States.[97]

Once an order has been made under the Act, the President is required to inform OFAC, who will notify financial institutions. Failure to comply with an order could result in a civil penalty of up to $250 000 or a criminal penalty which carries a maximum fine of $1m or a maximum custodial sentence of 20 years.[98] The powers were used in 1995 when President Bill Clinton issued Executive Order 12 947,[99] which blacklisted 12 'Terrorist Organisations which threaten to disrupt the Middle East Process'.[100] This became known as the 'Specially Designated Terrorist List'.[101] President Clinton also used these powers when he issued President Executive Order

---

[94]   Eckert, S. (2008), 'The US regulatory approach to terrorist financing', in T. Biersteker and S. Eckert (eds), *Countering the financing of terrorism*, Routledge, London, 209–233, at 209.

[95]   12 USC § 95a.

[96]   Donohue above, n 35 at 148.

[97]   § 1702 (a)(1)(b).

[98]   § 1705 (b) and (c).

[99]   Prohibiting Transactions With Terrorists Who Threaten to Disrupt the Middle East Peace Process, Exec. Order No. 12947, 60 Fed.Reg, 5079 (23 January 1995).

[100]   The list included Abu Nidal Organization, Democratic Front for the Liberation of Palestine, Hizballah, Islamic Gama'at, Islamic Resistance Movement, Jihad, Kach, Kahane Chai, Palestinian Islamic Jihad-Shiqaqi faction, Palestine Liberation Front-Abu Abbas faction, Popular Front for the Liberation of Palestine and the Popular Front for the Liberation of Palestine-General Command.

[101]   Ruff, K. (2006), 'Scared to donate: an examination of the effects of designating Muslim charities as terrorist organisations on the first amendment rights of

13 099,[102] which added Osama bin Laden to the 'Specially Designated Terrorist List'.[103] The Anti-terrorism and Effective Death Penalty Act sought to prevent persons within or outside the US 'from providing material support or resources to foreign organizations that engage in terrorist activities'.[104] This Act 'made it a crime to provide material support or resources to a foreign terrorist organisation'.[105] Furthermore, it made it a criminal offence if a person, 'knowing or having reasonable cause to know that a country is designated under the Export Administration Act as a country supporting international terrorism, engages in a financial transaction with the government of that country'.[106]

It wasn't until the al-Qaeda bombings in Africa in 1998 that the National Security Council, led by Richard Clarke, began to investigate, in conjunction with the State Department, FBI and CIA, the financial assets of Osama bin Laden.[107] However, it wasn't until 9/11 that 'the administrative structure suddenly and dramatically began to focus on the issue'.[108] Santoli noted that before 9/11 'the US did not actively concern itself with terrorist financing'.[109] President George Bush signed Presidential Executive Order 13 224 and the USA Patriot Act 2001, which 'turned the administration's policy 180 degrees',[110] from money laundering to terrorist financing.[111] This resulted in terrorist financing being propelled to the top of the government's financial crime agenda. The US response to terrorist financing was swift, with at least 20 federal agencies attempting to prevent and detect terrorist finances, each with their own policy. For example, the Department of Justice's policy is divided into four

---

Muslim donors', *New York University Journal of Legislation and Public Policy*, **9**, 447–502, at 455.

[102]   Prohibiting Transactions With Terrorists Who Threaten To Disrupt the Middle East Peace Process, Exec. Order No. 13099, 63 Fed.Reg. 45167 (20 August 1998).

[103]   Donohue above, n 35 at 148.

[104]   Murphy, S. (2000), 'US designation of foreign terrorist organisation', *American Journal of International Law*, **9**, 365–366, at 365.

[105]   Donohue above, n 35 at 149.

[106]   Anti-terrorism and Effective Death Penalty Act (1996), s. 312.

[107]   Donohue above, n 35 at 147.

[108]   *Ibid.*

[109]   See Santolli above, n 29 at 555–556.

[110]   Donohue above, n 35 at 160.

[111]   Conversely, and rather interestingly, Richard noted that parallels can be drawn between the US anti-money laundering strategies as outlined by its National Money Laundering Strategy. See Richard above, n 7 at 19.

parts,[112] while the Department of Treasury's is divided into six parts.[113] Conversely, the Council on Foreign Relations took the view that the US policy can be divided into three parts, intelligence gathering,[114] international co-operation,[115] and public designations under the International Emergency Economic Powers Act (1977).[116] Finally, some commentators have concluded that the US policy contains two objectives – to freeze terrorist assets and to disrupt their financial infrastructures.[117] Therefore, its policy is uncoordinated.[118] Nonetheless, the author argues that there are three central themes to the US policy, the criminalization of terrorist financing, the freezing of terrorist assets and the use of suspicious activity reports (SARs).

3.4.1 Criminalization of Terrorist Financing

The first law to criminalize terrorist financing was the Suppression of the Financing of Terrorism Convention Implementation Act 2002, which implemented the International Convention for the Suppression of the Financing of Terrorism. The Act made it a criminal offence to 'collect

---

[112] Firstly, it aims to criminalize terrorist financing. Secondly, the enforcement of terrorist crimes on known terrorist organizations and their followers. Thirdly, the identification of other terrorists and supporters of terrorist organizations through financial analysis. Finally, the freezing and confiscation of assets of identified terrorist organizations and their supporters. Department of Justice *United States Attorney's Bulletin: Terrorist Financing Issues* (Department of Justice: Washington, DC, 2003), p. 8.

[113] Firstly, it includes Presidential Executive Order 13 224. Secondly, the development and international implementation of UN Security Council Resolutions. Thirdly, the enactment of the USA Patriot Act 2001. Fourthly, engagement with international organizations such as the FATF. Fifthly, the establishment of Operation Green Quest. Finally, the sharing of information between the federal regulatory agencies.

[114] See Greenberg *et al* above, n 1 at 12.

[115] *Ibid.*

[116] *Ibid.*

[117] Raphaeli, N. (2003), 'Financing of terrorism: sources, methods, and channels', *Terrorism and Political Violence*, **15**(4), 59–82, at 59.

[118] It is important to note that in addition to the criminal sanctions outlined below civil proceedings are permitted under the Racketeer Influenced and Corrupt Organizations Act (1970) against people who fund international terrorist groups. For a more detailed explanation see Weiss, A. (2010), 'From the Bonannos to the Bin Ladens: the Reves operation or management test and the viability of civil RICO suits against financial supporters of terrorism', *Columbia Law Review*, May, 1123–1117 and Smith, J. and Cooper, G. (2009), 'Disrupting terrorist financing with civil litigation', *Western Reserve Journal of International Law*, **41**, 65–84.

or provide funds to support terrorist activities (or to conceal such fund-raising efforts), regardless of whether the offense was committed in the United States or the accused was a United States citizen'.[119] There are four terrorist financing offences under federal law. The first of these involves providing material support for commission of certain offences.[120] This 'makes it an offense to provide material support or resources intending that such material support be used to carry out violations of listed offense provisions'.[121] In order to secure a conviction, prosecutors must prove that the defendant provided or concealed or disguised material support or resources and that the defendant knew or intended that the material support or resources were to be used in violation of certain criminal offences.[122] The second criminal offence applies to 'providing material support or resources to a foreign terrorist organization'.[123] In order to obtain a prosecution, prosecutors must prove that the accused provided material support or resources to a foreign terrorist organization.[124] Furthermore, that the defendant acted with the knowledge that the organization is a designated terrorist organization; and the organization has engaged or engages in terrorist activity or the organization engages in terrorism.[125] The third offence applies to providing or collecting terrorist funds,[126] which criminalizes the provision or collection of funds for terrorist financing. A person is guilty of this offence if they acted wilfully and knew or intended that the funds were to be used in full, or in part, to carry out specified acts.[127] Furthermore, that the defendant provided or collected funds, directly or indirectly, by any means. The final federal

---

[119]   Title II of P.L. 107-197 (codified at 18 U.S.C. § 2339C).

[120]   18 U.S.C. § 2339A.

[121]   Financial Action Task Force *Third mutual evaluation report on anti-money laundering and combating the financing of terrorism – United States of America* (Financial Action Task Force: Paris, 2006) at p. 39.

[122]   The FATF stated that 'rather than providing funds, a conviction under this section requires provision of "material support or resources". This term is broadly defined to encompass virtually all tangible and intangible property (including currency, monetary instruments or financial securities) and services (including financial services), except for medicine or religious materials'. *Ibid.*

[123]   18 U.S.C. § 2339B.

[124]   A 'terrorist organization' is an organization that has been designated by the Secretary of State by virtue of the Immigration and Nationality Act (1952), s. 219 and Antiterrorism and Effective Death Penalty Act (1996), s. 302.

[125]   'Engage in terrorist activity' is defined by the Immigration and Nationality Act (1952), s. 212(a)(3)(B).

[126]   18 U.S.C. § 2339C(a).

[127]   There is no requirement under this offence for the prosecution to prove that the funds were actually used to carry out a terrorist act.

offence created relates to concealing or disguising either material support to terrorist organizations or funds used or to be used for terrorist acts.[128] The FATF reported in 2007 that '126 individuals had been charged with criminal violations of the specific terrorist financing . . . of those 54 so far have either pleaded guilty or been convicted'.[129] In order to be found guilty the defendant must knowingly conceal or disguise terrorist assets. Other criminal offences relating to terrorist financing include the violation of Presidential Executive Order 13 224 and Specially Designated Global Terrorists.[130]

The FATF described these provisions as 'very difficult legislation to follow and in some aspects seemingly unnecessarily complicated'.[131] In particular, the FATF's criticism of 'the terrorist financing provisions is that they are not self contained, in that many key terms such as "terrorist act", "terrorist activity" and "foreign terrorist organization" are defined by reference to other legislation. The need for cross referencing to other legislation makes it quite difficult to understand the elements of the offenses'.[132]

3.4.2 Asset Freezing

The second part of the policy is the freezing of terrorist assets, which is an integral part of the US response. Presidential Executive Order 13 224[133] sought to 'block [and freeze] all assets and interests in property of certain terrorists and individuals and entities materially supporting them'.[134] A total of 27 individuals and entities referred to by the Executive Order were listed as 'Specially Designated Global Terrorists', and by the end of 2001, 158 people and organizations had been added to the

---

[128]   18 U.S.C. § 2339C(c).
[129]   Financial Action Task Force above, n 121 at 43.
[130]   *Ibid.*, p. 42.
[131]   Financial Action Task Force above, n 121 at 43.
[132]   *Ibid.*, p. 42
[133]   The Executive Order was issued pursuant to the International Emergency Economic Powers Act 1977, s. 5 of the United National Participations Act 1945 and the United National Security Council Resolution 1214, Resolution 1267, Resolution 1333 and Resolution 1363. For a more detailed commentary on the International Emergency Economic Powers Act 1977 see Nice-Petersen, N. (2005), 'Justice for the designated: the process that is due to alleged US financiers of terrorism', *Georgetown Law Journal*, **93**, 1389–1392.
[134]   These powers already existed under previous US legislation, 'yet the new sanctions also significantly expanded on existing ones'. See Zagaris, B. (2004), 'The merging of the anti-money laundering and counter-terrorism financial enforcement regimes after September 11, 2001', *Berkeley Journal of International Law*, **22**, 123–157.

list.[135] Eckert noted that a majority of the announcements relating to the freezing of assets became known as the 'Rose Garden strategy'.[136] There are three important aspects of this law.[137] Firstly, it covers global terrorism. Secondly, it expands the class of targeted groups to include those who are associated with designated terrorist groups.[138] Thirdly, it clarifies the ability of the US to freeze and block terrorist assets abroad. The ability to freeze terrorist assets is often regarded as one of the 'most effective ways to combat terrorism'.[139] The government began to freeze assets and bank accounts across the globe which they believe to assist terrorists and their operations.

OFAC manages the freezing of assets of suspected or known terrorists,[140] and it maintains a Specially Designated National List.[141] OFAC has created a number of regulations which require banks to 'block the accounts and other assets of specified countries, entities and individuals; prohibit unlicensed trade and financial transactions with specified countries, entities and individuals'.[142] The Executive Order designated 27 groups and individuals as either a specially designated terrorist group or a foreign terrorist organization for the purposes of freezing assets.[143] The Department of Treasury reported that over 150 terrorist-related

---

[135]   Eckert above, n 94 at 214.

[136]   *Ibid.*, at 215.

[137]   Myers, J. (2003), 'Disrupting terrorist networks: the new US and international regime for halting terrorist finance', *Law and Policy in International Business*, **34**, 17–23, at 17.

[138]   McCulloch and Pickering are highly critical of a country's ability to proscribe organizations as terrorists because it 'expands dramatically executive power, undermines due process protections and provides states with powerful weapons with which to deal with political opposition'. See McCulloch, J. and Pickering, S. (2005), 'Suppressing the financing of terrorism – proliferating state crime, eroding censure and extending neo-colonialism', *British Journal of Criminology*, **45**(4), 470–486, at 470.

[139]   Hardister, above n 40, at 606.

[140]   For a more detailed commentary on the OFAC and the designation process see Nice-Petersen above, n 133 at 1394.

[141]   This list 'pulls together all of the terrorists and terrorist organizations as well as narcotic traffickers and others that are subject to economic sanctions and have their assets frozen'. See Richard above, n 7 at 34.

[142]   Klein, Laura (2008), *Bank Secrecy Act/Anti-Money Laundering*, Nova Science, New York, at p. 53. For an excellent commentary and review on the effectiveness of OFAC see O'Leary, R. (2010), 'Improving the terrorist finance sanctions process', *New York University Journal of International Law and Politics*, Winter, 549–590.

[143]   For a more detailed discussion of the US Government's ability to classify groups as specially designated terrorist group or a foreign terrorist organization see Crimm, N. (2004), 'High alert: the Government's war on the financing of

accounts have been blocked, more than 400 individuals and entities have been designated terrorists or terrorists' supporters and approximately 40 charities that were transferring money to al-Qaeda, Hamas and other terrorist groups have been designated and denied access to the US financial system.[144] Furthermore, 1439 suspected terrorist accounts have been frozen, containing $135m in assets.[145] Levitt warned 'when it comes to cracking down on terrorist financing, we have barely skimmed the surface'.[146] The FATF reported that by 2006 the US 'has designated 438 individuals and entities for terrorist and terrorist financing-related activities pursuant to Executive Order 13 224'.[147] In relation to the UN Security Council Resolutions the US has frozen/blocked a total of $281 372 910 worth of assets as follows: 24 Taliban-related individuals/entities totalling $264 935 075; 258 al-Qaeda-related individuals/entities totalling $9 322 159 and 21 other terrorist individuals/entities totalling $7 115 676.[148]

The freezing of assets has produced mixed results,[149] and the number of suspected accounts and assets frozen represents a small fraction of the funds available to terrorists.[150] Seldon warned that 'despite laudable goals, many asset seizures have undermined the faith of foreign investors in the US',[151] and he cited several failed prosecutions of individuals

---

terrorism and its implications for donors, domestic charitable organisations and global philanthropy', *William & Mary Law Review*, **45**, 1369–1451.

[144]   Department of Treasury *Office of Terrorism and Financial Intelligence – US Department of Treasury Fact Sheet* (Department of Treasury: Washington, DC, 2006) at p. 5. However, it is important to note that this figure does not include the $3.3bn of Iraqi assets that have been reclaimed since the fall of Saddam Hussein. See Shetterly, D. (2006), 'Starving the terrorists of funding: how the United States Treasury is fighting the war on terror', *Regent University Law Review*, **18**, 327–348, at 336.

[145]   Waszak above n 24, at 673. Richard noted that 'the government has identified 383 individuals and groups believed to have helped finance or otherwise support terror activities. Over $140m linked to al-Qaeda and other terrorists have been frozen worldwide. Of that, more than £37m has been frozen in the United States'. See Richard above, n 7 at 9.

[146]   Levitt, M. (2003), 'Stemming the flow of terrorist financing: practical and conceptual challenges', *The Fletcher Forum of World Affairs*, **27**(1), 59–70, at 61.

[147]   Financial Action Task Force above, n 121 at 58.

[148]   *Ibid.*

[149]   Weiss, M. (2004) *Terrorist Financing: Current efforts and policy issues for Congress: Report for Congress*, Washington, DC, Congressional Research Service, at p. 1.

[150]   See Navias above, n 30 at 59.

[151]   Seldon, R. (2003), 'The executive protection: freezing the financial assets of alleged terrorists, the constitution, and foreign participation in US financial markets', *Fordham Journal of Corporate & Financial Law*, **3**, 491–556, at 502.

and organizations who also had their assets frozen following 9/11.[152] The Department of Treasury defended its policy and states that terrorists are 'suffering financially as a result of our actions'.[153] However, it has been argued that this approach is misleading and that it is not the most appropriate mechanism to measure the success.[154] One of the most controversial aspects of this part of the policy is its stance towards Islamic charities.[155] The government claims that there is evidence that terrorists are financed by donations made to Islamic charities which are transferred to terrorists.[156] It has been estimated that al-Qaeda funds a large proportion of its operations through charitable donations.[157] Therefore, charities could be the second largest source of funding for al-Qaeda,[158] which has resulted in the government 'allocating substantial resources and efforts to blocking domestic organisations utilised in those fund raising efforts'.[159] One of the first Islamic charities to be classified as a terrorist organization was the Holy Land Foundation.[160] Since this announcement in December 2001, 26 other Muslim charities based in the US have also been given an identical classification, and had their assets frozen.[161] US authorities claim that all of these organizations supported terrorists.[162]

The government has been accused of being 'overzealous and using exaggerated facts to gain media attention'.[163] In a majority of these cases the charges of supporting terrorism were either dropped or the government were unable to obtain a conviction.[164] However, it must be pointed out that in November 2008, five of the organizers of the Holy Land

---

[152] *Ibid.*, at 503.

[153] Department of Treasury above, n 19, at 5.

[154] Eckert above, n 94 at 215–216.

[155] Ruff above n 101, at 448.

[156] Hardister above, n 40, at 605.

[157] Linn above n 21, at 200.

[158] Baron, B. (2005), 'The Treasury guidelines have had little impact overall on US international philanthropy, but they have had a chilling impact on US based Muslim charities', *Pace Law Review*, **25**, 307–320, at 315.

[159] See Crimm above n 143, at 1373.

[160] For a more detailed discussion about this particular charitable organization see Nice-Petersen above, n 133 at 1396–1400.

[161] See Ruff above n 101, at 449. The first three charities to be closed down by the US Administration were the Global Relief Foundation, Benevolence International Foundation and the Islamic American Relief Agency.

[162] Engel, M. (2004), 'Donating "bloody money": fundraising for international terrorism by United States charities and the government's efforts to constrict the flow', *Cardozo Journal of International and Company Law*, **12**, 251–296.

[163] Ruff above n 101, at 465.

[164] *Ibid.*, at 464–471.

Foundation were convicted of providing over $12 million to Hamas.[165] This part of the policy must be criticized because the evidence linking each of these organizations to the funding of terrorism was in the hands of federal prosecutors, who withheld it from the media, the public and the charities themselves who were accused of funding terrorism.[166] The government's policy toward the freezing of suspected terrorist assets is a short-term solution to a long-term problem. It is an ineffective response to the funding of international terrorism due to the vast array of sources of funding available. Nonetheless, the FATF concluded that the 'US has built a solid, well-structured system aimed at effectively implementing the UN sanctions . . . the statistics on the frozen terrorist related assets speak for themselves'.[167]

3.4.3 Reporting Requirements

The final part of the policy is the reporting requirements placed on financial and deposit-taking institutions.[168] The Currency and Foreign Transactions Reporting Act 1970 has been used to tackle terrorist financing and provides that 'reports should be made of records of cash, negotiable instruments, and foreign transactions'.[169] The Act allows the Secretary of the Treasury to impose regulations to ensure that information is recorded of financial transactions that have a 'high degree of usefulness in criminal, tax, or regulatory investigations or proceedings'.[170] The Act imposes burdensome obligations on overseas or foreign monetary transactions. In particular, people are compelled to 'keep records and file reports regarding transactions with foreign financial agencies, pursuant to rules promulgated by the Treasury Secretary. Monetary instruments of more than $10 000 that are exported from or imported into the United States must also be reported'.[171] Furthermore, the Intelligence Reform and Terrorism Prevention Act of 2004 requires the Treasury Secretary 'to issue regulations mandating the reporting of cross-border transmittals by

---

[165]   For an excellent discussion of this case see Nicols, G. (2008), 'Repercussions and recourse for specially designated terrorist organisations acquitted of materially supporting terrorism', *Review of Litigation*, **28,** 263–293.

[166]   Nice-Petersen above, n 133.

[167]   Financial Action Task Force above, n 121 at 58.

[168]   The FATF has influenced this part of the US terrorist financing policy by virtue of Recommendation 13 and Special Recommendation IV that apply to the reporting of suspicious transactions.

[169]   31 U.S.C. §§ 5311–5322.

[170]   12 U.S.C. § 1829b.

[171]   18 U.S.C. § 981(k).

certain financial institutions, and to submit a report to Congress on the Treasury Department's efforts to combat money laundering and terrorist financing'.[172]

The USA Patriot Act 2001 contains a comprehensive package of provisions which aimed to bolster the anti-terrorist financing regime.[173] The reporting requirements under Title III of the Act imposed significant administrative burdens on financial institutions that already had to comply with reporting requirements under the Bank Secrecy Act (BSA) 1970.[174] The Council on Foreign Relations took the view that 'Congress passed sweeping new anti-money laundering laws in part of the Patriot Act, many of which were quickly and diligently implemented by the Treasury Department'.[175] The Act increases the reporting obligations and permits the Department of Treasury to impose additional money laundering requirements on financial and credit institutions.[176] The Act introduced a series of regulations which are aimed at detecting terrorist finance prior to its introduction to the financial system.[177] This included, for example, the extension of the currency transaction reporting obligations under the BSA to all financial institutions; it authorized the introduction of measures to punish overseas financial institutions and countries for failing to stop money laundering; it stops correspondent accounts with certain money laundering institutions; and improves information sharing to oblige greater customer identification.[178] Under the Act, financial institutions are required to file a suspicious activity report (SAR) where they suspect the transaction is used for the purpose of terrorism.[179] Eckert took the view that this obligation 'enhances the financial footprint of transactions by requiring financial institutions to identify and verify the identity of new customers'.[180] The Act permits the Treasury Department to scrutinize

---

[172]   31 U.S.C. § 5317(c).
[173]   Department of Treasury above, n 19 at 10–11.
[174]   Title III is referred to as the International Money Laundering and Anti-terrorist Financing Act of 2001.
[175]   See Greenberg *et al* above, n 1 at 13.
[176]   Lyden noted that these provisions 'will have a negligible effect on the war against terrorism while creating serious headaches for financial institutions'. See Lyden, G. (2003), 'The International Money Laundering and Anti-terrorist Financing Act of 2001: Congress wears a blindfold while giving money laundering legislation a facelift', *Fordham Journal of Corporate & Financial Law*, **3**, 201–243.
[177]   USA Patriot Act 2001, ss. 311 to 330.
[178]   Eckert above, n 94 at 216.
[179]   USA Patriot Act 2001, s. 326.
[180]   Eckert above, n 94 at 216.

certain transactions and in some cases disallow them.[181] In particular, the Act permits the Department of Treasury to require supplementary reports and a higher level of due diligence from financial and deposit-taking institutions on areas of 'primary money laundering concern'.[182] The Act bans particular financial institutions from maintaining correspondent accounts for foreign shell banks and requires more due diligence controls.[183] Thirdly, it requires all financial institutions and businesses to comply with currency transaction reporting requirements of the BSA 1970.[184] Financial institutions were required to have in place an appropriate anti-money laundering programme.[185] The Department of Treasury was required to implement improved 'know your customer' regulations.[186] Furthermore, broker dealers are required to comply with the suspicious activity reporting obligations.[187] Finally, the Act seeks to encourage information-sharing between the government and financial institutions.[188] The impact of the USA Patriot Act 2001 is considerable. It has resulted in an increased level of record-keeping, report filing, and internal policing requirements.[189] For example, in 2006 FinCEN reported that financial institutions filed 919 230 SARs, an increase of 37 per cent when compared to the number of reports filed in 2004.[190] The imposition of more reporting requirements was inevitable following the attacks of 9/11 because one of the transactions used to fund the attacks was the subject of a SAR in September 2000.[191] It is questionable whether the 'filing of a SAR following these transactions [to fund 9/11] would have made a difference'.[192] The measures introduced

---

[181]   Stevens, P. and Bogle, T. (2002), 'Patriotic acts: Financial institutions, money laundering and the war against terrorism', *Annual Review of Banking Law*, **21**, 261–290, at 267–268.

[182]   USA Patriot Act, s. 311(a).

[183]   USA Patriot Act, s. 312.

[184]   USA Patriot Act, s. 365(a)(1).

[185]   USA Patriot Act 2001, s. 352(b).

[186]   USA Patriot Act 2001, s. 326.

[187]   USA Patriot Act 2001, s. 351.

[188]   USA Patriot Act 2001, s. 341.

[189]   Baldwin Jnr, above n 19, at 118.

[190]   FinCEN *The SAR Activity Review – By the Numbers* (FinCEN: Washington, DC, 2006) at p. 1.

[191]   Lee, R. *Terrorist Financing: The US and International Response Report for Congress* (Congressional Research Service: Washington, DC, 2002) at p. 19.

[192]   Roberts, M. (2004), 'Big brother isn't just watching you, he's also wasting your tax payer dollars: an analysis of the anti-money laundering provisions of the USA Patriot Act', *Rutgers Law Review*, **56**(2), 573–602.

by the USA Patriot Act 2001 may prove to be counterproductive.[193] Lee concluded that 'the plethora of reporting requirements creates a sort of "needle-in-the-haystack" problem for the authorities'.[194]

The imposition of more reporting regulations has generated 'depressingly few tangible results'.[195] However, it must be noted that according to recent statistical evidence from FinCEN, the number of reported instances of terrorist financing has fallen. For example, after peaking in 2004, the most recent 'SAR activity review' published by FinCEN stated that 'reported instances of Terrorist Financing decreased 26% in 2008, continuing a downward trend experienced since 2004'.[196] Conversely, in June 2010 FinCEN recorded that 'reports indicating Terrorist Financing increased 8% in 2009, making it the first such increase since 2004'.[197] Increasing the level of reporting requirements on financial institutions will not prevent terrorist financing. This part of the policy is predictable because a large percentage of the monies used to fund 9/11 were wired to the accounts of the terrorists directly through the US banking system. Nonetheless, a fundamental weakness of the reporting system is the inclusion of a 'threshold (of $5000 for financial institutions and $2000 for MSBs), which impacts, in particular, the effectiveness of the reporting requirement with respect to terrorist financing-related transactions, as the importance of tracking relatively low-value transactions has been highlighted in this field'.[198] Terrorists have developed a vast array of techniques to fund their activities without utilizing the financial services sector which does counter the object of the imposition of more reporting requirements.

One of the most determined and far reaching financial intelligence measures is the Terrorist Finance Tracking Programme (TFTP), which was established by Presidential Executive Order 13 224. The Department of Treasury initially targeted credit card companies to act as an early warning indicator if 'someone purchased items that could be used in bomb

---

[193]   The US Treasury Department reported that in 2001, there were 12.6 million currency transaction reports filed (these are required for transactions over $10 000) and 182 000 suspicious activity reports were filed with the Treasury Department. Department of Treasury above, n 19 at 6.

[194]   Lee above, n 191 at 18.

[195]   Department of Justice *United States Attorney's Bulletin: Terrorist Financing Issues* (Department of Justice: Washington, DC, 2003) at p. 82.

[196]   FinCEN *SAR Activity Review – By the Numbers* (FinCEN: Washington, DC, 2009d) at p. 5.

[197]   FinCEN *SAR Activity Review – By the Numbers Issue 14* (FinCEN: Washington, DC, 2010) at p. 5.

[198]   Financial Action Task Force above, n 121 at 146.

building'.[199] However, this proved extremely difficult to administer, so the Department of Treasury focused its attention to Western Union and the First Data Corporation, whose records were subpoenaed by the FBI.[200] Finally, the government was advised by a 'Wall Street executive' that it should target SWIFT.[201] The Society for Worldwide Interbank Financial Telecommunication, or SWIFT, is a financially owned co-operative that was established in Belgium in 1973 and it has been described as a 'shared worldwide data processing and communications link and a common language for international financial transactions'.[202] SWIFT has approximately 2000 members in 208 countries and it processes between 12m and 15m messages in a day.[203] Shrader took the view that 'in its most basic sense, SWIFT is a messaging system overseen by a committee drawn from major central banks and used by banks participating in international wire transfers'.[204] This scheme remained secret until it was uncovered by several US newspapers in 2006.[205] The use of the scheme was defended and it was described as an important weapon in the fight against terrorism.[206] Indeed, the Department of Treasury noted that the scheme has 'aided in the prevention of many terrorist attacks and in the investigation of many of the most visible and violent terrorist attacks and attempted attacks of the past decade'.[207] More recently, CNN reported that a 'Norwegian investigation into three men arrested Thursday for their alleged involvement in an al

---

[199]   Shea, C. (2008), 'A need for swift change: the struggle between the European Union's desire for privacy in international financial transactions and the United States' need for security from terrorists as evidenced by the SWIFT scandal', *Journal of High Technology Law*, **8**(1), 143–168, at 151.

[200]   *Ibid.*

[201]   Shea above, n 199 at 151.

[202]   Connorton, P. (2007), 'Tracking terrorist financing through SWIFT: when US subpoenas and foreign privacy law collide', *Fordham Law Review*, **76**, 283–322, at 287–288.

[203]   See Santolli above, n 29 at 559.

[204]   Shrader, J. (2007), 'Secrets hurt: how SWIFT shook up Congress, the European Union and the US banking industry', *North Carolina Banking Institute*, **11**, 397–420, at 400–401.

[205]   See Connorton above, n 202 at 284.

[206]   *Ibid.*, at 290–291.

[207]   Examples include the Bali bombings in 2002; the Madrid train bombings in 2004; the Van Gogh terrorist-related murder in the Netherlands in 2004; the bombings in London in 2005; the liquid bomb plot against transatlantic aircraft in 2006; the plan to attack New York's John F. Kennedy airport in 2007; the Islamic Jihad Union plot to attack sites in Germany in 2007; the attacks in Mumbai in 2008; and the Jakarta hotel attacks in 2009. See Department of Treasury *Terrorist financing tracking program questions and answers* (Department of Treasury: Washington, DC, 2010b) at p. 2.

Qaeda plot had also received support from the tracking program, using data collected before the end of last year and information stored in US based servers'.[208] The EU was concerned about the use of this programme and after negotiations it reached an agreement with the US which permitted the continued use of the scheme.[209] In July 2010 the US and the EU announced a new agreement had been reached on the sharing of bank data designed to track terrorist finances.[210] The BBC reported that 'under the new deal, the EU police agency Europol will assess whether specific data requests are necessary for the fight against terrorism before the data is sent to the US . . . the Commission will appoint EU officials to monitor the US investigators' actions'.[211] President Barak Obama welcomed the decision and stated that 'this new, legally binding agreement reflects significant additional data privacy safeguards but still retains the effectiveness and integrity of this indispensable counterterrorism program'.[212]

3.4.4 Conclusion

The government asserts that it has produced a comprehensive and successful policy toward the financing of terrorism.[213] This statement is supported by the convictions and controversial closure of the Holy Land Foundation for Relief and Development, Afghan Support Committee and the Revival of Islamic Heritage Society.[214] The Council of Foreign Relations notes that 'thanks to the leadership of President George W Bush, Congress, and the hard work of the Bush administration over the last year that

---

[208] CNN (2010), 'U.S. to share terror finance info with E.U.', 8 July 2010, available at http://news.blogs.cnn.com/2010/07/08/u-s-to-share-terror-finance-info-with-e-u/?iref=allsearch (accessed 14 July 2010).

[209] US authorities were allowed to use the scheme provided that the 'US agreed to (1) use data obtained through the SWIFT Program exclusively for counterterrorism purposes; (2) delete information unrelated to counterterrorism investigations on an ongoing basis; (3) retain data for no more than five years; (4) permit an EU official to monitor the program; and (5) publish the provisions of the agreement in the Federal Register'. See Connorton above, n 202 at 294.

[210] BBC (2010c), 'US to access Europeans' bank data in new deal', 8 July 2010, available at http://www.bbc.co.uk/news/10552630 (accessed 14 July 2010).

[211] *Ibid.*

[212] The White House (2010), 'Statement by the President on the U.S.-European Union Agreement on the Terrorist Finance Tracking Program', 8 July 2010, available at http://www.whitehouse.gov/the-press-office/statement-president-us-european-union-agreement-terrorist-finance-tracking-program (accessed 14 July 2010).

[213] Lee above, n 191 at 14.

[214] Department of Treasury above, n 19 at 6.

network has been disrupted'.[215] However, terrorists have adapted to the legislative changes introduced since 9/11 and they continue to have a vast array of sources of funding available. The impact of its provisions must be questioned, as al-Qaeda continues to inspire and finance terrorist attacks, a point illustrated by the failed car bomb attack in New York in May 2010.[216]

3.5   THE UNITED KINGDOM

The UK's terrorist financing policy can be contrasted with that of the US because it has been in place for a longer time. In 2002, HM Treasury published a report which outlined the important contribution made by the government towards targeting the sources of terrorist financing.[217] In 2007, the government launched 'The financial challenge to crime and terrorism', which 'sets out for the first time how the public and private sector would come together to deter terrorists from using the financial system, detect them when they did, and use financial tools to disrupt them'.[218] In 2010, HM Treasury stated that 'the government's aim is to deprive terrorists and violent extremists of the financial resources and systems needed for terrorist-related activity, including radicalisation'.[219] What can be deduced from these policy documents is that the UK's terrorist financing policy can be divided into three parts – the criminalization of terrorist financing, the freezing of terrorist assets and the use of SARs.

3.5.1   Criminalization of Terrorist Financing

The Prevention of Terrorism (Temporary Provisions) Act 1989 criminalized terrorist financing and allowed the government to seek the forfeiture of any money or other property which, at the time of the offence, the person had in his possession or under his control.[220] The UK has achieved some

---

215   See Greenberg *et al* above, n 1 at 1.

216   BBC (2010a), 'Car bomb found in New York's Times Square', 2 May 2010, available at http://news.bbc.co.uk/1/hi/world/americas/8656651.stm (accessed 14 July 2010).

217   HM Treasury *Combating the financing of terrorism – a report on UK Action* (HM Treasury: London, 2002).

218   HM Treasury above, n 37.

219   HM Treasury above, n 37 at 5.

220   Prevention of Terrorism (Temporary Provisions) Act 1989, s. 13. Also see Levi, M. (2010), 'Combating the financing of terrorism: a history and assessment

success in Northern Ireland against the Irish Republican Army by virtue of offences created by this Act.[221] However, the effectiveness of the Act was questioned and it resulted in a review of the UK's terrorist policy.[222] The consultation paper concluded that the terrorist financing provisions contained several weaknesses including the fact that there were only four terrorist financing convictions between 1978 and 1989.[223] Bell argues that 'there have been no successful prosecutions for terrorist funding offences in Northern Ireland over the last 30 years and the forfeiture provisions under the Prevention of Terrorism (Temporary Provisions) Act 1989 have never been utilised'.[224] The Home Office recommended that the scope of the terrorist financing provisions should be extended to fund-raising for all terrorist purposes.[225] The provisions were amended by the Terrorism Act 2000, which created five offences. Section 15 makes it a criminal offence for a person to solicit,[226] or to receive,[227] or provide money or property on behalf of terrorists if the person knows or has reasonable cause to suspect that such money may be used for the purpose of terrorism.[228] By virtue of section 16 a person commits an offence if he uses money or other property for terrorist purposes.[229] Furthermore, the person commits an offence if he possesses money or other property and he intends that it should be used, or has reasonable cause to suspect that it will be used for the purposes of terrorism.[230] Section 17 states that a person commits an offence if he enters into or becomes concerned in an arrangement in which money[231] or property is made available to another and the person knows or has cause to suspect that it may be used for terrorism.[232] A person breaches section 18 if he enters into or becomes concerned in an arrangement which

---

of the control of threat finance', *British Journal of Criminology*, **50**(4), 650–669, at 652.

[221] For a more detailed discussion of terrorist funding in Northern Ireland see Tupman, W. (1998), 'Where has all the money gone? The IRA as a profit-making concern', *Journal of Money Laundering Control*, **1**(4), 303–311.

[222] Home Office *Legislation against terrorism – a consultation paper* (Home Office: London, 1998b).

[223] *Ibid.*, at paragraph 6.14.

[224] Bell, R. (2003a), 'The confiscation, forfeiture and disruption of terrorist finances', *Journal of Money Laundering Control*, **7**(2), 105–125, at 113.

[225] Home Office above, n 222 at paragraph 6.15.

[226] Terrorism Act 2000, s. 15(1).

[227] Terrorism Act 2000, s. 15(2).

[228] Terrorism Act 2000, s. 15(3).

[229] Terrorism Act 2000, s. 16(1).

[230] Terrorism Act 2000, s. 16(2).

[231] Terrorism Act 2000, s. 17(1).

[232] Terrorism Act 2000, s. 17(2).

facilitates the retention or control by or on behalf of another person of terrorist property by concealment,[233] by removal from the jurisdiction,[234] by transfer to nominees[235] or in any other way.[236] It is a defence for a person charged under section 19 to prove that they neither knew, nor had reasonable cause to suspect that the arrangement was associated to terrorist property.[237] The Terrorism Act 2000 has had a limited impact. Bell noted that 'the primary difficulty for the prosecution in terrorist finance cases, however, is to prove beyond a reasonable doubt that the property is terrorist property'.[238]

Between 2001 and 2008 a total of 34 people have been charged with the fund raising offences under sections 15–19 of the Terrorism Act 2000.[239] Yet only a total of 10 people have been convicted of fund raising offences under the 2000 Act during the same time period.[240] However, Lord Carlile did note that 'there are some charges pending, and statistics to appear during 2009 are likely to demonstrate a high degree of vigilance by the authorities against the possession, potential transfer and use of terrorist funds'.[241] Bell realistically concluded that as 'a strategy against terrorist funding, this option is the most difficult from an investigative and prosecutorial perspective. Experience suggests, therefore, that only rarely will it be possible to prove terrorist finance charges, for example, where an exact tracing exercise has been carried out showing a financial trail between money in a particular account and arms purchases on behalf of a terrorist organisation'.[242]

The Terrorism Act 2000 grants law enforcement agencies additional investigative powers including financial information and account monitoring orders.[243] These have been described as 'an essential part of the legislation'.[244] The purpose of an account monitoring order is to

---

[233] Terrorism Act 2000, s. 18(1)(a).
[234] Terrorism Act 2000, s. 18(1)(b).
[235] Terrorism Act 2000, s. 18(1)(c).
[236] Terrorism Act 2000, s. 18(1)(d).
[237] Terrorism Act 2000, s. 18(2).
[238] Bell above, n 224 at 113.
[239] Home Office *Lord Carlile Report on the operation in 2008 of the Terrorism Act 2000 and of Part 1 of the Terrorism Act 2006* (Home Office: London, 2009) at p. 68.
[240] *Ibid.*, at 73. Also see Financial Action Task Force *Third mutual evaluation report: anti-money laundering and combating the financing of terrorism – the United Kingdom and Northern Ireland* (Financial Action Task Force: Paris, 2007) at p. 45.
[241] Home Office above, n 239 at 18.
[242] Bell above, n 224 at 113.
[243] Terrorism Act 2000, schedule 6.
[244] Home Office above, n 239 at 23.

permit law enforcement agencies to discover and recognize relevant bank accounts whilst undertaking a terrorist investigation. In order to obtain an account monitoring order, an application must be made by a police officer, at least at the rank of superintendent,[245] before a circuit judge,[246] who must be satisfied that '(a) the order is sought for the purposes of a terrorist investigation, (b) the tracing of terrorist property is desirable for the purposes of the investigation, and (c) the order will enhance the effectiveness of the investigation'.[247] Once an order has been granted, it will enable the police to require a financial institution . . . to provide customer information for the purposes of the investigation'.[248] Schedule 6 defines 'customer information' as including information about whether or not a business relationship exists or existed between a financial institution and a customer, the customer's account details, customer's name, address and date of birth.[249] Peddie, citing Lord Carlile's 2005 report on the performance of the Terrorism Act 2000, stated 'Lord Carlile opined that the financial information order system worked well and that there was a good level of co-operation between the police and financial institutions'.[250] The Terrorism Act 2000 states that if a person is convicted of an offence under Part III,[251] any property connected with the offence could be the subject of a forfeiture order.[252] This is referred to as criminal forfeiture.[253] The person subject to the order, once granted by a court, is required to give to a police officer as designated any property specified in the order.[254] The Terrorism Act 2000 also allows for Orders in Council to be made to permit foreign forfeiture orders to be recognized in England.[255]

The Anti-terrorism, Crime and Security Act 2001 amended the provisions for account monitoring orders, financial information orders and disclosure information orders. Under the 2001 Act, an account monitoring order may be granted by a Crown Court judge provided that the court is satisfied that the order is sought for the purposes of a terrorist

---

245   Terrorism Act 2000, schedule 6, paragraph 2(a).
246   Terrorism Act 2000, schedule 6, paragraph 2(b).
247   Terrorism Act 2000, schedule 6, paragraph 3.
248   Peddie, Jonathan (2008), 'Anti-terrorism legislation and market regulation', in W. Blair and R. Brent (eds), *Banks and financial crime – the international law of tainted money*, Oxford University Press, Oxford, 437–458, at 440.
249   Terrorism Act 2000, schedule 6, paragraph 7.
250   Peddie above, n 248 at 441.
251   Terrorism Act 2000, ss. 15–19.
252   Terrorism Act 2000, s. 23.
253   Terrorism Act 2000, s. 28.
254   Terrorism Act 2000, schedule 4.
255   Peddie above, n 248 at 443.

investigation, the tracing of terrorist property is desirable for the purposes of the investigation, and the order will enhance the effectiveness of the investigation.[256] Binning took the view that 'the effect of an account monitoring order is that the financial institution served with it must provide information of the description specified, for the period of the order and in accordance with it as to the time and place of the provision of information'.[257] The Anti-terrorism, Crime and Security Act 2001 states that a court can grant a Financial Information Order that compels a financial institution to disclose certain types of customer information for a terrorist investigation. A disclosure of information order allows for the disclosure of certain types of information and are very wide ranging. For example, they apply to any of the provisions listed in Schedule 4 of the Anti-terrorism, Crime and Security Act 2001.

Furthermore, the Counter-Terrorism Act 2008 contained a number of provisions which the government states are designed to enhance counter-terrorism powers. Under the Act, HM Treasury gained additional powers to direct financial institutions to carry out a graduated range of financial restrictions on business connected with jurisdictions of concern regarding money laundering and terrorist financing.[258] Part 1 of Schedule 7 outlines the conditions for giving a direction. HM Treasury liaises with the FATF who can dictate when appropriate action needs to be taken about a particular country due to the inherent risks of money laundering or terrorist financing.[259] These powers were used in 2008 after the FATF stated that it 'remains particularly concerned about Iran's failure to address the risk of terrorist financing and the serious threat this poses to the integrity of the international financial system'.[260] In response, HM Treasury issued a notice based on the advice of the FATF.[261] Additionally, if HM Treasury is of the opinion that a country poses a considerable threat to the UK's national interests due to an increased threat of money laundering of terrorist financing, it is permitted to issue a direction. Part 2 of Schedule 7 outlines the persons whom a direction may be given to. This includes,

---

[256]   Terrorism Act 2000, s. 38A.
[257]   Binning above, n 39 at 747.
[258]   Counter-Terrorism Act 2008, schedule 7.
[259]   Counter-Terrorism Act 2008, schedule 7, part 1.
[260]   Financial Action Task Force (2009) 'FATF Statement', 25 February 2009, available at http://www.fatf-gafi.org/dataoecd/18/28/42242615.pdf (accessed 3 August 2010).
[261]   HM Treasury (2009), 'HM Treasury warns businesses of serious threats posed to the international financial system', 11 March 2009, available at http://webarchive.nationalarchives.gov.uk/+/http://www.hm-treasury.gov.uk/press_26_09.htm (accessed 3 August 2010).

for example, people operating within the financial services sector.[262] The third part of Schedule 7 outlines the requirements that can be imposed by a direction. This includes, for example, imposing certain conditions on financial transactions or business relationships. The direction could also require an improved level of due diligence and that new transactions should not be entered into. Part 6 of Schedule 7 provides for the use of civil sanctions by the relevant enforcement authority. A civil sanction can be imposed if a person fails to comply with the obligation imposed by the direction. The Schedule 7 powers were used by HM Treasury in 2009 when it issued a 'Direction to the UK financial sector to cease all business relationships and transactions with Bank Mellat and Islamic Republic of Iran Shipping Lines'.[263] Goldby notes that 'the Order was made on the basis that "the Treasury believe that activity in Iran that facilitates the development or production of nuclear weapons poses a significant risk to the national interests of the United Kingdom."'[264] The Order was imposed due to the perceived increased threat posed by Iran.[265] The Order directs the financial sector to cease any business relationships with Bank Mellat and IRISL. This means that Bank Mellat is not allowed to conduct any financial transactions in the UK.[266] In 2009, Bank Mellat challenged the direction by HM Treasury.[267]

3.5.2 Asset Freezing

The Anti-terrorism, Crime and Security Act 2001 authorizes the seizure of terrorist cash anywhere in the UK,[268] the freezing of funds at the start of an investigation,[269] the monitoring of suspected accounts,[270] the imposition of requirements on people working within financial institutions to report where there are reasonable grounds to suspect that funds are destined for terrorism and to permit HM Treasury to freeze assets of

---

[262] Counter-Terrorism Act 2008, schedule 7, part 2 paragraph 3.
[263] Goldby, M. (2010), 'The Impact of Schedule 7 of the Counter-Terrorism Act 2008 on Banks and their Customers', *Journal of Money Laundering Control*, **13**(4), 351–71.
[264] *Ibid.*
[265] Goldby above, n 263.
[266] For a description of the losses suffered by Bank Mellat see *Bank Mellat v HM Treasury* [2010] EWHC 1332 (QB), para 2 and *Bank Mellat v HM Treasury* [2010] EWCA Civ 483, para 12.
[267] See *Bank Mellat v HM Treasury* [2010] EWHC 1332 (QB).
[268] Anti-terrorism, Crime and Security Act 2001, Sch. 1, Part 2.
[269] Anti-terrorism, Crime and Security Act 2001, ss. 4–16.
[270] Anti-terrorism, Crime and Security Act 2001, Sch. 1, Part 1.

foreign individuals and groups. Part II of the Act permits HM Treasury to freeze the assets of overseas governments or residents who have taken, or are likely to take, action to the detriment of the UK's economy or action constituting a threat to the life or property of a national or resident of the UK.[271] HM Treasury is allowed to make a freezing order if two statutory requirements are met. Firstly, it must reasonably believe that action threatening the UK's economy or the life or property of UK nationals or residents has taken place or is likely to take place.[272] Secondly, the persons involved in the action must be resident outside the UK or be an overseas government.[273] The freezing order prevents all persons in the UK from making funds available to, or for the benefit of, a person or persons specified in the order.[274] HM Treasury is also required to keep the freezing order under review and to determine whether it should continually be enforced over a period of two years.[275] HM Treasury has frozen the assets of individuals and organizations who were suspected of financing terrorism.[276] The government regularly updates a list of organizations and individuals whose accounts have been frozen.[277] Prior to 2001, HM Treasury froze £90m of terrorist assets, which contributed towards the fall of the Taliban in Afghanistan in 2002.[278] After this initial success HM Treasury has only been able to freeze a further £10m.[279] It has been suggested that this success can be measured in the actual amount of money frozen 'and though the headline figure thus generated is doubtless politically satisfying to some, it is not a measure of effectiveness'.[280] In July 2009, Lord Myners reported that 'as of the end of June 2009, a total of 237 accounts containing £607 661 of suspected terrorist funds were frozen in the UK'.[281] In October 2007, HM Treasury's Asset Freezing Unit was created. Until this date, the Bank

---

[271]   This provision repealed the Emergency Laws (Re-enactments and Repeals) Act 1964, s. 2.

[272]   The Act provides that HM Treasury is not required to prove actual detriment to freeze the assets of a suspected terrorist, but that a threat is sufficient.

[273]   Terrorism Act 2000, s. 4(1)(a) and (b).

[274]   Terrorism Act 2000, s. 5.

[275]   Terrorism Act 2000, ss. 7 and 9.

[276]   The freezing of assets is permitted by the Terrorism (United Nations Measures) Order 2006 (SI 2006/2657).

[277]   Terrorism Act 2000, Part II, Schedule 1.

[278]   Ryder, N. (2007a), 'A false sense of security? An analysis of the legislative approaches towards the prevention of terrorist finance in the United States and the United Kingdom', *Journal of Business Law*, November, 821–850, at 843.

[279]   HM Treasury above, n 217 at 27.

[280]   Ryder above, n 278 at 844.

[281]   15 July 2009: Column WS96.

of England had its own Financial Sanctions Unit, and this was transferred under the ambit of HM Treasury. The Asset Freezing Unit is responsible for legislation on financial sanctions, the implementation and administration of domestic financial sanctions, the designation of terrorist organizations, the implementation and administration of international financial sanctions in the UK, liaising with the Foreign and Commonwealth Office and collaborating with international partners to develop the international frameworks for asset freezing. The FATF concluded 'the UK has established a terrorist asset freezing regime which works well in practice. It has an effective domestic designation process which appears rapid, easy and efficient. The system can operate independently of the UN and EU listing mechanisms, where necessary'.[282] Therefore, the UK was fully compliant with the international standards and this resulted in the government stating that the UK was 'the first country to be awarded the fully compliant rating' in relation to asset freezing.[283]

The UK has implemented the Terrorism (United Nations Measures) Order 2006 to give legal effect to Security Council Resolution 1373.[284] The Order also gives effect to the enforcement of EC Regulation 2580/2001, which permits the designation of people within this regulation for such measures that relate to, *inter alia*, the freezing of funds, financial assets and economic resources.[285] HM Treasury took the view that the aim of the Order 'was enhanced to provide further restrictions on making funds, economic resources and financial services available to anyone who has been designated in the UK by the Treasury as a person suspected of committing, attempting to commit, participating in or facilitating acts of terrorism'.[286] By virtue of Article 4 of the Order, HM Treasury has been given the power to designate a person if four conditions are met. HM Treasury has reasonable grounds to suspect that a person is or may be (a) a person who commits, attempts to commit, participates in or facilitates the commission of acts of terrorism; (b) a person named in the Council Decision; (c) a person owned or controlled, directly or indirectly, by a designated person; or (d) a person acting on behalf of or at the direction of a designated person. Under Article 5 of the Order, HM Treasury is required to undertake appropriate measures to publicize the direction or to notify specific people and to inform the person identified in the direction. Furthermore,

---

282 Financial Action Task Force above, n 240 at 76.
283 HM Treasury above, n 37 at 11.
284 S.I. 2006/2657.
285 27 December 2001, on specific restrictive measures directed against certain persons and entities with a view to combating terrorism.
286 HM Treasury above n 116, at 25–26.

under Article 7 of the 2006 Order, a person is prohibited from 'dealing with funds, financial assets and economic resources of anyone who commits, attempts to commit, participates in or facilitates the commission of acts of terrorism; designated persons; anyone owned or controlled by them or anyone acting on their behalf of or at their direction'. The article makes it a criminal offence to contravene this prohibition. Article 8 of the Order prohibits making funds, financial assets, economic resources or financial services available to anyone in respect of whom Article 7 applies. The article makes it a criminal offence to contravene this prohibition.

The legality of the Terrorism (United Nations Measures) Order 2006 was challenged in *A v HM Treasury*.[287] Here, the appellants required orders from the court to quash the freezing of their assets under the 2006 Order.[288] Collins J decided that the orders granted should be set aside against five applicants on three grounds. Firstly, that parliamentary approval should have been sought and they should not have been made by Order in Council. Secondly, the court decided that it was impossible to determine how the test adopted by HM Treasury, that it had reasonable grounds for suspecting the applicants were or could be committing terrorists acts, could represent a necessary means of applying the relevant United Nations Resolution. Thirdly, that the 2006 Order created criminal offences that contravened the principle of legal certainty. The interpretation of the phrase 'economic resources' was crucial, and the court decided that the definition of this phrase meant that the family members of the applicants didn't know if they were breaching the Order or if they needed a licence from HM Treasury.[289] HM Treasury petitioned the Court of Appeal,[290] who considered four issues. Firstly, was the 2006 Order unlawful and should it be quashed? Secondly, what was the impact of the lack of procedural safeguards in the 2006 Order? Thirdly, did the offences created under Articles 7 and 8 of the Order satisfy the principles of legal certainty and proportionality? Finally, was the Al-Qa'ida and Taliban (United Nations Measures) Order 2006 unlawful because a person placed on the United Nations Sanctions Committee list has no appeal mechanism against that decision? The Court of Appeal held that the reasonable ground test adopted by HM Treasury did not go beyond the ambit of

---

[287]   [2008] EWHC 869.

[288]   One of the applicants unsuccessfully argued that an order granted against himself by the Al-Qa'ida and Taliban (United Nations Measures) Order 2006, S.I. 2006/2952 should be set aside.

[289]   For a more detailed discussion of this issue see *M v HM Treasury* [2008] UKHL 26.

[290]   *A v HM Treasury* [2008] EWCA Civ 1187.

Resolution 1373, but the requirement in the 2006 Order of 'or may be' did go further than the Resolution. Therefore, it determined that the directions granted by HM Treasury were quashed. Secondly, the Court of Appeal stated that the courts must be relied on to guarantee that satisfactory procedural protection is upheld for applicants under the Order.[291] Thirdly, the provisions of the licensing system under the Order were proportionate and legally certain. Finally, the Al-Qa'ida and Taliban (United Nations Measures) Order 2006 was lawful.

In response the government has introduced the Terrorism (United Nations Measures) Order 2009,[292] which provides that a direction will cease to have effect 12 months after it was made, but HM Treasury has the ability to renew a direction.[293] The Order revises the prohibition on making funds, economic resources and financial services available for the benefit of a designated person so that it only applies if the designated person obtains, or is able to obtain, a significant financial benefit. Furthermore, the ban on making funds, economic resources and financial services available directly to a designated person, as outlined above, is unaltered. Furthermore, the 2009 Order changes the prohibition on making economic resources available to a designated person by providing a defence to that person if they did not know and had no reasonable cause to suspect that economic resources which they provided to a designated person would be likely to be exchanged or used in exchange for funds, goods or services. The Financial Services Secretary to the Treasury, Lord Myners, took the view that 'overall, these changes will improve the operation of the asset-freezing regime, ensure that it remains fair and proportionate and help facilitate effective compliance by ensuring that prohibitions are more tailored and clearer in how they apply'.[294] The matter finally came before the Supreme Court who also considered the legitimacy of the Terrorism (United Nations Measures) Order 2006 and the Al-Qa'ida and Taliban (United Nations Measures) Order 2006. The Supreme Court determined that both of the Orders were *ultra vires* and HM Treasury swiftly responded by publishing the Draft Terrorist Asset Freezing Bill (2010) and implementing the Terrorist Asset-Freezing (Temporary Provisions) Act 2010.[295] Johnston and Nanopoulos took the view that the Act 'deems all of the impugned

---

[291] The Court of Appeal stated that the method adopted should be comparable with that adopted in *Secretary of State for the Home Department v MB* [2008] 1 A.C. 440.
[292] S.I. 2009/1747.
[293] S.I. 2009/1747, article 5.
[294] 15 July 2009: Column WS96.
[295] HM Treasury above, n 37.

Orders in Council under the 1946 Act to have been validly adopted and thus retains in force all directions made under those Orders; the Act will expire on 31 December 2010'.[296]

3.5.3 Reporting Requirements

Schedule 2 Pt III to the Anti-terrorism, Crime and Security Act 2001 inserted section 21A into the Terrorism Act 2000 and created the offence of failure to disclose for the regulated sector. A person commits an offence under this section if three conditions are met. The first condition is that the accused knows or suspects, or has reasonable grounds for knowing or suspecting that a person has committed an offence under sections 15 to 18 of the Terrorism Act 2000.[297] The second condition is that the information or other matter upon which the accused has based his knowledge or suspicion, or which gives reasonable grounds for such knowledge or suspicion, came to him in the course of a business that operates within the regulated sector.[298] The third condition is that the accused does not disclose the information or other matter to a constable or nominated officer, normally a money laundering reporting officer, as soon as practicable after he received the information.[299] Lord Carlile took the view that these reporting obligations are a 'still under-publicised duty, to which the only major statutory exception is genuine legal professional privilege'.[300] Since the introduction of the new section 21A, there have been no trials in which this new section have been tested.[301] A person does not commit an offence if he had a reasonable excuse for not disclosing the information or other matter or he is a professional legal adviser and the information or other matter came to him in privileged circumstances.[302] Lord Carlile took the view that 'this is a wide and still under-publicised duty'.[303] The Anti-terrorism, Crime and Security Act 2001 amended the Terrorism Act 2000 and inserted a defence of protected disclosures.[304] In order for this defence to be utilized, three conditions must be met. The first

---

[296] Johnston, A. and Nanopoulos, E. (2010), 'Case Comment: The new UK Supreme Court, the separation of powers and anti-terrorism measures', *Cambridge Law Journal*, **69**(2), 217–220, at 220.

[297] Terrorism Act 2000, s. 21A(2).

[298] Terrorism Act 2000, s. 21A(3).

[299] Terrorism Act 2000, s. 21A(4).

[300] Home Office above, n 239 at p. 23.

[301] *Ibid.*, at 18.

[302] Terrorism Act 2000, s. 21A.

[303] Home Office above, n 239 at 23.

[304] Terrorism Act 2000, s. 21B.

condition is that the information or other matter disclosed came to the person making the disclosure (the discloser) in the course of a business in the regulated sector.[305] The second condition is that the information or other matter causes the discloser to know or suspect, or gives him reasonable grounds for knowing or suspecting that a person has committed an offence as outlined above under sections 15 to 18 of the Terrorism Act 2000.[306] The third and final condition is that the disclosure is made to a constable or a nominated officer as soon as is practicable after the information or other matter comes to the discloser.[307] A new section 21ZA was inserted into the Terrorism Act in December 2007.[308] This amendment allows people to undertake unlawful acts provided there is consent by an authorized officer and its aim is to facilitate the discovery of offences. The amendments also aim to protect disclosures that are made after entering into such arrangements. Section 21ZC also provides a defence of reasonable excuse for not disclosing. An individual or organization who suspects that an offence has been committed under the Terrorism Act 2000 is required to complete a SAR, which is then sent to SOCA for processing.

Lord Carlile, in his annual report on the operation of the Terrorism Act 2000, commented that 'there are concerns in the business sector about difficulties of compliance and the serious consequences that may flow from this'.[309] In 2005 the Lander Review noted that 'in 2005, just under 2,100 of the total SARs (1%) were judged by the FIU terrorism team to be of potential interest in a terrorist context, of which about 650 were passed on to the NTFIU for more detailed investigation. There was a slight peak of reports of interest following the events of 7 and 21 July 2005'.[310] The number of terrorist-related SARs submitted between 2007 and 2008 was 956,[311] while the number was 703 between 2008 and 2009.[312] The usefulness of SARs in relation to terrorist financing was highlighted by SOCA who took the view that 'although the numbers continue to be small in

---

[305] Terrorism Act 2000, s. 21B(2).
[306] Terrorism Act 2000, s. 21B(3).
[307] Terrorism Act 2000, s. 21B(4).
[308] Terrorism Act 2000 and Proceeds of Crime Act 2002 (Amendment) Regulations 2007 (SI 2007/3398).
[309] Home Office above, n 239 at 19–20.
[310] Serious Organized Crime Agency *Review of the Suspicious Activity Reports Regime* (London: Serious Organized Crime Agency 2006) at p. 13.
[311] Serious Organized Crime Agency *The Suspicious Activity Reports Regime Annual Report 2008* (Serious Organized Crime Agency: London, 2009) at p. 42.
[312] Serious Organized Crime Agency *The Suspicious Activity Reports Regime Annual Report 2009* (Serious Organized Crime Agency: London, 2010) at p. 14.

proportion to the total numbers of SARs, their value can be significant, as has been demonstrated in previous years in which major terrorist incidents have taken place. All UK counter-terrorism investigations have a financial aspect to them, and the UKFIU Terrorist Finance Team has continued to provide support to these over the year'.[313]

3.5.4 Conclusion

The UK's terrorist financing policy was in place prior to the terrorist attacks in September 2001. The effectiveness of these measures must be questioned because only four people were convicted under the Prevention of Terrorism (Temporary Provisions) Act 1989. The ability to freeze terrorist assets has achieved some success under the Terrorism Act and the Anti-terrorism, Crime and Security Act. However, this is a short-term solution to a long-term problem. The final part of the policy is the use of financial intelligence obtained from SARs, which did little to prevent the terrorist attacks in July 2005.

3.6   CONCLUSION

Within ten days of the terrorist attacks in 2001, President George Bush proclaimed that his administration would stifle terrorist finances wherever they were held in the world. What followed can only be described as a plethora of legislation, rules and regulations aimed at preventing terrorist organizations from carrying out such attacks. The UN implemented several Resolutions aimed at financially crippling terrorists, which have to a large extent codified the international community's response to this type of financial crime. However, the implementation of these measures varies from nation state to nation state, so their universal application and implementation is difficult to determine. The actions of the FATF provide a welcome addition to the field of terrorist financing, but are these measures effective? If their objective is to starve terrorists of access to finances the simple answer is no, as graphically illustrated by the two terrorist attacks in Uganda.[314] If their objective is to impose a basic global legal framework then the answer is yes. However, as demonstrated in the previous chapter,

---

[313]   *Ibid.*, at 17.
[314]   BBC (2010b), '"Somali link" as 74 World Cup fans die in Uganda blasts', 12 July 2010, available at http://news.bbc.co.uk/1/hi/world/africa/10593771.stm (accessed 3 August 2010).

any global regime towards a specific type of financial crime is dependent on a number of factors. This includes, for example, co-operation between nation states and law enforcement agencies. However, there is little proof to date that the international response to 9/11 is working. The financial war on terror was ill-conceived and rushed. It has done little to limit the sources of finance available to terrorist groups. Therefore, irrespective of any legislation, improved methods of investigation, new powers for financial regulatory agencies or even an increased level of international co-operation, there is always the threat of a well-organized and self-funded terrorist cell, which operates under the radar of anti-terrorist financial legislation, which is capable of a terrorist attack.

3.6.1   United States

Prior to the terrorist attacks in 2001, the US policy towards terrorist financing was divided between several government departments and it concentrated on state sponsors of terrorism. It must be noted that the US prioritized tackling money laundering and fraudulent activities. The terrorist attacks on two US embassies in the late 1990s brought an immediate response from President Bill Clinton who prioritized tackling their finances. However, the terrorist attacks resulted in a complete overhaul of the terrorist financing policy after it was propelled to the top of the Department of Treasury agenda by President George Bush. The first part of the policy is the criminalization of terrorist financing and is found in four federal offences. These measures have resulted in a higher number of convictions than those achieved in the UK. At the forefront of the US war on terrorist financing is Executive Order 13 224, which had an immediate impact. The US authorities froze assets worth $135m of nearly 250 individuals and groups who were designated terrorist organizations. Part of this campaign was directed at US-based Islamic charities after it was reported that al-Qaeda received a large percentage of its monies from such organizations. A high-profile attempt to counter terrorist finance resulted in a number of Islamic charities having their assets frozen. What has this realistically achieved? It is controversial. It has alienated not only potential Islamic investors in the US but more importantly potential international partners who are needed to confront the problems caused by terrorist finance. The introduction of the terrorist financing reporting obligations by the USA Patriot Act 2001 would not have prevented the terrorist attacks. The inadequacies of the reporting mechanisms introduced by the BSA 1970 were highlighted by the 9/11 Commission, which reported that one of the terrorists had been the subject of a SAR in 2000. This SAR was one of over 1.2 million such reports filed with the US authorities between

1996 and 2003. The new regulations placed on the US banking sector are burdensome and the compliance costs are huge. The effectiveness of such a policy must therefore be questioned.

3.6.2 United Kingdom

The UK has had specific anti-terrorist financial legislation in place since 1989 and it has learnt a number of important lessons from the terrorist campaign conducted by the Irish Republican Army and other paramilitary organizations. The government has fully implemented UN Resolutions and it must be commended for going beyond the scope of its international obligations. The UK has adopted a similar approach towards the prevention of terrorist finance to that utilized by the US. The Terrorism Act 2000 overhauled the terrorist financing offences that yielded a derisory four convictions over a ten-year period. The amendments introduced by the 2000 Act have achieved a similar level of success, thus illustrating that the effectiveness of these provisions for criminalization of terrorist financing is limited. This could be explained by the sheer number of sources of financing available to terrorist organizations. The ability to freeze the assets of suspected terrorist organizations has been available since 1964, yet it was not until the fall of the Taliban that HM Treasury froze assets over £80m. The ability of the government to freeze the assets of terrorist organizations initially appeared to be an effective weapon against terrorist finance. Subsequently, HM Treasury has only frozen a further £10m of suspected terrorist assets. However, the ability to freeze the assets of suspected terrorists has been limited due to the decision in *A v HM Treasury*. Therefore, this part of the policy must be criticized because, like the US stance, it is a short-term solution to a long-term problem. The effectiveness of the reporting requirements under the Terrorism Act 2000 and the Anti-terrorism, Crime and Security Act 2001 must also be queried, due to the extensive sources of funding options available to terrorists.

4. Fraud

There is clear evidence that fraud is becoming the crime of choice for organised crime and terrorist funding. The response from law enforcement world-wide has not been sufficient. We need to bear down on fraud; to make sure that laws, procedures and resources devoted to combating fraud are fit for the modern age.[1]

4.1 INTRODUCTION

International efforts to tackle financial crime have concentrated on money laundering and terrorist financing. This is largely due to the United States of America (US)-led 'war on drugs' and the 'financial war on terrorism'. Fraud can be defined as 'persuading someone to part with something',[2] which includes 'deceit or an intention to deceive',[3] or an 'act of deception intended for personal gain or to cause a loss to another party'[4] and it 'involves the perpetrator making personal gains or avoiding losses through the deception of others'.[5] The international profile of fraud has increased significantly during the last two decades;[6] this is due, in part, to instances of corporate fraud relating to the collapse of the Bank of Credit and Commerce International,[7]

---

[1]   Wright, R. (2007), 'Developing effective tools to manage the risk of damage caused by economically motivated crime fraud', *Journal of Financial Crime*, **14**(1), 17–27, at 18.

[2]   Doig, Alan (2006), *Fraud*, Willan Publishing, Cullompton, at p. 19.

[3]   Ormerod, David and Williams, David (2007), *Smith's law of theft*, Oxford University Press, Oxford, at p. 9.

[4]   Serious Fraud Office (n/d), '*What is fraud?*', available at http://www.sfo.gov.uk/fraud/what-is-fraud.aspx (accessed 22 April 2010).

[5]   Financial Services Authority (n/d), 'Fraud', available at http://www.fsa.gov.uk/Pages/About/What/financial_crime/fraud/index.shtml (accessed 22 April 2010).

[6]   For an interesting discussion of the historical development of fraud see Robb, George (1992), *White-collar crime in modern England – Financial fraud and business morality 1845–1929*, Cambridge University Press, Cambridge.

[7]   For an excellent discussion see Arora, A. (2006), 'The statutory system of the bank supervision and the failure of BCCI', *Journal of Business Law*, August, 487–510.

Barings Bank,[8] Enron[9] and WorldCom.[10] Additionally, there are a number of fraudulent schemes that have targeted individuals including the 'Ponzi' fraud scheme by Bernard Madoff.[11] Large-scale fraud has also occurred in the European Union (EU) following the collapse of Parmalat and Vivendi,[12] and Jérôme Kerviel's fraudulent investments that cost SocGen £3.7bn.[13] The US has witnessed high profile frauds including Aldephia Communications, Qwest Communications International Inc, America Online, Xerox and Tyco International.[14] As a result of the global financial crisis, mortgage fraud is another major concern. The Federal Bureau of Investigation (FBI), citing research by The Prieston Group, estimated that the annual level of mortgage fraud in the US is $4–6bn.[15] The United Kingdom (UK) has also experienced large-scale instances of fraud. Examples include Polly Peck,[16]

---

[8]   For a general commentary of the collapse of Barings Bank see Proctor, L. (1997), 'The Barings collapse: a regulatory failure, or a failure of supervision?', *Brooklyn Journal of International Law*, **22**, 735–767.

[9]   Generally see Hurst, T. (2006), 'A post-Enron examination of corporate governance problems in the investment company industry', *The Company Lawyer*, **27**(2), 41–49.

[10]   See Sidak, J. (2003), 'The failure of good intentions: the WorldCom fraud and the collapse of American telecommunications after deregulation', *Yale Journal on Regulation*, **20**, 207–261.

[11]   It has been reported that the total amount of losses in the Madoff scandal could exceed $50bn. See Anderson, T., Lane, H. and Fox, M. (2009), 'Consequences and responses to the Madoff fraud', *Journal of International Banking and Regulation*, **24**(11), 548–555, at 548. Other examples include Victor Gomez, Toshihide Iguchi and Roberto Calvi. See Blanque, B. (2002), 'Crisis and fraud', *Journal of Financial Regulation and Compliance*, **11**(1), 60–70, at 61.

[12]   Abarca, M. (2004), 'The need for substantive regulation on investor protection and corporate governance in Europe: does Europe need a Sarbanes-Oxley?', *Journal of International Banking Law and Regulation*, **19**(11), 419–431, at 419.

[13]   Haines, J. (2009), 'The National Fraud Strategy: new rules to crackdown on fraud', *Company Lawyer*, **30**(7), 213.

[14]   Lunt, M. (2006), 'The extraterritorial effects of the Sarbanes-Oxley Act 2002', *Journal of Business Law*, May, 249–266, at 249. Other well known frauds include Rite Aid, Symbol Technologies Dynergy and Health South. See Brickey, K. (2004), 'White collar criminal law in comparative perspective: the Sarbanes-Oxley Act of 2002', *Buffalo Criminal Law Review*, **8**, 221–276, at 228. It is interesting to note that since 2003 the level of reported accountancy fraud has increased by approximately 300 per cent. See PriceWaterhouseCoopers *2009 Global Economic Crime Survey* (PriceWaterhouseCoopers: London, 2009) at p. 7.

[15]   Federal Bureau of Investigation (n/d), 'Mortgage fraud' available at http://www.fbi.gov/hq/mortgage_fraud.htm (accessed 22 April 2010).

[16]   Gallagher, J., Lauchlan, J. and Steven, M. (1996), 'Polly Peck: the breaking of an entrepreneur?' *Journal of Small Business and Enterprise Development*, **3**(1), 3–12.

the Mirror Group Pension Scheme,[17] Guinness[18] and the collapse of Barlow Clowes.[19] The calculation of fraud, like the other types of financial crime, is fraught with methodological difficulties.[20] For example, it has been estimated that it annually costs the US economy \$400bn,[21] and it has been conservatively suggested that the level of fraud in the UK is £13.9bn.[22] Conversely, the National Fraud Authority (NFA) noted that the figure was nearer £30bn.[23] Indeed, the Fraud Review stated that 'there are no reliable estimates of the cost of fraud to the economy as a whole',[24] and it has been argued that 'in monetary terms, fraud is on a par with Class A drugs'.[25] The threat of fraud should not be underestimated and it has been suggested that terrorists are increasingly using it to fund their illegal activities.[26]

Therefore, two important questions must be considered. Firstly, what can be done to tackle fraud? Secondly, can any lessons be learnt from the anti-money laundering and terrorist financing strategies previously outlined? At an international level, the United Nations (UN) and EU have adopted a rigorous stance towards the prevention of fraud and both institutions have introduced a number of measures. However, it is important to point out that their policies can be contrasted with those for money laundering and terrorist financing. For example, there is no international anti-fraud legal instrument, as there is for money laundering (Vienna and Palermo Conventions) and terrorist financing (International Convention for the Suppression of the Financing of Terrorism). Furthermore, the UN and EU

---

[17] Sarker, R. (1996), 'Maxwell: fraud trial of the century', *Company Lawyer*, **17**(4), 116–117.

[18] Sarker, R. (1994), 'Guinness – pure genius', *Company Lawyer*, **15**(10), 310–312.

[19] Doig above, n 2 at 9–12.

[20] Attorney General's Office *Fraud Review – Final Report* (Attorney General's Office: London, 2006) at p. 21. For a more detailed examination of the problems associated with determining extent of fraud see Levi, M. and Burrows, J. (2008), 'Measuring the impact of fraud in the UK: a conceptual and empirical journey', *British Journal of Criminology*, **48**(3), 293–318, at 297–298.

[21] Saksena, P. and Fox, M. (2004), 'Accounting fraud and the Sarbanes-Oxley Act', *International Company and Commercial Law Review*, **15**(8), 244–251, at 244.

[22] Levi, M., Burrows, J., Fleming, M. and Hopkins, M. *The Nature, Extent and Economic Impact of Fraud in the UK* (ACPO: London, 2007) at p. iii.

[23] National Fraud Authority *National Fraud Authority Annual Fraud Indicator* (National Fraud Authority: London, 2010) at p. 7.

[24] Levi and Burrows above, n 20 at 297.

[25] Sarker, R. (2007), 'Fighting fraud – a missed opportunity?', *Company Lawyer*, **28**(8), 243–244, at 243.

[26] Ryder, N. (2007a), 'A false sense of security? An analysis of legislative approaches to the prevention of terrorist finance in the United States of America and the United Kingdom', *Journal of Business Law*, November, 821–850, at 825.

are predominantly concerned with fraudulent activity that is committed against their institutions that relates to their finances. At a national level, it is possible to argue that some parts of the fraud policy are identical to the strategies towards money laundering and terrorist financing. For example, a common part of these policies is the criminalization of different types of financial crime and the reliance on financial intelligence. At a national level, the US and UK have implemented a number of legislative measures that criminalize a wide range of fraudulent activities. For example, in response to the threat posed by fraud to its financial sector Congress enacted the Bank Fraud Statute.[27] Another example was the Sarbanes-Oxley Act 2002, following unprecedented instances of accountancy fraud.[28] The Fraud Act 2006 was enacted after a 30-year campaign by the Law Commission in response to the problems with the Theft Acts (1968–94).

In addition to criminalizing fraud, both countries have established a large number of regulatory and law enforcement agencies with the specific task of fraud prevention. In the US, this includes the Department of Justice, which is supported by the United States Secret Service, the Federal Trade Commission (FTC), the FBI, Financial Crimes Enforcement Network (FinCEN) and several fraud task forces. In the UK there is the Serious Fraud Office (SFO) and the NFA is supported by the Financial Services Authority (FSA), the Serious Organized Crime Agency (SOCA), the National Fraud Reporting Centre (NFRC) and HM Revenue and Customs (HMRC). An effective anti-fraud policy is reliant on the co-operation of deposit-taking institutions and other members of the financial services sector. These firms are expected to provide financial intelligence of suspected instances of fraud to regulators and law enforcement agencies. The importance of financial intelligence in the fight against money laundering and terrorist financing has already been demonstrated in Chapters 2 and 3, and it also plays a pivotal role in the battle against fraud. In the US a wide range of institutions are obliged to submit suspicious activity reports (SARs) to FinCEN highlighting suspected instances of fraud. This is also the position in the UK where institutions are obliged to report allegations of fraud to SOCA.

Therefore, this chapter identifies the policies adopted by the UN and the EU towards the prevention of fraud. It comments on the extent to which the respective anti-fraud policies and legislative measures have influenced the strategies adopted in the US and the UK. In both countries, the fraud policy can be divided into three parts:

---

[27] Title 18 U.S.C. § 1344.
[28] H.R. 3763 Pub. L. 107-204.

1. criminalization of fraudulent activities;
2. regulatory agencies; and
3. anti-fraud reporting requirements.

The next part of the chapter investigates the impact of the anti-fraud strategies of the UN and the EU.

4.2 INTERNATIONAL MEASURES

4.2.1 United Nations

The UN has not implemented a single anti-fraud convention and its policy is directed towards its own finances. For example, the UN Development Programme (UNDP) has its own fraud policy which provides:

> UNDP is committed to preventing, identifying and addressing all acts of fraud against UNDP as well as third parties involved in UNDP activities. To this effect, UNDP will raise awareness of fraud risks, implement controls aimed at preventing fraud and establish a procedure applicable to the detection of fraud and the enforcement of this policy. This policy aims to prevent and detect fraud involving UNDP staff members, consultants, contractors, and/or other parties with a business relationship to UNDP.[29]

This policy is concerned with three types of fraud. Firstly, fraud committed to obtain undue financial benefits or entitlements under UN staff regulations and rules.[30] Secondly, fraud involving third parties.[31] Finally, fraud committed to cause the 'organization to act in a manner other than it would have acted with the full knowledge of the genuine information'.[32] Furthermore, the UNDP is also concerned about the risk of procurement fraud.[33] Similarly, the UN Office for Project Services (UNOPS) fraud policy provides:

---

[29] United Nations Development Programme *Fraud policy statement* (United Nations Development Programme: New York, 2007) at p. 2.

[30] This includes rental subsidy, insurance claims, education grants, tax reimbursement, travel costs and misuse of funds.

[31] Examples include collusion with contractors, kickbacks and reporting false expenditure.

[32] This includes for example false curricula vitae and fraudulent appraisal reports or certificates.

[33] United Nations Development Programme (n/d), 'Programme and Operations Policies and Procedures', available at http://content.undp.org/go/

UNOPS is committed to preventing, identifying and addressing all alleged acts of fraud or attempted fraud against UNOPS. To this effect, UNOPS will enforce this policy by raising awareness of fraud risks, implementing controls aimed at preventing fraud and establishing procedures for the detection, investigation and reporting of fraud.[34]

UNOPS policy concentrates on fraud to obtain undue financial benefits or entitlements under the United Nations Staff Regulations and Rules, fraud involving third parties which includes collusion with contractors, and fraud committed to induce the UN to act in an illegal manner.[35] However, there are a number of UN instruments that refer to fraud, including the UN Convention on Independent Guarantees and Stand-by Letters of Credit,[36] the UN Convention against Transnational Organized Crime[37] and UN Security Council Resolution 1373.[38] The UN's policy prioritizes frauds either committed by its employees or committed against the UN. Therefore, a direct comparison can be made with the approach adopted by the EU.

4.2.2 European Union

The policy adopted by the EU towards fraud can be contrasted with its efforts against money laundering and terrorist financing. It concentrates on frauds committed against the EU, and it doesn't impose any anti-fraud obligations on Member States.[39] The origins of its strategy can be traced to the creation of the Common Agricultural Policy which resulted in the number of allegations of fraud increasing.[40] However, it was not until the 1970s that the EU began to realize the threat to its finances posed

---

userguide/cap/procurement/fraud-corrupt-practices/?lang=en (accessed 4 August 2010).

[34]   United Nations Office for Project Services *UNOPS policy to address fraud* (United Nations Office for Project Services: New York, 2008) at p. 1.

[35]   *Ibid.*

[36]   See Xiang, G. and Buckley, R. (2003), 'Comparative analysis of the standard of fraud required under the fraud rule in letter of credit law', *Duke Journal of Comparative and International Law*, **13**, 293–336.

[37]   General Assembly resolution 55/25 of 15 November 2000.

[38]   Adopted by the Security Council at its 4385th meeting, on 28 September 2001.

[39]   See for example the EU's Convention on the Protection of the EC's financial interests [OJ C 316, 27.11.1995] and the EU's 2001 Framework Decision 'combating fraud and counterfeiting of non-cash means of payment'.

[40]   Ruimschotel, D. (1994), 'The EC budget: ten per cent fraud? A policy analysis approach', *Journal of Common Market Studies*, **32**(3), 320–342, at 320.

by fraud.[41] The legal basis of its fraud policy is found in Article 5 of the Treaty of Rome,[42] under which Member States are required to certify that the Council Regulations that outline the policies of the EU are not damaged by fraudulent activities.[43] Furthermore, Article 280 of the EU Treaty provides that Member States are required to combat fraud and other criminal activities that will affect the financial interests of the EU.[44]

An important part of the EU's fraud policy is the European Court of Auditors, which acts as an independent reviewer of the EU's finances.[45] It determines whether any fraud has been committed against the EU and identifies whether or not the fiscal procedures have been recorded, and properly implemented in lawful method to guarantee efficiency and effectiveness.[46] The Court of Auditors has highlighted instances of fraud on several occasions to the European Parliament;[47] however, its efforts have been hampered because it is not entitled or allowed to undertake any anti-fraud investigations.[48] This problem was raised by the European Parliament's Committee of Budgetary Control who recommended that a 'flying squad' should be created to investigate allegations of fraud.[49] As a result, 'Unité de coordination de la lutte anti-fraude' (UCLAF) was established in 1987 and became operational in 1988, with the objective of dealing

---

[41]   Pujas, C. (2003), 'The European Anti-Fraud Office (OLAF): a European policy to fight against economic and financial fraud?', *Journal of European Public Policy*, **10**(5), 778–797, at 780. The amount of fraud committed against the EU is impossible to determine, yet recent estimates suggest that the figure on an annual basis is €1 000 000 000. See Xanthaki, H. (2010), 'What is EU fraud? And can OLAF really combat it?', *Journal of Financial Crime*, **17**(1), 133–151, at 133.

[42]   Article 5 provides that 'Member States shall take all appropriate measures whether general or particular, to ensure fulfilment of the obligations arising out of this Treaty, or resulting from action taken by the institutions of the Community. They shall facilitate the achievement of the Community tasks'.

[43]   Ruimschotel above, n 40 at 330.

[44]   See Council Regulation (EC, Euratom) No 2988/95 of 18 December 1995 on the protection of the European Communities financial interests.

[45]   The European Court of Auditors was established by the Treaty of Brussels in 1975. For a more detailed discussion about the general role of the European Court of Auditors see Quirke, B. and Pyke, C. (2002), 'Policing European Union Expenditure: A Critical Appraisal of the Transnational Institutions', *Journal of Finance and Management in Public Services*, **2**(1), 21–32, at 23–25.

[46]   European Court of Auditors (n/d), 'About us', available at http://eca.europa.eu/portal/page/portal/aboutus (accessed 3 August 2010).

[47]   Pujas above, n 41 at 780.

[48]   *Ibid.*

[49]   White, S. (1999), 'Investigating EC Fraud: The metamorphosis of UCLAF', *Journal of Financial Crime*, **6**(3), 255–260, at 256.

with fraud against the EU.[50] UCLAF was created as a result of an increase in financial irregularities within the EU and the resulting criticism.[51] Its effectiveness was limited due to its small number of 'desk bound' staff[52] and its disorganized structure,[53] both of which inhibited its ability to effectively investigate fraud.[54] UCLAF's position became precarious following the reported loss of £600m of humanitarian aid to fraudulent activities.[55] The Court of Auditors recommended the establishment of an autonomous anti-fraud agency[56] and the European Anti-Fraud Office, OLAF, was born in 1999.[57] OLAF's objective was to assist EU institutions to combat fraud and other financial indiscretions.[58] Therefore, a comparison can be made between the anti-fraud provisions of the Treaty of Rome and the objectives of OLAF, to protect the financial interests of the EU, not to impose any direct anti-fraud obligations on its Member States. OLAF is respon-

---

[50]   Tupman, B. (2000), 'The sovereignty of fraud and the fraud of sovereignty: OLAF and the wise men', *Journal of Financial Crime*, **8**(1), 32–46, at 43.

[51]   Quirke, B. (2007), 'Critical appraisal of the role of UCLAF', *Journal of Financial Crime*, **14**(4), 460–473, at 460. Tupman also noted that UCLAF was the European Commission's response where 'a picture is emerging of criminal networks slimming down, specialising and becoming more and more market responsive'. See Tupman, W. (1994), 'You Should Have Read the Small Print: The European Commission's Post-Maastricht Response to Fraud', *Journal of Financial Crime*, **2**(2) 107–114, at 107.

[52]   White above, n 49 at 256.

[53]   Pujas above, n 41 at 781. See in particular Doig, A. (1996), 'A fragmented organizational approach to fraud in a European context', *European Journal on Criminal Policy and Research*, **3**(2), 48–73.

[54]   Tupman above, n 50 at 33.

[55]   Quirke and Pyke above, n 45 at 29. Also see House of Lords, Select Committee on the European Communities, Fraud against the European Communities, Session 1988–1989, 5th Report, HL paper 27, para. 205, as cited in Skiadas, D. (1998), 'EC: The Role of the European Court of Auditors in the Battle against Fraud and Corruption in the European Communities', *Journal of Financial Crime*, **6**(2), 178–185, at 179.

[56]   Quirke, B. (2010), 'OLAF's role in the fight against EU Fraud: Do too many cooks spoil the broth?', *Crime, Law and Social Change*, **53**(1), 97–108, at 97. In particular, White stated that the Court of Auditors 'recommended that consideration should be given to the establishment of a separate unit, to which any suspicion of corruption would automatically be communicated and which would have the authority and resources to undertake any necessary investigation'. White above, n 49 at 257.

[57]   Pujas above, n 41 at 782.

[58]   Commission Decision of 28 April 1999 establishing the European Anti-Fraud Office (OLAF) (OJ 1999 L136). Vlogaret, Johan and Pesta, Michal (2008), 'OLAF fighting fraud and beyond' in S. Brown (ed.), *Combating international crime – the longer arm of the law*, Routledge, London, 77–87, at 77.

sible for the 'fraud-proofing of EC legislation',[59] and it has the ability to conduct administrative investigations,[60] which are defined as inspections and other appropriate measures performed by OLAF staff to determine the quality of the allegation under investigation. There are two types of investigations – internal and external. Internal investigations relate to financial discrepancies within the EU and alleged staff misconduct,[61] while external investigations relate to activities that occur outside the EU.[62] The effectiveness of these investigations is limited due to OLAF's inability to independently initiate them,[63] although it is permitted to assist other Member States by sharing information and financial intelligence.[64]

OLAF's performance has been limited due to the 'shadow of UCLAF'[65] and its relationship with Eurojust, the EU's Judicial Co-operation Unit. Eurojust was created to fight organized crime by improving the level of co-operation during investigations and prosecutions that occur in more than one Member State.[66] The relationship has been described as 'rather troubling',[67] a position that worsened after Eurojust asserted that it saw OLAF as a competitor rather than a colleague.[68] Furthermore, OLAF has no enforcement powers and only makes recommendations.[69] The extension

---

[59] House of Lords European Union Committee *Strengthening OLAF, the European Anti-Fraud Office* (House of Lords European Union Committee: London, 2004) at p. 11.

[60] Vlogaret and Pesta above, n 58 at 77.

[61] *Ibid.*, at 79. For a discussion of the EU's anti-fraud enforcement policy see White, S. (2010), 'EU anti-fraud enforcement: overcoming obstacles', *Journal of Financial Crime*, **17**(1), 81–99.

[62] Vlogaret and Pesta above, n 58 at 79.

[63] *Ibid.*

[64] Vlogaret and Pesta above, n 58 at 78. One of the highest profile cases involving OLAF related to the Lesotho Water Project in South Africa. Following an investigation several people were convicted of bribery and corruption. See *Sole v The Crown* C of A (Cri) 5 of 2002 (unreported). For a more detailed discussion of this case see Letsika, O. (2004), 'Creating a corruption-free zone through legislative instruments: some reflections on Lesotho', *Journal of Financial Crime*, **12**(2), 185–191 and Darroch, F. (2003), 'The Lesotho corruption trials – a case study', *Commonwealth Law Bulletin*, **29**(2), 901–975.

[65] Quirke above, n 56 at 99.

[66] 2002/187/JHA: Council Decision of 28 February 2002 setting up Eurojust with a view to reinforcing the fight against serious crime, Official Journal L 063, 06/03/2002 P. 0001 – 0013. Pujas noted that it was 'a temporary unit of judicial co-operation . . . in charge of fighting serious transnational crime'. See Pujas above, n 41 at 784.

[67] Quirke above, n 56 at 99.

[68] House of Lords European Union Committee above, n 59 at 12.

[69] Vlogaret and Pesta above, n 58 at 84.

of EU membership to 27 countries has resulted in OLAF attempting to deal with different national approaches towards fraud in addition to the different approaches adopted by Member States.[70] Interestingly, some Member States have protected their own national financial interests before those of the EU.[71] Therefore, the objective of the EU's fraud policy is to protect its own financial interests, a position that can be contrasted with its strategy on money laundering and terrorist financing.

What becomes clear after reviewing the respective policies of the UN and the EU is that they prioritize tackling fraudulent activities against their own finances, a position that can be contrasted with their policies towards money laundering and terrorist financing. Therefore, it can be concluded that the measures implemented by the UN and the EU have had a minimal impact on the strategies adopted in the US and the UK, and it is to these issues that the chapter now turns.

4.3   UNITED STATES OF AMERICA

The US anti-fraud policy can be contrasted with its stance towards money laundering and terrorist financing. For example, there is no 'strategy document' that offers a valuable insight and overview into the mechanisms and measures employed to tackle fraud. What will become clear from the discussion below is that the US criminalizes a very broad range of fraudulent activities and since the introduction of the Mail Fraud Statute 1872, a glut of anti-fraud statutes have been introduced. Furthermore, the US doesn't benefit from a specialized anti-fraud office like OLAF; the responsibilities are shared amongst a variety of regulators. For example, its anti-fraud efforts are led by the primary regulator, the Department of Justice, which is supported by the investigative and prosecutorial tools of the FBI. Any successful fraud strategy is dependent on the quality of the financial intelligence provided by deposit-taking institutions and other financial intermediaries to its financial intelligence unit, in this case FinCEN. The US anti-fraud policy can be divided into three parts, each of which will now be discussed in turn:

1.   criminalization of fraudulent activities;
2.   regulatory agencies; and
3.   anti-fraud reporting requirements.

---

[70]   Quirke above, n 56 at 101.
[71]   Tupman above, n 51 at 108.

4.3.1 Criminalization

The prevention of fraud is an essential part of many criminal statutes and it shows no signs of abating.[72] Podgor stated that 'the scope of fraud is problematic in that there is no specific group of statutes designated in the federal code as fraud statutes and no consistent definition'.[73] The Mail Fraud Statute[74] criminalizes mistreating the post office in continuance with any fraudulent activity.[75] Prosecutors must prove that the defendant intended to create a scheme to defraud the post office and it is not obligatory for the false representation to be communicated by mail, only that the mail system was to be used to conduct the fraudulent activity.[76] Elder noted that 'the mail fraud statute occupies a unique position in federal criminal law as one of the last broad and amorphous criminal statutes'.[77] Indeed, it has been argued that the judiciary have allowed the Mail Fraud Statute to become a 'nonspecific' fraud statute[78] and that prosecutors have abused its scope to cover the legislative abnormalities left by Congress.[79] For example, the Statute has been used by prosecutors as a launch pad for money laundering prosecutions.[80] Coffee and Whitehead stated that 'federal prosecutors have long followed the maxim when in doubt charge

---

[72] Podgor, E. (1999), 'Criminal fraud', *American University Law Review*, **48**, 729–768, at 730.

[73] *Ibid.*, at 740.

[74] Act of June 8, 1872, ch. 335, § 301, 17 Stat. 283, 323, 18 U.S.C. § 1341. As cited in Henning, P. (1995), 'Maybe it should be called federal fraud: the changing nature of the Mail Fraud Statute', *Boston College Law Review*, May, 435–477. Also see Kessimian, P. (2004), 'Business fiduciary relationships and honest services fraud: a defense of the statute', *Columbia Business Law Review*, 197–230, at 201.

[75] Mogin, P. (2002), 'Refining in the Mail Fraud Statute', *Champion*, **26**, 12–17, at 13.

[76] Weintraub, L. (1987), 'Crime of the century: use of the Mail Fraud Statute against authors', *Boston University Law Review*, **67**, 507–549, at 524. Also see Gagliardi, J. (1993), 'Back to the future: federal mail and wire fraud under 18 U.S.C. § 1343', *Washington Law Review*, **68**, 901–921, at 903 and Brown, M. (2008), 'Prosecutorial discretion and federal mail fraud prosecutions for honest services fraud', *Georgetown Journal of Legal Ethics*, **21**, 667–682, at 669.

[77] Elder, J. (1998), 'Federal mail fraud unleashed: revisiting the criminal catch-all', *Oregon Law Review*, **77**, 707–733, at 707.

[78] Orr, K. (2006), 'Fencing in the frontier: a look into the limits of mail fraud', *Kentucky Law Journal*, **95**, 789–809, at 791. For a similar view see Molz, T. (1997), 'The Mail Fraud Statute: an argument for repeal by implication', *University of Chicago Law Review*, **64**, 983–1007, at 983.

[79] Molz above, n 79 at 984. This had led to the Mail Fraud Statute being commonly referred to as a 'catch all' law.

[80] Mogin above, n 75 at 14. Indeed, Henning concluded that the 'statute became

mail fraud'[81] and the Statute has also been described as the 'prosecutor's secret weapon'.[82] Therefore, it can be argued that the Statute is one of the most important and powerful prosecutorial tools available.[83] The judiciary has attempted to limit the ability of prosecutors to abuse the Statute,[84] and in *McNally v United States* the Supreme Court restricted the scope of the Statute to cases involving crimes against property rights.[85] Congress reacted swiftly and implemented the Anti-Drug Abuse Act 1988,[86] which extended the scope of the Statute to offer protection to the 'intangible right of honest services'.[87] The Mail Fraud Statute was amended by the Violent Crime Control and Law Enforcement Act 1994 to include any parcel 'sent or delivered by any private or commercial interstate carrier'.[88] Therefore, the Mail Fraud Statute now 'covers a full range of consumer frauds, stock frauds, land frauds, bank frauds, insurance frauds, and commodity frauds, but [also] areas as blackmail, counterfeiting, election fraud, and bribery'.[89] The Mail Fraud Statute is used in conjunction with the Wire Fraud Statute 1952, which states:

---

a strategic tool in fighting political corruption and increasingly sophisticated economic misconduct'. See Henning above, n 74 at 438.

[81]   Coffee J. and Whitehead, C., 'The Federalization of Fraud: Mail and Wire Fraud Statutes', in *White Collar Crime: Business and Regulatory Offenses*, § 9.01, at 9-2 (O. Obermaier and R. Morvillo (eds), 1990) as cited in Mogin above, n 75 at 13.

[82]   Greenwood, L. (2008), 'Mail and wire fraud', *American Criminal Law Review*, **45**, 717–740, at 717. The Act has also been referred to as the prosecutor's '"Stradivarius", "Colt 45", or "UZI"' and Judge Ralph K. Winter described the impact of the Statute as a 'hydrogen bomb on stealth aircraft'. See Kessimian above, n 74 at 198.

[83]   Weintraub above, n 76 at 523.

[84]   Podgor, E. (1998), 'Mail fraud: redefining the boundaries', *Saint Thomas Law Review*, **10**, 557–570, at 560. Examples of this judicial contempt for the aggressive actions of federal prosecutors include *United States v Jackson* 26 F.3d 999 (10th Cir. 1994) and *United States v Frost* 125, F.3d 346, 369–70 (10th Cir.1994).

[85]   483 U.S. 350 (1987). For a more detailed commentary on this case see Dean, J. and Green Jr, D. (1988), '*McNally v United States* and its effect on the federal Mail Fraud Statute: will white collar criminals get a break?', *Mercer Law Review*, **39**, 697–716.

[86]   Pub. L. 100-690, Title VII, §7603(a), 102 Stat. 4181, 4508.

[87]   18 U.S.C.A. § 1346. For a discussion of the approach adopted by the judiciary towards the Mail Fraud Statute prior to the Supreme Court decision in *McNally* see Gagliardi above, n 76 at 901. Henning noted that Congress added to Title 18 a new section 1346 which states in its entirety, 'the term "scheme or artifice to defraud" includes a scheme or artifice to deprive another of the intangible right of honest services'. See Henning above, n 74 at 463.

[88]   Pub. L. 103-322, § 108 Stat. 1796.

[89]   Greenwood, L. (2008), 'Mail and wire fraud', *American Criminal Law Review*, **45**, 717–740, at 719.

Whoever, having devised or intending to devise any scheme or artifice to defraud, or for obtaining money or property by means of false or fraudulent pretenses, representations, or promises, transmits or causes to be transmitted by means of wire, radio, or television communication in interstate or foreign commerce, any writings, signs, signals, pictures, or sounds for the purpose of executing such a scheme or artifice, shall be fined under this title or imprisoned.[90]

In order for a person to be convicted prosecutors must prove that there was a 'scheme to defraud that includes a material deception; with the intent to defraud; while using the mail, private commercial carriers, and/ or wires in furtherance of that scheme; that did result or would have resulted in the loss of money or property or the deprivation of honest services'.[91] The Wire Fraud Statute has been described as the 'first line of defence against fraudulent activity'[92] and that it provides prosecutors with a broad range of prosecutorial measures.[93] The courts have expanded the application of the Wire Fraud Statute to an ever increasing number of methods of communication and it also applies to a wide range of fraudulent activities.[94]

Another example of legislation designed to prevent fraud is the Bank Fraud Act, which was introduced as part of the Comprehensive Crime Control Act 1984.[95] The Act was a reaction to a large number of fraudulent schemes that targeted financial institutions[96] and the Supreme Court's

---

[90] 18 U.S.C. § 1343.

[91] Stuart, C. (2009), 'Mail and wire fraud', *American Criminal Law Review*, **46**, 813–835, at 816.

[92] NuraKami, K. (1987), 'Mail and wire fraud', *American Criminal Law Review*, **24**, 623–637, at 623.

[93] Blumel, R. (2005), 'Mail and wire fraud', *American Criminal Law Review*, **42**, 677–698, at 678. For an excellent commentary on judicial precedent in this area see Robinson, J. (2008), 'The federal Mail and Wire Fraud Statutes: correct standards for determining jurisdiction and venue', *Willamette Law Review*, **44**, 479–540, at 482–507.

[94] Blumel above, n 93 at 678.The scope of the Wire Fraud Statute was extended in 1994 via the Senior Citizens Against Marketing Scams Act, Pub. L. No. 103-322, Title XXV, § 250006, 108 Stat. 1796, 2087 (1994).

[95] S Rep No. 98-225, 98th Cong, 2d Sess 377. U.S.C. § 1344.

[96] Madia, M. (2005), 'The Bank Fraud Act: a risk of loss requirement?', *University of Chicago Law Review*, **72**, 1445–1471, at 1445. It is important to note that this was not the only law passed by Congress to combat such fraudulent schemes. Other notable laws included the Financial Institutions, Reform, Recovery, and Enforcement Act 1989 and the Comprehensive Thrift and Bank Fraud Prosecution and Taxpayer Recovery Act 1990. For an interesting commentary on these laws see Rowlett, J. (1993), 'The chilling effect of the Financial

decision in *Williams v United States*.[97] Here, the court held that people who participate in fraudulent activities such as 'check-kiting'[98] could not be prosecuted for making a misleading statement to the financial institution.[99] The Department of Justice was forced to abandon many fraud-related prosecutions and Congress passed the Bank Fraud Act which criminalizes schemes that intend to deceive or obtain finances from federally-insured financial institutions.[100] The Act criminalizes cheque forging, credit card fraud, student loan fraud, mortgage fraud and false financial transactions between offshore shell banks and domestic banks.[101] The scope of the Bank Fraud Act was further extended by the Financial Institutions Reform, Recovery and Enforcement Act 1989,[102] to include the 'financial kingpin crime', which imposes a life sentence for defendants who manage so-called financial crime enterprises.[103] The Major Fraud Act 1988 was instituted to

---

Institutions Reform, Recovery, and Enforcement Act of 1989 and the Bank Fraud Prosecution Act of 1990: has Congress gone too far?', *American Journal of Criminal Law*, **20**, 239–262.

[97]   458 U.S. 279. See for example Fischer, A. and Sheppard, J. (2008), 'Financial institutions fraud', *American Criminal Law Review*, **45**, 531–578, at 533.

[98]   'Check-kiting' is defined as 'the drawing of checks on an account in one bank and depositing them in an account in a second bank when neither account has sufficient funds to cover the amounts drawn. Due to the delay created by the collection of funds by one bank from the other, an artificial balance is created'. See Madia above, n 96 at 1446.

[99]   Delone and Gwartney stated that the 'Congress passed § 1344 in reaction to this ruling primarily to give the government the means to prosecute check-kiting'. See Delone, C. and Gwartney, S. (2009), 'Financial institutions fraud', *American Criminal Law Review*, **46**, 621–670, at 623.

[100]   Biskupic, S. (1999), 'Fine tuning the bank statute: a prosecutor's perspective', *Marquette Law Review*, **82**, 381–403, at 382. The Bank Fraud Act provides 'whoever knowingly executes or attempts to execute, a scheme or artifice (1) to defraud a financial institution; or (2) to obtain any of the money, funds, credits, assets, securities, or other property owned by, or under the custody or control of, a financial institution, by means of false or fraudulent pretenses, representations, or promises, shall be fined not more than $1m or imprisoned not more than 30 years, or both'.

[101]   Delone and Gwartney above, n 99 at 625. The Bank Fraud Act does not extend to money laundering, the bribery of bank officials and fraud committed by a bank on its customers.

[102]   Pub.L. No. 101-73, 103 Stat. 187 (1989).

[103]   Sussman, R. (1991), 'Protecting clients from the government's thermonuclear war on bank fraud', *American Law Institute – American Bar Association Continuing Legal Education ALI-ABA Course of Study*, **C646**, 213–260, at 215.

tackle procurement fraud,[104] but its scope is limited to frauds that exceed $1m.[105]

The notorious accountancy frauds at Enron and WorldCom resulted in the introduction of the Sarbanes-Oxley Act 2002.[106] Its objective is to improve the level of regulation for the accountancy profession and to deter fraudulent and unethical behaviour.[107] The Act increases the maximum penalty for wire and mail fraud from five years' to twenty years' imprisonment[108] and it provides prosecutors several new weapons that can be used in fraud cases.[109] This includes the codification of securities fraud as a federal crime and the criminalizing of the early destruction of corporate audit records. The impact of the criminal sanctions has been criticized, being described as 'needlessly redundant'.[110] Brickey concluded that 'Sarbanes-Oxley's criminal provisions are more an expression of symbolic political outrage than they are a reasoned response to a public policy question'.[111] Despite this concern, the Securities Fraud Statute 2003 was introduced following a number of securities frauds that resulted in investors losing over $40bn.[112] Under this legislation a person is guilty of an offence where he 'knowingly executes, or attempts to execute, a scheme or artifice to defraud any person in connection with any security of an issuer with a class of securities registered' and 'obtain, by means of false or fraudulent pretenses, representations, or promises, any money or property in connection with the purpose or sale of any security of an issuer with a

---

[104]   MacKay, S. (1992), 'Major fraud against the United States', *Army Lawyer*, September, 7–14, at 8. Liro stated that 'in the late 1980s, a series of well-publicized defense contractor abuses brought the ordinarily obscure topic of government contracting to the public eye'. See Liro, C. (2000), 'Prosecution of minor subcontractors under the Major Fraud Act of 1988', *Michigan Law Review*, **99**, 669–695, at 669–670.

[105]   MacKay above, n 104.

[106]   Pub. L. No. 107-204, 116 Stat. 745 (2002).

[107]   Saksena, P. (2009), 'The Sarbanes-Oxley Act and occupational fraud: does the law effectively tackle the real problem?', *International Company and Commercial Law Review*, **20**(2), 37–43, at 37.

[108]   Sarbanes-Oxley Act 2002, s. 903.

[109]   Brickey above, n 14 at 229. More specifically see Sarbanes-Oxley Act of 2002, Title VIII Corporate and Criminal Fraud Accountability and Title IX White Collar Crime Penalty Enhancements.

[110]   Brickey, K. (2003), 'From Enron to WorldCom and beyond: life and crime after Sarbanes-Oxley', *Washington University Law Review*, **81**, 357–382, at 359.

[111]   *Ibid.*

[112]   Pazicky, L. (2003), 'A new arrow in the quiver of federal securities fraud prosecutors: section 807 of the Sarbanes-Oxley Act of 2002', *Washington University Law Quarterly*, **81**, 801–828, at 801.

class of securities registered'.[113] The Securities Fraud Statute had three objectives:

1. to plug the holes in the existing securities and criminal fraud legislation;[114]
2. to enable prosecutors to initiate criminal proceedings for 'unforeseen classes of schemes'; and
3. to deter people from committing securities fraud by imposing a 25-year custodial sentence.[115]

Pazicky stated that the Act 'significantly impacts securities fraud prosecutions because the government will no longer need to prove the defendant's use of the interstate mail or wire systems. Also, the flexibly written statute will enable prosecutors to keep up with the most complex new fraud schemes and target the most egregious and deceitful scams'.[116]

Another area of concern in addition to the mail, wire and securities fraud legislation is health care fraud. It has been estimated that the US government spends over $550bn per year on its Medicare and Medicaid health programmes,[117] which resulted in Blank *et al* stating that 'it is no surprise that criminals view health care fraud as a lucrative field for illicit profit'.[118] The extent of health care fraud is $13bn per year.[119] Legislation to prevent such fraud includes the Medicaid False Claims Statute which criminalizes 'false statements or representations in connection with any application for claim of benefits or payments of the disposal of assets under a federal health care program'.[120] In order to achieve a prosecution four elements must be proven. Firstly, that the accused made, or caused to be made, a statement or representation of material fact in an application for payment or benefits under a federal health care programme.[121]

---

[113]   If convicted a maximum sentence of 25 years may be imposed.

[114]   Pazicky above, n 112 at 801–802.

[115]   *Ibid.*

[116]   *Ibid.*

[117]   Blank, S., Kasprisin, J. and White, A. (2009), 'Health Care Fraud', *American Criminal Law Review*, **46**, 701–759, at 703. Hereafter Blank *et al.*

[118]   *Ibid.*

[119]   Blank *et al* above, n 117 at 703.

[120]   42 U.S.C. § 1320a-7b(a). For a more detailed discussion of this Act see Shaffer, C. (2007), 'The impact of Medicaid reforms and false claims enforcement: limiting access by discouraging provider participation in Medicaid programs', *South Carolina Law Review*, **58**, 995–1023.

[121]   See generally *United States v Laughlin*, 26 F.3d 1523, 1526 (10th Cir. 1994). As cited in Blank *et al* above, n 117 at 707.

Secondly, that the statement or representation was indeed false.[122] Thirdly, that the defendant knowingly and wilfully made the statement,[123] and finally, that the defendant knew that the statement was false.[124] If the defendant is convicted of an offence under this statute, it is punishable by a fine and/or a custodial sentence of up to five years.[125] The Medicaid Anti-Kickback Statute is broad and applies to all divisions of the health care industry.[126] Under this, the prosecution must prove that the defendant knowingly and wilfully solicited or received remuneration in return for, or to induce, referral of programme-related business.[127] Other examples of statutes designed to tackle health care fraud include the Health Insurance Portability and Accountability Act 1996,[128] which according to some commentators is the 'most comprehensive attempt to fight fraud in federal health care programs'.[129] The Act provides a sustainable source of funding to counteract health care fraud by broadening the scope of the Anti-Kickback Statute to include all health care programmes and increases prosecutorial powers.[130] The Act makes it illegal for anyone to knowingly and wilfully defraud any health care benefit programme or to obtain by means of false representations any money or property of a health care benefit programme; make false or fictitious statements 'in any matter involving a health care benefit program'; embezzle, convert, or steal any funds, property, or assets of a health care benefit programme, or obstruct, delay, or mislead the investigation of federal health care offences.[131] Prosecutors are also able to use the False Claims Act,[132] the

---

[122]   *Ibid.*

[123]   See *United States v Catton*, 89 F.3d 387, 392 (7th Cir. 1996) as cited in Blank *et al* above, n 117 at 707.

[124]   See *United States v Laughlin*, 26 F.3d 1526-1527 (10th Cir. 1994) as cited *ibid.*

[125]   42 U.S.C. § 1320a-7b(a)(6)(i).

[126]   42 U.S.C. § 1320a-7b(b).

[127]   42 U.S.C. § 1320a-7b(b)(1). For a more detailed explanation of this offence see *Hanlester Network v Shalala* (1995), 51 F.3d at 1400 and *McClatcey v United States* (2000) 217 F.3d 823.

[128]   Pub. L. No. 104-191, 110 Stat. 1936.

[129]   Blank *et al* above, n 117 at 736. For an interesting discussion of this Act see Eddy, A. (2000), 'The effect of the Health Insurance Portability and Accountability Act of 1996 on health care fraud in Montana', *Montana Law Review*, **61**, 175–221.

[130]   *Ibid.*

[131]   Blank *et al* above, n 117 at 738.

[132]   18 U.S.C. § 287 (2006). For a detailed commentary on the link between the False Claims Act and health care fraud see Girard, V. (2009), 'Punishing pharmaceutical companies for unlawful promotion of approved drugs: why the False Claims Act is the wrong rx', *Journal of Health Care Law and Policy*, **12**, 119–158.

False Statements Act,[133] the Social Security Act,[134] and the Mail and Wire Fraud Statutes.

The Computer Fraud and Abuse Act is also used in the fight against fraud as it 'protects against various crimes involving "protected computers." Due to the fact that "protected computers" include those used in interstate commerce or communications, the statute covers any computer attached to the Internet, even if all the computers involved are located in the same state'.[135] Under the Act, a person can be held 'criminally or civilly liable for obtaining government protected information, obtaining information from a protected computer by means of interstate communication, accessing a government computer, obtaining anything of value by fraudulent means from a protected computer except for computer use worth less than $5000 in a one-year period, causing damage to a protected computer and/or its data or programming, trafficking in passwords in some situations, and threatening to damage a protected computer and/or its data or programming for purposes of extortion'.[136] Moreover, the Identity Theft and Assumption Deterrence Act 1998 criminalized identity theft,[137] specifically, conduct that 'knowingly transfers or uses, without lawful authority, a means of identification of another person with the intent to commit, or aid, or abet, any unlawful activity'.[138] According to the Department of Justice, 'this offense, in most circumstances, carries a maximum term of 15 years' imprisonment, a fine, and criminal forfeiture of any personal property used or intended to be used to commit the

---

[133] 18 U.S.C. § 1001 (2006). See generally Halverson, A. and Olson, E. (2009), 'False statements and false claims', *American Criminal Law Review*, **46**, 555–587.

[134] 42 U.S.C. § 1320a-7b(a).

[135] Initially, the Act criminalized three narrow types of conduct. Firstly, it made it a criminal offence to access a computer without permission, or where such permission was granted, to exceed that permission, with the purpose of obtaining classified information that would damage the US. Secondly, the Act criminalized conduct where computers were used to obtain records or information of a financial institution. Thirdly, the Act criminalized conduct that intended to 'modify, destroy, or disclose information in, or prevent authorized use of, a computer operated for or on behalf of the US if such conduct would affect the government's use of the computer'. See Kleindienst, K., Coughlin, T. and Pasquarella, J. (2009), 'Computer crimes', *American Criminal Law Review*, **46**, 315–392, at 331–333.

[136] Boyer, S. (2009), 'Computer Fraud and Abuse Act: abusing federal jurisdiction?', *Rutgers Journal of Law and Public Policy*, **6**(3), 661–702, at 667.

[137] Pub. L. No. 105-318, 112 Stat. 3007 (1998) (codified as amended 18 U.S.C. § 1028 (1990)).

[138] 18 U.S.C. § 1028(a)(7).

offense'.[139] Therefore, the Act affords high penalties for this fraudulent activity and allows the Federal Trade Commission to take a lead role in the fight against identity theft.[140] Finally, credit card fraud was traditionally covered by the Truth in Lending Act,[141] the Mail Fraud Statute and the Wire Fraud Statute. These measures have been amended by the Credit Card Fraud Act 1984.[142] Other fraud statutes include the Marriage Fraud Act 1986 and the Civil Tax Fraud Statute.[143]

A large number of fraud statutes have been introduced in the US, each of which criminalizes a different type of fraudulent activity. However, it must be noted that the most popular fraud statutes are the Mail and Wire Fraud Statutes, which have become generic fraud statutes. The US approach towards the criminalization of fraud is a legislative minefield gripped by uncertainties. Federal prosecutors are able to abuse the scope of the fraud statutes seeking prosecutions for a broad range of offences. There are too many fraud statutes and codification into a single fraud statute is recommended. However, this is not a view shared by all commentators. Podgor took the view that:

> although consistency is promoted, a single fraud statute may be more cumbersome than beneficial. The vast circumstances to which fraud applies necessitate an array of different provisions. Some consistency in the statutory construction could enhance the interpretative process. Consolidation, deletion of redundant statutes, and the writing of specific provisions would heighten the prosecution of criminal fraud. Most important, however, is the need for limitations on generic fraud statutes.[144]

There appears to be no desire from within the US to amend its legislative approach towards fraud and it is highly likely that the introduction of more fraud statutes will continue.

---

[139]   Department of Justice (n/d), 'Identity theft and identity fraud' available at http://www.justice.gov/criminal/fraud/websites/idtheft.html (accessed 19 March 2010). It is important to note that methods of committing identity theft could breach other fraud statutes. For example, credit card fraud (18 U.S.C. § 1029), computer fraud (18 U.S.C. § 1030), mail fraud (18 U.S.C. § 1341), wire fraud (18 U.S.C. § 1343), or financial institution fraud (18 U.S.C. § 1344).

[140]   Saunders, K. and Zucker, B. (1999), 'Counteracting identity fraud in the information age: the Identity Theft and Assumption Deterrence Act', *Cornell Journal of Law and Public Policy*, **8**, 661–675, at 673.

[141]   15 U.S.C. § 1643.

[142]   18 U.S.C. § 1029. See for example the commentary by Faro, E. (1990), 'Telemarketing fraud: is RICO one answer?', *University of Illinois Law Review*, Summer, 675–710.

[143]   I.R.C. § 6663.

[144]   Podgor above, n 72 at 768.

4.3.2   Regulatory Agencies

The second part of the fraud policy involves federal agencies and several fraud task forces. There is a link between criminalization and the agencies that investigate and prosecute fraudulent activities. The primary regulators are federal government departments, who lead the fight against fraud. For example, the Department of Justice has its own Fraud Section which investigates and prosecutes complicated fraud cases and also constitutes a rapid anti-fraud response unit. Importantly, the Fraud Section performs a crucial role in the development of the Justice Department's anti-fraud policy, which involves implementing legislation, crime prevention measures, providing training and public education.[145] Furthermore, the Fraud Section also synchronizes interagency investigations and international enforcement efforts. The Fraud Section also contains several interagency fraud working groups:

1.   Hurricane Katrina Fraud Task Force
2.   Identity Theft Task Force
3.   National Procurement Fraud Task Force
4.   Securities and Commodities Fraud Working Group
5.   Interagency Bank Fraud Enforcement Working Group
6.   Mortgage Fraud Working Group
7.   Mass-Marketing Fraud Working Group
8.   Consumer Protection Initiatives Committee

In 2007–2008, the Fraud Section initiated approximately 100 investigations, filed 80 indictments, charged 160 defendants and achieved 156 fraud-related convictions.[146] Another part of the Department of Justice that plays an important role in the US anti-fraud strategy is the FBI, whose priorities are divided into two areas – national security and criminal. It is under the second priority that the FBI seeks to tackle what it refers to as 'white collar crime', and especially fraud, which is illustrated by its 'White-Collar Crime: Strategic Plan'.[147] The strategic plan provides the FBI with six strategic objectives, five of which relate to fraud:

---

[145]   Department of Justice (n/d), 'Fraud Section', available at http://www.justice.gov/criminal/fraud (accessed 19 March 2010).
[146]   Department of Justice *Fraud Section Activities Report Fiscal Year 2008* (Department of Justice: Washington, DC, 2008a) at p. 2.
[147]   Federal Bureau of Investigation *White-Collar Crime: Strategic Plan* (Federal Bureau of Investigation: Washington, DC, 2007b).

1. to cut the levels of corporate fraud by targeting those groups or individuals engaged in major corporate fraud schemes;
2. to reduce the levels of health care frauds;
3. to lower the fraud committed by organized criminals against financial institutions;
4. to trim down the impact of telemarketing, insurance, and investment frauds, and
5. to address those investigative matters which represent the most significant economic losses within federally-funded procurement, contract, and entitlement programmes, environmental crimes, bankruptcy fraud, and anti-trust offences.

The FBI has also been charged with tackling mortgage fraud and it has been boosted by the Fraud Enforcement and Recovery Act 2009.[148] The Act had three objectives. Firstly, to improve the levels of responsibility and accountability for frauds that had arisen during the financial crisis. Secondly, it provided a substantial increase in funding for the Department of Justice and other law enforcement agencies to tackle mortgage fraud. The Act has permitted the government to provide an additional $500m for 2010 and 2011 to increase the levels of government enforcement activity.[149] The Department of Justice has been given $330m to investigate instances of mortgage fraud and to pursue any potential prosecutions that arise. Finally, the Act seeks to clarify several problematic areas of fraud and money laundering statutes.[150] The funding is essential given the complexity of the fraudulent activity that has arisen due to the financial crisis. The FBI has been able to undertake numerous detailed investigations into allegations of mortgage fraud.[151]

---

[148] Ryder, Nicholas and Chambers, Clare (2010), 'The credit crunch and mortgage fraud – too little too late? A comparative analysis of the policies adopted in the United States of America and the United Kingdom', in S. Kis and I. Balogh (eds), *Housing, housing costs and mortgages: trends, impact and prediction*, Nova Science, New York, pp. 1–22.

[149] *Ibid.*

[150] This includes for example important amendments to the False Claims Act following the Supreme Court decision in *Allison Engine Co v United States ex rel, Sanders* 553 U.S. ___ (2008), 128 S. Ct. 2123 (2008). Furthermore, several important amendments were made to several fraud statutes including the definition of 'proceeds' in money laundering (18 U.S.C. § 1956). This was an attempt to overcome the shortcomings of the decision of the Supreme Court in *United States v Santos* (2008) (No. 06-1005) 461 F. 3d 886, affirmed.

[151] For example, the FBI announced in November 2009 that it brought fraud charges against 100 defendants involved in illegally obtaining loans totalling

In addition to the FBI, the US Secret Service plays also an important role in fraud prevention.[152] Its original aim was to investigate the counterfeiting of US currency and to ensure that the payment and financial systems are protected. In 1984, the responsibilities of the Secret Service grew to include the protection against and the investigation of financial institution fraud, computer fraud,[153] access device fraud, and telecommunications fraud. It is important to note that it also investigates allegations of money laundering. Winn and Govern took the view that:

> the Secret Service has concurrent jurisdiction with the Department of Justice for financial crimes and primary jurisdiction for crimes involving financial infrastructure and bank payment systems. This includes both domestic and international access device fraud, debit and credit cards, identity theft, false identification, and computer fraud.[154]

Its remit was further extended by the USA Patriot Act 2001 which requires it to establish and coordinate the Electronic Crimes Task Force.[155] Other deferral agencies include the Postal Inspection Service, the Federal Trade Commission (FTC) and the Securities and Exchange Commission (SEC). The Postal Inspection Service performs an important role in fraud prevention and its objective is to protect and maintain the integrity of the US postal system. The Postal Inspection Service addresses mail and identity

---

$400m in connection with over 700 properties. See Department of Justice (2009), 'Mortgage Fraud Surge Investigation Nets More Than 100 Individuals Throughout Middle District of Florida', Press Release, 4 November 2009, available at http://tampa.fbi.gov/dojpressrel/2009/ta110409.htm (accessed 15 March 2010).

[152] For a brief discussion of its role see United States Secret Service *Fiscal Year 2008 – Annual Report* (United States Secret Service: Washington, DC, 2009) at p. 34.

[153] The Secret Service has retained jurisdiction over computer fraud and other crimes since the early part of the 1980s. Urbelis noted that the 'Computer Fraud and Abuse Act of 1984 charged the Secret Service with the responsibility and authority of investigating computer crime'. See Urbelis, A. (2005), 'Towards a more equitable prosecution of cybercrime: concerning hackers, criminals and the national security', *Vermont Law Review*, **29**, 975–1008, at 976.

[154] Winn, J. and Govern, K. (2009), 'Identity theft: risks and challenges to business of data compromise', *Temple Journal of Science, Technology & Environmental Law*, **28**, 49–63, at 59.

[155] The Act states that '[t]he Director of the United States Secret Service shall take appropriate actions to develop a national network of electronic crime task forces, based on the New York Electronic Crime Task Force model, throughout the United States, for the purpose of preventing, detecting, and investigating various forms of electronic crime including potential terrorist attacks against critical infrastructure and financial payment systems'. See 107 H.R. 3162.

fraud and it seeks to protect customers from mail fraud schemes including boiler room fraud, health care fraud, advance fee fraud, insurance fraud and other consumer frauds. In 2006/2007 for example, it investigated 38 000 allegations of mail fraud,[156] and in 2007 it reported that '40 percent of Postal Inspectors' arrests related to mail theft'.[157] Additionally, the FTC attempts to tackle identity theft and internet fraud. The FTC reported that 'internet-related complaints accounted for 46% of all reported fraud complaints, with monetary losses of over \$335m'.[158] It seeks to provide information, advice and guidance for consumers and businesses to prevent identify theft.[159] Finally, the SEC seeks to 'protect investors, maintain fair, orderly, and efficient markets, and facilitate capital formation'.[160] The Securities Act 1933 provides that the SEC has two principal objectives.[161] Firstly, to ensure that investors receive financial and other significant information concerning securities being offered for public sale. Secondly, to prohibit deceit, misrepresentations, and other fraud in the sale of securities. In particular, the SEC is concerned with 'promoting the disclosure of important market-related information, maintaining fair dealing, and protecting against fraud'.[162] The SEC has extensive enforcement powers to tackle securities fraud and insider trading by virtue of the Sarbanes-Oxley Act 2002.[163]

The primary agencies are assisted by several secondary bodies, that were created following a number of high profile frauds.[164] For example,

---

[156] Maskaleris, S. (2007), 'Identity theft and frauds against senior citizens: "who's in your wallet?"', *Experience*, **18**, 14–32, at 16.

[157] Postal Services Inspectorate *2007 Annual Report of Investigations* (Postal Services Inspectorate: Washington, DC, 2008) at p. 2.

[158] Federal Trade Commission *Consumer fraud and identity theft complaint data: January–December 2005* (Federal Trade Commission: Washington, DC, 2006) as cited in Corbett, P. (2007), 'Prosecuting the internet fraud case without going for broke', *Mississippi Law Journal*, **76**, 841–873, at 843.

[159] See for example Federal Trade Commission (n/d), 'Fighting back against identity theft', available at http://www.ftc.gov/bcp/edu/microsites/idtheft// (accessed 26 March 2010).

[160] Securities and Exchange Commission (n/d), 'The Investor's Advocate: How the SEC Protects Investors, Maintains Market Integrity, and Facilitates Capital Formation', available at http://www.sec.gov/about/whatwedo.shtml (accessed 26 March 2010).

[161] As amended through P.L. 111-72, approved 13 October 2009.

[162] Securities and Exchange Commission above, n 160.

[163] Public Law 107-204, 30 July 2002, 116 Stat. 745.

[164] Arogeti took the view that these institutions were 'a direct response to an epidemic of corporate fraud, igniting a fear amongst investors about the future of the marketplace'. Arogeti, J. (2006), 'How much co-operation between government

the Corporate Fraud Task Force (CFTF) was established due to the collapse of Enron and WorldCom.[165] President George Bush stated that it 'is time to reaffirm the basic principles and rules that make capitalism work – truthful books and honest people, and well-enforced laws against fraud and corruption'.[166] The CFTF originated from President Bush's 'ten-point plan to improve corporate responsibility and protect America's shareholders'.[167] This initiative was based on three principles – information accuracy and accessibility, management accountability, and auditor independence.[168] Presidential Executive Order 13 271 permitted the Attorney General to establish within the Department of Justice the CFTF,[169] with the rationale that, collectively, these agencies 'would help send Bush's emphatic message: dishonest corporate leaders will be exposed and punished'.[170] The CFTF had three functions:

1. to determine and recommend the investigation and prosecution of a broad range of financial crimes;[171]
2. to make recommendations to the Attorney General to determine the allocation of the resources for the investigation and prosecution of significant financial crimes;[172] and

---

agencies is too much? Reconciling *United States v Scrushy*, the Corporate Fraud Task Force, and the nature of parallel proceedings', *Georgia State University Law Review*, **23**, 427–453, at 427.

[165]   Griffin, L. (2007), 'Compelled co-operation and the new corporate criminal procedure', *New York University Law Review*, **82**, 311–382, at 314.

[166]   Exec. Order No. 13 271, 67 Fed. Reg. 46 091 (9 July 2002).

[167]   The White House (n/d), 'The President's Leadership in Combating Corporate Fraud', available at www.whitehouse.gov/infocus/corporateresponsibility/ (accessed 6 July 2010). This is known as the 'Thompson Memo', named after its author, the then Deputy Attorney General Larry Thompson. See Wray, C. and Hur, R. (2006), 'Corporate criminal prosecution in a post-Enron world: the Thompson Memo in theory and practice', *American Criminal Law Review*, **43**, 1095–1188, at 1101.

[168]   Corporate Fraud Task Force *First year report to the president* (Department of Justice: Washington, DC, 2003) at 1.4.

[169]   Presidential Executive Order 13 271, 9 July 2002, article 2. Membership of the Corporate Fraud Task Force comprised the Deputy Attorney General, the Assistant Attorney General (Criminal and Tax Divisions), the Director of the Federal Bureau of Investigation and United States Attorneys from several states.

[170]   *Ibid.*

[171]   For the purposes of this Presidential Executive Order financial crime includes mail fraud, money laundering, accounting fraud and tax-based frauds.

[172]   Presidential Executive Order 13 271, 9 July 2002.

3. to make recommendations to improve the levels of co-operation and collaboration between federal agencies, and to amend laws and regulations to tackle financial crime.[173]

The beneficiaries of the CFTF were the Department of Justice and the SEC, whose anti-fraud budgets were significantly expanded.[174] In its lifetime, the CFTF presented three reports to the President. For example, in 2003 it reported that it had successfully secured over 250 corporate fraud convictions, initiated nearly 300 investigations and charges had been filed against 354 defendants. Furthermore, as a result of these legal proceedings, US courts imposed financial sanctions totalling $2.5bn between July 2002 and March 2003.[175] In its second report the CFTF illustrated its achievements by referring to several high profile convictions, including Martha Stewart and Frank Quattrone, and the imposition of a record civil penalty of $2.25bn against WorldCom.[176] In this report, the CFTF stated that it had successfully secured over 500 convictions for corporate fraud and that 960 individuals had been charged with corporate fraud-related crime. Furthermore, it had reclaimed over $160m for the victims of the Enron fraud.[177] In its final report, the Task Force noted that it has obtained approximately 1300 corporate fraud convictions,[178] and this resulted in Arogeti noting that 'there is no doubt that the creation of the Task Force is a leading factor in the record number of criminal securities

---

[173] *Ibid.* The Corporate Fraud Task Force outlined the reasons for its creation: 'in establishing his Corporate Fraud Task Force, the President called on us to clean up corruption in the board room, restore investor confidence in our financial markets, and to send a loud and clear message that corporate wrongdoing will not be tolerated. Numerous high-profile acts of deception in corporate America had shaken the public's trust in corporations, the financial markets, and the economy. A few dishonest individuals hurt the reputations of many honest companies and executives. They hurt workers who committed their lives to building the companies that hired them. They hurt investors and retirees who placed their faith in the promise of growth and integrity'. See Corporate Fraud Task Force above, n 168 at 1.4.

[174] For example, the Department of Justice's budget was increased by $24.5m whilst the Securities and Exchange Commission's budget increased by 73 per cent. See Hurt, C. (2008), 'The under civilization of corporate law', *Journal of Corporation Law*, **33**, 361–445, at 379.

[175] Corporate Fraud Task Force *Second year report to the president* (Department of Justice: Washington, DC, 2003) at p. iii.

[176] *Ibid.*, at para. 2.2.

[177] Corporate Fraud Task Force above, n 175 at 2.3.

[178] Corporate Fraud Task Force *Report to the president* (Department of Justice: Washington, DC, 2008) at p. ii.

prosecutions that have been brought to date'.[179] The impact of the CFTF was immense and it diligently has assisted the Department of Justice in pursuit of fraudsters in the wake of the collapse of Enron and WorldCom.

The Identity Theft Task Force (ITTF) was established by Presidential Executive Order 13 402 in 2006.[180] It is chaired by the Attorney General, in conjunction with the Chairman of the FTC,[181] and it examines the effectiveness of the legislative measures utilized by law enforcement agencies to investigate, prosecute and to recover the proceeds of identity theft.[182] It also liaises with federal agencies to assess how the government can implement appropriate safety mechanisms to protect the information it and businesses hold. In April 2007, the ITTF published its 'Strategic Plan',[183] and made four recommendations aimed at improving the US policy towards identity theft:

1. federal agencies should reduce the unnecessary use of people's Social Security numbers;
2. national standards should be established to require the private sector to safeguard personal data and to provide notice to consumers when a breach occurs that poses a significant risk of identity theft;
3. federal agencies should implement a broad, sustained awareness campaign to educate consumers, the private sector, and the public sector on deterring, detecting, and defending against identity theft; and
4. a National Identity Theft Law Enforcement Center should be created to allow law enforcement agencies to coordinate their efforts and information more efficiently.[184]

---

[179]   Arogeti above, n 164 at 432.

[180]   Presidential Executive Order 13402, 10 May 2006. The Executive Order 'charged 15 federal departments and agencies with crafting a comprehensive national strategy to combat more effectively this pernicious crime, which afflicts millions of Americans each year and, in some cases, causes devastating damage to its victims'. See Identity Theft Task Force *The President's Identity Theft Task Force Report* (Identity Theft Task Force: Washington, DC, 2008) at p. vii.

[181]   Dent, R. (2008), 'The role of banking regulation in data theft and security', *Review of Banking and Financial Law*, **27**, 381–392, at 385–386.

[182]   Lafferty, I. (2007), 'Medical Identity Theft: The Future of Health Care is Now – Lack of Federal Law Enforcement Efforts Means Compliance Professionals Will Have to Lead the Way', *Health Care Compliance*, **9**(1), 11–20, at 17.

[183]   Identity Theft Task Force *Combating identity theft: a strategic plan* (Identity Theft Task Force: Washington, DC, 2007).

[184]   *Ibid.*, at p. 4. For an excellent discussion of the US strategy towards identity theft see Marron, D. (2008), '"Alter reality": governing the risk of identity theft', *British Journal of Criminology*, **48**(1) 20–38.

Additionally, the National Procurement Fraud Task Force (NPFTF) was established in 2006 with the aim of preventing, detecting and prosecuting those involved in procurement and grant fraud. This Task Force, like those already referred to, is led by the Department of Justice and its membership consists of the FBI, the Department of Justice Inspector General and other federal agencies. The NPFTF concentrates its anti-fraud efforts on pursuing civil and criminal enforcement which includes concentrating on such issues as misuse of classified and procurement-sensitive information, false claims, grant fraud, fraud involving foreign military sales and public corruption associated with procurement fraud. In 2010, the Department of Justice announced that the ambit of the NPFTF would be extended to include combating Recovery Act fraud, in addition to procurement and grant fraud. The NPFTF has established the following objectives relating to procurement, grant, and Recovery Act fraud:

1. increase coordination and strengthen partnerships among all Inspectors General, law enforcement, and the Department of Justice to fight fraud more effectively;
2. assess existing government-wide efforts to combat fraud and work with audit staff and contracting staff both inside and outside of government to detect and report fraud;
3. increase and accelerate civil and criminal prosecutions and administrative actions to recover ill-gotten gains resulting from fraud;
4. educate and inform the public about fraud;
5. identify and remove barriers to preventing, detecting, and prosecuting fraud; and
6. encourage greater private sector participation in the prevention and detection of fraud.

In an attempt to codify the role and responsibilities of the secondary anti-fraud agencies President Barak Obama established the interagency Financial Fraud Task Force in 2009.[185] This is led by the Department of Justice,[186] and replaces the CFTF and seeks to 'build upon efforts already underway to combat mortgage, securities and corporate fraud by increasing coordination and fully utilizing the resources and expertise of the

---

[185] Presidential Executive Order 13 519.
[186] Federal Bureau of Investigation (2009), 'President Obama Establishes Interagency Financial Fraud Enforcement Task Force', available at http://www.fbi.gov/pressrel/pressrel09/taskforce_111709.htm (accessed 29 November 2009).

government's law enforcement and regulatory apparatus'.[187] The Task Force has three functions:

1. to provide advice to the Attorney General for the investigation and prosecution of a wide range of financial crimes;[188]
2. to make recommendations to the Attorney General to improve the levels of cooperation amongst federal, state and local authorities; and
3. to synchronize the law enforcement between the federal, state and local authorities.

The Department of Justice has admirably led the US fight against fraud and it is assisted by the extensive investigative and prosecutorial powers of the FBI. Furthermore, there are many primary federal agencies including the Secret Service, SEC and FTC that also play an active role in the US anti-fraud policy. The achievements of these agencies are not in question, but there is a great deal of overlap between them and many perform identical functions. The primary regulators are assisted by several fraud task forces, or secondary regulators, which are led by the Department of Justice, who concentrate on specific types of fraud. It would be very easy to argue that there are too many anti-fraud regulators in the US and that the position could be rectified by creating a unifying anti-fraud office, like OLAF for instance. The Department for Justice must be commended for acting as an effective umbrella organization that provides guidance and support. However, it is important to note that these agencies do not have access to a government anti-fraud policy, a position that can be completely contrasted with the government's stance towards money laundering and terrorist financing. It is strongly contended that the US anti-fraud policy would benefit from such a strategy document that outlines achievable and proportionate targets so that the success of the US anti-fraud policy can be accurately measured.

4.3.3 Reporting Obligations

The final part of the US fraud policy is the imposition of anti-fraud reporting obligations and the use of financial intelligence supplied via currency transaction reports (CTR) or suspicious activity reports (SARs). SARs are filed by depository institutions, the securities and futures industry, and casinos and card clubs; the forms contain boxes where these institutions

---

[187] *Ibid.*
[188] This includes for example bank, mortgage, loan, and lending fraud; securities and commodities fraud; retirement plan fraud; mail and wire fraud; tax crimes and money laundering.

can report instances of certain types of fraud. These include cheque fraud, commercial loan fraud, consumer loan fraud, credit card fraud, debit card fraud, mortgage loan fraud and wire transfer fraud. The SAR contains a narrative section, which allows the institution to summarize the apparent illegal activity. The benefits of this part of the US anti-fraud policy have been illustrated during the financial crisis where FinCEN reported, in 2008, the total number of fraud-related SARs was 63 173, with estimated fraud losses exceeding $1.5bn. In 2009, FinCEN reported that 'in the third quarter of 2009, depository institution filers submitted 15 697 mortgage loan fraud SARs, a 7.5 percent increase over the same period in 2008'.[189] In 2009, 40 901 such reports were submitted to FinCEN by the end of April. As a result of the financial intelligence provided, the FBI has undertaken 2440 investigations, started 965 cases and obtained 354 convictions since the beginning of the global financial crisis in 2007.[190]

However, in relation to fraud Linn noted that 'nonbank lenders, mortgage brokers and other real estate professionals were not subject to the Bank Secrecy Act's (BSA) provisions, including mandatory mortgage fraud reporting requirements'.[191] Members of many professions are required by the USA Patriot Act 2001 to have in place an anti-money laundering programme.[192] This includes the development of internal anti-money laundering procedures and controls, the appointment of a compliance officer, the creation of a training scheme to encourage employees to detect and prevent money laundering, and an independent audit to be carried out to determine the effectiveness of the anti-money laundering procedures.[193] However, the USA Patriot Act does not contain the term 'real estate'. Linn concluded that:

> regrettably, at the height of the subprime lending boom, trade groups representing non-bank mortgage lenders, mortgage brokers, real estate agents, and other persons involved in real estate closing and settlements, successfully resisted efforts by the Department of Treasury to impose BSA regulations on them.[194]

---

[189] FinCEN *Mortgage loan fraud update – suspicious activity report filings from 1 July – 30 September 2009* (FinCEN: Washington, DC, 2009) at p. 2.
[190] Federal Bureau of Investigation above, n 15.
[191] Linn, C. (2009), 'The way we live now: the case for mandating fraud reporting by persons involved in real estate closings and settlements', *Journal of Financial Crime*, **16**(1), 7–27, at 20.
[192] Uniting and Strengthening America by Providing Appropriate Tools Required to Intercept and Obstruct Terrorism Act (2001), s. 352(a).
[193] Tellechea, A. (2008), 'Economic crimes in the capital markets', *Journal of Financial Crime*, **15**(2), 214–222, at 217.
[194] Linn, above n 191 at 10.

There are a number of possible reasons as to why the federal agencies have been reluctant to impose compulsory reporting obligations on the real estate industry, such as cost,[195] the increase of defensive reporting,[196] and increased level of regulation and perhaps, somewhat surprisingly, the real estate industry felt that they were not at threat from financial crime. This reluctance is very surprising as there is increasing evidence that criminals and terrorists are exploiting this loophole to hide their proceeds of crime and commit fraud. Linn recommended that 'extending mandatory fraud reporting requirements to the real estate industry makes sense for another reason. The real estate industry in the US is fragmented, with many participants regulated by a patchwork of federal, state and local agencies. The fragmented nature of the real estate industry in the US, which many now agree was a regulatory weakness during the subprime era, could have been used to some advantage'.[197] The benefits of the reporting requirements and the resultant financial intelligence were emphasized by the FBI in its White Collar Crime Strategy. The FBI has identified six strategic objectives, all of which specifically address the importance of intelligence. For example, in relation to the first strategic objective, the FBI stated that its first priority action was to 'expand the intelligence base through private sector and community outreach specifically focused on private industry personnel, government regulators, and all levels of law enforcement'.[198]

The US has adopted a robust stance towards fraud. It has criminalized a very wide range of fraudulent activities and these provisions have been effectively used by prosecutors. The Department of Justice and the FBI have benefited from an unprecedented level of funding which has been provided by successive presidential administrations. This is especially the case regarding mortgage fraud which has seen an unprecedented number of investigations and prosecutions brought by the FBI. Furthermore, the US fraud policy has been assisted by the creation of a number of specialized fraud task forces which have been established to initiate criminal and civil proceedings and support the activities of the FBI. However, as outlined above the effectiveness of these agencies must be questioned as many of them perform the same function. There are too many federal agencies

---

[195]   See for example Roberts, M. (2004), 'Big brother isn't just watching you, he's also wasting your tax payer dollars: an analysis of the anti-money laundering provisions of the USA Patriot Act', *Rutgers Law Review*, **56**(2), 573–602, at 592.

[196]   Leong, A. (2007a), 'Chasing dirty money: domestic and international measures against money laundering', *Journal of Money Laundering Control*, **10**(2), 141–156, at 141.

[197]   Linn, above n 191, at 11.

[198]   Federal Bureau of Investigation above, n 147.

tackling fraud, a factor which has also adversely affected the US terrorist financing policy. The US strategy would benefit from the creation of a single economic crime agency. Once again, the importance of financial intelligence in the battle against financial crime should not be underestimated. The usefulness and appropriateness of the financial intelligence provided to FinCEN and the FBI has become a central tenet of the US anti-fraud strategy. It is interesting to note that the UK has adopted an almost identical policy toward fraud.

4.4   THE UNITED KINGDOM

> Historically, there was a lack of authoritative statistics in the area on the scale of fraud in the UK, posing a policy challenge for the UK government. Additionally, the criminal law and court procedure, which are at the heart of an effective anti-fraud strategy, were complex and largely ineffective . . . outdated and inflexible legislation prevented many large fraud cases from being brought to court at all.[199]

The UK fraud policy is similar to that adopted in the US and is divided into three parts:

1.   criminalization of fraudulent activities;
2.   regulatory agencies; and
3.   anti-fraud reporting requirements.

Fraud has been propelled from its traditional tertiary position, behind money laundering and terrorist financing, to the top of the government's financial crime agenda. This is due to the publication of the Fraud Review and the introduction of the Fraud Act 2006.[200] Sarker takes the view that 'a fresh crop of anti-fraud initiatives, reviews and legislation has sprung up, ostensibly demonstrating how fighting fraud is a top priority in the UK'.[201] However, this is not a view shared by all commentators and it has been argued that 'little has changed to reverse the perception of fraud as a low priority'.[202] The Fraud Review (the Review) was commissioned by the Attorney General 'to recommend ways of reducing fraud and the

---

[199]   Haines above, n 13 at 213.
[200]   The government announced that it intended to introduce a radical overhaul of the laws on fraud in its 2005 general election manifesto. Labour Party *Labour Party manifesto – Britain forward not back* (Labour Party: London, 2005).
[201]   Sarker above, n 25 at 243.
[202]   *Ibid.*

harm it does to the economy and society'.[203] The Review considered three questions:

1.   what is the level of fraud?
2.   what is the appropriate role of the government in dealing with fraud?
3.   how could government resources be spent to maximize value for money?[204]

The Review was unable to accurately outline the extent of fraud. In relation to its second task, it concluded that the government has two functions – to protect public money from fraudsters and to protect consumers and businesses against fraud. The Review recommended that the government should adopt a holistic approach towards fraud and develop a national strategy. Furthermore, it recommended the creation of the NFA to develop and implement the strategy. It also suggested that a NFRC should be created so that businesses and individuals could report fraud. The NFRC has been operating since October 2009,[205] as actionfraud.org.[206] The National Fraud Intelligence Bureau (NFIB) is the agency dedicated to analyse and assess fraud, employing analysts from both law enforcement and the private sector. Fourthly, the Review suggested that a national lead police force should be established based on the City of London Police Fraud Squad.[207]

4.4.1   Criminalization

The UK's legislative framework towards fraud can be contrasted with that in the US. Prior to the Fraud Act, it comprised eight statutory deception offences in the Theft Acts (1968 and 1978) and the common law offence of conspiracy to defraud.[208] The offences created by the Theft Act

---

[203]   Attorney General's Office above, n 20 at 4.

[204]   *Ibid.*, at 4–5.

[205]   National Fraud Authority (2009a), 'National Fraud Reporting Centre's "0300" line launches in the West Midlands', available at http://www.attorneygeneral.gov.uk/nfa/WhatAreWeSaying/NewsRelease/Documents/NFRC%20 launch%2026%20Oct%2009.pdf (accessed 3 March 2010).

[206]   Action Fraud (n/d), 'Action Fraud', available at http://www.actionfraud. org.uk/ (accessed 13 March 2010).

[207]   Attorney General's Office above, n 20 at 10. The effectiveness of this decision has been questioned. See for example Rider, B. (2009), 'A bold step?', *Company Lawyer*, **30**(1), 1–2, at 1.

[208]   The Theft Act 1968 was a creation of the Criminal Law Revision Committee: Theft and Related Offences, Cmnd. 2977, May 1966. Other noteworthy attempts

1968 were difficult to enforce.[209] Therefore, it led to the introduction of the Theft Act 1978, which did little to rectify the problems.[210] The Home Office noted that it 'is not always clear which offence should be charged, and defendants have successfully argued that the consequences of their particular deceptive behaviour did not fit the definition of the offence with which they have been charged'.[211] In 1998, the then Home Secretary Jack Straw MP asked the Law Commission to examine the law on fraud.[212] In 1999 it published a Consultation Paper which distinguished between two types of fraudulent offences – dishonesty and deception.[213] The Law Commission concluded that while the concerns expressed about the existing law were valid they could be met by extending the existing offences in preference to creating a single offence of fraud.[214] The Law Commission published its final report in 2002 with the Fraud Bill.[215] The Fraud Act came into force on 15 January 2007;[216] it overhauls and widens the criminal offences available in respect of fraudulent and deceptive behaviour.[217] The new offence, punishable by imprisonment of up to 10 years and/or an

---

to tackle fraud before the Fraud Act were the Prevention of Fraud (Investments) Act 1958 and the Financial Services Act 1986.

[209]   See generally Kiernan, P. and Scanlan, G. (2003), 'Fraud and the Law Commission: the future of dishonesty', *Journal of Financial Crime*, **10**(3), 199–208.

[210]   For a useful discussion of the law of theft see Doig above, n 2 at 22–35. Wright concluded that the laws were 'fragmented, disparate and over specific'. See Wright above, n 1 at 18.

[211]   *Ibid.* For a more detailed illustration of this problem see generally *R v Preddy* [1996] AC 815, 831.

[212]   Specifically the Law Commission were asked 'to examine the law on fraud, and in particular to consider whether it: is readily comprehensible to juries; is adequate for effective prosecution; is fair to potential defendants; meets the need of developing technology including electronic means of transfer; and to make recommendations to improve the law in these respects with all due expedition. In making these recommendations to consider whether a general offence of fraud would improve the criminal law'. See HC Debates 7 April 1998 c.176-177WA.

[213]   Law Commission *Legislating the Criminal Code: Fraud and Deception – Law Commission Consultation Paper no. 155* (Law Commission: London, 1999).

[214]   The Law Commission also published an informal discussion paper in 2000. See Law Commission *Informal discussion paper: fraud and deception – further proposals from the criminal law team* (Law Commission: London, 2000).

[215]   For an analysis of the Law Commission's report see Kiernan and Scanlan above, n 209.

[216]   The Fraud Act 2006 (Commencement) Order 2006, S.I. 2006/3500.

[217]   For a detailed commentary and analysis of the Fraud Act see Ormerod. D. (2007), 'The Fraud Act 2006 – criminalising lying?', *Criminal Law Review*, March, 193–219. However, it is important to note that not all of the offences under the Theft Act 1968 have been abolished. For example false accounting (Theft Act 1968, s. 17), the liability of company directors (Theft Act 1968, s. 18), false

unlimited fine can be committed in three different ways – fraud by false representation,[218] fraud by failing to disclose information[219] and fraud by abuse of position.[220] Dennis argued that the Act 'represents the culmination of a law reform debate that can be traced back more than 30 years'.[221] Scanlan takes the view that the Fraud Act 2006 'provides prosecutors with a broad range offence of fraud'.[222] This clearly represents a significant improvement on the statutory offences of the Theft Acts and the common law offence of conspiracy to defraud.

4.4.2 Regulatory Authorities

There are a broad range of regulatory agencies that attempt to combat fraud.[223] It is important to note that this part of the UK policy can be contrasted with that in the US, where the Department of Justice is the primary agency. There is no single government department that plays such an active role in the UK, where the most prominent agency is the SFO. This was established following the 'era of financial deregulation' in the 1980s, an era that resulted in London attracting 'foreign criminals, including "mademen" from the US Mafia, the "Cosa Nostra", who were now in London taking advantage of the new climate of enterprise, offering securities scams, commodity futures trading frauds and other forms of investment rip-offs'.[224] Bosworth-Davies noted that 'almost

---

statements by company directors (Theft Act 1968, s. 19) and dishonest destruction of documents (Theft Act 1968, s. 20(1)).

[218] Fraud Act 2006, s. 2.

[219] Fraud Act 2006, s. 3.

[220] Fraud Act 2006, s. 4.

[221] Dennis, I. (2007), 'Fraud Act 2006', *Criminal Law Review*, January, 1–2, at 1.

[222] Scanlan, G. (2008), 'Offences concerning directors and officers of a company: fraud and corruption in the United Kingdom – the present and the future', *Journal of Financial Crime*, **15**(1), 22–37, at 25.

[223] This includes for example the SFO, FSA, NFA, Office of Fair Trading (OFT), SOCA and HMRC. Indeed Wright stated that 'it is reassuring that the newly formed Serious Organized Crime Agency . . . will have non-fiscal fraud as one of its major priorities'. See Wright above, n 1 at 14. Doig opined that agencies that tackle fraud can be categorized as either revenue-collecting organizations, organizations involved in benefit payments, regulatory organizations, non-departmental public sector organizations, governmental organizations and police forces within public sector. See Doig above, n 53 at 54.

[224] Bosworth-Davies, R. (2009), 'Investigating financial crime: the continuing evolution of the public fraud investigation role – a personal perspective', *Company Lawyer*, **30**(7), 195–199, at 196.

overnight, London became the fraud capital of Europe and every con-man, snake-oil salesman, grafter and hustler turned up'.[225] To tackle these problems the SFO, an independent government department, was created with both investigative and prosecutorial powers.[226] The impetus for introducing the Criminal Justice Act 1987 and creating the SFO was the Fraud Trials Committee Report, commonly known as the 'Roskill Report'. The government established the independent committee of inquiry in 1983. The Roskill Committee considered the introduction of more effective means of fighting fraud through changes to the law and criminal proceedings.[227] The Committee criticized the staffing levels of the agencies policing fraud, and that there was a great deal of overlap between them. Roskill concluded that 'co-operation between different investigating bodies in the UK was inefficient, and the interchange of information or assistance between our law enforcement authorities was unsatisfactory'.[228] The Roskill Committee made 112 recommendations, of which all but two were implemented.[229] Its main recommendation was the creation of a new unified organization responsible for the detection, investigation and prosecution of serious fraud cases. The result was the SFO, which has jurisdiction in England, Wales and Northern Ireland, but not Scotland.[230] It is headed by a director, who is appointed and account-able to the Attorney General. Under the Act, the SFO has the ability to search property and compel persons to answer questions and produce documents provided it has reasonable grounds to do so.[231] The SFO

---

[225] *Ibid.*

[226] See generally Wright, R. (2003), 'Fraud after Roskill: A view from the Serious Fraud Office', *Journal of Financial Crime*, **11**(1), 10–16.

[227] The Committee was asked to 'consider in what ways the conduct of crimi-nal proceedings in England and Wales arising from fraud can be improved and to consider what changes in existing law and procedure would be desirable to secure the just, expeditious and economical disposal of such proceedings'. See Fraud Trials Committee Report (1986) HMSO.

[228] *Ibid*, p. 8.

[229] For a detailed commentary of the Roskill Commission see Levi, M. (2003), 'The Roskill Fraud Commission revisited: an assessment', *Journal of Financial Crime*, **11**(1), 38–44.

[230] Criminal Justice Act 1987, s. 1.

[231] Criminal Justice Act 1987, s. 2. It is important to note that the SFO has other investigative and prosecutorial powers under the Fraud Act 2006, the Theft Act 1968, the Companies Act 2006, the Serious Crime Act 2007, the Serious Organised Crime and Police Act 2005, the Proceeds of Crime Act 2002 and the Regulation of Investigatory Powers Act 2000.

has a budget of £44.6m per year, it employs 303 staff and has 86 active cases.[232] It sees its mission as:

> to protect society from extensive, deliberate criminal deception which could threaten public confidence in the financial system. We investigate fraud and corruption that requires our investigative expertise and special powers to obtain and assess evidence to successfully prosecute fraudsters, freeze assets and compensate victims.[233]

The SFO determines whether or not to investigate the matter if the allegation meets the following criteria:

1. Does the value of the alleged fraud exceed £1m?
2. Is there an international element to the fraud?
3. Is it likely to cause widespread public concern?
4. Does the case require specialized knowledge?
5. Does the SFO need to use its investigative powers?

The SFO also considers the seriousness of the case and its complexity and will investigate investment fraud, bribery and corruption, corporate fraud and public sector fraud.

The effectiveness of the SFO has been questioned following a number of high profile failed prosecutions. Mahendra describes the notorious failures of the SFO as reminiscent of 'watching the England cricket team – a victory being so rare and unexpected that it was a cause of national rejoicing'.[234] Indeed, Wright notes that 'because the SFO operates in the spotlight, the beam falls on the unsuccessful as well as the victorious. Indeed it shines with blinding brightness on the ones that get away'.[235] The prosecutorial inadequacies of the SFO were highlighted by the 'Review of the Serious Fraud Office'.[236] The Review compared the performance of the SFO with the US Attorney's Office for the Southern District of New York and the Manhattan District Attorney's Office and concluded that 'the discrepancies in conviction rates are striking'.[237] The Review noted that

---

[232] Serious Fraud Office *Achievements 2009–2010* (Serious Fraud Office: London, 2010) at p. 3.

[233] Serious Fraud Office *SFO Budget 2009–2010* (Serious Fraud Office: London, 2010) at p. 3.

[234] Mahendra, B. (2002), 'Fighting serious fraud', *New Law Journal*, **152**(7020), 289.

[235] Wright above, n 226 at 10.

[236] de Grazia, J. *Review of the Serious Fraud Office – Final Report* (Serious Fraud Office: London, 2008).

[237] *Ibid.*, at pp. 3–4.

between 2003 and 2007 the SFO's average conviction rate was 61 per cent, whilst the conviction rates in the two aforementioned case studies were 91 per cent and 97 per cent respectively.[238] In September 2007, the Crown Prosecution Service announced the creation of the Fraud Prosecution Unit, now referred to as the Fraud Prosecution Division,[239] which was established following the collapse of the Jubilee Line fraud trial.[240] The Unit will limit its involvement to suspected instances of fraud exceeding £750000, cases involving the corruption of public officials, fraud on government departments, fraud on overseas governments, complicated money laundering cases and any other matter that it feels is within its remit.[241] In October 2008, HM Crown Prosecution Service Inspectorate concluded that there 'has been a positive direction of travel in terms of successful outcomes (convictions), which stood at a creditable 85% of the defendants proceeded against in 2007–2008; underlying casework quality, which is characterised by strong legal decision-making and active case progression; and the development of management systems and leadership profile'.[242] Bosworth-Davies took the view that 'it [the Serious Fraud Office] was not the great success that Roskill envisaged, and its activities were marked out by 20 years of professional jealousy and internal squabbling among its component teams'.[243] Conversely, the performance of the SFO is hampered by the complexity of the crimes it investigates.[244] Wright noted that the SFO was 'always kept short of resources and instead of being a unified fraud office, was just another, more sophisticated, prosecution agency'.[245]

The first secondary agency that tackles fraud is the FSA.[246] The FSA stated that its fraud policy can be divided into four parts – a direct

---

[238]   de Grazia above, n 236.

[239]   Crown Prosecution Service (2009), 'DPP announces new head of Fraud Prosecution Division', available at http://www.cps.gov.uk/news/press_releases/136_09/ (accessed 22 January 2010).

[240]   Masters, J. (2008), 'Fraud and money laundering: the evolving criminalisation of corporate non-compliance', *Journal of Money Laundering Control*, **11**(2), 103–122, at 104.

[241]   *Ibid.*

[242]   HM Crown Prosecution Service Inspectorate *Review of the Fraud Prosecution Service* (HM Crown Prosecution Service Inspectorate: London, 2008) at p. 5.

[243]   Bosworth-Davies above, n 224 at 198.

[244]   Wright above, n 226 at 10.

[245]   *Ibid.*

[246]   Financial Services Authority *Developing our policy on fraud and dishonesty – discussion paper 26* (Financial Services Authority: London, 2003).

approach,[247] increased supervisory activity,[248] promoting a more joined-up approach[249] and Handbook modifications.[250] The FSA requires senior management to take responsibility for managing the risk of fraud and that firms are required to have in place effective controls and instruments that are proportionate to the risk the firm faces.[251] The FSA encourages firms to maintain their systems and controls, thematic work, improving the whistle-blowing arrangement, amending the financial crime material in the FSA Handbook and ensuring that the financial services sector, trade associations and the government continue to communicate the risk of fraud to customers.[252] To implement this policy the FSA has been given an extensive array of enforcement powers, some of which it has utilized to combat fraud. It is a prosecuting authority for both money laundering, and certain fraud-related offences,[253] and has the power to impose a financial penalty where it establishes that there has been a contravention by an authorized person of any requirement.[254] The FSA fined Capita Financial Administration Limited £300 000 for poor anti-fraud controls,[255] and in May 2007 fined BNP Paribas Private Bank £350 000 for weaknesses in its systems and controls which allowed a senior employee to fraudulently

---

[247]   This would have seen the FSA focusing its efforts on specific types of fraud or dishonesty which constitute the greatest areas of concern, and where they can make a difference.

[248]   This would include, for example, considering the firms' systems and controls against fraud in more detail in its supervisory work, including how firms collect data on fraud and dishonesty.

[249]   The third approach would involve the FSA liaising closely with the financial sector and other interested parties in order to achieve a more effective approach towards fraud prevention in the financial services sector.

[250]   The final proposed method would include codification and clarification of the relevant fraud risk management provisions of the Handbook.

[251]   Financial Services Authority (2004c),'The FSA's new approach to fraud – Fighting fraud in partnership', speech by Philip Robinson, 26 October 2004, available at http://www.fsa.gov.uk/Pages/Library/Communication/Speeches/2004/SP208.shtml (accessed 3 August 2010).

[252]   *Ibid.*

[253]   For example, in 2008 the FSA successfully prosecuted William Radclyffe for offences under the Theft Acts, the Financial Services Act 1986 and the Financial Services and Markets Act 2000. See '"Fake" stockholder sentenced to 15 months', available from http://www.fsa.gov.uk/pages/Library/Communication/PR/2008/011.shtml (accessed 28 March 2010).

[254]   Financial Services and Markets Act 2000, s. 206(1).

[255]   Financial Services Authority (2006a), 'FSA fines Capita Financial Administrators Limited £300,000 in first anti-fraud controls case', available at   http://www.fsa.gov.uk/pages/Library/Communication/PR/2006/019.shtml (accessed 16 March 2006).

transfer £1.4m out of the firm's clients' accounts without permission.[256] Furthermore, it has fined the Nationwide Building Society £980 000 for 'failing to have effective systems and controls to manage its information security risks',[257] and Norwich Union Life £1.26m for not 'having effective systems and controls in place to protect customers' confidential information and manage its financial crime risks'.[258] The FSA also has the power to ban authorized persons and firms from undertaking any regulated activity.[259] In 2008, the FSA fined and/or banned 12 mortgage brokers for submitting false mortgage applications. In 2007, the FSA only imposed five bans. In 2008, the FSA prohibited 24 separate brokers and issued fines in excess of £500 000.[260] In the first half of 2009, the level of fines imposed by the FSA had already exceeded this figure. In addition to imposing sanctions on fraudsters the FSA has also enabled victims of fraud to recover losses suffered at the hands of companies involved in share fraud activity.[261] The FSA has concentrated its financial crime policy on money laundering, largely at the expense of fraud, in order to meet its statutory objective to reduce financial crime. Its recent efforts to tackle fraud, especially mortgage fraud, have been fast tracked due to the problems associated with the global financial crisis. The FSA should have equally prioritized the different types of financial crime it is required to tackle under FSMA 2000, and not exclusively concentrate its efforts on money laundering. Furthermore, there is a clear overlap between the investigative and prosecutorial responsibilities of the FSA and SFO.

The most recent agency created to tackle fraud is the NFA.[262] The objectives of the NFA include creating a criminal justice system that is sympathetic to the needs of victims of fraud by ensuring that the system operates

---

[256] Financial Services Authority *Financial Services Authority Annual Report 2007/2008* (Financial Services Authority: London, 2008a), p. 23.

[257] Financial Services Authority (2007b), 'FSA fines Nationwide £980 000 for information security lapses', available at http://www.fsa.gov.uk/pages/Library/Communication/PR/2007/021.shtml (accessed 14 February 2007).

[258] Financial Services Authority (2007c), 'FSA fines Norwich Union Life £1.26m', available at http://www.fsa.gov.uk/pages/Library/Communication/PR/2007/130.shtml (accessed 4 November 2009).

[259] Financial Services and Markets Act 2000, s. 56.

[260] National Fraud Authority above, n 23 at 16.

[261] In February 2010 the FSA recovered £270 000 for defrauded investors who were advised to buy shares in Eduvest plc. Financial Services Authority (2010), 'FSA returns £270 000 to victims of share fraud', available at http://www.fsa.gov.uk/pages/Library/Communication/PR/2010/032.shtml (accessed 21 March 2010).

[262] National Fraud Authority *The National Fraud Strategy – A new approach to combating fraud* (National Fraud Authority: London, 2009b) at p. 10.

more effectively and efficiently,[263] to discourage organized criminals from committing fraud in the UK and to increase the public's confidence in the response to fraud.[264] Professor Barry Rider stated that the NFA:

> has an impressive list of strategic aims: tackling the key threats of fraud that pose the greatest harm to the United Kingdom; the pursuit of fraudsters effectively, holding them to account and improving victim support; the reduction of the UK's exposure to fraud by building, sharing and acting on knowledge; and securing the international collaboration necessary to protect the UK from fraud.[265]

The NFA's Interim Chief Executive Sandra Quinn boldly claimed that 'we can respond quickly and effectively to the fraud threat'.[266] This level of optimism was not shared by Bosworth-Davies who stated that the NFA 'will last about as long as the unlamented Asset Recovery Agency'.[267] An important measure introduced by the NFA was the publication of the National Fraud Strategy, which is an integral part of the government's fraud policy.[268] Under this, the NFA's priorities are:

1. tackling the threats presented by fraud;
2. acting effectively to pursue fraudsters and holding them to account;
3. improving the support available to victims;
4. reducing the UK's exposure to fraud by building the nation's capability to prevent it; and
5. targeting action against fraud more effectively by building, sharing and acting on knowledge and securing the international collaboration necessary to protect the UK from fraud.[269]

Despite the fanfare announcement by the government that it had created the NFA, one fundamental question must be asked: will it actually make any difference towards the overall effectiveness of the UK's fraud policy? If

---

[263] For a more detailed discussion of how this is to be achieved see The Attorney General's Office *Extending the powers of the Crown Court to prevent fraud and compensate victims: a consultation* (Attorney General's Office: London, 2008).

[264] National Fraud Authority (2008), 'UK toughens up on fraudsters with new anti-fraud authority', available at http://www.attorneygeneral.gov.uk/NewsCentre/Pages/UKToughensUpOn%20FraudstersWithNewAnti-FraudAuthority.aspx (accessed 2 October 2008).

[265] Rider above, n 207 at 1.

[266] National Fraud Authority above, n 264.

[267] Bosworth-Davies above, n 224 at 199.

[268] National Fraud Authority above, n 262 at 3.

[269] *Ibid.*

we are to believe that the extent of fraud in the UK is somewhere between £14bn and £30bn, how is it possible for an agency to make any valuable dent in this statistic if it only has a budget of £29m over a three-year period? Another secondary agency is the Office of Fair Trading (OFT) which 'is chiefly concerned with the protection of consumers. It also regulates competition amongst businesses but this is approached from a consumer protection perspective'.[270] The OFT has three regulatory objectives – investigation of whether markets are working well for consumers, enforcement of competition laws and enforcement of consumer protection laws. It is important to note that the OFT has its own fraud policy.[271] The objectives of the OFT are similar to the FTC's, in that it seeks to inform and protect consumers from fraudulent scams.[272] Furthermore, the OFT works and co-operates with other agencies such as the SFO,[273] and it also liaises with overseas agencies.[274] As previously outlined in this book, SOCA is the UK's Financial Intelligence Unit, and it plays an integral part in the fight against financial crime. Finally, HMRC deals with such issues as VAT fraud, alcohol fraud[275] and oil fraud.[276]

The effectiveness of these anti-fraud agencies must be questioned and can be contrasted with those in the US. There is a considerable degree of overlap between the SFO and the FSA; both have extensive investigative and prosecutorial powers that seek to achieve the same objective. The failures of the SFO are well documented, whilst the FSA's effectiveness must be questioned because of its obsession with combating money laundering. It is recommended that a single financial crime agency should be established to co-ordinate the UK's fraud policy with extensive investigative and prosecutorial powers. Such an idea was first mooted by

---

[270]   Kiernan, P. (2003), 'The regulatory bodies fraud: its enforcement in the twenty-first century', *Company Lawyer*, **24**(10), 293–299, at 295.

[271]   Office of Fair Trading *Prevention of fraud policy* (Office of Fair Trading: London, n/d).

[272]   See for example Office of Fair Trading *Scamnesty 2010 campaign strategy* (Office of Fair Trading: London, 2009).

[273]   See for example Office of Fair Trading *Memorandum of understanding between the Office of Fair Trading and the Director of the Serious Fraud Office* (Office of Fair Trading: London, 2003).

[274]   See for example Office of Fair Trading (2005), 'OFT and Nigerian financial crime squad join forces to combat spam fraud', available at http://www.oft.gov.uk/news-and-updates/press/2005/210-05 (accessed 2 August 2010).

[275]   See for example HM Revenue and Customs Renewal of the 'Tackling Alcohol Fraud' Strategy (HM Revenue and Customs: London, 2009).

[276]   See HM Customs and Excise *Oils Fraud Strategy: Summary of Consultation Responses; Regulatory Impact Assessment* (HM Customs and Excise: London, 2002).

Fisher who recommended the creation of a 'single "Financial Crimes Enforcement Agency" to tackle serious fraud, corruption and financial market crimes'.[277] This recommendation has been supported by the Conservative party who would establish an Economic Crime Agency that would do the work of the SFO, the Fraud Prosecution Service and the OFT. The then Shadow Chancellor George Osborne MP stated that 'we are very, very bad at prosecuting white-collar crime. We have six different government departments, eight different agencies and the result is that these crimes go unpunished'.[278] Following the 2010 general election, the coalition government outlined its desire to create a single agency to tackle financial crime. The government stated:

> we take white collar crime as seriously as other crime, so we will create a single agency to take on the work of tackling serious economic crime that is currently done by, among others, the Serious Fraud Office, Financial Services Authority and Office of Fair Trading.[279]

However, it is likely that the 'financial crisis' could scupper the government's plans to create such an agency.[280] The Fraud Advisory Panel writing in March 2010 took the view that due to the current climate the time is not right for an economic crime agency.[281]

4.4.3   Reporting Obligations

The UK has a strong history of utilizing financial intelligence as part of its broader financial crime strategy, a point clearly illustrated by the anti-money laundering reporting provisions of the Proceeds of Crime Act 2002 (PCA 2002) and the duty to report any suspected instances of terrorist financing under the Terrorism Act 2000. The Fraud Review noted that

---

[277]   Fisher, J. *Fighting Fraud and Financial Crime: A new architecture for the investigation and prosecution of serious fraud, corruption and financial market crimes* (Policy Exchange: London, 2010) at p. 3.

[278]   Timesonline (2010), 'Conservatives confirm plans for single Economic Crime Agency', available at http://timesonline.typepad.com/law/2010/04/conservatives-confirm-plans-for-single-economic-crime-agency.html (accessed 26 April 2010).

[279]   HM Government *The Coalition: our programme for government* (HM Government: London, 2010) at p. 9.

[280]   Leigh, D. and Evans, R. (2010), 'Cost of new economic crime agency could prove prohibitive', available at http://www.guardian.co.uk/business/2010/jun/02/economic-crime-agency-scheme-cost (accessed 12 July 2010).

[281]   See generally Fraud Advisory Panel *Roskill Revisited: Is there a case for a unified fraud prosecution office?* (Fraud Advisory Panel: London, 2010).

'fraud is massively underreported. Fraud is not a police priority, so even when reports are taken, little is done with them. Many victims therefore, don't report at all. So the official crime statistics display just the tip of the iceberg and developing a strategic law enforcement response is impossible because the information to target investigations does not exist'.[282] If a suspected fraud is committed against a bank it is reported to its Money Laundering Reporting Officer (MLRO). Successful frauds are reported to SOCA. Conversely, it is left to individual banks to determine whether or not to report the fraud to the police. In 2007, the Home Office announced that victims of credit card, cheque and online banking fraud are to report the matter to banks and financial institutions.[283] However, the obligation to report allegations of fraud is not as straightforward, but nonetheless still important. The primary statutory obligation for reported instances of fraud is contained under the PCA 2002.[284] It is a criminal offence under the 2002 Act to fail to disclose via a SAR where there is knowledge, suspicion or reasonable grounds to know or suspect that a person is laundering the proceeds of criminal conduct. Successful fraud is defined as money laundering for the purpose of this Act.[285] Furthermore, the Act specifies that members of the regulated sector are required to report their suspicions 'as soon as reasonably practical' to SOCA via their Money Laundering Reporting Officer. There is no legal obligation to report unsuccessful or attempted frauds to the authorities because any attempted frauds will not give rise to any legal criminal proceedings that are available for money laundering, and fall outside the scope of the mandatory reporting obligations under the PCA 2002. Ultimately, the decision lies with the police whether or not an investigation will be conducted. The Home Office has advised that the police should only investigate where there are good grounds to believe a criminal offence has been committed.[286]

Furthermore, members of the regulated sector are obliged to report fraud to the FSA in the following circumstances:

(1) it becomes aware that an employee may have committed a fraud against one of its customers; or

---

[282] Attorney General's Office above, n 20 at 7.
[283] Home Office (n/d), 'Fraud', available at http://www.crimereduction.home-office.gov.uk/fraud/fraud17.htm (accessed 7 December 2009).
[284] Proceeds of Crime Act 2002, s. 330.
[285] It is important to note that the Proceeds of Crime Act 2002 applies to serious crime, which includes fraud.
[286] Home Office *Home Office circular 47/2004 Priorities for the investigation of fraud cases* (Home Office: London, 2004a).

(2) it becomes aware that a person, whether or not employed by it, may have committed a fraud against it; or
(3) it considers that any person, whether or not employed by it, is acting with intent to commit a fraud against it; or
(4) it identifies irregularities in its accounting or other records, whether or not there is evidence of fraud; or
(5) it suspects that one of its employees may be guilty of serious misconduct concerning his honesty or integrity and which is connected with the firm's regulated activities or ancillary activities.[287]

In determining whether or not the matter is significant, the firm must consider:

(1) the size of any monetary loss or potential monetary loss to itself or its customers (either in terms of a single incident or group of similar or related incidents);
(2) the risk of reputational loss to the firm; and
(3) whether the incident or a pattern of incidents reflects weaknesses in the firm's internal controls.[288]

The FSA Handbook also provides that 'the notifications under SUP 15.3.17R are required as the FSA needs to be aware of the types of fraudulent and irregular activity which are being attempted or undertaken, and to act, if necessary, to prevent effects on consumers or other firms'.[289] Therefore, 'a notification under SUP 15.3.17R should provide all relevant and significant details of the incident or suspected incident of which the firm is aware'.[290] Furthermore, 'the firm may have suffered significant financial losses as a result of the incident, or may suffer reputational loss, and the FSA will wish to consider this and whether the incident suggests weaknesses in the firm's internal controls'.[291] If the fraud is committed by representatives or other Approved Persons, the FSA has the power to withdraw its authorization and the possibility of prosecution.

The UK's policy towards fraud has gained momentum under the previous government, a willingness shared by the new coalition administration. However, there is still scope for improvement in the initiatives that have been introduced to tackle fraud. For example, the effectiveness of the criminalization of fraud has been limited by the inadequacies of the Theft Acts and the common law offence, a position that has been improved by

---

[287]   SUP 15.3.17R.
[288]   SUP 15.3.18G.
[289]   SUP 15.3.19G.
[290]   SUP 15.3.19G.
[291]   SUP 15.3.20G.

the introduction of the Fraud Act. However, concerns still remain about the enforcement of these offences by the SFO and the Crown Prosecution Service (CPS) following the collapse of several high profile cases of fraud. It is simply too early to determine if the Fraud Act has made any difference to the prosecution of fraudsters. The Coalition government must be commended for recognizing the need to create a single economic crime agency. The reporting of instances of suspected fraudulent activities is fragmented with a number of different reporting mechanisms available. This causes confusion and delay.

4.5   CONCLUSION

The influence of the international community on the US and the UK anti-fraud policies can be contrasted with money laundering and terrorist financing. It is clear that both the UN and the EU consider fraud to be a significant problem, but interestingly, neither has imposed any significant obligations on either the US or the UK.

4.5.1   United States of America

The US has adopted an extremely robust and aggressive policy towards fraud. It has a long legislative history of criminalizing fraudulent activities. The Mail Fraud Statute is often used in conjunction with the Wire Fraud Statute and represents a formidable tool in the armoury of federal prosecutors. The other fraud statutes referred to in this chapter are reactionary. For example, the Sarbanes-Oxley Act of 2002 was introduced following the accountancy frauds at Enron and WorldCom. Similarly, the Bank Fraud Statute was implemented due to the threat posed towards the US banking sector in the early 1980s. Other examples of statutes that have been introduced include the Credit Card Fraud Act, the Marriage Fraud Act and the Civil Fraud Statute. Therefore, the US has adopted what can be classified as a 'shotgun' approach towards the criminalization of fraud. Therefore, there are too many fraud statutes. This creates confusion and uncertainty amongst defendants and prosecutors. To overcome this confusion, prosecutors are heavily reliant on the breadth of the provisions afforded to them by the Mail and Fraud Statutes. It can be argued that the actions of prosecutors have resulted in these statutes becoming a 'generic' fraud Act. Prosecutors have also used them to prosecute for other offences including money laundering, bribery and corruption. Therefore, in order to strike an appropriate balance between the rights of defendants and prosecutors, it is suggested that the US anti-fraud policy would benefit from a single unifying fraud statute. This would provide more certainty for those facing prosecution and it would prevent federal prosecutors from being able to use the current fraud statutes to seek prosecution for other types of financial crime.

There are a large number of primary and secondary agencies that investigate and prosecute suspected instances of fraud. The Department of Justice plays a very important role in the implementation of the US anti-fraud policy. Its Fraud Unit plays a lead role in the battle against identity theft and it is a member of several fraud task forces created by the government. The FBI has been granted extensive investigative powers and provided additional funding. This has been clearly illustrated in its aggressive investigative and prosecutorial stance towards mortgage fraud. The Department of Treasury's financial intelligence unit, FinCEN, plays a fundamentally important function in the fight against fraud. The information provided by deposit-taking institutions to FinCEN has proved an effective tool in the fight against fraud. In addition to the regulatory agencies there are several fraud task forces that have led the fight against corporate and identity fraud. However, these are only short-term measures to a long-term problem and it is highly likely that more fraud-related task forces will be created. Nonetheless, this part of the anti-fraud policy can be deemed a very appropriate model that should be followed in the UK, despite the clear overlap between the jurisdictions of some of the primary and secondary agencies. Nonetheless, the US fraud policy can be contrasted with its anti-money laundering and terrorist financing policy in that there is no 'strategy document' and, as outlined above, such a document would enable a more focused anti-fraud strategy with achievable targets.

4.5.2   United Kingdom

The UK fraud policy has gathered pace following the publication of the Fraud Review in 2006, but is still in a state of flux. The policy adopted is very similar to that adopted in the US, but the criminalization of fraud can be contrasted with the approach in the US. The UK has a single Fraud Act, which criminalizes different types of fraudulent activities and provides prosecutors with new powers to tackle fraud. The second part of its anti-fraud policy concerns primary and secondary agencies, and it is this part that is in need of fundamental reform. There is no single agency that takes a lead role in tackling fraud; there are simply too many agencies performing the same function, a position that is worsened by the fact that not one government department performs a similar function to the Department of Justice. For example, HM Treasury has been charged with developing and implementing the UK's policies towards money laundering and terrorist financing, yet it has very little to do with the UK's fraud policy. Furthermore, the Home Office has been charged with tackling the problems associated with organized crime, but does little to tackle fraud. Therefore, it is recommended that a single government department is given the task of tackling all types of financial crime; it seems logical that this task is given to HM Treasury, given its experience with money laundering and terrorist financing.

Another example of the overlap between anti-fraud agencies relates to the fact that both the SFO and FSA have the ability to conduct investigations and initiate prosecutions. The NFA has been given a three-year budget of £29m to tackle an industry that is worth £30bn. Therefore, it faces an improbable mission to reduce the extent of fraud with a very small budget. This makes little or no sense. The UK government should develop a unitary financial crime agency that incorporates the functions of the agencies outlined above. It is possible to argue that this process has already started with the merger of several agencies including the National Crime Squad, the National Criminal Intelligence Service and the Assets Recovery Agency into SOCA. The final part of the UK's policy can be contrasted with that of the US. The primary legislation that imposes reporting obligations is the PCA 2002, under which fraud is reported to SOCA. However, in some circumstances allegations of fraud are reported to banks and the police and the regulated sector reports to the FSA. The system needs clarification and it has not been assisted by the creation of the NFRC. In the US, allegations of fraud are reported to FinCEN, and it is suggested that the UK should adopt a similar reporting strategy and that all suspicious transactions relating to fraud should be reported to SOCA.

5. Insider dealing

Andrew H. Baker*

Two of the largest and most successful securities markets in the world, the USA and the UK, provide the benchmark for the regulation of insider trading.[1]

5.1 INTRODUCTION

Gordon Gekko said 'the most valuable commodity I know of is information'.[2] The quote is from a fictional Hollywood character but that character was apparently based on real persons engaged in the securities industry during the 1980s, and whatever the fiction, the fact remains that information is one of the most valuable commodities in the financial services industry.[3] Indeed, McCoy and Summe took the view that during the 1980s 'insider trading scandals occupied the front pages of not only the trade papers, but also quotidian tabloids. Assailed for its unfairness and characterised by some as thievery, insider trading incidents increased calls for stricter regulation of the market-place and its participants'.[4] Insider trading, as referred to in the United States (US), is referred to as insider dealing in the United Kingdom (UK) and it can be defined as 'the unfair use of material, non-public information concerning an issue of securities – [it] threatens to undermine the integrity of the national securities mar-

---

* Liverpool John Moores University, Law School.

[1] McCoy, K.A. and Summe, P. (1998), 'Insider trading regulation: a developing state's perspective', *Journal of Financial Crime*, **5**(4), 311–346, at 311.

[2] This quote was also used as a title to an article by Burger, R. and Davies, G. (2005a), 'The most valuable commodity I know of is information', *Journal of Financial Regulation and Compliance*, **13**(4), 324–332.

[3] It is said that Gordon Gekko is an amalgamation of persons including, among others, Ivan Boesky and Michael Milken, both of whom were convicted of securities fraud. It is said that Gekko's 'greed is good speech' was based on one made by Ivan Boesky, given at the University of California, Berkeley in 1986, where he stated that 'greed is alright, by the way I think greed is healthy. You can still be greedy and feel good about yourself'.

[4] McCoy and Summe above, n 1 at 311.

kets'.[5] Insider trading is a sophisticated crime as its complexity 'continues to increase because of new methods to conceal insider trading on material non-public information throughout the intertwined global financial markets'.[6] Insider trading has also been referred to as a 'cancerous greed on Wall Street'.[7] As Hudson notes 'information is the key to securities markets'.[8] A person in possession of material information is in an advantageous position in relation to a person without that information when making investment decisions. Those that have information stand to make financial gains or mitigate a substantial loss of money, if that information is used to their advantage. Takeovers and mergers present the ideal opportunity for insider dealing and market abuse generally. Information before and during the bid is highly price sensitive, information which can have a significant impact on the share price of the companies involved, particularly the issuing company.[9] It is with reference to takeovers and mergers that much of the insider dealing and market abuse debate revolves. The question in respect of this chapter is what limits, sanctions and penalties should be and are placed on the access and use of information in the financial services industry.

The core focus of this chapter is to discuss the provisions designed to ensure the integrity of securities markets and the legislation aimed at tackling insider dealing and market manipulation in the financial services sector. Although a long-standing part of US law this is a relatively new arena for UK lawmakers and regulators. The US criminalized insider trading by virtue of the Securities and Exchange Act 1934.[10] However, the 'Supreme Court determined that the statute was aimed at the prohibition of fraud in connection with the purchase or sale of securities'.[11] Lambert

---

[5] Colvin, O. (1991), 'A dynamic definition of and prohibition against insider trading', *Santa Clara Law Review*, **31**, 603–640, at 603. For an excellent discussion of the interpretation of insider trading see Anabtawi, I. (1989), 'Toward a definition of insider trading', *Stanford Law Review*, **41**, 377–399.

[6] Pearson, T. (2008), 'When hedge funds betray a creditor committee's fiduciary role: new twists on insider trading in the international financial markets', *Review of Banking and Financial Law*, **28**, 165–220, at 168.

[7] Cox, C. and Fogarty, K. (1988), 'Basis of insider trading law', *Ohio State Law Journal*, **49**, 353–372, at 353.

[8] Hudson, Alistair (2009) *The Law of Finance*, Sweet & Maxwell, London, at p. 972.

[9] Hannigan, Brenda (2009) *Company Law*, Oxford University Press, Oxford.

[10] Naylor, J. (1990), 'The use of criminal sanctions by UK and US authorities for insider trading: how can the two systems learn from each other? Part 1', *Company Lawyer*, **11**(3), 53–61, at 53.

[11] McCoy and Summe above, n 1 at 312.

argued that 'the insider trading prohibition explicitly prohibits certain types of trading on the basis of material, non-public information'.[12] In the UK legislation has existed in some form since 1939 but it was only in the 1980s and 1990s when comprehensive legislative provisions appeared with the broader task of keeping the securities industry clean for investor confidence.[13] Before embarking on a discussion and analysis of the restrictions that the law places on the use of information in this context it is useful to start with the question on whether restrictions should be in place at all.[14] This debate stems from the decision of the Securities and Exchange Commission (SEC) to denounce insider trading in the infamous *Cady Roberts* case.[15] There is strong argument from some quarters that the use of information not generally available to the market, conferring a benefit on the persons in receipt of that information should not face any restrictions on its use to make a profit or avoid a loss.[16] This is the liberal economic argument and it is held that the market itself will correct any problems perceived with this issue. The seminal work in this area was done in the 1960s by Professor Manne,[17] when he advocated that insider trading was actually an efficient method of compensating insiders.[18] A further argument against prohibiting insider dealing is the perceived lack of a victim. In analysing insider trading cases it is difficult to pinpoint a

---

[12]   Lambert, T. (2006), 'Overvalued equity and the case for an asymmetric insider trading regime', *Wake Forest Law Review*, **41**, 1045–1129, at 1050.

[13]   This was based on the premise that 'the principles of confidentiality and trust, which are essential to the operations of the commercial world, are betrayed by insider dealing and public confidence in the integrity of the system which is essential to its proper function is undermined by market abuse'. Per Judge LCJ in *R v McQuoid* [2009] EWCA Crim 1301. This is an appeal against a sentence in the first conviction under the Criminal Justice Act 1993 brought by the Financial Services Authority. For a brief discussion of the history of insider dealing in the UK see Naylor above, n 10 at 55–56.

[14]   For an interesting discussion see Bauman, T. (1984), 'Insider trading at common law', *University of Chicago Law Review*, **51**, 838–867, at 847–854 and Carlton, D. and Fischel, D. (1983), 'The regulation of insider trading', *Stanford Law Review*, **35**, 857–895, at 872–882.

[15]   See Prentice, R. and Donelson, D. (2010), 'Insider trading as a signaling device', *American Business Law Journal*, **47**, 1–73, at 1.

[16]   For an excellent review on this point see Hannigan, Brenda (1994) *Insider Dealing*, Longman, London.

[17]   See particularly Manne, Henry (1966) *Insider Trading on the Stock Market*, Free Press, New York.

[18]   Painter, R. (1999–2000), 'Insider trading and the stock market thirty years later', *Case Western Reserve Law Review*, **50**, 305–311. Also see Harris, D. and Herzel, L. (1989), 'USA: do we need insider trading laws?', *Company Lawyer*, **10**(1), 34–35.

person or persons who lose out as a result of another dealing on the basis of privileged information, so if there is no apparent loser why create the prohibition in the first place? This has long been a problem in the debate over whether or not to prohibit the activity. The counter argument to the premise that insider dealing is a 'victimless' crime is that the victim is the market for securities as a whole, insomuch as the victim is anyone who has or intends to invest in securities, which given that many pension funds invest in securities arguably creates a very large class of victims. These investors are not in possession of the same information as those with 'inside information' and thus not able to make a fully informed decision. If there is consensus to fight insider dealing then there has been some debate as to which path to take. It is important to note that both the US and the UK have adopted different policies towards insider dealing that will be discussed later in this chapter.[19]

5.2 INTERNATIONAL COMMUNITY

5.2.1 United Nations

The United Nations does not have a policy towards insider dealing, a position that can be contrasted with its stance towards the other types of financial crime considered in this book.

5.2.2 European Union

There is some uncertainty as to the commencement of the European Union's (EU) policy towards insider dealing. For example, it has been argued that the EU's regulation of insider dealing was influenced by US regulations.[20] Furthermore, its policy was also influenced by the fact that several European countries had introduced laws to tackle insider dealing.[21] In 1987 the EU published its draft Insider Dealing Council

---

[19]   Naylor above, n 10 at 53.
[20]   Hansen, J. (2002), 'The new proposal for a European Union directive on market abuse', *University of Pennsylvania Journal of International Economic Law*, **23**, 241–268, at 250.
[21]   This included for example France, Sweden, Denmark, Norway and the United Kingdom.

Directive,[22] which was introduced in 1989.[23] The aim of the proposal was to 'ensure equality of opportunity to all investors'.[24] Furthermore, the Directive seeks to 'provide minimum standards for insider dealing laws throughout the Community'.[25] The Directive was implemented in the UK via the Criminal Justice Act 1993 (CJA 1993),[26] and it contains a number of provisions that have influenced the UK's policy toward insider dealing. For example, Article 3 'requires a prohibition on insiders possessing inside information from (a) disclosing that information to any third person unless such disclosure is made in the normal course of the exercise of his employment, profession or duties; or (b) recommending or procuring a third party, on the basis of inside information, to acquire or dispose of transferable securities'. Additionally, the EU introduced the Market Abuse Directive in 2003,[27] which was instigated via the Financial Services and Markets Act 2000 (FSMA).[28] The Market Abuse Directive 'prohibits abusive behaviour such as insider dealing and market manipulation. It creates obligations aimed at deterring abuses, such as insiders lists, suspicious transaction reporting, and disclosure of trades by managers of issuers. It also requires issuers to disclose inside information'.[29]

---

[22]   The original Directive was published in May 1987 (Directive 7310/87) and amended in October 1988 (Directive 8810/88). The Directive was adopted on 13 November 1989.

[23]   Council Directive 89/592/EEC.

[24]   Cantos, F. (1989), 'EEC draft directive on insider dealing', *Journal of International Banking Law*, **4**(4), N174–176, at 174.

[25]   Ashe, M. (1992), 'The directive on insider dealing', *Company Lawyer*, **13**(1), 15–19, at 15.

[26]   For an interesting discussion of the implementation of the Insider Dealing Directives and Market Abuse Directives see the British Institute of International and Comparative Law *Comparative implementation of EU directives (1) – insider dealing and market abuse* (British Institute of International and Comparative Law: Corporation of London, 2005).

[27]   Market Abuse Directive 2003/6 ([2003] OJ L96/16). The 'European Commission published the proposed Directive 'on insider dealing and market manipulation (market abuse) on 30 May 2001'. See McKee, M. (2001), 'The proposed EU market abuse directive', *Journal of International Financial Markets*, **3**(4), 137–142, at 137. In 2009, the EU Commission instigated a call for evidence as part of its ongoing review of the effectiveness of the Market Abuse Directive. See European Commission (2009), 'Call for evidence review of Directive 2003/6/EC on insider dealing and market manipulation (Market Abuse Directive)', available at   http://ec.europa.eu/internal_market/consultations/docs/2009/market_abuse/call_for_evidence.pdf (accessed 12 August 2010).

[28]   Financial Services and Markets Act 2000, s.118–118C.

[29]   Ed. (2009), 'Commission seeks evidence in review of Market Abuse Directive', *Company Law Newsletter*, **252**, 4–5, at 4.

Importantly, the Directive requires Member States to 'require that any person professionally arranging transactions in financial instruments who reasonably suspects that a transaction might constitute insider dealing or market manipulation shall notify the competent authority without delay'.[30] The use of suspicious transaction reports (STRs) has become an integral part of the UK's insider dealing policy and is managed by the Financial Services Authority (FSA). Therefore, comparisons can be drawn between the EU's anti-money laundering strategy and its market abuse strategy by the use of STRs.

What becomes clear after reviewing the international measures is that the UN has not implemented any legal instruments to tackle insider dealing. Conversely, the EU has introduced a series of measures designed to tackle insider dealing and market abuse. The policy adopted by the UN towards insider dealing can be contrasted with its strategies towards money laundering and terrorist financing yet compared to its stance towards fraud. The EU's policy towards insider dealing and market abuse is very similar to that adopted towards money laundering and terrorist financing, yet it can be contrasted with its fraud strategy. This response is unsatisfactory given the global nature of securities and investments. Pitt and Hardison warned that:

> the internationalization of the securities markets not only facilitates global investing, but also creates new opportunities for insider trading. For example, unscrupulous traders may seek to trade through accounts in jurisdictions with secrecy and blocking laws that purport to preclude the disclosure to foreign agencies of information regarding their accounts. Internationalization also may result in insider trading if foreign investors persist in engaging in conduct that, although permitted in their home markets, violates the laws of other countries.[31]

The inadequacies of the response to insider dealing by the international community have frustrated the US who has sought to 'encourage' other nation states to implement insider trading laws.[32] Nnona argued that 'the SEC has also exported US insider trading laws to other jurisdictions,

---

[30]   Market Abuse Directive 2003/6 ([2003] OJ L96/16), Article 6(9).

[31]   Pitt, H. and Hardison, D. (1992), 'Games without frontiers: trends in the international response to insider trading', *Law and Contemporary Problems*, **55**, 199–229, at 203–204.

[32]   For example the US authorities influenced Switzerland to introduce insider trading laws in 1988. For a more detailed discussion see Hanneman, J. (1997), 'The evolution of co-operation between authorities in the United States of America and Switzerland in the enforcement of insider trading laws', *Wisconsin International Law Journal*, **16**, 247–270.

as part of the crusade to stem insider trading globally'.[33] Furthermore, the SEC 'has increasingly felt the need to extend the reach of its insider trading regulation beyond the US, in order to effectively protect the US markets and investors from the impact of insider trading involving transactions with multi-jurisdictional features'.[34] The SEC is assisted by the International Securities Enforcement Cooperation Act 1990 which 'has improved substantially the SEC's ability to co-operate with the securities regulators of other countries'.[35] Furthermore, SEC has assisted overseas regulators in the freezing of assets and imposing sanctions on 'securities professionals who have been found negligent or guilty by foreign security authorities'.[36] The SEC has agreed a Memorandum of Understanding with numerous foreign jurisdictions,[37] entered into Mutual Assistance Treaties and is a member of the International Organization of Securities Commissions.[38] The extraterritorial provisions available to the SEC are similar to those powers provided to the Department of Treasury as part of the US policy towards money laundering and terrorist financing as outlined previously in this book. The next part of this chapter investigates the US policy towards insider trading.

5.3   UNITED STATES OF AMERICA

The regulation and prosecution of insider trading in the United States has been, by far, the most vigorous of any country in the world.[39]

---

[33]   Nnona, G. (2001), 'International insider trading: reassessing the propriety and feasibility of the US regulatory approach', *North Carolina Journal of International Law and Commercial Regulation*, **27**, 185-253, at 201.

[34]   *Ibid.*, at 195.

[35]   H.R. 1396, 101st Cong. (1990). See Mann, M. and Barry, W. (2005), 'Developments in the internationalisation of securities enforcement', *International Lawyer*, **39**, 667–696, at 672. For a more detailed discussion on the levels of co-operation with overseas regulators see Securities and Exchange Commission *International co-operation in securities law enforcement* (Securities and Exchange Commission: Washington, DC, 2004).

[36]   Wolf noted that 'the SEC can impose sanctions on foreign securities professionals who have been found negligent or guilty by foreign security authorities via section 203'. Wolf, P. (1995), 'International securities fraud: extraterritorial subject matter jurisdiction', *New York International Law Review*, **8**, 1–22, at 22.

[37]   For an excellent discussion of this see Jimenez, P. (1990), *Harvard International Law Journal*, **31**, 295–311.

[38]   Diamong, E. (1992), 'Outside investors: a new breed of insider traders?', *Fordham Law Review*, **60**, 316–347, at 348.

[39]   Pitt and Hardison above, n 31 at 200.

5.3.1 Criminalization

US anti-insider trading provisions stem from the aftermath of the 1929 Wall Street 'Crash' and the subsequent Great Depression. It is generally agreed that the prohibition stems from the enactment of the Securities and Exchange Act of 1934, which created the SEC.[40] However, Bainbridge noted that initially 'insider trading was regulated by state corporate law', which was to be amended by the 1934 Act. Naylor noted that the most important feature of the Act was that it criminalized insider trading and 'granted the SEC the authority to bring civil penalties against violators of the statute'.[41] However, there is some doubt as to whether Congress actually intended to prohibit insider trading with the legislation.[42] The origin of the prohibition is arguably in Sections 10(b) and 16(b) of the Securities and Exchange Act; however, neither section actually specifically states a prohibition against insider trading.[43] Interestingly, Bainbridge noted that neither of these 'prohibited insider trading until 1961, thirty-seven years after the 1934 Act was passed and nineteen years after the SEC promulgated the rule'.[44]

Both sections are primarily anti-fraud provisions but have been widely interpreted by the SEC to include a prohibition against insider trading. Additionally the sections themselves do little without the SEC drawing up rules under which the provisions apply, which in the case of Section 10(b) is undertaken by Rule 10(b)-5. Again, though, there is no mention of a prohibition against insider trading here. Section 16 is even narrower in requiring directors, corporate officers and those persons with over 10 per cent shareholdings to report trades in equity securities of their firms on a monthly basis; however, there is a six-month limit on this requirement. The reality of the US position is that the actual insider trading prohibition is a construction of the US judiciary,[45] only loosely based on the original

---

[40] Naylor, J. (1990), 'The use of criminal sanctions by UK and US authorities for insider trading: how can the two systems learn from each other? Part 2', *Company Lawyer*, **11**(5), 83–91, at 83.

[41] *Ibid.*, at 85.

[42] Bainbridge, S. (1985), 'A critique of Insider Trading Sanctions Act of 1984', *Virginia Law Review*, **71**, 455–498, at 459.

[43] For an interesting discussion of the approach adopted by the judiciary toward the interpretation of this offence see Jain, N. (2004), 'Significance of mens rea in insider trading', *Company Lawyer*, **25**(5), 132–140.

[44] Bainbridge, S. (1986), 'The insider trading prohibition: a legal and economic enigma', *University of Florida Law Review*, **38**, 35–68, at 38. See *re Cady, Roberts & Co* 40 S.E.C. 907 (1961).

[45] McCoy and Summe above, n 1 at 311.

legislation;[46] a point conceded by the SEC in confirming that the courts, on its urging, have played the largest role in defining insider trading law.[47] This is unsatisfactory and it has been argued that 'when Charles Dickens wrote "the law is a[n] ass" he might well have been describing the law governing insider trading'.[48] Rakoff and Eaton argued that there is an additional mechanism to tackle insider trading: 'Rule 14e-3, which directly prohibits insider trading but only in the context of tender offers'.[49] In reality the SEC cannot be said to have been particularly quick on the uptake of the prohibition. As Bainbridge notes Rule 10(b)-5, upon which the whole prohibition properly stands, wasn't brought forward until 1942, some eight years after the Act, possibly evidencing Congress's lack of intention that Section 10(b) was designed to be an insider trading prohibition provision at all.[50] However, it is arguable that it was the SEC's rule-making powers coupled with its strong will to provide clean and efficient markets that led the judiciary to essentially outlaw insider trading. Despite its criminalization, insider trading was largely ignored by the authorities until the 1980s,[51] when US courts decided that 'private citizens could maintain civil suits against insider traders upon demonstrating a loss due to the violation'.[52] As a result the SEC instigated civil proceedings and brought the first criminal prosecution under the 1934 Act.[53] It has been argued that 'scandals involving such modern-day Al Capones as Ivan Boesky and Dennis Levine have motivated Congress to enact strong measures to combat insider trading'.[54]

---

[46] Bainbridge, S. (2004), *An Overview of US Insider Trading Law: Lessons for the EU*, Research Paper No.05-5, UCLA, School of Law, Law and Economic Research Paper Series, available from http://ssrn.com/abstract=654703 (accessed 1 June 2010).

[47] Newkirk, T. and Robertson, M. (1998), 'Speech given at the 16th International Symposium on Economic Crime', Jesus College, Cambridge, 19 September 1998, available from http://www.sec.gov/news/speech/speecharchive/1998/spch221.htm (accessed 1 June 2010).

[48] Fisch, J. (1991), 'Start making sense: an analysis and proposal for insider trading', *Georgia Law Review*, **26**, 179–251, at 179.

[49] Rakoff, J. and Easton, J. (1996), 'How effective is US enforcement in deterring insider trading?', *Journal of Financial Crime*, **6**(3), 283–287, at 283.

[50] Bainbridge above, n 46.

[51] Naylor above, n 40 at 85.

[52] *Ibid*. See in particular *Kardon v National Gypsum Co*, 69 F. Supp. 512 (E.D. Penn. 1946), affirmed, and *Superintendent of Insurance v Bankers Life & Cas. Co.* 404 US 6 (1971).

[53] Naylor above, n 40 at 84.

[54] O'Connor, M. (1989), 'Toward a more efficient deterrence of insider trading: the repeal of section 16(b)', *Fordham Law Review*, **58**, 309–381, at 309.

The weaknesses of the enforcement provisions of the 1934 Act were illustrated by the fact that the Insider Trading Sanction Act 1984 (ITSA) was introduced to improve the regulatory performance of the SEC.[55] The SEC was granted additional enforcement powers under the Insider Trading and Securities Fraud Enforcement Act of 1988. O'Connor noted that this provided 'control person liability; express private rights of action, and bounties for informants in order to promote the detection and successful prosecution of insider trading. Congress also enhanced deterrence by increasing the criminal penalties for insider trading violations'.[56] However, Bainbridge concluded that the number of convictions achieved under the 1988 Act remained 'small in comparison to the number of violations. Consequently, adoption of ITSA has created an enforcement regime which couples large nominal sanctions with low probabilities of enforcement. The result is a system where a very few are punished very severely in order to enforce the prohibition against insider trading'.[57] Furthermore, the 1988 Act 'offered informants a "bounty" in the amount of ten percent of civil penalties recovered from insider traders apprehended on the basis of the informant's information'.[58] The harshness of the imposition of a civil penalty was illustrated in 2002 by Martha Stewart.[59]

The US courts 'defined insider trading to encompass a broad range of activity. In the 1970s, the courts initially proposed the "possession theory" to define the offence'.[60] Even then progress was slow and it was not until 1961 that the US properly started out on the road of prohibiting insider trading when in *Re Cady Roberts & Co.* the SEC expressed its view that corporate officers not only owe a duty to the company but also to shareholders. However, the SEC properly came down against insider trading in the landmark judgment in *SEC v Texas Gulf Sulphur* which stated that anyone who possesses material non-public information had two options, disclose it, or abstain.[61] The *Texas Gulf Sulphur* decision was dealt a blow by the US Supreme Court in 1980, in rejecting the equality of access basis that *Texas Gulf Sulphur* was founded upon. In *Chiarella v US*, the Supreme Court brought the law back to its fiduciary duty origins, so it

---

[55]   Pub. L. No. 98-376.
[56]   O'Connor above, n 54 at 309.
[57]   Bainbridge above, n 44 at 42.
[58]   Joo, T. (2007), 'Legislation and legitimation: Congress and insider trading in the 1980s', *Indiana Law Journal*, 82, 575–622, at 578.
[59]   Shen, H. (2008), 'A comparative study of insider trading regulation enforcement in the US and China', *Journal of Business & Securities Law*, **9**, 41.
[60]   Naylor above, n 40 at 84.
[61]   401 F.2d 833 2nd Cir 1968.

seemed that only those with a true fiduciary duty to the company could be caught by the insider trading prohibition.[62] The solution to this problem according to Rakoff and Easton was the 'development of the so-called "misappropriation theory" of Rule 10b-5 liability, which separates the "fraud" and the "trading" aspects of insider trading into two distinct components. Under this theory, any person who steals ("misappropriates") inside information from anyone to whom he owes a fiduciary duty also thereby commits a fraud (by not disclosing the theft)'.[63]

In *Dirks v SEC*, the Supreme Court noted that the prohibition did extend beyond just those in a fiduciary relationship, to the so-called 'tippee' in so much that the information in the tippee's possession comes from a person who is in a fiduciary relationship with the company whose securities are involved.[64] Bainbridge took the view that 'the decision's limited practical impact on enforcement, its unique facts, and its focus on objective criteria convinced the committee [SEC] that *Dirks* would not adversely affect enforcement if construed narrowly by the courts'.[65] Nonetheless, US legislature introduced the ITSA[66] and the Insider Trading and Securities Fraud Enforcement Act of 1988 to alter the focus of the definition.[67] McCoy and Summe noted that the 1984 Act provided:

> the federal courts were permitted to impose civil monetary penalties up to three times the illegal profits earned, or losses avoided, by virtue of the insider trading. Criminal monetary penalties also increased from a previous maximum of $10 000 to $100 000. Under s. 32(a), between $10 000 and $100 000 could be fined for each insider trading offence, coupled with imprisonment for up to five years. In addition, the SEC's enforcement authority was enlarged to include individuals who aided and abetted insider trading.[68]

This is a view supported by Bainbridge who noted that the aim of the Act was 'to increase the deterrent effect of the insider trading prohibition . . .

---

[62]   445 US 222 (1980). See Livingston, J. and Salavert, D. (1990), 'An overview of the US law of insider trading', *International Business Law Journal*, **1**, 149–152, at 149. For a more detailed discussion of this case see Prakash, S. (1999), 'Our dysfunctional insider trading regime', *Columbia Law Review*, **99**. 1491–1550, at 1501–1502.

[63]   Rakoff and Easton above, n 49 at 284. For a more detailed discussion of rule 10b see Lee, I. (2002), 'Fairness and insider trading', *Columbia Business Law Review*, 119–192, at 124–129.

[64]   462 US 646 (1983).

[65]   Bainbridge above, n 42 at 483.

[66]   McCoy and Summe above, n 1 at 317.

[67]   Naylor above, n 40 at 84.

[68]   McCoy and Summe above, n 1 at 317.

The Act creates a civil penalty of up to three times the profit gained, or loss avoided, through trading while in possession of material non-public information'.[69] It is important to note that both the 1984 and 1988 legislation did not clarify the definition of insider trading. Therefore, the different approaches resulted in Naylor concluding 'the statute, regulations, and court cases still fail to provide a precise definition of what constitutes insider trading'.[70] As Bainbridge notes, *Dirks* did not fully answer the question of how far the US prohibition truly extends, when the information is from a non-insider, and is non-public and material.[71] Thus illustrating the SEC's commitment to tackle insider trading they began to develop the misappropriation theory. This theory has found favour with the US Supreme Court and in *US v O'Hagan* where a lawyer was not in a fiduciary position yet was still guilty of the offence as he was held to still owe a fiduciary duty to the source of the information and had misappropriated it for his own profit.[72] This of course opens up a much wider class of persons caught by the insider trading prohibition. Mistry argues that the misappropriation theory makes the US enforcement of insider trading more effective as it provides for a more elastic relationship between insider and issuer than the UK regime requires.[73] To clarify the position in respect of insider dealing the SEC has created Rules 10b5-1 and 10b5-2.[74] The first of these provides that a person commits insider trading if he trades on the basis of material non-public information if a trader is aware of the material non-public information when making the purchase or sale. The second covers the misappropriation theory position and provides that a person receiving confidential information under circumstances specified in the rule would owe a duty of trust or confidence and thus could be liable under the misappropriation theory. It is evident from a discussion about the US position that the SEC as regulatory body and the US courts, including the Supreme Court, have played an enormous role in prohibiting insider trading even though it is arguable that Congress in 1934 did not have

---

[69] Bainbridge above, n 42 at 456.

[70] Naylor above, n 40 at 84.

[71] Bainbridge above, n 42 at 456.

[72] Loke, A. (2006), 'From the fiduciary theory to information abuse: the changing fabric of insider trading law in the UK, Australia and Singapore', *The American Journal of Comparative Law*, **54**(1), 123–172.

[73] 521 US 642 (1997). See Mistry, H. (2002), 'Battle of the regulators: is the US system of securities regulation better provided for than that which operates in the United Kingdom?', *Journal of International Financial Markets*, **4**(4), 137–142.

[74] This has been described as 'the key provision of US insider trading law'. Livingston and Salavert above, n 62 at 149.

such a prohibition in mind, and in the face of strong intellectual argument against such a prohibition.

Due to the inadequacies of the Securities Exchange Act, the SEC has used several other legislative measures to tackle insider trading. For example, the Racketeer Influence and Corrupt Organizations Act 1970 (RICO) provided that it was only necessary for prosecutors to illustrate that 'a defendant committed securities fraud twice within any ten-year period. Prosecutors also favoured the stiff penalties imposed for a RICO conviction'.[75] O'Connor argued that 'securities violations and mail and wire fraud violations may serve as predicate acts to establish a pattern of racketeering activity under RICO'.[76] Furthermore, the Mail and Wire Fraud Statutes provide prosecutors with extensive enforcement powers that have been used in instances of insider trading.[77] The Sarbanes-Oxley Act 2002 introduced a new insider trading embargo that 'is linked to trading blackouts affecting a significant percentage of US participants in individual account retirement plans that hold employer equity securities. Additionally, the Act requires that new blackout notices be provided to defined contribution retirement plan participants and beneficiaries even when insiders are not restricted from trading and even though the retirement plan holds no employer securities'.[78] Shen concluded that:

> with these weapons, the SEC has become notably unforgiving of insider trading violations. For example, on July 11, 2003, Samuel Waksal, former president and CEO of ImClone Systems, was sentenced for his illegal insider trading to eighty-seven months (more than seven years) in prison and was ordered to pay a $3 million fine and $1.26 million in restitution.[79]

Shen noted that 'each year, the SEC brings approximately fifty enforcement actions against insider trading and the DOJ brings approximately eighteen indictments'.[80] Like other regulatory agencies, the SEC is permitted to seek equitable relief for the benefit of investors by virtue of the Securities Exchange Act 1934 and the Securities Enforcement Remedies and Penny Stock Reform Act 1990.[81] Despite the rigorous approach

---

[75] McCoy and Summe above, n 1 at 318.
[76] O'Connor above, n 54 at 340. The use of RICO to prosecute insider trading was famously illustrated in *Carpenter v. United States* 108 S. Ct. 316 (1987).
[77] McCoy and Summe above, n 1 at 319.
[78] Levitt, B. (2003), 'Sarbanes-Oxley insider trading prohibitions affect insiders outside the US', *International Company and Commercial Law Review*, **14**(9), 293–299, at 299.
[79] Shen above, n 59.
[80] *Ibid.*
[81] Ashe, M. (2009), 'The long arm of the SEC', *Company Lawyer*, **30**(7),

adopted by the SEC toward enforcing the insider trading provisions a number of concerns have been raised regarding their 'over enthusiasm' demonstrated during their investigations.[82] Furthermore, it has been noted by commentators that the SEC needs to rebuild its reputation after failing to act on six complaints alleging misconduct by Bernard Madoff between 2002 and 2006.[83]

The US policy towards insider trading is well established and administered by the SEC. However, its effectiveness has been limited by a number of factors including the courts' inconsistent interpretation of 'insider trading' and an initial reluctance by the SEC to pursue the offences outlined above. This enforcement stance has fundamentally changed with the increased coverage and exposure of insider trading since the 1980s and therefore direct comparisons can be made with the US anti-money laundering policy. Rakoff concluded that the effectiveness of the US system is 'inherently difficult to assess since it is impossible to ascertain the number of people who were tempted but were in fact deterred, or the number of people who were not deterred but escaped detection. Still, we are not entirely without clues'.[84] Kamman and Hood took the view that 'the development of US insider trading law is a long and convoluted history'.[85]

5.3.2 Reporting Obligations

The second part of the US insider trading policy is linked with its fraud policy as discussed in Chapter 4. Deposit-taking institutions are obliged to report allegations of fraudulent activity via currency transaction reports (CTRs) or suspicious activity reports (SARs). In particular, they are required to complete FinCEN Form 101 'Suspicious Activity Report by the Securities and Futures Industries'. SARs are filed by

---

193–194, at 193. See in particular the decision of the Court of Appeal in *US Securities and Exchange Commission v Manterfield* [2009] EWCA Civ 27.

[82] See for example Newkirk, T. (2001), 'Conflicts between public accountability and individual privacy in SEC enforcement actions', *Journal of Financial Crime*, **8**(4), 319–324.

[83] Harris, J. (2010), 'Getting over Madoff: how the SEC must restore its credibility', *Company Lawyer*, **31**(2), 33–34, at 33. For an in-depth discussion of the performance of the SEC see Securities and Exchange Commission *Investigation of Failure of the SEC to Uncover Bernard Madoff's Ponzi Scheme – Public Version* (Securities and Exchange Commission: Washington, DC, 2009).

[84] Rakoff and Easton above, n 49 at 285–286.

[85] Kamman, T. and Hood, R. (2009), 'With the spotlight on the financial crisis, regulatory loopholes, and hedge funds, how should hedge funds comply with insider trading laws?', *Columbia Business Law Review*, **2**, 357–467, at 363.

depository institutions, the securities and futures industry, and casinos and card clubs; the forms contain boxes where these institutions can report instances of certain types of fraud, especially securities fraud. A wide range of fraudulent activities are linked with insider trading. FinCEN reported that 'securities fraud, including market manipulation, insider trading and fictitious trading, was reported in 23 percent of the SAR-SFs reviewed'.[86] FinCEN reported a 29 per cent increase in the reported number of insider trading suspicious transactions between 2007 and 2008.[87] The information gathered from SARs has been used by the SEC to conduct numerous investigations concerning insider trading.[88] Another reporting mechanism utilized by the SEC in the fight against insider trading is the Securities Observation, News Analysis and Regulation System, or Sonar. Sonar was established in 2001 by NASD to monitor various stock markets to detect insider trading and fraud.[89] Shen noted that

> when there is a price movement in a particular stock that exceeds predetermined parameters, an 'alert' will be generated by SONAR, which will be further reviewed by several groups of regulatory analysts and investigators. The system generates around 50-to-60 alerts per day and a number of these are referred to the SEC for further investigation. The NYSE also uses sophisticated technology and pattern recognition system to monitor volume and price movements of all publicly traded stocks on a realtime basis. Where there is sufficient circumstantial evidence of insider trading and where the powers of the stock exchange are inadequate for addressing it, a referral will be made to the SEC.[90]

5.4   UNITED KINGDOM

5.4.1   Criminalization

It was not until the Companies Act 1980 that insider dealing was properly criminalized and later consolidated into the Company Securities (Insider

---

[86]   FinCEN *Mortgage loan fraud connections with other financial crime: an evaluation of suspicious activity reports filed by money service businesses, securities and futures firms, insurance companies and casinos* (FinCEN: Washington, DC, 2009b) at 7.

[87]   FinCEN *Suspicious activity review – trends, tips and issues,* Issue 15 (FinCEN: Washington, DC, 2009a) at p. 9.

[88]   *Ibid.,* at 18.

[89]   Goldberg, H., Dale, K., Lee, D., Shyr, P. and Thakker, D. (2003) *The NASD Securities Observation, News Analysis & Regulation System (SONAR),* available from http://www.aaai.org/Papers/IAAI/2003/IAAI03-002.pdf (accessed 12 August 2010).

[90]   Shen above, n 59.

Dealing) Act 1985. Further reform was introduced by the Insider Dealing Directive,[91] which was enacted as Part V of the CJA 1993. The Act contains three offences of insider dealing,[92] namely an 'insider' who deals in price-affected securities,[93] encouraging another to deal in price-affected securities,[94] and a disclosure offence relating to inside information by a party to another otherwise than in the proper performance of the functions of their employment, office or profession.[95] The *actus* and *mens rea* for each of the offences differ, the exception being one common *actus reus* factor of an individual charged with insider dealing who must have 'inside information' as an 'insider'. Under the dealing head the accused must also deal on a regulated market or be, or rely on a professional intermediary. The provision does not extend to abstention from dealing, so the accused must actually deal in the relevant securities, which for the purposes of the legislation are 'price-affected securities'. The *mens rea* element for the dealing offence is that the accused has knowledge that the information they possess is 'inside information' and that he or she is an 'insider', whether primary or secondary. In reference to the encouraging offence the additional *actus reus* requirement is that the accused must encourage another person to deal in price-affected securities. In this instance the person so encouraged does not have to deal, so long as they knew or had 'reasonable cause to believe that the dealing would take place'.[96] The *mens rea* for the encouraging offence is that they know that they are an 'insider' in possession of 'insider information' and that they know or have reasonable cause to believe that the dealing will take place. In this case the prosecution need only show reasonable belief that the person encouraged will deal. This part of the offence ensures that a person who would be caught by the primary insider dealing offence does not attempt to circumvent it by encouraging another to do the dealing instead. With regard to the disclosure offence, the additional *actus reus* element is that the accused disclosed the information 'otherwise than in the proper performance of the functions of his employment, office or profession, to another person',[97] the *mens rea* simply being that the accused knows that he is in possession of 'inside information' as an 'insider'.

The overall nature of the offence is that an 'insider' is in possession of

---

[91] 89/592.
[92] Criminal Justice Act 1993, s. 52.
[93] Criminal Justice Act 1993, s. 52(1).
[94] Criminal Justice Act 1993, s. 52(2)(a).
[95] Criminal Justice Act 1993, s. 52(2)(b).
[96] Criminal Justice Act 1993, s. 52(2)(a).
[97] Criminal Justice Act 1993, s. 52(2)(b).

'inside information' and undertakes prohibited activities as set out in the Act.[98] The provisions in the Act thus lead to a number of important issues, in relation to the information, who has it and how it is being used. The prohibition against insider dealing in the Act relates to relevant securities, and while wider than previous provisions is by no means totally comprehensive.[99] There are no real surprises in the list of securities contained in the legislation, and they include such securities as shares, debt securities, warrants, depositary receipts, options, futures, and contracts for differences.[100] One of the narrowing factors of the legislation is that the offence must take place on a regulated market,[101] defined as 'any market, however operated',[102] with the specific markets identified by an order made by HM Treasury, which lists the usual suspects. This focus on regulated markets precludes face to face deals between individuals, presumably leaving it up to the individuals concerned to ensure equality of information.[103]

Key in the legislation is the notion of inside information, as to be in breach of the provision the 'insider' must be in possession of information that is described as 'inside information'. What amounts to 'inside information' is information that relates to particular securities or to a particular issuer of securities;[104] is specific or precise;[105] has not been made public;[106] and if it were made public would be likely to have a significant effect on the price of any securities.[107] The section also moves on to specify a narrower definition of securities in that they must be 'price-affected securities' only,[108] meaning that if, and only if, the information was made public it would likely have a significant effect on the price of those securities.[109] What is meant by 'having a significant effect on the price of securities' is an important question to answer. The fact that the word 'significant' appears

---

[98]   Stallworthy, M. (1993), 'The United Kingdom's New Regime for the Control of Insider Dealing', *International Company and Commercial Law Review*, 4(12), 448–453.

[99]   Stallworthy above, n 98.

[100]   Stallworthy above, n 98.

[101]   Criminal Justice Act 1993, s. 52(3).

[102]   Criminal Justice Act 1993, s. 60(1).

[103]   Contrast this with the early provision in the USA where only face to face deals and not anonymous markets were caught by the legislation.

[104]   Criminal Justice Act 1993, s. 56(1)(a). The provision notes that this does not include securities generally or issuers of securities generally.

[105]   Criminal Justice Act 1993, s. 56(1)(b).

[106]   Criminal Justice Act 1993, s. 56(1)(c).

[107]   Criminal Justice Act 1993, s. 56(1)(d).

[108]   Criminal Justice Act 1993, s. 56(2).

[109]   *Ibid.*

suggests that this is a narrowing of the prohibition, in so much as not all 'insider trading' would be caught. The prohibition only applies where the securities in question would be or have been impacted to higher degree, for example a major increase in the share price, rather than any slight movement. As Lomnicka notes this would rule out trivial price movements, leaving only information that would have a much more pronounced impact on a security's price.[110] The inside information must be specific or precise, leading to the conclusion that the provision relates to something clearly identifiable or something clearly defined,[111] and it is argued that the more specific the information is the more price sensitive it will be.[112] It is interesting that the provision states 'specific' *or* 'precise' allowing for an either or position to be taken, arguably allowing a broader approach to be taken where the inside information does not display exact precision.[113]

The prohibition also states that the inside information must not yet have been made public for the offence to have been committed, so that any information that is in the public domain cannot lead to the committal of the offence. The CJA 1993 outlines in some detail when it would be considered that the information was in the public domain, and thus no longer was inside information.[114] A key element here is that research and diligence is rewarded. 'Made public' does not have to mean an overt statement made by the issuer of securities; it could be information and data contained in accessible reports that one diligent market participant has found and used. This would not be caught by the prohibition. Another key element in the legislation is that the prohibition relates only to an insider who is in possession of 'inside information', knowing that it is inside information;[115] and has it, and knows that he has it, from an inside source.[116] The section continues on to state that an insider has information from an inside source if and only if he has it through being a director, employee or shareholder of an issuer of securities;[117] or having access to the information by virtue

---

[110]   Lomnicka, E. (1994), 'The New Insider Dealing Provisions: Criminal Justice Act 1993, Part V', *Journal of Business Law*, March, 173–188.

[111]   *Ibid.*

[112]   Zekos, G. (1999), 'Insider trading under the EU, USA and English laws: a well recognised necessity or a distraction?', *Managerial Law*, **41**(5), 1–35.

[113]   Lomnicka above, n 110. The example given in this article is that an indication that profits will exceed expectation will be caught even though it lacks the specific amount of the profit increase.

[114]   Criminal Justice Act 1993, s. 59.

[115]   Criminal Justice Act 1993, s. 57(1)(a).

[116]   Criminal Justice Act 1993, s. 57(1)(b).

[117]   Criminal Justice Act 1993, s. 57(2)(a)(i).

of his employment, office or profession;[118] or the direct or indirect source of his information is a director, employee or shareholder of an issuer of securities.[119]

While not specified in the legislation the insider itself is subdivided into primary and secondary insider. The primary insider is one which receives or has the information by virtue of being the issuer or closely connected with the issuer, and would include people who in the ordinary course of their business acquire price-sensitive information. In essence a primary insider is one who acquires inside information about price-sensitive information likely to have a significant impact on their price by virtue of his relationship with the company. Classes of people who would fall into this category include directors, employees and shareholders. Secondary insiders acquire inside information from a primary insider knowing that it is unpublished price-sensitive information, and commit the offence if they then deal or encourage others to deal. Examples of this could be office cleaners. While the criminal justice provisions arguably have a narrow focus, requiring an individual who is an 'insider' in possession of 'inside information', 'dealing' or 'encouraging' other individuals to deal, in 'proscribed securities', on a 'regulated market', there does exist one provision that in effect widens the scope of the offence. This is contained in section 52 which extends the reach of the criminal prohibition to certain 'off market' transactions where either the 'person dealing relies on a professional intermediary or is himself acting as a professional intermediary'.[120] This broadening of the offence allows a wider range of market transactions to come under the legislations remit.[121] What amounts to a professional intermediary is defined in section 59,[122] and is in essence a person who carries on a business or is employed by a business that deals in securities, for example a stockbroker. The sanctions for insider dealing are contained in section 61 and amount to six months' imprisonment and/or a fine on summary conviction and seven years' imprisonment and/or a fine for conviction on indictment. The Act does provide for a number of defences, namely that the 'insider' did not expect the dealing to result in a profit attributable to the fact that the information in question was price-sensitive information in relation to the securities;[123] or he believed on reasonable grounds that the information had been disclosed widely enough to ensure that none of

---

118   Criminal Justice Act 1993, s. 57(2)(a)(ii).
119   Criminal Justice Act 1993, s. 57(2)(b).
120   Criminal Justice Act 1993, s. 52(3).
121   Stallworthy above, n 98.
122   Criminal Justice Act 1993.
123   Criminal Justice Act 1993, s. 53(1)(a).

those taking part in the dealing would be prejudiced by not having the information;[124] or that he would have done what he did even if he had not had the information.[125] In addition, further defences are listed in Schedule 1 of the Act.[126] As well as the criminal insider dealing provisions discussed above, English law also criminalizes the intentional misleading of financial markets. Such a provision is contained in section 397 FSMA 2000 which makes it an offence to make statements, promises or forecasts knowing that they are materially misleading, false or deceptive; where the person dishonestly conceals material facts; or recklessly makes a statement, promise or forecast which is materially misleading, false or deceptive.[127]

5.4.2 The Market Abuse Regime

The fact that the criminal provisions to counter insider dealing in the CJA were largely unsuccessful are a matter of considerable comment.[128] The standard of proof required has proved a major hurdle for the criminal law, for transactions can appear quite opaque and difficult to understand, and often happen between very small groups of individuals. The government's answer to the problem of the lack of convictions was to 'fill the regulatory gap'.[129] The new approach to tackling abuse is 'The Market Abuse Regime', arguably reflecting that the focus was not merely on insider dealing but the whole ambit of activities that could affect the probity of the financial markets. Indeed, one of the key aims of the Market Abuse Regime is to give the FSA maximum flexibility in its task by requiring a lower standard of proof than needed to secure a criminal conviction.[130] The concept of a civil regime in the UK itself is not new, and was a hotly debated topic during the passage of the CJA, but was obviously felt to be

---

[124]   Criminal Justice Act 1993, s. 53(1)(b).
[125]   Criminal Justice Act 1993, s. 53(1)(c).
[126]   Criminal Justice Act 1993.
[127]   For an analysis of FSMA 2000, s. 397, its predecessor provision, Financial Services Act 1986, s. 47 see Barnett, W. (1996), 'Fraud enforcement in the Financial Services Act 1986: an analysis and discussion of s.47', *Company Lawyer*, **17**(7), 203–210.
[128]   See for example Alcock, A. (2002), 'Market abuse', *Company Lawyer*, **23**(5), 142–150 and Linklater, L. (2001), 'The Market Abuse Regime: setting standards in the twenty-first century', *Company Lawyer*, **22**(9), 267–272.
[129]   See Filby, M. (2004), 'Part VIII Financial Services and Markets Act: filling insider dealing's regulatory gaps', *Company Lawyer*, **23**(12), 363–370.
[130]   Swan, E. (2004), 'Market abuse: A new duty of fairness', *Company Lawyer*, **25**(3), 67–68.

a step too far at that time.[131] The obvious lack of success of the criminal provisions within the CJA put civil enforcement squarely back on the agenda. The overall aim of FSMA 2000 was to provide a comprehensive regulatory structure to oversee all financial services operations. To enable this to happen, it gives considerable power to the FSA to make rules in pursuit of its statutory objectives. The five objectives are maintaining market confidence,[132] ensuring financial stability,[133] promoting public awareness,[134] protecting consumers,[135] and reducing financial crime.[136] Arguably tackling market abuse covers three of the stated objectives, and if the market abuse provisions are used innovatively can help to promote public awareness also. Therefore it is important not to narrowly interpret the market abuse provisions but to make reference to the wider role of the FSA in keeping markets clean and efficient for investor confidence to blossom, protecting individual consumers against misselling and reducing the incidence of financial crime, in particular fraud on investors.[137] And while the Code of Market Abuse[138] section of the Handbook will play a central role in controlling market abuse reference must also be made to the Handbook generally, in particular the High Level Standards such as Principles of Business,[139] and Senior Management Arrangement, Systems and Controls,[140] and the specific Handbooks such as Supervision,[141] Decision Procedures and Penalties Manual,[142] Disclosure Rules and Transparency Rules[143] and the Listing Rules.[144]

The new Market Abuse Regime has been described as 'novel',[145] 'con-

---

[131]   See Ed. (1993), 'Insiders beware!', *Company Lawyer*, **14**(11), 202.

[132]   Financial Services and Markets Act 2000, s. 3.

[133]   Financial Services and Markets Act 2000, s. 3A. This section was inserted by the Financial Services Act 2010 in response to the global financial crisis.

[134]   Financial Services and Markets Act 2000, s. 4.

[135]   Financial Services and Markets Act 2000, s. 5.

[136]   Financial Services and Markets Act 2000, s. 6.

[137]   Note that during the preparation of this chapter the new Conservative/ Liberal Democrat coalition announced major reforms to bank and financial services regulation, with much of the FSA's role in supervising banks and the maintenance of financial stability being moved to the Bank of England. The final outcome of the proposed reforms was not known at the time of writing.

[138]   MAR.

[139]   PRIN.

[140]   SYSC.

[141]   SUP.

[142]   DEPP.

[143]   DTR.

[144]   LR.

[145]   Linklater above, n 128.

troversial'[146] and the 'new witchcraft'.[147] These comments arguably stem from the civil enforcement mechanisms contained within the provisions. The new regime is designed to complement the criminal provisions of the Criminal Justice Act 1995 (CJA 1995), to run in parallel and in addition to, not to replace and substitute them.[148] While the regime only came into force in 2001 it has already been subject to a major revision by virtue of the Market Abuse Directive (MAD) which aimed to set a minimum standard across EU markets,[149] while also bringing in a new focus on preventing market abuse occurring in the first place. The Directive was the first of the provisions to be brought through using the Lamfalussy process designed to speed up the implementation of provisions forming part of the EU's 'Financial Services Action Plan', and was designed to bring a level of uniformity to the Community's approach to tackling market abuse.[150] The Market Abuse Regime came into force on 1 July 2005.[151]

FSMA provides that market abuse can take a number of forms and that it constitutes behaviour that occurs in relation to '(i) qualifying investments admitted to trading on a prescribed market, (ii) qualifying investments in respect of which a request for admission to trading on such a market has been made, or (iii) in the case of subsection (2) or (3) behaviour, investments which are related investments in relation to such qualifying investments, and falls within any one or more of the types of behaviour set out in subsections (2) to (8)'.[152] Part VIII FSMA 2000 applies to all persons whose actions have an effect on the market, irrespective of whether they are required to seek authorization or have an exemption. It is interesting to note the distinction here from the criminal insider dealing provisions in that market abuse can be committed by juristic persons, not merely individuals as was the case in the CJA. In a similar vein to the insider dealing provisions the market abuse must occur in relation to qualifying investments traded on a prescribed market, however both are wider in scope than under the 1993 Act.

---

[146] Alcock above, n 128.

[147] Alcock, A. (2001), 'Market abuse – the new witchcraft', *New Law Journal*, **151**, 1398.

[148] Sykes, A. (1999), 'Market abuse: a civil revolution', *Journal of International Financial Markets*, **1**(2), 59–67.

[149] 2003/6/EC.

[150] Hansen, J. (2007), 'MAD in a hurry: the swift and promising adoption of the EU Market Abuse Directive', *European Business Law Review*, **15**(2), 183–221.

[151] Amendments made to FSMA 2000 by the Financial Services and Markets Act 2000 (Market Abuse) Regulations 2005, SI 2005/381.

[152] Financial Services and Markets Act 2000, s. 118.

The original UK regime contained three categories that would amount to market abuse, being misuse of information,[153] creating false and misleading impressions,[154] and distorting the market.[155] The areas introduced by the Directive cover broadly similar ground to the UK regime already in place; however, they are narrower than those of the original FSMA regime,[156] as the Directive rolls back the UK market abuse regime in force at that time. Since the introduction and enactment of the Directive the prohibition has been expanded to include seven types of behaviour, albeit under two broad headings.[157] Haynes states, 'the essence of the regime . . . has remained the same since the passing of the FSMA, which is that certain types of behaviour are deemed to be in breach of the Act'.[158] The first three types of behaviour relate to the misuse of inside information or of information which is not yet generally available, while the second four relate to various types of market manipulation. Unlike the criminal provisions of the CJA the Market Abuse Regime does not require the 'prosecuting' authority to show intent on the part of the market participant,[159] a cause for initial concern explained by the government on the basis that the Market Abuse Regime was not primarily about catching errant individuals but about providing clean and efficient financial markets.[160] As Swan notes, this leads to the potential of market abuse being committed by 'mistake' and as such it is clearly possible that the offence can be committed negligently,[161] although in a response to the Joint Committee on Financial Services and Markets the FSA did note that they do not 'propose to prosecute people for accidental offences'.[162] This lack of intent requirement has now been confirmed by the Court of Appeal.[163]

The FSA is required to publish a code of conduct outlining what the

---

[153]   Financial Services and Markets Act 2000, s. 118(2)(a).

[154]   Financial Services and Markets Act 2000, s. 118(2)(b).

[155]   Financial Services and Markets Act 2000, s. 118(2)(c).

[156]   Burger, R. and Davies, G. (2005b), 'What's new in market abuse – Part 2', *New Law Journal*, **155**, 964.

[157]   MAD categorized the offences broadly as insider dealing and market manipulation.

[158]   Haynes, A. (2007), 'Market abuse: an analysis of its nature and regulation', *Company Lawyer*, **28**(11), 323–335, at 323.

[159]   MAR1.2.6G.

[160]   Alcock above, n 147.

[161]   Swan above, n 130.

[162]   Joint Committee on Financial Services and Markets, First Report, para 265 available at http://www.publications.parliament.uk/pa/jt199899/jtselect/jtfinser/328/32809.htm (accessed 8 July 2010).

[163]   *Winterflood Securities Ltd and others v Financial Services Authority* [2010] EWCA Civ 423; [2010] WLR (D) 101.

FSA's responsibilities are in respect of guarding against market abuse.[164] The Code of Market Conduct (MAR) of the FSA Handbook is 'central'[165] to the operation of the Market Abuse Regime, described by others as the 'backbone' of the regime.[166] The original version only stated what behaviour did not amount to market abuse.[167] However, later versions have included examples of what amounts to market abuse, thus giving clear guidelines to market participants of the types of behaviour to avoid. The code is designed to provide assistance and guidance in ascertaining whether behaviour amounts to market abuse.[168] The code is quick to point out that it is not an exhaustive description of all types of behaviour amounting to market abuse,[169] nor is it an exhaustive description of all factors to be taken into account in the determination of whether behaviour is market abuse.[170] The Code of Market Conduct also contains two so-called 'safe harbours', outlining behaviour that will not amount to market abuse, these being share buy-back schemes and price stabilization programmes associated with new issues.[171]

What then amounts to behaviour that would be regarded as market abuse? In determining such behaviour we have to look to both the Act and the Code of Market Conduct to see what is and what isn't behaviour amounting to market abuse. Unsurprisingly the first of the seven is the classic offence of insider dealing,[172] requiring an 'insider' to deal, or try to deal, on the basis of 'inside information'. The second form of behaviour caught by the regime is improper disclosure,[173] where the 'insider' discloses 'inside information' to another person without permission. The FSA gives the example of a company employee who on finding out that his company has become the target of a takeover, buys or sells shares before that information becomes public.[174] The improper disclosure provision is designed

---

[164] Financial Services and Markets Act 2000, s. 119.
[165] Linklater above, n 128 at 269.
[166] Sabalot, D. and Everett, R. (2004) *Financial Services and Markets Act 2000*, Butterworths New Law Guide LexisNexis, at 270.
[167] These are termed 'safe harbours' in which the activity is not subject to the prohibition.
[168] MAR1.1.2G; Note anything marked with a 'C' is behaviour that does not constitute market abuse – MAR1.1.4G.
[169] MAR1.1.6G.
[170] MAR1.1.7G.
[171] MAR 1.10 and Annex 1.
[172] Financial Services and Markets Act 2000, s. 118(2).
[173] Financial Services and Markets Act 2000, s. 118(3).
[174] Financial Services Authority (2008f), 'Why market abuse could cost you money – The revised Code of Market Conduct is here to help protect you',

to catch the 'insider' if he then tells a friend or work colleague. The classic example of the potential for market abuse surrounding takeovers and mergers has long been seen, and has been a primary concern for the FSA and its predecessor organizations. The FSA noted that while it felt that the statistics were improving, the level of informed price movements ahead of takeover announcements was causing concern.[175] However, the trend has more recently been a cause for concern again, with abnormal price movements seen in over 30 per cent of takeovers, the highest level for five years.[176] The third type of behaviour caught by the legislation is misuse of information[177] not generally available, which would have an effect on an investor's decision about the terms on which to deal. The FSA example[178] for this type of behaviour is the employee who learns that his company is about to lose a significant contract that would have an overall effect on the price of securities of that company. An example could be that a government order for an aircraft carrier is to be cancelled.

This is the first of the two so-called 'super-equivalent provisions' that have been specifically retained by the FSA even though they were not part of the Directive, and as such go further than was required by the Directive. The super-equivalent provisions catch more potentially abusive practices as they retain the term 'behaviour' as opposed to the Directive's more specific terminology,[179] the Directive requiring some positive action by the market participant.[180] This provision utilizes the regular user test as a basis of ascertaining whether or not market abuse has been committed. It is clear from the examples in the Code of Market Conduct that this is a broader approach than the Directive required as there is no need for the person in possession of the information to be an 'insider', and in the

---

available at http://www.fsa.gov.uk/pubs/public/market_abuse.pdf (accessed 29 June 2010).

[175] Financial Services Authority (2007a) 'Market Watch. Market Division: Newsletter on market conduct and transaction reporting issues', available at http://www.fsa.gov.uk/pubs/newsletters/mw_newsletter21.pdf (accessed 30 June 2010).

[176] Wachman, R. (2010), 'Suspicious share trading before takeover news at five-year high', available at http://www.guardian.co.uk/business/2010/jun/10/fsa-takeover-suspicious-trading (accessed 30 June 2010).

[177] Financial Services and Markets Act 2000, s. 118(4)(a) & (b).

[178] Financial Services Authority above, n 174.

[179] Financial Services Authority (2004b), 'UK Implementation of EU Market Abuse Directive', available from http://www.fsa.gov.uk/pubs/other/eu_mad.pdf (accessed 5 July 2010).

[180] Sheikh, S. (2008), 'FSMA Market Abuse Regime: a review of the sunset clauses', *International Company and Commercial Law Review*, **19**(7), 234–236.

example of an 'insider' having lunch with a non-insider friend, telling him of a proposed takeover, and then the friend placing a bet on the basis of this information, the friend will be liable to action by the FSA.[181] Neither does the information need to be 'inside information'; the focus here is on relevant information not generally available, known by its acronym RINGA. As this is retained from the pre-Directive regime, and extends further than the Directive's provisions, it is designed for use only in situations where the first two provisions do not apply, sweeping up behaviour that would slip through the MAD net.[182] The super-equivalent provisions are subject to a sunset clause[183] originally to trigger on 30 June 2008,[184] and subsequently extended to 31 December 2009.[185] This has been further extended to 31 December 2011,[186] arguably showing that the UK authorities believe that maintaining the flexibility of these super-equivalent provisions is an important component of the Market Abuse Regime, at least until the EU has completed its review of the Market Abuse Directive, and possibly a mistrust that the European minimum standard may not be sufficiently strong to deal with market abuse, a valid point where the large UK securities market is concerned.

The fourth type of behaviour is manipulating transactions,[187] where trades or the placing of orders to trade give a false or misleading impression of the supply of, or demand for, one or more investments, thus raising the price of the investment to an artificial or abnormal level.[188] The fifth type of behaviour is manipulating devices,[189] where a person trades or places orders to trade, employing fictitious devices or any other form of deception or contrivance. The sixth form of behaviour surrounds dissemination[190] where a person gives out information conveying a false or misleading impression about an investment or issuer of an investment

---

[181] MAR1.5.10E, Para (1).

[182] Loke above, n 72.

[183] Sheikh above, n 180.

[184] Financial Services and Markets Act 2000 (Market Abuse) Regulations 2005 (SI 2005/381).

[185] Financial Services and Markets Act 2000 (Market Abuse) Regulations 2008 (SI 2008/1439).

[186] Financial Services and Markets Act 2000 (Market Abuse) Regulations 2009 (SI 2009/3128).

[187] Financial Services and Markets Act 2000, s. 118(5)(a) & (b).

[188] See for example *Queen v Securities and Futures Authority Ltd. Disciplinary Appeal Tribunal of the Securities and Futures Authority Limited, ex parte Bertrand Fleurose* [2001] EWHC Admin 292; [2001] 2 All ER (Comm) 481.

[189] Financial Services and Markets Act 2000, s. 118(6).

[190] Financial Services and Markets Act 2000, s. 118(7).

knowing that this information is false and misleading. The final type of behaviour is distortion and misleading behaviour[191] that gives a false and misleading impression of either the supply of, or demand for, an investment; or behaviour that otherwise distorts the market in an investment. This is the second of the super-equivalent provisions, and while the first one deals with the misuse of information, the second is concerned with market manipulation and distortion in particular. Again, the objective regular user test is applied, and again these provisions are to be applied where the behaviour does not fall within the definition of the other sections dealing with market manipulation, misleading impressions and distortion.

A key element in the pre-Directive UK provision is the notion of the regular user. The original version of the legislation required that the behaviour in question occurring in relation to qualifying investments satisfying one or more of the conditions set had to be regarded by a 'regular user of that market who is aware of the behaviour as a failure on the part of the person or persons concerned to observe the standard behaviour reasonably expected of a person in his or their position in relation to the market'.[192] The regular user test sets up an objective and hypothetical standard against which market participants can be judged, and has been seen as a sophisticated financial services equivalent of the reasonable man standard used to judge whether a person has breached their duty of care in an action for negligence.[193] The regular user test was not included in the MAD; however, it has been retained by the FSA in support of the so-called super-equivalent provisions, albeit with the protection of a sunset clause, thus the regular user test now only applies to Sections 118(4) and 118(8) FSMA 2000.

In much the same way as the criminal insider dealing provisions, to be caught by the provisions the information must be 'inside information', held by an 'insider'; simply having inside information is not of itself sufficient.[194] One clear improvement as a result of the MAD is that issuers of securities are now required to produce insider lists of people with access to 'inside information'.[195] What constitutes an 'insider' is contained in Section 118B FSMA 2000 listing a number of criteria to be taken into

---

[191] Financial Services and Markets Act 2000, s. 118(8).

[192] Financial Services and Markets Act 2000, s. 118(1)(c), pre-Market Abuse Directive.

[193] See *Blyth v Birmingham Waterworks* (1856) 11 Ex Ch 781; see also *Hall v Brooklands Auto Racing Club* [1933] 1 KB 205.

[194] Davies, P. (2008), *Gower and Davies Principles of Modern Company Law*, Sweet & Maxwell, London.

[195] See now DTR 2.8, FSA Handbook.

consideration. Thus to be an insider the person will have the 'inside information' as a result of being a director or shareholder of the issuer of the securities,[196] holding capital of an issuer,[197] having access to inside information as a result of their employment, profession or duties,[198] or as a result of criminal activities.[199] Additionally the person is an insider if he has obtained by other means information which he knows, or could reasonably be expected to know, is inside information.[200] Again the Code of Market Conduct provides information on what an insider would look like.[201] In essence the code lays out a set of criteria where if a person is in possession of inside information, such as a senior manager in an organization that is the target of a takeover, then he will be classified as an insider for the purpose of the market abuse provisions.

It is quite transparent that the definition of 'insider' primarily relates to a person in possession of 'inside information', and therefore it is arguable that the definition of 'inside information' is the key to being able to bring a successful action for market abuse against that 'insider'. What amounts to inside information is contained in Section 118C(2) and (3) FSMA 2000 with guidance again provided in the Code of Market Conduct.[202] The provisions are split between qualifying or related investments which are not commodity derivatives[203] and those which are commodity derivatives.[204] For both elements information is 'inside information' if it is of a precise nature and is not generally available,[205] and relates, directly or indirectly to issuers of qualifying investments or qualifying investments themselves,[206] and in the case of commodities to one or more derivatives.[207] In relation to qualifying investments the requirement is that the information would have a significant effect on the price of the qualifying or related investments.[208] In relation to commodities it is 'inside information' if users on such markets would expect to receive such information in

---

196 Financial Services and Markets Act 2000, s. 118B(a).
197 Financial Services and Markets Act 2000, s. 118B(b).
198 Financial Services and Markets Act 2000, s. 118B(c).
199 Financial Services and Markets Act 2000, s. 118B(d).
200 Financial Services and Markets Act 2000, s. 118B(e).
201 MAR 1.2.7, 1.2.8E and 1.2.9G.
202 MAR 1.2.10.
203 Financial Services and Markets Act 2000, s. 118C(2).
204 Financial Services and Markets Act 2000, s. 118C(3).
205 Financial Services and Markets Act 2000, s. 118C(2)(a) & 118C(3)(a).
206 Financial Services and Markets Act 2000, s. 118C(2)(b).
207 Financial Services and Markets Act 2000, s. 118C(3)(b).
208 Financial Services and Markets Act 2000, s. 118C(2)(c).

accordance with any accepted practices on those markets.[209] The different section dealing with commodities reflects the physical nature of commodities, and as such markets for commodities may have access to information in different forms.[210] 'Precise' is defined in Section 118C(5) FSMA as if it indicates circumstances that exist or may reasonably be expected to come into existence or an event that has occurred or may reasonably be expected to occur,[211] and is specific enough to enable a conclusion to be drawn as to the possible effect of those circumstances or that event on the price of qualifying investments or related investments.[212] This is not a particularly well-defined section and could conceivably lead to some debate. The question remains of how precise or how specific the 'inside information' needs to be. If too specific then the FSA will struggle to bring successful enforcement actions. It is submitted that this is the correct approach in so much that the requirement for inside information should not be overly restricted by a requirement of too great a specificity. Many issues have an impact on the price of securities and a broad approach is to be welcomed.[213]

In addition to the need to be precise the information needs to be 'likely to have a significant effect on the price of those qualifying investments or related investments'.[214] In similar fashion to the older criminal provisions this requirement leads to the conclusion that for the prohibition to apply the action on the part of the person accused of market abuse must be more than trivial, in that minor movements in the prices of qualifying investments will not amount to market abuse. Exactly what will amount to market abuse is a matter for the FSA to determine, and a trawl through the Authority's enforcement actions list will give some idea as to what 'significant' will mean in practice.[215] Thus, the FSA will consider what the reasonable investor would be likely to do; the more significant the price movement gained from the 'inside information' the more likely that the FSA will see it as 'significant' within the meaning of the provision.[216]

---

[209] Financial Services and Markets Act 2000, s. 118C(3)(c).
[210] Hudson above, n 8 at 282.
[211] Financial Services and Markets Act 2000, s. 118(C)(5)(a).
[212] Financial Services and Markets Act 2000, s. 118(C)(5)(b).
[213] For a look at Finnish case law on the issue of what is precise see Hayrynen, J. (2008), 'The precise definition of inside information?', *Journal of International Banking Law and Regulation*, **23**(2), 64–70.
[214] Financial Services and Markets Act 2000, s. 118C(6).
[215] See Financial Services Authority (n/d), 'Enforcement Notices, Financial Services Authority', available from http://www.fsa.gov.uk/pages/About/What/financial_crime/market_abuse/library/notices/index.shtml (accessed 1 July 2010).
[216] Hudson above, n 8 at 284.

A further key issue is whether or not the information has been made public. Information is only 'inside information' if it 'is not generally available',[217] and once it is regarded as generally available it ceases to be information for the purposes of market abuse. Section 118C(8) and the Code of Market Conduct provide the provision and assistance, and examples to determine whether or not information is to be regarded as generally available.[218] These include information disclosed in the proper manner to a prescribed market,[219] publicly available documents,[220] only available on payment of a fee,[221] and obtained by analysing or developing other information which is generally available.[222] It is not relevant if the information is only available outside the UK,[223] nor is it relevant if the analysis is only possible by a person with considerable financial 'resources, expertise or competence'.[224] The example given in the Code of Market Conduct is that of a passenger on a train seeing a burning factory and calling his broker to sell shares in that company; this will not amount to market abuse as the information will be deemed to be generally available.[225] Information is available in many forms today and so it can be a difficult question as to whether information is no longer to be regarded as 'inside information' and will be a matter for evidence. What does come through is that the professional and talented market analyst and broker are protected against accusations of market misconduct, providing of course the source of their information is not 'inside information'. The professional and thorough analysis of the broker will not fall foul of the regime, even if the information is paid for and if the information is not generally available to the market as a whole, unless of course they have done the same research. One of the new and innovative features required by the MAD was the introduction of more proactive measures to prevent market abuse. In this the MAD required a system of suspicious transaction reporting,[226] and while not a new phenomenon by any means to the financial sector in respect

---

[217] Financial Services and Markets Act 2000, s. 118C(2)(a), 118C(3)(a) and 118C(4)(b).
[218] MAR1.2.12E.
[219] MAR1.2.12E, Para (1).
[220] MAR1.2.12E, Para (2).
[221] MAR1.2.12E, Para (3).
[222] MAR1.2.12E, Para (5).
[223] MAR1.2.13E, Para (1).
[224] MAR1.2.13E, Para (2).
[225] MAR1.2.14G.
[226] Article 6.9 MAD.

of money laundering[227] it was a new requirement for suspected market abuse.[228]

5.4.3 Enforcement

It is arguable that the primary function of the Market Abuse Regime is to punish market abusers, and to that end Part VIII FSMA 2000 is actually entitled 'Penalties for Market Abuse'. While this was the position of the original iteration of the Act the MAD required Member States' regulatory authorities to attempt to prevent market abuse occurring, and this is evident in the way that the Code of Market Conduct elucidates examples of what amounts to market abuse and who commits it. By doing this market participants should be able to ascertain when they are coming dangerously close to committing the prohibited activities contained in Part VIII FSMA 2000. However, it remains that the Market Abuse Regime plays a vital role in bringing market abusers to book. To this aim the FSA has considerable power to undertake investigations into alleged market abusers. These powers are contained in Part XI FSMA 2000, which allows the FSA to appoint professionals to undertake general investigations under section 167 or investigations in particular cases under Section 168. The types of cases relevant to section 168 include insider dealing[229] and market abuse.[230] To bring a disciplinary action the FSA must be satisfied that a person has engaged in market abuse,[231] or has encouraged another person to undertake behaviour which if he had engaged in such action would amount to market abuse.[232] The outcome of such investigations is sent to the Regulatory Decisions Committee, an administrative decision maker to decide whether or not to bring disciplinary actions against an individual.

If the FSA proposes that it is to take action it must issue a warning notice,[233] and likewise a warning notice must be issued if it proposes to impose a penalty stating the amount of the intended penalty,[234] and if the proposal is to publish a censure, a warning notice setting out the terms of

---

[227] Proceeds of Crime Act 2002.
[228] Detailed suspicious transaction reporting requirements are contained in the Supervision Handbook (SUP) at SUP 15.10.
[229] Financial Services and Markets Act 2000, s. 168(2)(a).
[230] Financial Services and Markets Act 2000, s. 168(2)(d).
[231] Financial Services and Markets Act 2000, s. 123(1)(a).
[232] Financial Services and Markets Act 2000, s. 123(1)(b).
[233] Financial Services and Markets Act 2000, s. 126(1).
[234] Financial Services and Markets Act 2000, s. 126(2).

the censure.[235] Equally the FSA must issue decision notices in respect of decisions to take action against a person,[236] imposition of a penalty,[237] or publication of a censure statement.[238] An important check and balance here is that if the FSA decides to take action against a person, that person may refer the matter to the Financial Services and Markets Tribunal, an independent tribunal set up to hear appeals against FSA decisions. Where market abuse has been proved, the FSA has a number of options dependent on the severity of the abuse. Firstly, at the upper end it may impose a financial penalty of an unlimited amount under Section 123.[239] Additionally the FSA has the power to publicly censure market participants,[240] and apply for injunctive[241] or restitutionary[242] remedies. The FSA also has the power to order restitution itself.[243] As part of the measures to ensure greater transparency and to head off civil liberties concerns the FSA is required to publish a 'Statement of policy'[244] outlining how it intends to implement its penalties regime, detailing when and how it will impose penalties and the amount of any penalty imposed along with other relevant factors.[245] As with the insider dealing provisions any imposition of a penalty does not render any transaction void or unenforceable;[246] to ensure orderly compliance, however, the FSA may apply for or make restitutionary orders by virtue of Part XXV FSMA 2000.[247]

The FSA retains the power to bring criminal prosecutions for insider dealing[248] under the CJA; however, it is arguable that the authority has been slow in progressing down this route, attracting criticism,[249] preferring to use financial penalties as its main enforcement mechanism, with some commentators wondering if the FSA would ever get round to commencing criminal prosecutions for insider dealing at all.[250] Rider notes that in

---

[235] Financial Services and Markets Act 2000, s. 126(3).
[236] Financial Services and Markets Act 2000, s. 127(1).
[237] Financial Services and Markets Act 2000, s. 127(2).
[238] Financial Services and Markets Act 2000, s. 127(3).
[239] Financial Services and Markets Act 2000, s. 123(1).
[240] Financial Services and Markets Act 2000, s. 123(3).
[241] Financial Services and Markets Act 2000, s. 381.
[242] Financial Services and Markets Act 2000, s. 383.
[243] Financial Services and Markets Act 2000, s. 384.
[244] Financial Services and Markets Act 2000, s. 124.
[245] See DEPP 6 Decision Procedure and Penalties Manual FSA Handbook.
[246] Financial Services and Markets Act 2000, s. 131.
[247] Financial Services and Markets Act 2000, ss. 382, 383 and 384.
[248] Financial Services and Markets Act 2000, s. 402(1)(a).
[249] Haines, J. (2008), 'FSA determined to improve the cleanliness of markets: custodial sentences continue to be a real threat', *Company Lawyer*, **29**(12), 370.
[250] Burger and Davies above, n 2 at 326.

the early days of the FSA there seemed to be a culture of reluctance on the part of the authority's senior management to acknowledge that one of its tasks was to reduce the incidence of financial crime and combat market abuse, after so long as a self-regulating club.[251] There does, however, now seem to be some evidence that the FSA is beginning to get tougher with insider dealers and more criminal prosecutions are likely in the future.[252] Alexander[253] notes the increasing FSA intensity in referring to a speech by Margaret Cole, Director of the FSA's Enforcement Division, where she emphasized that the FSA would be seeking to increase the number of criminal prosecutions it brings,[254] with others within the FSA calling it '. . . one of the most significant changes in our approach'[255] and that shortly after this speech the FSA obtained its first conviction for insider dealing. This increase in intensity and focus toward criminal prosecutions has borne fruit with the first criminal conviction for insider dealing brought by the FSA in which a solicitor was sentenced to eight months for passing on information to his father-in-law about an impending takeover.[256] Additionally the courts have recently given a green light to the FSA to use its prosecutorial powers in confirming that the FSA is able to bring prosecutions under the CJA without recourse to the Secretary of State or Director of Public Prosecutions.[257] It is also clear that the reach of the FSA is expanding as a result of its more aggressive approach to dealing with market abuse stretching out beyond traditional securities markets and into the debt markets.[258]

One of the most controversial and initially confusing elements of the Market Abuse Regime has surrounded the nature of the offence. As noted the intention of Part VIII FSMA 2000 is to introduce a civil enforcement regime parallel to the criminal provision contained in the CJA 1995. The

---

[251] Rider, B. (2008), 'Where angels fear!', *Company Lawyer*, **29**(9), 257–258.

[252] Haines above, n 249.

[253] Alexander, R, (2009a), 'Corporate crimes: are the gloves coming off?', *Company Lawyer*, **30**(11), 321–322.

[254] Financial Services Authority (2008d), 'After dinner remarks at Cambridge Symposium on economic crime', available at http://www.fsa.gov.uk/pages/Library/Communication/Speeches/2008/0901_mc.shtml (accessed 1 July 2010).

[255] Financial Services Authority (2008e), 'FSA and enforcing the Market Abuse Regime' available at http://www.fsa.gov.uk/pages/Library/Communication/Speeches/2008/1106_js.shtml (accessed 16 July 2010).

[256] Financial Services Authority (2009b), 'Solicitor and his father-in-law found guilty in FSA insider dealing case', available at http://www.fsa.gov.uk/pages/Library/Communication/PR/2009/042.shtml (accessed 4 July 2010).

[257] See *R (Uberoi and Another) v City of Westminster Magistrates' Court* [2008] EWHC 3191 (Admin); [2009] 1 WLR 1905.

[258] See for example Peat, R., Mason, I. and Bazley, S. (2010), 'Market abuse in the debt markets – a new FSA case', *Company Lawyer*, **31**(2), 50.

confusion is not helped by the terms used to describe the regime, such as 'offence' and 'prosecute',[259] words normally associated with criminal sanctions. The introduction of the civil enforcement mechanisms forced the FSA to consult[260] beyond their original intention due to the volume of comments on their original consultation[261] outlining how the FSA was to properly implement the provisions. The key issue here is whether or not the so-called civil sanctions are compatible with the European Convention on Human Rights as incorporated into English law by the Human Rights Act 1998, a relevant question when a decision of the FSA has been referred to the Financial Services and Markets Tribunal.[262] Section 123 FSMA 2000 merely states that the FSA has to be 'satisfied' that market abuse or encouraging such activity has occurred, which doesn't seem to be a particularly high standard. This argument relates to whether the civil penalties in the regime can accurately be described as civil or whether they are more akin to criminal sanctions. The controversy has centred on the two key issues of the reduced burden of proof required to prove market abuse as opposed to the criminal standard required by the criminal provisions of the CJA 1995, or whether or not the allegation of market abuse is a criminal charge, subject to the usual protections.[263]

The civil liberty concerns dogged the entire passage of the legislation. The Joint Committee on Financial Services and Markets questioned the lack of certainty of the regime, especially the lack of any requirement of intent to commit market abuse.[264] The government's response to this concern was to explain that the civil regime of the FSMA 2000 was not focused on the moral culpability of the individual but with ensuring the efficiency of the market.[265] The issue was subject to a detailed investigation by Lord Lester of Herne Hill and Javan Herberg who stated:

---

[259]   Filby above, n 129.

[260]   Financial Services Authority (1999), 'Feedback statement on responses to Consultation Paper 10: Market Abuse', available at http://www.fsa.gov.uk/pubs/cp/cp10_response.pdf (accessed 5 July 2010).

[261]   Financial Services Authority (1998), 'Consultation Paper 10: Market Abuse Part 1: Consultation on a draft Code of Market Conduct', available at http://www.fsa.gov.uk/pubs/cp/cp10.pdf (accessed 5 July 2010).

[262]   Conceicao, C. (2007), 'The FSA's approach to taking action against market abuse', *Company Lawyer*, **29**(2), 43–45.

[263]   Additionally there have been concerns that the Market Abuse Regime lacks the certainty required by Article 7 ECHR.

[264]   Joint Committee on Financial Services and Markets (1999), First Report, para 264, available at http://www.publications.parliament.uk/pa/jt199899/jtselect/jtfinser/328/32809.htm (accessed 8 July 2010).

[265]   *Ibid.*, at para 265.

> In our view, it would be very surprising if the Article 6 protections which plainly apply to the criminal offence of insider trading were not to apply to the very similar offences of misuse of privileged information.[266]

They also felt that there was insufficient distinction between the custodial sanction in the criminal provisions of the CJA and Financial Services Act 1986, and the financial penalties in the Market Abuse Regime, and that the nature and severity of the penalty also points to the criminal nature of the market abuse offences.[267] The concerns led the government to make significant amendments to the regime to include protections. The issue has now been subject to judicial commentary in the *Fleurose* case which although involving the FSA's predecessor authority, the Securities and Futures Authority, is nevertheless instructive.[268] The case involved a securities trader who was suspended from the register and ordered to pay £175 000. He subsequently applied for and was refused judicial review. At first instance Morison J considered the leading European Court of Human Rights case on the classification of civil or criminal provisions in *Engel v Netherlands*.[269] The consideration applied was whether the contracting state has classified the case as subject to disciplinary law or criminal law, what is the nature of the offence charged, and what is the nature and severity of the penalty that was or might be imposed. After a thorough investigation of the authorities Morison J dismissed the appeal, feeling that on balance the proceedings should be classified as civil in nature. Fleurose further applied to the Court of Appeal against this refusal on the grounds that the disciplinary hearings had involved the determination of a criminal charge and that his right to a fair trial had been impinged; both in contravention of his Article 6 ECHR rights. The Court of Appeal dismissed his appeal on the basis that the proceedings of the Securities and Futures Exchange had not involved the determination of a criminal charge.[270] Interestingly, the Financial Services and Markets Tribunal in *Davidson and Tatham*[271]

---

[266] Joint Committee on Financial Services and Markets above, n 264 at annex C, para 32.

[267] *Ibid.*, Annex C, paras 34 and 35.

[268] *R. (On the application of Fleurose) v Securities and Futures Authority Ltd* [2001] EWCA Civ 2015; [2002] IRLR 297.

[269] [1976] 1 EHRR 647. *Queen v Securities and Futures Authority Ltd. Disciplinary Appeal Tribunal of the Securities and Futures Authority Limited, ex parte Bertrand Fleurose* [2001] EWHC Admin 292; [2001] 2 All ER (Comm) 481.

[270] *Ibid.*

[271] Financial Services and Markets Tribunal Case 031, available at http://www.tribunals.gov.uk/financeandtax/Documents/decisions/FSMTribunal/DavidsonAndTatham.pdf (accessed 7 July 2010).

concluded that the penalty for market abuse is a criminal charge for the purposes of Article 6 ECHR,[272] however, the Tribunal concluded that Article 6 did not deal with the burden of proof:

> although we have decided that these are criminal charges for the purposes of Article 6, there is no provision in Article 6 that the appropriate standard of proof is the criminal standard. We are of the view that the civil standard of proof is sufficiently strong enough to establish what has to be established in these references.[273]

The Tribunal undertook a thorough investigation of the authorities on how to approach the burden of proof issues in civil cases which are analogous to criminal provisions, noting that in such cases the standard should be amended to take account of the seriousness of the offence and the severity of the sanction, stating:

> In the light of the authorities we conclude that there is a single standard of proof on the balance of probabilities but that it is flexible in its application. The more serious the allegation, or more serious the consequences if the allegation is proved, the stronger must be the evidence before we should find the allegation proved on the balance of probabilities.[274]

In *Davidson and Tatham* the Tribunal concluded that as the allegations and sanctions against the accused were very serious[275] then a strict approach to the standard of proof would be needed, requiring 'cogent evidence to establish'.[276] In the *Parker* case the Tribunal noted 'it is difficult to draw a meaningful distinction between the standard we must apply and the criminal standard'.[277] This approach will undoubtedly make it increasingly difficult to prove that market abuse has taken place, placing in jeopardy the entire raison d'être of the legislation. This would show that where the Tribunal judges the offence to be serious the standard of proof required will be virtually the same as the criminal standard,[278] prompting Alcock to note that 'the standard is unlikely to be much, if any easier than bringing a prosecution'.[279]

---

[272] *Ibid.*

[273] Financial Services and Markets Tribunal Case above, n 271.

[274] *Ibid.*

[275] A penalty of £750000 had been imposed on Davidson and £100000 on Tatham. Financial Services and Markets Tribunal Case above, n 271.

[276] *Ibid.*

[277] Conceicao above, n 262 at 44.

[278] Burger, R. (2007), 'A principled front in the war against market abuse', *Journal of Financial Regulation and Compliance*, **15**(3), 331–336.

[279] Alcock, A. (2007), 'Five years of market abuse', *Company Lawyer*, **28**(6), 163–171, at 164.

5.4.4   Reporting of Suspicious Transactions

The final part of UK policy towards market abuse is the reporting of suspicious transactions and therefore comparisons can be drawn with similar provisions outlined above for money laundering and fraud. The obligation to report suspected dealings of market abuse was a result of the Market Abuse Directive, which was implemented on 1 July 2005. In determining whether or not to report the transaction, the firm or individual must have reasonable grounds of suspicion which is the same test as utilized by the PCA 2002. The FSA has its own rules for the reporting of suspicious transactions which provide that:

> a firm which arranges or executes a transaction with or for a client in a qualifying investment admitted to trading on a prescribed market and which has reasonable grounds to suspect that the transaction might constitute market abuse must notify the FSA without delay.[280]

If a firm or individual does not file a suspicious transaction report the FSA has the ability to impose a financial penalty.

5.5   CONCLUSION

From the above discussion we can see that contrary to some arguments the decision to prohibit insider dealing market abuse behaviour is one that has gained favour and momentum over time.

5.5.1   United States of America

It was doubtful that initial US laws actually meant to prohibit such activity, however through a proactive SEC and a largely co-operative judiciary the practice of insider trading has been tackled with zeal and, in no small measure, ingenuity. The US has adopted a very tough stance towards insider trading, which was criminalized in 1934. However, the criminal provisions were not enforced by the SEC for a number of years. There are many reasons why insider trading criminal provisions were not effectively enforced. For example, this includes the initial judicial attitude towards the interpretation of insider trading. The enforcement powers of the SEC were broadened during the 1980s which resulted in the SEC pursuing more

---

[280]   Financial Services Authority *FSA Handbook – SUP (Supervision)* (Financial Services Authority: London, 2008b) at SUP 15.10.2.

civil penalties against those who breached the insider trading provisions. The SEC, due to the inadequacies of the international insider trading legislative measures, has taken the initiative and has influenced several other countries to criminalize such activities.

5.5.2 United Kingdom

The criminalization of insider dealing in the UK is largely seen as a failure as a result of the high burden of proof required in such difficult evidentiary cases. The attempt to address this perceived failure has come in the form of a civil regime enacted as part of FSMA 2000. Whether or not this regime has more success is difficult to judge even nine years after enactment, partly due to the requirements of the Market Abuse Directive making alterations only four years after it first came into force. It is certainly evident that the level of fines remains high and this coupled with a more aggressive approach taken by the FSA, particularly in respect of criminal prosecutions for insider dealing, should allow it to claim success in its mission, at least in respect of market abuse. However, it is possible to argue that this is largely due to the decision by the coalition government to abolish the FSA by 2012. Challenges will undoubtedly remain. The perception of the victimless crime and the ongoing difficulties in proving the offence will remain problematic areas, especially if the Financial Services and Markets Tribunal applies a criminal standard of proof to the more important cases, an issue which could bring the Market Abuse Regime to a halt. As Rider notes, the compromises in respect of the civil liberties issues have resulted in civil offences as difficult to prove as the criminal ones they were designed to remedy.[281] However, if, as was evident in the US, the FSA and the UK courts maintain the energy and focus displayed in the last few years, then the future augers well for the Market Abuse Regime, albeit with significant challenges.

---

[281] Rider, B. (2010), 'An abominable fraud?', *Company Lawyer*, **31**(7), 197–198.

6. The confiscation and forfeiture of the illicit proceeds of crime

> The first and most important legal tool for depriving offenders of illegal profits is confiscation of the proceeds of crime.[1]

6.1 INTRODUCTION

An integral part of the global financial crime strategy is the ability of law enforcement agencies to deprive organized criminals, drug cartels and terrorists of their illegal earnings. Nelen argued that 'by dismantling their organisations financially, criminals must be hit at their supposedly more vulnerable spot: their assets'.[2] This is a view supported by the Financial Action Task Force (FATF) who noted that:

> a robust system of provisional measures and confiscation is an important part of an effective anti-money laundering and counter-terrorist financing regime. Confiscation prevents criminal property from being laundered or reinvested either to facilitate other forms of crime or to conceal illicit proceeds.[3]

There are a broad range of mechanisms to tackle the proceeds of crime including forfeiture provisions, criminal and civil confiscation regimes and taxation procedures. Forfeiture has been defined as 'the surrender or loss of property or rights without compensation'.[4] There are traditionally

---

[1] Stessens, Guy (2000) *Money laundering: a new international law enforcement model*, Cambridge University Press, Cambridge, at p. 29.

[2] Nelen, H. (2004), 'Hit them where it hurts most? The proceeds of crime approach in the Netherlands', *Crime, Law & Social Change*, **41**(5), 517–534, at 517. Also see Smellie, A. (2004), 'Prosecutorial challenges in freezing and forfeiting proceeds of transnational crime and the use of international asset sharing to promote international cooperation', *Journal of Money Laundering Control*, **8**(2), 104–114, at 104.

[3] Financial Action Task Force *Best Practices Confiscation (Recommendations 3 and 38)* (Financial Action Task Force: Paris, 2010) at p. 3.

[4] Gallant, Michelle (2005) *Money laundering and the proceeds of crime*, Edward Elgar, Cheltenham, at p. 54.

four types of forfeiture: criminal forfeiture,[5] the forfeiture of items related to convictions,[6] the forfeiture of objects *malem in se*[7] and civil forfeiture.[8] It is important to note that forfeiture 'has now become an integral part of the confiscation regimes which are defined as a governmental decision through which property rights can be affected as a consequence of a criminal offence'.[9] The United Nations (UN) Convention against Illicit Traffic in Narcotic Drugs and Psychotropic Substances, or Vienna Convention, provides that confiscation is 'the permanent deprivation of property by order of a court or other competent authority'.[10] There are three types of confiscation – confiscation of the proceeds of the instrumentalities of crime, confiscation of the *objectum sceleris* and confiscation of the proceeds of crime.[11] It is not the intention of this chapter to provide a detailed historical account of the evolution of these powers but to provide a critique of their effectiveness.[12]

The ability to forfeit or confiscate the proceeds of crime provides law enforcement agencies with an effective, yet controversial weapon against organized criminals. The international measures that permit the confiscation of illicit profits include the Vienna Convention,[13] Council of Europe Convention on Laundering, Search, Seizure and Confiscation of the Proceeds from Crime 1990,[14] the International Convention for

---

[5]   Criminal forfeiture was abolished by virtue of the Forfeiture Act 1870.

[6]   See for example Misuse of Drugs Act 1971, s. 27.

[7]   This forfeiture measure ensures the removal of dangerous and prohibited goods from the public domain.

[8]   These powers have been extensively used in customs legislation. See Proceeds of Crime Act 2002, s. 298.

[9]   Stessens above, n 1 at 30.

[10]   United Nations Convention against Illicit Traffic in Narcotic Drugs and Psychotropic Substances, 20 December 1988, 1582 UNTS 165, 170, Article 1(f). Forfeiture has also been referred to as the power granted to a court 'to take property that is immediately connected with an offence'. See Oxford Analytica Ltd (2004), 'Country report: anti-money laundering rules in the United Kingdom' in M. Pieith and G. Aiolfi (eds), *A comparative guide to anti-money laundering: a critical analysis of systems in Singapore, Switzerland, the UK and the USA*, Edward Elgar, Cheltenham, pp. 265–345, at 290.

[11]   Stessens above, n 1 at 30. Confiscation is defined as 'depriving the offender of the proceeds or profits of crime'. *Ibid.*

[12]   For a more detailed account of the history of the use of forfeiture see Gallant above, n 4 at 54–74.

[13]   United Nations Convention against Illicit Traffic in Narcotic Drugs and Psychotropic Substances, 20 December 1988, 1582 UNTS 165, 170.

[14]   European Treaty Series – No. 141, Strasbourg, 8.XI.1990.

the Suppression of the Financing of Terrorism 1999,[15] UN Convention Against Transnational Organized Crime 2000,[16] the UN Convention against Corruption 2003,[17] the Council of Europe Convention on Laundering, Search, Seizure and Confiscation of the Proceeds from Crime and on the Financing of Terrorism 2005[18] and UN Security Council Resolution 1373/2001.[19] The US forfeiture measures are to be found in the Comprehensive Drug Abuse Prevention and Control Act 1970,[20] the Comprehensive Crime Control Act 1984, the Civil Asset Forfeiture Reform Act 2000 and the USA Patriot Act 2001. The UK provisions regarding confiscation came into existence as a result of the decision *R v Cuthbertson*,[21] and are contained in the Proceeds of Crime Act 2002 (PCA).[22] The ability to confiscate the proceeds of crime has become an integral part of the financial crime policies in the US and the UK. However, its use has been criticized because in some circumstances there is no need for a criminal trial and it has been described as 'legalized theft' and 'unconstitutional'. The next part of the chapter illustrates the strategy adopted by the UN and the European Union (EU) towards the confiscation of the proceeds of crime.

6.2 INTERNATIONAL COMMUNITY

The international community has recognized the importance of tackling the proceeds of crime and has implemented a series of legal measures.[23] Commentators have argued that such measures are an integral part of

---

[15] Adopted by the General Assembly of the United Nations in resolution 54/109 of 9 December 1999.

[16] Adopted by the General Assembly of the United Nations in its resolution 55/25 of 15 November 2000. This is commonly referred to as the Palermo Convention.

[17] General Assembly resolution 58/4 of 31 October 2003.

[18] Council of Europe Treaty Series – No. 198, Warsaw, 16.V.2005.

[19] SC Res. 1373, UN SCOR, 56th Sess., 4385th Mtg. Article 1(a).

[20] Blumenson, E. and Nilsen, E. (1998), 'Policing for profit: the drug war's hidden economic agenda', *University of Chicago Law Review*, **65**, 35–114, at 37.

[21] [1981] AC 470.

[22] It is important to note that confiscation measures relating to terrorism are contained in the Terrorism Act 2000 and the Anti-terrorism, Crime and Security Act 2001.

[23] Verbruggen, F. (1997), 'Proceeds-orientated criminal justice in Belgium: backbone or wishbone of a modern approach to organised crime?', *European Journal of Crime, Criminal Law and Criminal Justice*, **5**(3), 314–341, at 317.

the battle against organized crime and terrorism.[24] The first measure, the Vienna Convention, provides that signatories should adopt measures to enable the restraint, seizure and confiscation of the proceeds and instruments of drug trafficking.[25] The scope of the requirements is limited to the laundering of drug proceeds, not of the proceeds of other criminal offences.[26] Sproule and Saint-Denis took the view that the provisions of the Vienna Convention 'can be properly viewed as a major breakthrough in attacking the benefits derived from drug trafficking activities and are a forceful endorsement of the notion that attacking the profit motive is essential if the struggle against drug trafficking is to be effective'.[27] The Palermo Convention stated that signatories should implement measures to permit the confiscation of the proceeds of criminal offences created by the Convention and to include 'property, equipment or other instrumentalities used in or destined for use in offences covered by this Convention'.[28] The ambit of the Council of Europe Convention on Laundering, Search, Seizure and the Confiscation of the Proceeds of Crime was broader than the scope of the Vienna Convention because it applied to the confiscation of the proceeds of *any* offence.[29] It stated that 'each Party shall adopt such legislative and other measures as may be necessary to enable it to confiscate instrumentalities and proceeds or property the value of which corresponds to such proceeds'.[30] The scope of the international confiscation measures was extended by the International Convention for the Suppression of the Financing of Terrorism. This provides that signatories should take appropriate measures for the identification, detection, freezing or seizure of any funds

---

[24] See for example Young, Simon (2009a), 'Civil forfeiture for Hong Kong: issues and prospects', in S. Young (ed.), *Civil forfeiture of criminal property – legal measures for targeting the proceeds of crime*, Edward Elgar, Cheltenham, at pp. 278–320. Indeed, Borgers and Moors stated that 'the legislation on confiscation of the proceeds of crime has developed into an important instrument in the fight against all forms of crime. This development was stimulated to no small degree by the drafting of various international treaties and conventions'. See Borgers, M. and Moors, J. (2007), 'Targeting the proceeds of crime: bottlenecks in international cooperation', *European Journal of Crime*, **15**(1), 1–22, at 1.

[25] UN Convention Against the Illicit Traffic in Narcotic Drugs and Psychotropic Substances, or the Vienna Convention (1988), article 5.

[26] Stessens above, n 1 at 23.

[27] Sproule, D. and Saint-Denis, P. (1989), 'The UN Drug Trafficking Convention: an ambitious step', in *Canadian year book of international law* p. 263.

[28] UN Convention Against Transnational Organized Crime (2000), article 12.

[29] Stessens above, n 1 at 30.

[30] The Council of Europe Convention on Laundering, Search, Seizure and Confiscation of the Proceeds from Crime (1990), article 2.

for the purposes of possible forfeiture.[31] Furthermore, UN Security Council Resolution 1373 was implemented to tackle terrorist financing in response to the terrorist attacks in 2001.[32] In 2003, the UN Convention Against Corruption extended the scope of the confiscation procedures to corruption and other offences created by the Convention.[33] In addition to these measures, the FATF provides that:

> countries should adopt measures . . . including legislative measures, to enable their competent authorities to confiscate property laundered, proceeds from money laundering or predicate offences, instrumentalities used in or intended for use in the commission of these offences, or property of corresponding value, without prejudicing the rights of bona fide third parties.[34]

The Council of Europe Convention on Laundering, Search, Seizure and Confiscation of the Proceeds from Crime and on the Financing of Terrorism provides that signatories should implement legislation that permits the confiscation of 'instrumentalities and proceeds or property the value of which corresponds to such proceeds and laundered property'.[35] These measures have been implemented by the international community in recognition of the problems caused by organized criminals, drug cartels and terrorists. Furthermore, these measures are 'concerned not so much with punishing individuals for their past wrongs but with achieving specific criminal justice objectives including disgorging offenders of their ill-gotten gains, disabling the financial capability of criminal organisations and compensating victims of crime'.[36] The international instruments also recognize the increasing levels of sophistication for organized criminals who wish to disguise their wealth, money launderers who want to distance themselves from their criminal activities and terrorists pursuing their illegal goals. It has also been argued that there

---

[31]   International Convention for the Suppression of the Financing of Terrorism (1999), article 8.

[32]   Young above, n 24 at 280.

[33]   UN Convention Against Corruption (2003), article 31. For a more detailed analysis and commentary see Webb, P. (2005), 'The United Nations Convention Against Corruption – global achievement or missed opportunity?', *Journal of International Economic Law*, **8**(1), 191–229.

[34]   Financial Action Task Force above, n 3.

[35]   Council of Europe Convention on Laundering, Search, Seizure and Confiscation of the Proceeds from Crime and on the Financing of Terrorism (2005), article 3.

[36]   Young, Simon (2009b), 'Introduction', in S. Young (ed.), *Civil forfeiture of criminal property – legal measures for targeting the proceeds of crime*, Edward Elgar, Cheltenham, pp. 1–10, at 1.

is a 'consensus among the international law enforcement community that the epic scale of money laundering and profitability of organised crime in general can be dismantled by the co-ordinated and aggressive pursuit of asset recovery'.[37] The international community has recognized the weaknesses in the respective criminal justice systems and introduced the controversial civil confiscation and forfeiture regimes. It is clear that the measures introduced by the international community to permit the confiscation of illicit proceeds of crime have influenced the stance adopted by the US and the UK. The next part of the chapter reviews the use of forfeiture powers in the US where it has become the linchpin of their fight against drug cartels, organized criminals and terrorists.

6.3   THE UNITED STATES OF AMERICA

The United States has led the world in anti-crime legislation and enforcement action by targeting the proceeds of crimes. The array of the US legal instruments and powers is equalled in no other country.[38]

Civil forfeiture laws have been an integral part of the US anti-crime strategy since 1789.[39] However, the introduction of criminal forfeiture provisions in the 1970s was linked with the US-led 'war on drugs'.[40] Gallant took the view that 'the primary instrument the US used to attack the financial element of crime is forfeiture'.[41] Law enforcement agencies use the forfeiture provisions because of imposed budgetary restrictions, the pursuit of economic self-sufficiency and a change of policy from targeting crimes to pursuing illegally obtained assets.[42] The forfeiture powers also act as a deterrent,[43] a view outlined by Cassella who noted that 'there

---

[37]   Rees, Edward, and Fisher, Richard (2008) *Blackstone's guide to the Proceeds of Crime Act 2002*, Oxford University Press, Oxford, at p. 1.

[38]   Evans, J. (1996), 'International money laundering: enforcement challenges and opportunities', *Southwestern Journal of Law and Trade in the Americas*, **2**, 195–221, at 197.

[39]   Cassella, Stefan (2009), 'An overview of asset forfeiture in the United States', in S. Young (ed.), *Civil forfeiture of criminal property – legal measures for targeting the proceeds of crime*, Edward Elgar, Cheltenham, pp. 23–51, at 24.

[40]   Blumenson and Nilsen above, n 20 at 35.

[41]   Gallant above, n 4 at 75.

[42]   Blumenson and Nilsen above, n 20 at 40.

[43]   See Blanchard, A. (2006), 'The next step in interpreting criminal forfeiture', *Cardozo Law Review*, **28**, 1415–1445, at 1422–1423.

is also the matter of the message that is sent to the community of law abiding citizens when a notorious gangster or fraud artist is stripped of the trappings of what may have appeared to be an enviable lifestyle'.[44] The forfeiture provisions have also been used to compensate the victims of crime by recovering property lost as a result of the criminal activity.[45] A comparison can be made between the forfeiture provisions and the US money laundering and fraud measures already discussed in this book. Namely, that there are multiple statutes that permit the forfeiture of the proceeds of a wide range of criminal offences. There is no generic statute that allows the forfeiture of either instruments used in the crime or part of the profits resulting from the offence. Therefore, forfeiture is only possible when allowed by a specific law. Cassella took the view that 'most federal criminal statutes now authorize the forfeiture of assets as part of the punishment that may be imposed when a defendant is convicted'.[46]

6.3.1   Forfeiture Legislation

The US legislative approach to the forfeiture of the proceeds of crime is ingrained with its battle against drugs.[47] Gallant took the view that this approach was 'vigorously endorsed by the Reagan administration'.[48] To counter these problems Congress decided to excavate the criminal forfeiture provisions in the 1970s to tackle the 'war on drugs'[49] and the battle against organized crime.[50] The Racketeer Influenced and Corrupt Organizations Act (RICO) was introduced as part of the Organized Crime and Control Act 1970, and it had two objectives. Firstly, to restrict the growth of criminal enterprises. Importantly, the Act referred to the term 'proceeds which is thought to encompass all property purchased with and traceable to criminal profits, including any appreciation in the value

---

[44]   Cassella above, n 39 at 31–32.

[45]   *Ibid.*, at 31.

[46]   Cassella, S. (2004c), 'The forfeiture of property involved in money laundering offences', *Buffalo Criminal Law Review*, **7**, 583–660, at 585.

[47]   See Johnson, B. (2002), 'Restoring civility – the Civil Asset Forfeiture Reform Act 2000: baby steps towards a more civilised civil forfeiture system', *Indiana Law Review*, **35**, 1045–1085.

[48]   Gallant above, n 4 at 74.

[49]   See Garretson, H. (2008), 'Federal criminal forfeiture: a royal pain in the assets', *Southern California Review of Law & Social Justice*, **18**, 45–77, at 46.

[50]   Linn, C. (2004), 'International asset forfeiture and the Constitution: the limits of forfeiture jurisdiction over foreign assets under 28 U.S.C. § 1355(B)(2)', *American Journal of Criminal Law*, **31**, 251–303, at 255–256.

not attributable to a criminal activity'.[51] However, the Supreme Court in *United States v Santos* restricted the interpretation of proceeds to 'net profits, not gross receipts, of unlawful activity'.[52] Secondly, to target the so-called 'kingpins of crime'.[53] It has also been argued that another purpose of the Act was to 'slow the infiltration of organised crime into legitimate business organisations'.[54] RICO allows for the forfeiture of 'property acquired or maintained through the racketeering activity and any interest that the defendant has in the racketeering enterprise itself'.[55] Furthermore, the Comprehensive Drug Abuse and Prevention Act 1970[56] and the Organized Crime Control Act 1970 attempted to revive the use of civil *in rem* forfeitures in the battle against drugs.[57] The Organized Crime Control Act criminalized racketeering participation in commercial ventures and imposed a maximum prison sentence of 25 years, a \$25 000 fine and permitted the forfeiture of 'all interests held in contravention of the statute'.[58] The Department of Justice is permitted to bring civil forfeiture proceedings against illegal goods or property that was either used or

---

[51]   Stessens above, n 1 at 51.

[52]   128, S. Ct. 2020, 2025, 2031 (2008). Gurule took the view that the decision of the Supreme Court 'restricts the scope of the money laundering statute'. See Gurule, J. (2009a), 'Does "proceeds" really mean "net profits"? The Supreme Court efforts to diminish the utility of the federal money laundering statute', *Ave Maria Law Review*, **7**, 339–390, at 339.

[53]   Gallant above, n 4 at 77.

[54]   Malani, A. (1999), 'The scope of criminal forfeiture under RICO: the appropriate definition of "proceeds"', *University of Chicago Law Review*, **66**, 1289–1316, at 1296.

[55]   Cassella, above n 39 at 36. For a more detailed discussion about RICO see Tarlow, B. (1983), 'RICO revisited', *Georgia Law Review*, **17**, 291–424.

[56]   18 USC § 1963. For an interesting historical account of this law see Schecter, M. (1990), 'Fear and loathing and the forfeiture laws', *Cornell Law Review*, **75**, 1151–1183, at 1155–1157.

[57]   Pub. L. No. 91-513, 1970 U.S.C.C.A.N (84 Stat.) 1437 (codified as amended at 21 USC § 801-971). It is important to note that the 'War on Drugs' was instigated by President Nixon in 1973 and it has been described as an 'extraordinary failure'. See Blumenson and Nilsen above, n 20 at 37. However, numerous declarations of war on drugs have been made by successive administrations. See for example Durkin, C. (1990), 'Civil forfeiture under federal narcotics law: the impact of the shifting burden of proof upon the Fifth Amendment privilege against self-incrimination', *Suffolk University Law Review*, **24**, 679–705, at 679.

[58]   For a detailed discussion of the historical development of forfeiture law in the US see Maxeiner, J. (1977), 'Bane of American Forfeiture Law: Banished at Last?', *Cornell Law Review*, **62**(4), 768–802, at 792–793.

obtained whilst breaking federal narcotics laws.[59] These provisions were unproductive because they were restricted to people who were convicted of involvement in a 'continuing criminal enterprise'.[60] The forfeiture laws were extended in 1978 to include the criminal proceeds derived from the sale of narcotics.[61] The Comprehensive Crime Control Act 1984 broadened the provisions to include 'real property' purchased with the illegal proceeds.[62] It has been argued that this 'amendment greatly expanded the policy and scope of civil forfeiture by authorising *in rem* actions, which provide few of the constitutional guarantees that are attached to criminal indictment'.[63]

Importantly, the Comprehensive Crime Control Act allows the proceeds of civil forfeiture to be placed in a special forfeiture fund held at the Department of Justice and the Department of Treasury.[64] The Act also introduced the equitable sharing programme that allowed law enforcement agencies to share a large proportion of the seized or forfeited assets.[65] The National Assets Seizure and Forfeiture Fund has proved to be successful; by the 1990s, $500m was annually deposited and nearly $1.4bn of property was held.[66] The Asset Forfeiture Programme, which is administered by the Department of Justice, 'plays a critical and key role in disrupting and dismantling illegal enterprises, depriving criminals of the proceeds of illegal activity, deterring crime, and restoring

---

[59]   21 USC § 881(a). The Act also applied to money, negotiable instruments, securities, items of value and property that was used for criminal purposes. See Petrou, P. (1984), 'Due process implications of shifting the burden of proof in forfeiture proceedings arising out of illegal drug transactions', *Duke Law Journal*, September, 822–843, at 824. For a detailed discussion of the interpretation of section 881 see Speta, J. (1990), 'Narrowing the scope of civil drug forfeiture: section 881, substantial connection and the Eighth Amendment', *Michigan Law Review*, **89**, 165–210.

[60]   Nelson, S. (1994), 'The Supreme Court takes a weapon from the drug war arsenal: new defences to civil drug forfeiture', *Saint Mary's Law Journal*, **26**, 157–201, at 159.

[61]   21 USC §§ 801–969 (1982) 881(a).

[62]   Saltzburg, D. (1992), 'Real property forfeitures as a weapon in the government's war on drugs: a failure to protect innocent ownerships', *Boston University Law Review*, **72**, 217–242, at 218.

[63]   Nelson above, n 60 at 159–160.

[64]   Johnson above, n 47 at 1049–1050.

[65]   Stessens above, n 1 at 57.

[66]   Stahl, M. (2009), 'Asset forfeiture, burdens of proof and the war on drugs', *Journal of Criminal Law and Criminology*, **83**, 274–337, at 274–275. Cassella noted that the figure was $600m per year. See Cassella above, n 39 at 23.

property to victims'.[67] Since 2006, over \$2bn has been forfeited by virtue of the Asset Forfeiture Programme.[68] The fund has been assisted by the National Asset Forfeiture Strategic Plan.[69] The mission of the Strategic Plan is to:

1. provide a strategic framework to enhance the capability, reach, and effectiveness of the Programme;
2. provide direction to the asset forfeiture community to ensure that the Programme's mission is carried out effectively and efficiently;
3. enable Programme participants to manage and expand this important and vital law enforcement tool;
4. ensure maximum participation by all Programme participants and determine appropriate areas of growth; and
5. advocate for the resources needed to support and grow the Programme.[70]

The Plan has four intentional objectives that seek to increase the efficiency of asset forfeiture – communication, programme resources, case development and execution, and programme growth.[71]

The new millennium saw the introduction of the Civil Asset Forfeiture Act (2000) and the USA Patriot Act 2001. The 2000 Act applies to all civil forfeiture proceedings started on or after 23 August 2000, and it represented the most significant amendment to the US forfeiture laws since 1789.[72] The Act made a number of significant changes to the civil forfeiture laws.[73] Firstly, it introduced a series of technical requirements that federal agencies must comply with. Secondly, the 2000 Act established measures for employing legal representation for impoverished defendants.[74] Thirdly, the Act made some significant changes to the burden of

---

[67] Department of Justice *National Asset Forfeiture Strategic Plan 2008–2012* (Department of Justice: Washington, DC, 2008b) at p. 5.

[68] *Ibid.*, at p. 3.

[69] *Ibid.*, at p. 3.

[70] *Ibid.*, at p. 7.

[71] *Ibid.*, at p. 9.

[72] Cassella, S. (2001), 'The Civil Asset Forfeiture Reform Act of 2000: expanded government forfeiture authority and strict deadlines imposed on all parties', *Journal of Legislation*, **27**, 97–151, at 97.

[73] Johnson above, n 47 at 1070–1072.

[74] Chi noted that the forfeiture laws prior to the 2000 Act failed to 'provide legal representation for defendants, as guaranteed by the Sixth Amendment'. Chi, K. (2002), 'Follow the money: getting to the root of the problem with civil asset forfeiture in California', *California Law Review*, **90**, 1635–1673, at 1641.

proof, which demands the government to meet 'a preponderance of the evidence standard'.[75] Prior to the introduction of the Act, 'all property was deemed forfeit once the government showed probable cause that the property was used to facilitate a narcotics crime or was derived from a narcotics crime'.[76] Fourthly, the 'innocent owner' requirement has been retained. Fifthly, the Act 'contains provisions that allow a claimant to petition the presiding court for a determination of whether the forfeiture violates the Excessive Fines Clause of the Eighth Amendment'.[77] The 2000 Act modernized the US forfeiture laws, yet despite the safeguards outlined above, faults remain.[78] For example, the dubious motivation or 'perverse incentives' of law enforcement agencies[79] towards appropriating property for their own gain remains questionable.[80] This is supported by several examples where law enforcement agencies have confiscated property from people who have not been charged with any criminal offences.[81] The Act has not resulted in a decrease in the amount of money forfeited and it has been argued that it 'has not proven to be an obstacle to federal law enforcement agencies. In fact, most people familiar with the program agree that the number of forfeitures is set to rise'.[82]

Following the terrorist attacks in 2001, the USA Patriot Act 2001 extended the ability of the federal government and law enforcement agencies to seize and forfeit the assets of terrorists.[83] Gallant noted that the terrorist attacks 'pushed terrorism to the top of the crime control agenda, rivalling, if not overtaking, the illegal drugs trade as the foremost evil in need of immediate attendance'.[84] The extensive scope of the forfeiture powers under the 2001 Act were noted by Cassella:

---

[75]   Johnson above, n 47 at 1075.

[76]   *Ibid.*, at p. 1058.

[77]   *Ibid.*, at p. 1072.

[78]   Cassella above, n 72 at 150–151.

[79]   Moores, E. (2009), 'Reforming the Civil Asset Forfeiture Reform Act', *Arizona Law Review*, **51**, 777–803, at 786.

[80]   Johnson above, n 47 at 1070–1074.

[81]   See for example the story of Luther and Meredith Ricks as cited in Moores above, n 79 at 782.

[82]   *Ibid.*, at pp. 783–784.

[83]   Cassella, S. (2002), 'Forfeiture of terrorist assets under the USA Patriot Act of 2001', *Law and Policy in International Business*, **34**, 7–15, at 7. For a more detailed discussion of these powers see Thomas, J. and Roppolo, W. (2010) 'United States of America', in M. Simpson, N. Smith and A. Srivastave (eds), *International guide to money laundering law and practice*, Bloomsbury Professional, Haywards Heath, pp. 1095–1138, at 1128–1133.

[84]   Gallant above, n 4 at 105.

once the government establishes that a person, entity, or organisation is engaged in terrorism against the United States, its citizens or residents, or their property, the government can seize and ultimately mandate forfeiture of all assets, foreign or domestic, of the terrorist entity, whether those assets are connected to terrorism or not.[85]

The 2001 Act permits forfeiture of all assets, whether overseas or national, involved in arranging acts of terrorism, assets retained or obtained for the purposes of conducting acts of terrorism.[86] Civil and criminal forfeiture is permitted in terrorist cases for all of the proceeds of all specified activities including support and the financing of terrorism,[87] terrorist activities[88] and for collecting or providing funds for terrorist purposes.[89] Gallant took the view that 'terrorism is to the Bush administration what illegal drugs were to President Ronald Reagan. In organising its response to the destruction of 2001, the Bush administration immediately implemented a proceeds-orientated strategy whose target was the financial component of terrorist activity'.[90]

6.3.2 What can be Forfeited?

There are three types of forfeiture procedures available in the US: administrative forfeiture, criminal forfeiture and civil forfeiture. Administrative forfeiture is the most popular procedure and it relates to unchallenged cases which are pursued by federal law enforcement agencies as a 'non judicial' matter that results in the court ordering the transfer of title to the government.[91] Administrative forfeiture is limited to four categories of assets:

1. where its value does not exceed $500 000 per item;
2. where its importation is illegal;
3. where it is a means of transport used in moving or storing controlled substances; and
4. where it is currency or a monetary instrument of any value.[92]

---

85 Cassella above, n 83 at 8.
86 Gallant above, n 4 at 105.
87 Title 18 USC §§2339A, 2339B and 2339C.
88 Title 18 USC § 981(a)(1)(g).
89 Title 18 USC § 981(a)(1)(h).
90 Gallant above, n 4 at 75.
91 Cassella, S. (2004b), 'Overview of asset forfeiture law in the United States', *South African Journal of Criminal Justice*, **17**(3), 347–367, at 353.
92 18 USC § 983(a)(1) and (2) and 19 USC § 1602.

Administrative forfeiture proceedings are brought by the seizing agency, while judicial proceedings are brought before a judge. Criminal and civil forfeitures are 'judicial matters, requiring the commencement of a formal action in a federal court'.[93] Criminal forfeiture is an integral part of a criminal case which is imposed by a court on the defendant, once convicted.[94] This is also referred to as *in personam*, which means that it is against the individual; it involves the prosecution indicting the property used in or obtained with the proceeds of the illegal activity. If the defendant is found guilty, criminal forfeiture proceedings are conducted in court before a judge and they could result in a decision of forfeiting property either used or obtained in the crime. Furthermore, the defendant will be required to pay a financial penalty, recompense the victims, and disgorge the proceeds of the crime or the property utilized in the commission of the criminal offence.[95] Therefore, criminal forfeiture proceedings are part of the sentencing practice[96] and have been described as 'a powerful law enforcement tool that is rapidly becoming a fixture in federal criminal practice'.[97] US law provides for the forfeiture of the proceeds of over 200 federal and state crimes.[98] This includes the federal offences of fraud and theft, whilst at a state level examples include arson, robbery, gambling and drug trafficking offences.[99] The courts have extensive powers to confiscate the drug proceeds and any personal or real property utilized in the commission of a drug offence.[100] The most potent forfeiture provisions apply to money laundering, which allows the forfeiture of all the property involved in the commission of the money laundering offence.[101]

---

[93]   Cassella above, n 39 at 35.

[94]   The US criminal forfeiture statute is found at 18 USC § 982.

[95]   Cassella, S. (2008), 'The case for civil recovery: why in rem proceedings are an essential tool for recovering the proceeds of crime', *Journal of Money Laundering Control*, **11**(1), 8–14, at 9.

[96]   Cassella above, n 91 at 355.

[97]   Cassella, S. (2004a), 'Criminal forfeiture procedure: an analysis of developments in the law regarding the inclusion of a forfeiture judgment in the sentence imposed in a criminal case', *American Journal of Criminal Law*, **32**, 55–103, at 102–103.

[98]   18 USC § 981(a)(1)(c).

[99]   Cassella above, n 39 at 33. These measures can also be used for violations of the Trafficking Victims Protection Act (2000); see Soto, J. (2004), 'Show me the money: the application of the asset forfeiture provisions of the Trafficking Victims Protection Act and suggestions for the future', *Penn State International Law Review*, **23**, 365–381.

[100]   Under 21 USC §§ 853(a) and 881(a) (Criminal and civil forfeiture respectively).

[101]   Cassella above, n 39 at 35.

Civil forfeiture is the most controversial forfeiture provision.[102] The action is taken *in rem*, and is taken against the property, not the defendant, or *in personam*. This means that the government acts as a civil plaintiff and anybody who challenges the proceedings is referred to as the claimant.[103] The proceedings are a separate action from any criminal proceedings against the defendant. The Supreme Court in *United States v Various Items of Personal Property* stated that 'it [in rem] is the property which is proceeded against and, by resort to a legal fiction, held guilty and condemned as though it were conscious instead of inanimate and insentient'.[104] Stessens noted that 'the concept of civil forfeiture logically follows from relation-back doctrine; given the fact that the state is, by legal fiction, deemed to be the owner of the property from the moment the offence was committed'.[105] Civil forfeiture permits the government to control property that has been obtained with the proceeds of illegal activities or used in conjunction with drug-related offences.[106] Maxeiner stated that 'theoretically, the owner is not punished because the forfeiture is directed against the property'.[107] Therefore, it is dependent on the myth that the property is capable of illegal behaviour.[108]

Civil forfeiture proceedings are extremely popular with law enforcement agencies. For instance, if prosecutors are unable to obtain a criminal conviction they are able to initiate proceedings against property and not the defendant.[109] Cassella surmised that civil forfeiture proceedings are beneficial to law enforcement agencies because they require a lower burden of proof and there is no need for a criminal conviction.[110] Civil forfeiture proceedings are popular amongst law enforcement agencies because they are an 'easy way to deprive criminals of the fruits of their acts'.[111] Their popularity has led to accusations that the 'government may be tempted to 'fill its coffers' by seizing property for minor offenses'.[112] Stessens was extremely critical of these measures and stated that 'it is fundamentally wrong to investigate and prosecute criminal activities with a view to the financial profits arising from them will accrue to government'.[113]

---

[102] The civil forfeiture statute is found at 18 USC § 981.
[103] Cassella above, n 83 at 9.
[104] 82 US 577, 581 as cited in Stessens above, n 1 at 39.
[105] *Ibid.*, at p. 41.
[106] Saltzburg, above n 62 at 217.
[107] Maxeiner above, n 58 at 768.
[108] Gallant above, n 4 at 83.
[109] Chi above, n 74 at 1639–1640.
[110] Cassella above, n 91 at 360–362.
[111] Moores above, n 79 at 779.
[112] Johnson above, n 47 at 1069.
[113] Stessens above, n 1 at 57.

The problems associated with civil forfeiture relate to burdensome procedural requirements, and that the forfeiture is 'limited to property traceable to the offence', which in many instances is impossible to determine.[114] Other criticisms include the potential unfair treatment of so-called 'innocent owners' whose property could be forfeited because of the illegal activity of another party which they could not have anticipated.[115] Indeed, Chi noted that:

> civil asset forfeiture in the United States has evolved from a rarely employed legal fiction into the favourite weapon in the arsenal of law enforcement agencies. For all its constitutional implications, the fundamental defect of civil asset forfeiture is economic, not procedural. Procedural reform of the process, however progressive, will promote little actual change in the absence of a transformation of the financial incentives that motivate law enforcement groups to find and employ loopholes at the local and federal levels.[116]

It has also been argued that the use of civil forfeiture procedures violates the Double Jeopardy clause of the US Constitution when it is used in conjunction with a criminal prosecution.[117] Similarly, Nelson argued that 'civil drug forfeiture is an important weapon in the war on drugs. However, the broad language of the Forfeiture Statute, coupled with the zealousness of the drug war, erodes important constitutional safeguards'.[118] Meyer took the view that 'while civil forfeiture may be an effective tactic, in many cases it is not a fair one'.[119]

6.3.3   Conclusion

US forfeiture laws have become an integral part of its fight against organized crime, drug cartels and terrorism. The use of such powers is very popular amongst law enforcement agencies because it is a means to generate revenue and, in effect, permits these agencies to become self-sufficient.[120] It is extremely difficult to determine whether or not these

---

[114]   Cassella above, n 91 at 362–363.
[115]   Johnson above, n 47 at 1054.
[116]   Chi above, n 74 at 16.
[117]   However, this argument has been dismissed by the Supreme Court in *United States v Ursery* (1996) 518 US 267.
[118]   Nelson above, n 60 at 200.
[119]   Meyer, C. (1991), 'Zero tolerance for forfeiture: a call for reform of civil forfeiture law', *Notre Dame Journal of Law, Ethics and Public Policy*, **5**, 853–887, at 854.
[120]   Gallant above, n 4 at 76.

measures are successful. Indeed, Gallant concluded that 'having long embarked on the strategy, whether the United States' proceeds orientated mechanism achieves any tangible results is problematic'.[121] The FATF stated that:

> the US has made a priority of the recovery of criminal assets and is systematically and vigorously pursuing seizure and confiscation. To achieve that goal law enforcement can count on a comprehensive and solid legal basis, and on the support of specialists. The forfeiture system is quite flexible to offer the possibility to use the most effective and adequate procedure: civil, criminal or administrative. If the money laundering statutes are not applicable or suitable for any reason, there are a series of related penal provisions the authorities can and do use frequently to recover the criminal assets.[122]

Evidently, law enforcement agencies prefer to use the civil forfeiture procedures for a number of contentious reasons; for example, the lower burden of proof required and that there is no need to successfully obtain a criminal conviction. More importantly, the civil forfeiture route does not offer the same level of constitutional safeguards as the criminal forfeiture procedures. Therefore, it is imperative that an appropriate balance is achieved between protecting the constitutional rights of the accused whilst allowing law enforcement agencies the ability to tackle the problems associated with drugs, organized crime and terrorism. This is an impossible objective to achieve and it is likely, as terrorists and organized criminals continue to show increasing levels of sophistication to hide their illicit gains, that law enforcement agencies will continue to excessively use forfeiture powers.

The use of forfeiture powers has revolutionized law enforcement in the US and they have contributed towards the urgent desire of law enforcement agencies to become self-sufficient. Cassella noted that 'by making judicious and strategic use of the various procedures, federal prosecutors can greatly enhance their ability to control and deter criminal activity and to recover the proceeds of crime for the benefit of the victim'.[123] In its 2006 Mutual Evaluation Report the FATF concluded that the 'US system for freezing, seizing and forfeiture is quite robust and is achieving good results. There are, however, some weaker areas'.[124]

---

[121] *Ibid.*
[122] Financial Action Task Force *Third mutual evaluation report on anti-money laundering and combating the financing of terrorism – United States of America* (Financial Action Task Force: Paris, 2006) at p. 49.
[123] Cassella above, n 91 at 367.
[124] Financial Action Task Force above, n 122 at p. 51.

6.4   THE UNITED KINGDOM

There are three forfeiture mechanisms in the UK: the forfeiture of property, forfeiture of cash at borders and confiscation resulting from a criminal conviction.[125] Additionally, there are four asset recovery procedures provided by the PCA. This includes criminal confiscation, civil recovery and tax. Where the Crown Prosecution Service (CPS) has obtained a criminal conviction, it, or the Serious Organized Crime Agency (SOCA), is permitted to apply for a Confiscation Order so that they can recover the financial gain by the defendant. The Assets Recovery Agency (ARA) was given the task of administering and implementing the provisions of the PCA 2002, but due to its poor performance, its remit was transferred to SOCA. The Serious Crime Act 2007 extended the civil recovery and tax powers of SOCA to other prosecuting authorities. These new powers go further than the customary criminal conviction and are often used when the assets in question are in the UK, but the defendant is out of the country or has fled. Civil recovery allows agencies in the UK to initiate civil proceedings where the property has been illegally obtained. SOCA is permitted to impose taxes provided it has 'reasonable grounds' to suspect that the income gained is the result of criminal conduct and a company's profits are chargeable to corporation tax and are a result of criminal conduct.

The power to confiscate the proceeds of crime from convicted defendants is a recent phenomenon.[126] The need for effective confiscation powers was highlighted by the decision in *R v Cuthbertson*.[127] The defendants were convicted of conspiracy offences to manufacture and provide Lysergic Acid Diethylamide, or LSD. The Crown attempted to rely on the Misuse of Drugs Act (1971)[128] to 'secure the forfeiture of assets linked to illegal drugs offences'.[129] Here, £750000 of criminal proceeds was traced to the offenders and retained. However, the funds had to be released after

---

[125]   Leong, Angela (2009), 'Asset recovery under the Proceeds of Crime Act 2002: the UK experience', in S. Young (ed.), *Civil forfeiture of criminal property – legal measures for targeting the proceeds of crime*, Edward Elgar, Cheltenham, pp. 187–227, at 188.

[126]   Although the Crown had the power of forfeiture until 1870 when this process was abolished by the Forfeiture Act 1870. See Alldridge, B. (2002), 'Smuggling, Confiscation and Forfeiture', *Modern Law Review*, **65**(5), 781–791, at 781.

[127]   *R v Cuthbertson* [1981] AC 470, which came to be known as the 'Operation Julie' case.

[128]   s. 27(1).

[129]   Gallant above, n 4 at 24.

the House of Lords held that existing powers to confiscate items used in the commission of an offence could not be used. In particular, the court decided that 'the forfeiture powers under section 27 of the Misuse of Drugs Act 1971 were restricted to the physical items used to commit the offence'.[130] More importantly, the House of Lords stated that the defendants had not been convicted under the 1971 Act, but of a conspiracy offence under the Criminal Law Act 1977.[131] As a result of the decision, the Hodgson Committee was established with the aim of improving the confiscation regime for drug trafficking offences.[132] Its recommendations led to the enactment of the Drug Trafficking Offences Act 1986, which 'imposed a mandatory obligation on the court to confiscate the proceeds of drug trafficking offences'.[133] Therefore, a comparison can be made between the US and UK approaches towards initially targeting the illegal profits derived from the sale of narcotics. The aims of the 1986 Act were clear and broad, yet 'there were anomalies in the legal regime, which has developed in a piecemeal fashion. And there are significant deficiencies in the use of legislative provisions'.[134] The 1986 Act was amended in 1988 by the Criminal Justice Act, which contained confiscation provisions for all non-drug indictable offences and several explicit summary offences.[135] Importantly, the Criminal Justice (International Co-operation) Act 1990 permitted legal mutual assistance in confiscation and the Criminal Justice Act 1993 implemented Article 3 of the Vienna Convention.[136] These provisions were extended by the Drug Trafficking Act 1994,[137] and the Proceeds of Crime Act 1995.[138] The impact of these measures has been questioned by many commentators. Indeed, Leong concluded that 'the major weakness of this early legislation [Drug Trafficking Act] was that only the proceeds of drug trafficking could be confiscated, and it failed to attack

---

[130]   Leong above, n 125 at 188.
[131]   *Ibid.* See in particular the comments by Lord Diplock in *R v Cuthbertson* [1980] 2 All ER 401, at 406.
[132]   Profits of Crime and their Recovery: the Report of a Committee chaired by Sir Derek Hodgson: 1984: Cambridge Studies in Criminology.
[133]   Leong above, n 125 at 189.
[134]   Cabinet Office *Recovering the Proceeds of Crime – A Performance and Innovation Unit Report* (Cabinet Office: London, 2000) at p. 5.
[135]   Criminal Justice Act 1988, ss. 71–89. Leong took the view that the 1988 Act 'extended the confiscation legislation to include all non-drug indictable offences, and specified summary offences from which peculiarly high profits could be gained'. Leong above, n 125 at 191.
[136]   *Ibid.*, at p. 192.
[137]   Drug Trafficking Act 1994, ss. 1–41.
[138]   Proceeds of Crime Act 1995, ss. 1–2.

the proceeds of non-drug trafficking crime'.[139] The Home Office Working Group on Confiscation commented that the UK's confiscation regime was not as successful as anticipated.[140] Rider concluded that 'the amounts actually taken out of the criminal pipe line . . . are derisory'.[141] Statistical evidence also illustrates the ineffectiveness of the legislation.[142] The Joint Committee on Human Rights stated that in 2000 'the gross receipts from confiscation orders amounted to about £30m'.[143] According to Saunders and Watson only 20 per cent of drug trafficking cases between 1998 and 2003 resulted in confiscation orders.[144] The Performance and Innovation Unit (PIU) concluded that the 'pursuit and recovery of criminal assets in the UK is failing to deliver the intended attack on the proceeds of crime'.[145]

6.4.1   The Proceeds of Crime Act 2002

The general election in 1997 resulted in a fundamental overhaul of the UK's strategy toward the illicit profits generated in the UK. In 1999, the then Prime Minister Tony Blair announced that the PIU would consider and review the current policies and legislation towards the pursuit of and removal of criminal assets.[146] He stated that 'seizing criminal assets deprives criminals and criminal organizations of their financial

---

[139]   Leong above, n 125 at 197.

[140]   Home Office *Working Group on Confiscation Third Report: Criminal Assets* (Home Office: London, 1998) at p. 2. Mumford and Alldridge added that 'the original UK confiscation legislation failed to generate significant sums because the burden was placed on the prosecution'. See Mumford, A. and Alldridge, P. (2002), 'Taxation as an adjunct to the criminal justice system: the new Assets Recovery Agency regime', *British Tax Review*, **6**, 458–469, at 463.

[141]   Rider, B. (2001), 'Wrongdoers' Rights', *Company Lawyer*, **22**(3), 87.

[142]   It must however be noted that 'data on the level of confiscation and enforcement is not collected in any systematic way'. See Cabinet Office above, n 134 at para. 4.18. A confiscation order is a court order 'against a convicted defendant to pay the state a sum equivalent to the proceeds that he has gained by crime'. See Alldridge above, n 126 at 782.

[143]   Joint Committee on Human Rights *Joint Committee on Human Rights – Third Report – The Proceeds of Crime Bill* (Joint Committee on Human Rights: London, 2001) at para 4. See also Bell, R. (2003b), 'The seizure, detention and forfeiture of cash in the UK', *Journal of Financial Crime*, **11**(2), 134–149.

[144]   Saunders, N. and Watson, B. (2003), 'Confiscation orders under the New Proceeds of Crime Act', *New Law Journal*, **152**(7066), 183–185, at 183.

[145]   Cabinet Office above, n 134 at para. 1.7.

[146]   *Ibid.*, at para. 1.1.

lifeblood'.[147] The PIU report was the driver of the reform process, and recommended that an Asset Confiscation Agency should be created, that should focus on financial investigations and both the money laundering and confiscation regimes should be consolidated under one piece of primary legislation.[148] Furthermore, it suggested increased use of the taxation of the proceeds of crime.[149] The PCA received Royal Assent on 24 July 2003, is spread over 462 sections and 'was introduced into Parliament in fulfilment of an election promise'.[150] It was described as 'a radical piece of legislation'.[151] The most controversial aspect of the legislation is the creation of the ARA,[152] which according to the National Audit Office (NAO) was established to 'put an end to the champagne lifestyle that many criminals were perceived to enjoy'.[153] One commentator noted that 'the establishment of the Assets Recovery Agency will be the most visible sign of POCA's implementation so far as the public is concerned'.[154]

6.4.2   What can be Confiscated?

The ARA had three policy objectives – to disrupt criminal enterprises, to promote the use of financial investigation and to operate in accordance with its visions and values.[155] It has been noted by one commentator that these aims are 'consistent with the Government's Asset Recovery

---

[147]   Cabinet Office above, n 134 at para. 2.4.

[148]   Cabinet Office above, n 134 at 118–120. The report made several other recommendations relating to the taxation of illegal profits and international co-operation but these are beyond the scope of this book.

[149]   Leong above, n 125 at 201.

[150]   Fisher, J. (2003), 'A review of the new investigation powers under the Proceeds of Crime Act 2002', *Journal of International Banking Law*, **18**(1), 15–23, at 15.

[151]   *Ibid.*

[152]   The Assets Recovery Agency was created on 13 January 2003 as a non-ministerial department which was answerable to the Home Office. See Leong, A. (2006), 'Civil recovery and taxation regime: are these powers under the Proceeds of Crime Act 2002 working?', *Company Lawyer*, **27**(12), 362–368, at 362. Mumford and Alldridge described the creation of the ARA as a 'radical departure' from the previous confiscation regimes. Mumford and Alldridge above, n 140 at 459.

[153]   National Audit Office *The Assets Recovery Agency – Report by the Comptroller and Auditor General* (National Audit Office: London, 2007) at p. 4.

[154]   Fisher above, n 150 at 15.

[155]   Assets Recovery Agency *Annual Report 2003/2004* (Assets Recovery Agency: London, 2004) at p. 4 as cited in Leong above, n 152 at 362.

Strategy'.[156] Under the Act, the ARA has four mechanisms that enable it to recover assets – criminal confiscation, civil recovery, taxation and the seizure and forfeiture of cash.[157] If a defendant has been convicted or has been committed for sentencing in the Crown Court, the ARA is permitted to ask the court to grant a confiscation order.[158] However, before the court will grant such an order, it has to be satisfied that two important questions have been answered. Firstly, whether the defendant has a criminal lifestyle.[159] A defendant is regarded to have a criminal lifestyle if one of the following three conditions is met, and there has to be a minimum benefit of £5000 for the final two conditions to be met:

1. it is a 'lifestyle offence' as specified in Schedule 2 of PCA;
2. it is part of a 'course of criminal conduct'; and
3. it is an offence committed over a period of at least 6 months and the defendant has benefited from it.

Secondly, whether or not the defendant has profited from the illegal behaviour.[160] Once the court feels that this criterion has been met, it will determine a 'recoverable amount' and grant a confiscation order that compels the defendant to pay.[161] In relation to criminal confiscation the FATF concluded that the provisions:

> appear to be working reasonably well in practice. The steady increase in restraint and confiscation and recovery figures, combined with positive feedback received from a range of law enforcement and prosecution agencies involved with the use of the new provisions, demonstrates an increased appreciation and understanding of the effective use of criminal confiscation to interrupt money laundering activities.[162]

The second method, civil recovery, allows the ARA to initiate civil proceedings in the High Court if a criminal prosecution is

---

[156] *Ibid.*

[157] According to Leong 'the concept of civil recovery is similar to the forfeiture power under the Racketeer Influenced and Corrupt Organizations Act 1970, which does not rely on the individual being convicted but instead allows civil forfeiture on irrebuttable presumptions without a prior criminal conviction'. Leong above, n 152 at 362.

[158] Proceeds of Crime Act 2002, s. 6.

[159] Proceeds of Crime Act 2002, ss. 10 and 75.

[160] Proceeds of Crime Act 2002, s. 307.

[161] Proceeds of Crime Act 2002, s. 7.

[162] Financial Action Task Force *The third mutual evaluation report: anti-money laundering and combating the financing of terrorism – the United Kingdom of Great Britain and Northern Ireland* (Financial Action Task Force: Paris, 2007) at p. 61.

unachievable.[163] Kennedy took the view that 'some commentators suggest that civil recovery is being introduced as a "quick and cheap" method of going after criminal assets'.[164] The Act creates an extended regime of civil recovery for property which has been obtained via illegal conduct and a cash forfeiture system for monies recovered by police and customs officers.[165] The ARA is not allowed to commence proceedings on its own initiative but it is allowed to do so when cases are referred to it where there is insufficient evidence to proceed with a criminal trial, or where the Crown Prosecution Service has decided against pursuing the case due to the public interest criteria, where confiscation proceedings are unsuccessful due to procedural mistakes and where the defendant has died or even is abroad.[166] In order for SOCA to initiate civil recovery or tax proceedings a number of criteria must be fulfilled:

1. recoverable property has been identified and has an estimated value of at least £10 000;[167]
2. recoverable property has been acquired in the last 12 years (20 years for tax);
3. recoverable property includes property other than cash, cheques and the like (although cash can be recovered in addition to other property);
4. there is evidence proven to civil standards of criminal conduct;
5. for tax cases there must be reasonable suspicion that untaxed income has resulted from criminality.[168]

Proceedings are commenced in the High Court for a recovery order against any person holding the proceeds of crime.[169] The High Court

---

[163] Proceeds of Crime Act 2002, s. 240(2).

[164] Kennedy, A. (2005), 'Justifying the civil recovery of criminal proceeds', *Company Lawyer*, **26**(5), 137–145, at 141.

[165] Briggs noted that 'confiscation of the proceeds of crime was described as the new big idea for controlling criminal behaviour'. See Briggs, J. (2006), 'Criminal confiscation, civil recovery and insolvency under the Proceeds of Crime Act 2002', *Insolvency Intelligence*, **19**(10), 145–150, at 145.

[166] Leong above, n 152 at 363.

[167] Proceeds of Crime Act 2002, s. 287 and the Proceeds of Crime Act 2002 (Financial Threshold for Civil Recovery) Order 2003, S.I. 2003/175.

[168] Leong above, n 152 at 363.

[169] Proceeds of Crime Act (2002), ss. 240(1)(a) and 243(1). For a detailed commentary on the civil recovery regime under the Proceeds of Crime Act 2002, see Kennedy, A. (2006), 'Civil recovery proceedings under the Proceeds of Crime Act 2002: the experience so far', *Journal of Money Laundering Control*, **9**(3), 245–264.

determines on a balance of probabilities and 'provides for retrospective application to property unlawfully obtained before the Act came into force'.[170] The ARA must be able to demonstrate on a balance of probabilities that there is some evidence of criminality. The respondent has the reverse burden of proof and must illustrate the lawful origin of the assets.[171] Additionally, where civil confiscation dealings have been instigated, it is possible for SOCA to apply for an Interim Receiving Order and an Interim Administrative Order.[172] This allows for the detention, custody or preservation of property and that the property will be held by an interim receiver. The FATF concluded that the introduction of the civil recovery scheme 'is another positive development in the UK regime'.[173]

The third recovery method is taxation and it enables the ARA to tax any income, benefit or turnover where the respondent is unable to legitimize the source.[174] This is a very important tool in the fight to end the champagne lifestyle of organized criminals.[175] The PIU Report articulated its frustration at the underuse of these powers:

> many criminal organisations generate substantial revenues that go untaxed . . . the powers of the Inland Revenue to raise assessments and enforce removal of assets against those shown to have undeclared income and wealth are considerable. The Inland Revenue can consider income over an extended period in raising a tax assessment, and it is able to impose additional fines. This means that much, and in some cases all, of a criminal's illegally obtained wealth can be removed by taxation. But the powers are generally little used against individuals suspected of benefiting from crime, despite the fact that they may be openly living beyond their means.[176]

---

[170]   Fisher above, n 150.
[171]   Leong above, n 125 at 209.
[172]   Proceeds of Crime Act 2002, s. 246.
[173]   Financial Action Task Force above, n 162 at 62.
[174]   These powers originated in the US and have been used 'as a weapon against organised crime through the outstanding work of the Internal Revenue Service's Criminal Investigation Division'. See Lusty, D. (2003), 'Taxing the untouchables who profit from organised crime', *Journal of Financial Crime*, **10**(3), 209–228, at 212. For a more detailed discussion of the Internal Revenue Service see Baker, G. (1994), 'Your worst nightmare: an accountant with a gun! The criminal investigation division of the Internal Revenue Service: its past, present, and future', *Georgia State University Law Review*, **11**, 331–379.
[175]   For a discussion of the rationale of these powers see Cabinet Office above, n 134 at 90–95 and Kennedy, A. (2007a), 'An evaluation of the recovery of criminal proceeds in the United Kingdom', *Journal of Money Laundering Control*, **10**(1), 33–46, at 40–42.
[176]   Cabinet Office above, n 134 at para. 1.38.

Under the Act, the ARA, which assumed the taxation work of the Inland Revenue, must be satisfied that it has reasonable grounds to suspect that 'income, profits or gains arising or accruing to a person (including a company) in respect of a chargeable period are chargeable to tax and arise or accrue as a result of that person's, or another's, criminal conduct'.[177] The seizure and forfeiture of cash allows a law enforcement officer to seize any cash if he has reasonable grounds for suspecting that it is '(a) recoverable property, or (b) intended by any person for use in unlawful conduct'.[178] Furthermore, the officer 'may also seize cash part of which he has reasonable grounds for suspecting to be '(a) recoverable property, or (b) intended by any person for use in unlawful conduct, if it is not reasonably practicable to seize only that part'.[179] The Act also introduces a wide range of investigative powers including confiscation investigation,[180] civil recovery investigation,[181] and money laundering investigation.[182] The ARA is also able to obtain a series of orders including a production order,[183] disclosure order,[184] customer information order,[185] and an account monitoring order.[186]

The final method afforded towards targeting the illicit proceeds of crime is seizure and forfeiture, which is used if a person is convicted of an offence that relates to the funding of terrorism.[187] The Terrorism Act 2000 states that the court 'may make a forfeiture order'.[188] This means that if a person is convicted of an offence under the Terrorism Act 2000 the court may order the forfeiture of money or property that was in the defendant's possession or control.[189] Bell questioned the effectiveness of these orders and stated that 'producing evidence even to the civil standard may be difficult in many cases'.[190] Furthermore, Bell concluded 'while making

---

[177]   Proceeds of Crime Act 2002, s. 317(1)(a) and (b).
[178]   Proceeds of Crime Act 2002, s. 294(1).
[179]   Proceeds of Crime Act 2002, s. 294(2). This part of the Act replaces and extends the scheme created by the Drug Trafficking Act 1994.
[180]   Proceeds of Crime Act 2002, s. 341(1).
[181]   Proceeds of Crime Act 2002, s. 341(2).
[182]   Proceeds of Crime Act 2002, s. 341(4).
[183]   Proceeds of Crime Act 2002, s. 345(4).
[184]   Proceeds of Crime Act 2002, s. 357(4) and (5).
[185]   Proceeds of Crime Act 2002, s. 363(5).
[186]   Proceeds of Crime Act 2002, s. 371(4).
[187]   Terrorism Act 2000, ss. 15–19.
[188]   Terrorism Act 2000, s. 23.
[189]   Terrorism Act 2000, s. 23(2).
[190]   Bell, R. (2003a), 'The confiscation, forfeiture and disruption of terrorist finances', *Journal of Money Laundering Control*, **7**(2), 105–125, at 113.

small civil forfeitures can be worthwhile as a disruptive approach, it has little long-term value unless the cash can be tracked back to its origin and becomes useful in detecting a terrorist funding source and those who rely upon it'.[191] Furthermore, the Anti-terrorism, Crime and Security Act 2001 allows the police to confiscate cash where they have reasonable grounds for suspecting that the cash is intended for use for the purposes of terrorism, or that it represents the assets of a proscribed organization, or it represents property obtained through terrorism, or is property that has been earmarked as terrorist property.[192] A court is permitted to confiscate the money in civil proceedings provided it is satisfied that the cash is terrorist cash.[193] Under Schedule 1 of the Act, the police are allowed to initiate forfeiture proceedings against terrorists but 'also bring forfeiture proceedings against any third party recipient of terrorist property who is not a bona fide purchaser for value of the property'.[194]

6.4.3   Reform

The performance of the ARA, which has been assessed by 'key performance indicators',[195] is rather impressive in its first few years of operation. For example, in 2003/2004 the ARA met one of its three objectives.[196] In both 2004/2005 and 2005/2006 the ARA performed significantly better and achieved three out of its five objectives.[197] In 2006/2007, the ARA met all its intended objectives for the first time.[198] The initial success of the ARA was succinctly stated in 2006 by a commentator who stated:

> to summarise the performance of Assets Recovery Agency since its establishment in 2003, the Assets Recovery Agency has disrupted a total of 160 criminal enterprises, obtained 23 confiscation orders of a value of £13.5 million in the

---

[191]   *Ibid.*, at 114.

[192]   This is referred to as 'terrorist cash'.

[193]   Anti-terrorism, Crime and Security Act 2001, s. 1 and sch. 1.

[194]   Society for Advanced Legal Studies (2003), 'Forfeiture of terrorist property and tracing: sub-group 4: impact of the initiatives on other areas of the law', *Journal of Money Laundering Control*, **6**(3), 261–268, at 262.

[195]   Leong above, n 152 at 364.

[196]   See Assets Recovery Agency *Annual Report 2003/2004* (Assets Recovery Agency: London, 2004).

[197]   See Assets Recovery Agency *Annual Report 2004/2005* (Assets Recovery Agency: London, 2005) and see Assets Recovery Agency *Annual Report 2005/2006* (Assets Recovery Agency: London, 2006).

[198]   Assets Recovery Agency *Annual Report 2006/2007* (Assets Recovery Agency: London, 2007) as cited in Leong, A. (2007b), 'The Assets Recovery Agency: future or no future?', *Company Lawyer*, **28**(12), 279–380, at 380.

criminal confiscation cases, and obtained £9.6 million worth of recovery orders, voluntary settlement and tax agreements in 24 cases. However, only £9.2 million of receipts were actually realised and collected in the tin box.[199]

Charles Clarke MP, then Home Secretary, boldly proclaimed that the ARA has taken over £120m from criminals.[200] He said that 'the tough powers introduced in the Proceeds of Crime Act are really starting to bite, making it harder for criminals to hold on to the profits of their illegal activities'.[201] This marks a clear and significant improvement on the previous incumbent legislation. However, according to Leong 'a common criticism was that in the first three years of its existence the ARA cost £60m but only managed to retrieve £8m'.[202] This is a view supported by the House of Commons Committee of Public Accounts who noted that during 2005/2006 the ARA only recovered £23m, when its total expenditure for that year was £65m.[203] Nelen added 'the explanations for the disappointing financial results of the proceeds of crime policy can be found in both a weak policy theory and in defective law enforcement'.[204] The government must accept some responsibility for the failings of the ARA because it set unachievable targets. This is a view supported by the FATF who noted that 'the targets originally set may have been overly optimistic'.[205]

For example, the target for recovery of proceeds of crime in 2006/2007 was £125m. This was later increased to £250m by 2009/2010, 'with the longer term vision to detect up to £1bn'.[206] Furthermore, the PIU Report suggested that the recovery regime had the potential to be cost effective'.[207] It is possible to criticize not only the impact of the above legislation but the political expectation of such laws. Nelen states 'there were very high expectations in the Netherlands . . . with regard to the potential outcome of the legislation to deprive criminals of assets'.[208] The Dutch Ministry of Justice

---

[199] Leong above, n 152 at 364.
[200] BBC (2005), 'New laws target criminal's case', available at http://news.bbc.co.uk/1/hi/uk/4294581.stm (accessed 8 March 2005).
[201] *Ibid.*
[202] Leong above, n 198 at 380.
[203] House of Commons Committee of Public Accounts *Assets Recovery Agency – 5th Report of Session 2006/2007* (House of Commons Committee of Public Accounts: London, 2007) at p. 5.
[204] Nelen above, n 2 at 521.
[205] Financial Action Task Force above, n 162 at 62.
[206] Home Office *Rebalancing the criminal justice system in favour of the law-abiding majority. Cutting crime, reducing reoffending and protecting the public* (Home Office: London, 2006) at p. 36.
[207] Cabinet Office above, n 134 at 23.
[208] Nelen above, n 2 at 520.

estimated that the financial remuneration of the law would 'exceed the value of 200 million euros'.[209] These opportunities 'worked like a boomerang' for two reasons.[210] Firstly, the Dutch government was accused of abusing its power. Secondly, the government was also accused of putting too much pressure on the prosecution services and the police.

Another criticism of the ARA was its performance against organized criminals, one commentator taking the view that 'the Assets Recovery Agency is likely to concentrate on attacking the criminal assets of around 400 major crime bosses in the UK, the so-called untouchables, who are estimated to have a combined wealth of £440m'.[211] Sproat took the view that 'there are around 400 organised crime bosses in the UK with an amassed criminal wealth of approximately £440m. So called "dirty-money" – or assets derived from crime represents around 2% of the UK's GDP or £18bn. The exercise of the legal tools provided by the Serious Organized Crime and Police Act 2005 and the Proceeds of Crime Act 2002 is expected to have a considerable impact in terms of bringing organised criminals to justice'.[212] Smellie took the view 'the only sure way of putting the "Mr Bigs" out of business is to confiscate their proceeds of crime. Other remedies taken, such as sanctions and blacklisting of foreign states and persons deemed associated with "King Pins", have been of little more than symbolic effect'.[213] However, Kennedy warned 'the effectiveness of civil recovery must also be considered in terms of not just how much money it removes but from whom it is removed. While it is important that the activities of the "Mr Bigs" of crime are affected, it is also important that those who act as criminal role models in local communities are likewise affected'.[214] Kennedy, citing Levi and Osofsky, stated that 'relatively few "Mr Bigs" had been convicted in the courts and, consequently, few were available to have their assets confiscated'.[215]

Morris took the view that 'the Proceeds of Crime Act 2002 . . . continues to generate some rather eccentric problems'.[216] The Home Office Working

---

209   *Ibid.*
210   Nelen above, n 2 at 521.
211   Fisher above, n 150 at 15.
212   Sproat, P. (2009), 'To what extent is the UK's anti-money laundering and asset recovery regime used against organised crime?', *Journal of Money Laundering Control*, **12**(2), 134–150, at 134.
213   Smellie above, n 2 at 104.
214   Kennedy above, n 164 at 144.
215   Levi, M. and Osofsky, L. *Investigating, seizing and confiscating the proceeds of crime* (Home Office: London, 1995).
216   Morris, P. (2004), 'The importance of being appropriate', *Journal of International Banking Law and Regulation*, **19**(7), 258–260, at 259.

Group on Confiscation stated that the UK's approach to confiscation was not as successful as originally hoped.[217] Furthermore, it has been argued that the UK approach was 'never designed for the complexities of national or international recovery of criminal proceeds from high level offenders'.[218] In 2007, the NAO published a critical report (the Report) of the ARA, which concluded that 'problems in recovering assets have been due to poor quality referrals – particularly in the early days; defence representations, including a few cases relating to the Human Rights Act 1998; and weaknesses in the Agency's internal processes'.[219]

The performance of the ARA has been adversely affected for a number of reasons. For example, at the date of the report only a small number of police forces and local authorities had referred a case. Furthermore, its management of cases is weak and it has experienced a high turnover of staff. Finally, in several instances, the fees for court-appointed receivers exceeded the assets recovered.[220] This particular problem was commented upon by the *Guardian* in September 2006 which stated 'one problem for the ARA is the laborious machinery devised by the Home Office when first setting up the Agency. The ARA was required to hire outside accountants . . . to act as court-appointed advisors'.[221]

An important factor that limited the effectiveness of the ARA was its relationship with the European Convention on Human Rights.[222] The Home Office stated that it was necessary to 'reach an appropriate balance between the right of the individual to legal enjoyment of property and the rights of society to reclaim illegally derived assets'.[223] The PIU report stated that the safeguards included 'a £10 000 *de minimis* threshold; the burden of proof remaining with the State; the provision of civil legal aid; compensation provisions; and organisational management arrangements

---

[217]   Home Office *Home Office Working Group on Confiscation* (Home Office: London, 1998a).

[218]   Kennedy, A. (2004), 'Justifying the civil recovery of criminal proceeds', *Journal of Financial Crime*, **12**(1), 8–23, at 20.

[219]   National Audit Office above, n 153 at p. 5.

[220]   *Ibid.*

[221]   *The Guardian* (2006a), 'Solicitor's saga highlights problems facing cash recovery unit: unrealistic figure targets for agency accused of sweeping aside civil liberties' available from http://www.guardian.co.uk/uk/2006/sep/29/ukcrime.davidleigh (accessed 4 August 2010).

[222]   Similar provisions have already been tested in the European Court of Human Rights. See *M v Italy* Application 12386/86, decision of 15 April 1991, *Riela v Italy* Application 52439/99, decision of 4 September 2001 and *Arcuri v Italy* Application 52024/99, decision of 5 July 2001.

[223]   Leong above, n 152 at 362.

to ensure that the civil forfeiture route is not adopted as a "soft option" in place of criminal proceedings'.[224] Rider noted that 'despite considerable efforts on the part of the government and its advisors to tone down the new provisions for civil enforcement and to inject a greater degree of impartiality into the process, there are still many who are eagerly awaiting the first opportunity to attack the integrity of the new regime'.[225] The relationship between confiscation orders and the right to peaceful enjoyment of property was tested in *Phillips v United Kingdom*.[226] The European Court of Human Rights held that confiscation orders in drug trafficking cases were lawful and did not breach Article 1 of Protocol No.1 of the European Convention on Human Rights.[227] The European Court of Human Rights reached a similar decision in *Raimundo v Italy*.[228] Article 6 of the Convention applies to 'a person who is facing an application for a confiscation order following conviction'.[229] Article 6(1) provides that every person is entitled to a fair and public hearing within a reasonable time by an independent and impartial tribunal established by law, subject to a criminal charge.[230] Article 6(2) and (3) applies to those charged with criminal offences only, and provides specific examples of the duties under Article 6(1) to secure a fair trial. Article 6(2) 'includes the presumption of innocence amongst the specific rights constituting the right to a fair trial'.[231] However, the presumption of innocence may be set aside by public interest considerations.[232]

Another controversial issue is the reverse burden of proof. The judiciary regards the change in burden of proof as justifiable 'as long as the defendant has already been convicted, because there is no consequent interference

---

[224]   Cabinet Office above, n 134 at para. 5.2.4.

[225]   Rider above, n 141 at 87.

[226]   [2001] Crim LR 817.

[227]   The Joint Committee on Human Rights noted that this decision illustrates that confiscation orders in such cases are compatible with the conditions in *Phillips*. They warned, however, that 'the Proceeds of Crime Bill . . . makes it possible to impose confiscation orders on defendants whose level of criminal activity differs widely'. See Joint Committee on Human Rights above, n 143 at para. 24.

[228]   [1994] HR CD 6.

[229]   See Joint Committee on Human Rights above, n 143 at para. 16.

[230]   Article 6(1) applies to criminal charges and the determination of civil rights and obligations.

[231]   Mumford and Alldridge above, n 140 at 462.

[232]   See for example *Salabiaku v France* (1991) 13 EHRR 379, *R v Lambert* [2001] UKHL 37, *Director of the Assets Recovery Agency v Walsh* [2004] NIQB 21, 18 and *R (The Director of the Assets Recovery Agency) v He & Cheng* [2004] EWCH 3021.

with the presumption of innocence'.[233] Mumford and Alldridge noted that 'challenges to the switch in the burden of proof in confiscation proceedings were dismissed on this ground by the Privy Council, the European Court of Human Rights and the House of Lords'.[234] For example, in *McIntosh v Lord Advocate*, the Judicial Committee of the Privy Council considered the compatibility of Article 6(2) and the assumptions made under section 3(2) of the Proceeds of Crime (Scotland) Act 1998.[235] The court decided that Article 6(2) had no application.[236] One of the most controversial aspects of the 2002 Act is the burden of proof and its relationship with the European Convention on Human Rights. The PCA provides that 'the burden of proof has to be placed on the holder of property to show that property in his hands was lawfully obtained'.[237] Another area of conflict between the PCA and the Convention is Article 7 and the freedom from retrospective penalties.[238] A relevant case here is *Welch v. United Kingdom*,[239] where the court deemed that confiscation orders are a vital, albeit draconian, power to stop the scourge of drug smuggling.

6.4.4   Serious Organized Crime Agency

The government announced its intention to establish SOCA in February 2004, following an extensive Home Office review of organized crime.[240] The Serious Organized Crime and Police Act has given SOCA three objectives. Firstly, the prevention and detection of serious organized crime.[241] Secondly, the mitigation of the consequences of such crime.[242] Thirdly, the function of gathering, storing, analysing and disseminating of information.[243] Harfield took the view that 'the Agency will investigate

---

[233]   Mumford and Alldridge above, n 140 at 463.

[234]   *Ibid.*

[235]   [2001] 3 WLR 107.

[236]   Prior to the Privy Council decision, the Scottish Court of Appeal decided that the Scottish Proceeds of Crime Act was 'contrary' to the European Convention on Human Rights.

[237]   Mumford and Alldridge above, n 140 at 462.

[238]   No one shall be held guilty of any criminal offence on account of any act or omission which did not constitute a criminal offence under national or international law at the time when it was committed. There is little case law under Article 7.

[239]   20 EHRR 247.

[240]   Home Office *One Step Ahead – A 21st century strategy to defeat organised crime* (Home Office: London, 2004b).

[241]   Serious Organized Crime and Police Act 2005, s. 2(1)(a).

[242]   Serious Organized Crime and Police Act 2005, s. 2(1)(b).

[243]   Serious Organized Crime and Police Act 2005, s. 3.

crime in order to provide evidence to support prosecutions [and] it will have police powers'.[244] The government announced in 2007 that SOCA would take over the assets recovery function of the ARA,[245] which was subsequently abolished by the Serious Crime Act 2007.[246] John Reid MP, the then Home Secretary, stated that this would 'create a more effective law enforcement agency with a wider range of skills and expertise'.[247] There are a number of reasons why the government decided to merge the ARA with SOCA. Firstly, to improve the work already conducted by the ARA and improve the overall effectiveness of the civil confiscation regime. Secondly, to build upon the recommendations made in the NAO report in relation to the performance of the ARA. Thirdly, the underachievement of the ARA.[248] Leong added that 'the rationale behind the merger . . . is to streamline the work carried out by law and order agencies so as to widen the skills and expertise as well as achieving better economies of scale in the fight against serious organised crime'.[249] In 2008, SOCA announced that 'the operational element of the work of the ARA will merge into SOCA the Serious Organized Crime Agency . . . [this] means SOCA will now have both criminal and civil powers to reduce harm caused to individuals and communities in the UK by organised crime'.[250]

SOCA has been granted new powers under the Serious Crime Act 2007.[251] The Act introduced new measures to prevent serious crime, including Serious Crime Prevention Orders which allow courts to impose restrictive conditions on those proved to be involved in serious crime.[252]

---

[244]   Harfield, C. (2006), 'SOCA: a paradigm shift in British policing', *British Journal of Criminology*, **46**(4), 743–761 at 743. For a more detailed commentary on the creation of the Serious Organized Crime Agency see Bowling, B. and Ross, J. (2006), 'The Serious Organized Crime Agency – should we be afraid?', *Criminal Law Review*, December, 1019–1034.

[245]   Home Office *Asset Recovery Action Plan – a consultation document* (Home Office: London, 2007) at p. 21. Vernon Coaker MP via a Written Ministerial Statement outlined some of the reasons for the reform in January 2007. See HC Deb 11 January 2007, c21-222WS.

[246]   See the Serious Crime Act 2007 (Amendment of the Proceeds of Crime Act 2002) Order 2008 2008/949 and Serious Crime Act 2007, s. 74.

[247]   Home Office above, n 245 at p. 3.

[248]   Leong above, n 198 at 380.

[249]   Leong, A. (2008), 'Passing the buck!', *Journal of Money Laundering Control*, **11**(2), 101–102, at 101.

[250]   Serious Organized Crime Agency (2008a), 'Merger of SOCA and ARA strengthens government drive to deprive criminals of their assets', available at www.soca.gov.uk (accessed 4 August 2010).

[251]   Serious Crime Act 2007, ss. 75–86.

[252]   Sproat above, n 212 at 136.

SOCA is allowed to 'monitor the financial affairs of "serious acquisitive criminals" from the point of sentence for up to 15 years (up to 20 years where an individual is imprisoned for life) by use of a financial reporting order'.[253] Sproat took the view that financial reporting orders 'would be obtained in cases of criminals convicted of a qualifying offence who law enforcement believes pose a long-term threat'.[254] Qualifying offences include tax evasion, money laundering, counterfeiting and drugs trafficking.[255] Kennedy stated that:

> the effect of the order is to require the offender to make reports containing specified particulars of his financial affairs. Failure to comply (or inclusion of false or misleading information) is a criminal offence punishable with up to a year's imprisonment. The White Paper envisaged that these would be ancillary orders, taking effect after the offender's release from imprisonment and could constitute a requirement to file detailed six monthly returns setting out income, assets and expenditure. Released offenders might be obliged to report all bank accounts and credit cards being used, and be forbidden to carry out transactions using any other route.[256]

The first reported instance of a court granting a Financial Reporting Order was *R v Abdullah Babyasin*.[257] Similarly, in 2007, Terry Adams, a convicted money launderer, was also subject to a Financial Reporting Order.[258] In February 2008, Northampton Police and Northamptonshire Crown Prosecution Service obtained a Financial Reporting Order against Shaun Davies.[259] SOCA reported that it had successfully obtained its

---

[253] *Ibid.*, at 138. For information relating to the practicalities of Financial Reporting Orders see Crown Prosecution Service *Financial Reporting Orders Sections 76 & 79–81 SOCPA 2005* (Crown Prosecution Service: London, n/d).

[254] It is likely that such qualifying offences are created by the Fraud Act 2006 and the lifestyle offences listed in Schedule 2 of the Proceeds of Crime Act (2002). Sproat above, n 212 at 136.

[255] See the Fraud Act (2006) and the Proceeds of Crime Act (2002), Schedule 2.

[256] Kennedy, A. (2007b), 'Winning the information wars: collecting, sharing and analysing information in asset recovery investigations', *Journal of Financial Crime*, **14**(4), 372–404, at 382.

[257] 19 June 2005 at Woolwich Crown Court. See *The Guardian* (2006b), 'Turkish drug gang leader jailed for 22 years', available at http://www.guardian.co.uk/uk/2006/may/16/drugsandalcohol.drugstrade (accessed 4 August 2010).

[258] *The Guardian* (2007), 'Crime boss Adams faces ruin after trial', available at http://www.guardian.co.uk/uk/2007/may/19/ukcrime.sandralaville (accessed 4 August 2010).

[259] Northamptonshire Police (2009), 'Financial reporting order among the first in country', available at http://www.northants.police.uk/default.aspx?id=18341&d b=old&datewant=yes (accessed 4 August 2010).

first conviction for a person breaching a Financial Reporting Order. Roy Williams was convicted on 14 April 2008 and given a three month custodial sentence for breaching the Financial Reporting Order which is to run concurrently with his 8-year sentence for drug and fraud-related offences.[260] The Director General of the SOCA, Bill Hughes states:

> As we have always said, our action against criminals does not conclude when they are behind bars. Financial Reporting Orders are not of the most powerful tools to deprive criminals of their ill-gotten gains. We are committed to driving serious organised criminals out of business through lifetime management of offenders and we will go after their assets no matter how large or small the amount.[261]

The suitability of Financial Reporting Orders has been questioned on the grounds that they potentially breach the European Convention on Human Rights.[262] In November 2008, SOCA stated that following legal advice it was no longer able to name convicted criminals because it would breach their right to family and private life under Article 8 of the European Convention on Human Rights.[263] Financial Reporting Orders were initially used in a test case in 2003, where Essex police were prevented from using a picture of a prolific convicted burglar and car thief, Gary Ellis, on a wanted style poster.[264]

6.4.5   Conclusion

The UK's approach towards the confiscation of criminally obtained assets is very similar to that in the US. It initially targeted the drugs trade and now it has expanded to incorporate a broader range of criminal offences. The decision in *R v Cuthbertson* illustrated the need for reform and what followed was a number of different ineffective statutes

---

[260] Serious Organized Crime Agency (2008b), 'Serious Organized Crime Agency secures first conviction under new power', available at www.soca.gov.uk (accessed 4 August 2010).

[261] *Ibid.*

[262] Kennedy above, n 256 at 382. Financial Reporting Orders were initially proposed by the Home Office in 2004, see Home Office above, n 240 at p. 53.

[263] The Telegraph (2008), 'Naming and shaming criminal masterminds "infringes their human rights"', available at http://www.telegraph.co.uk/news/uknews/law-and-order/3439645/Naming-and-shaming-criminal-masterminds-infringes-their-human-rights.html (accessed 12 November 2008).

[264] For a more detailed commentary of this case see Melville-Brown, A. and Burgess, D. (2003), 'The right to be rehabilitated – can you ever escape your past?', *Entertainment Law Review*, **14**(4), 88–90.

that did little to improve the position. The recommendations of the PIU report represented a fundamental change in the legislative policy towards recovering the proceeds of criminal activity. The ARA was initially successful, recovering over £260m of illicit assets, but due to the ill-advised aspirations of the Home Office, its existence was short lived. The ARA performed a very important task and has laid the foundations for SOCA to continue to tackle the illicit finances generated by organized criminals in the UK.

6.5 CONCLUSION

This chapter has clearly illustrated the importance of tackling the illicit profits of organized criminals, drug cartels and terrorists. Several international institutions, including the UN, the EU and the FATF, have implemented a series of international legal instruments to tackle the proceeds of crime. However, it must be noted that these measures have been, once again, influenced by measures introduced by the US in the 1970s. The scope of the international measures, as contained in the Vienna Convention 1988, was initially limited to the proceeds of drug-related sales, but was broadened following the implementation of the Palermo Convention (2000) which extended the scope of the confiscation proceedings to more criminal offences. However, it is important to note that the EU adopted a slightly different policy towards tackling the proceeds of crime. For example, the Council of Europe Convention on Laundering, Search, Seizure and the Confiscation of the Proceeds from Crime 1990 was broader in scope than the Vienna Convention as it applied to the confiscation of the proceeds of any offence. The breadth of the international measures was strengthened as a result of the terrorist attacks on 11 September 2001, which resulted in the implementation of Security Council Resolution 1373.

6.5.1 The United States of America

Nonetheless, as with the global policy towards money laundering, the US has been the 'flag bearer' of tackling the proceeds of crime since the declaration of war on drugs by President Richard Nixon in the 1970s. This policy was reaffirmed by President Ronald Reagan in the 1980s. Comparisons can be made between the US policy towards the proceeds of crime and its strategy towards fraud, money laundering, terrorist financing and insider dealing for two reasons. Firstly, there is not one single piece of legislation that deals with all forms of forfeiture. Secondly, there is no one single agency that has been set up with the specific task of administering the pursuit of the illicit proceeds of crime. Nonetheless, the US has adopted an extremely tough stance towards the proceeds of crime, and the scope of its forfeiture powers is extensive. The ability of law enforcement and federal agencies to seek the forfeiture of the proceeds of crime has become a vital part of the US criminal justice system. Of the three types of forfeiture procedures available, administrative, civil and criminal, it is the use of the civil forfeiture route that is the most popular method utilized by these agencies for a number of controversial issues outlined above. Nonetheless, these measures will still continue to be used by federal and law enforcement agencies despite the concerns raised by many commentators.

6.5.2   The United Kingdom

The need to confiscate the proceeds of crime was graphically illustrated by the decision of the House of Lords in *R v Cuthbertson*. However, the introduction of several statutory instruments did little to quell the level of criticism aimed at these ineffective and toothless laws. The publication of the report by the Performance and Innovation Unit in 2000 galvanized attempts by the government to tackle the illicit proceeds of crime. The creation of the ARA and the implementation of the Proceeds of Crime Act 2002 were seen to place the UK at the forefront of the fight against organized criminals, terrorists and drug cartels. Indeed, it was proclaimed by successive Home Secretaries that the ARA would become self-sufficient and that it would end the so-called 'champagne lifestyle' of the organized criminals residing in the UK. However, these goals were ill-advised and resulted in the government setting unachievable targets for the ARA. The ARA was not given sufficient time and resources to tackle the proceeds of crime, and the government wanted a quick fix to what can be described as a long-term problem. SOCA has been given a much wider remit than the ARA; in addition to administering the UK's confiscation regime, it also acts as its Financial Intelligence Unit. In recognition of this, the government granted SOCA an extensive array of law enforcement tools designed to tackle organized criminals. SOCA has benefited from the groundwork and foundations laid by the ARA, with many of the uncertainties presented by the relationship between the PCA and the European Convention on Human Rights being clarified. However, it is worth noting that additional powers granted to SOCA by the Serious Crime Act (2007) have also been challenged by the rights afforded by the European Convention.

What can be concluded is that forfeiture and confiscation procedures are here to stay and that they form a central pillar of the global, regional and national financial crime measures despite the concerns afforded by civil liberty groups. Organized criminals, drug cartels and terrorists have continued to show a remarkable level of sophistication that enables them to hide their illicit profits in an array of mechanisms, which provide sufficient distance between them to avoid prosecution by law enforcement agencies. This is clearly illustrated in the UK, where SOCA faces a difficult battle to tackle the increasing number of organized criminals and their illicit profits. This clearly demonstrates the importance of allowing law enforcement agencies to tackle the finances of organized criminals, drug cartels and terrorists.

7.   Regulators and agencies

> If these activities are to be suppressed and hopefully, in the long term, substantially eliminated it will require the collective will and commitment of the public and private sector working together.[1]

7.1   INTRODUCTION

A large number of regulators and agencies have been established at an international, regional and national level to implement the financial crime policies identified in this book. Efforts by the international community to tackle financial crime have been largely led by the United Nations (UN), the Financial Action Task Force (FATF) and its regional affiliates, the European Union (EU), and supported by the International Monetary Fund (IMF), the World Bank Group, the Egmont Group, the Basle Committee and the Wolfsberg Group. The chapter divides the regulators and agencies in the United States of America (US) and the United Kingdom (UK) into three categories:

1.   Primary
2.   Secondary
3.   Tertiary

The US financial crime policy is led by three government departments, the Department of Treasury, the Department of Justice and the State Department, its primary regulators. The Department of Treasury plays a fundamental role in the development of the US anti-money laundering and counter-terrorist financing policies. The Department of Justice manages the investigation and prosecution of a wide range of financial crimes including money laundering, terrorist financing, fraud and insider dealing. The State Department represents the US on a number of international organizations including the UN Sanctions and Counter-Terrorism

---

[1]   Drage, John (1993), 'Countering money laundering: the response of the financial sector', in H. Macqueen (ed.), *Money Laundering*, Edinburgh University Press, Edinburgh, 60–70.

Committee, the FATF and the G-8 Roma-Lyon Group. Furthermore, it is the 'lead agency and a major source of funding for the provision of foreign AML/CFT training and technical assistance'.[2] The primary agencies are assisted by a number of secondary agencies that include the Office of Terrorism and Financial Intelligence, Office of Terrorist Financing and Financial Crime, Office of Intelligence and Analysis, Office of Foreign Assets Control and the Treasury Executive Office for Asset Forfeiture which are subsidiaries of the Treasury Department. The Department of Justice has a number of ancillary sections which include Asset Forfeiture and Money Laundering Section, Criminal Division, Counterterrorism Section, Criminal Division, National Drug Intelligence Center and the Office of International Affairs. The State Department is supported by the Bureau of Economic and Business Affairs, Bureau of International Narcotics and Law Enforcement Affairs, and State's Office of the Coordinator for Counterterrorism. The tertiary agencies can be divided into three categories, law enforcement, financial regulatory bodies and interagency groups that include several financial crime task forces.

The financial crime policies of the UK are led by HM Treasury, the Home Office and the Foreign and Commonwealth Office, the primary agencies. HM Treasury is responsible for initiating and implementing the UK's anti-money laundering and counter-terrorist financing policies. HM Treasury represents the UK during the drafting and implementation of the EU's Money Laundering Directives. Furthermore, it manages the UK's terrorist freezing obligations on the FATF. The Home Office administers the police forces, the Serious Organized Crime Agency (SOCA); it manages the assets recovery strategy and the counter-terrorism strategy. The Foreign and Commonwealth Office has a limited involvement in the UK's financial crime strategies but it does manage the UK's commitment to UN treaties and international agreements. These are supported by several secondary regulators which can be divided into two categories, criminal justice and financial sector agencies. The tertiary agencies include a number of trade associations.

---

[2]   Financial Action Task Force *Third mutual evaluation report on anti-money laundering and combating the financing of terrorism – the United States of America* (Financial Action Task Force: Paris, 2006) at p. 18.

7.2   INTERNATIONAL COMMUNITY

7.2.1   United Nations

The UN has led the global battle against financial crime by implementing a number of anti-money laundering instruments including the UN Convention against Illicit Traffic in Narcotic Drugs and Psychotropic Substances (1988)[3] and the UN Convention against Transnational Organized Crime (2000). Additionally, the UN provides assistance to member countries via its Global Programme Against Money Laundering and its Office for Drug Control and Crime Prevention.[4] Both of these initiatives seek to enable their members to comply with the global anti-money laundering standards.[5] The Office for Drug Control and Crime Prevention has drafted model laws including the 'Model Legislation on Laundering, Confiscation and International Cooperation in Relation to the Proceeds of Crime' and in response to its expansion into the realm of counter-terrorist financing 'the Model Money-Laundering, Proceeds of Crime and Terrorist Financing'.[6] The Global Programme against Money Laundering was created in 1995 with the aim of conducting research and providing technical support when required by member states.[7] Furthermore, the Programme also 'runs the Anti-Money Laundering International Database on the International Money Laundering Information Network'.[8] The UN has also undertaken the lead role in relation to terrorist financing, a point illustrated by its Declaration to Eliminate International Terrorism (1994),[9] the International Convention for the Suppression of the Financing of Terrorism (1999)[10]

---

[3]   United Nations Convention against Illicit Traffic in Narcotic Drugs and Psychotropic Substances (1988).

[4]   For a more detailed discussion of the Office for Drug Control and Crime Prevention see http://www.unodc.org/.

[5]   Bachus, A. (2004), 'From drugs to terrorism: the focus shifts in the international fight against money laundering after September 11, 2001', *Arizona Journal of International and Comparative Law*, **21**, 835–872, at 856.

[6]   Zagaris, B. (2004), 'The merging of anti-money laundering and counter-terrorism financial enforcement regimes after September 11, 2001', *Berkeley Journal of International Law*, **22**, 123–157, at 137–139.

[7]   Shehu, A. (2005), 'International initiatives against corruption and money laundering: an overview', *Journal of Financial Crime*, **12**(3), 221–245, at 228.

[8]   *Ibid.*

[9]   United Nations A/RES/49/60 84th plenary meeting, Measures to eliminate international terrorism, 9 December 1994.

[10]   Article 4.

and the implementation of several Security Council Resolutions following the terrorist attacks in September 2001.[11] However, it must be noted that the UN has not implemented any international legislative measures to tackle fraud or insider dealing. Its fraud policies prioritize fraudulent activities on its finances.

7.2.2 Financial Action Task Force

The FATF, like the UN, plays a central role in the fight against money laundering and terrorist financing, but a very limited role in the battle against fraud and insider dealing. Its own website states 'the priority of the FATF is to ensure global action to combat money laundering and terrorist financing, and concrete implementation of its 40+9 Recommendations throughout the world'.[12] It was created in 1989, and is described as 'one of the first collaborative international efforts targeting money laundering'.[13] Indeed, Bachus noted that 'the FATF's charge was to examine anti-money laundering measures, particularly those regarding illicit funds from the drug trade'.[14] This point is demonstrated by the publication of its 40 Recommendations in 1996.[15] Its emphasis broadened to include terrorist financing following the terrorist attacks in 2001, when the FATF published the 'Special Recommendations'.[16] Jackson stated that the FATF had three important tasks: 'to spread the anti-money laundering message worldwide, to monitor the implementation of its Forty Recommendations among FATF members, and to review money laundering trends and countermeasures'.[17] The FATF 'monitors members' progress in implementing necessary measures, reviews money laundering and terrorist financing

---

[11] A more detailed discussion of these issues can found in Chapter 3.

[12] Financial Action Task Force (n/d), 'Mandate' available at http://www.fatf-gafi.org/pages/0,3417,en_32250379_32236846_1_1_1_1_1,00.html (accessed 4 August 2010).

[13] Dellinger, L. (2008), 'From dollars to pesos: a comparison of the US and Colombian anti-money laundering initiatives from an international perspective', *California Western International Law Journal*, **38**, 419–454, at 433.

[14] Bachus above, n 5 at 849.

[15] Financial Action Task Force (n/d), 'Forty recommendations', available at www.fatf-gafi.org/document/28/0,3343,en_32250379_32236920_33658140_1_1_1_1,00.html (accessed 6 August 2010).

[16] Financial Action Task Force (n/d), '9 special recommendations on terrorist financing', available at www.fatf-gafi.org/document/9/0,3343,en_32250379_32236920_34032073_1_1_1_1,00.html (accessed 6 August 2010).

[17] Jackson, C. (2004), 'Combating the new generation of money laundering: regulations and agencies in the battle of compliance, avoidance, and prosecution in a post-September 11 world', *Journal of High Technology Law*, **3**, 139–171, at 154.

techniques and counter-measures, and promotes the adoption and implementation of appropriate measures globally'.[18] The FATF is assisted by several regional affiliates which include the Asia/Pacific Group on Money Laundering,[19] the Caribbean Financial Action Task Force,[20] the Council of Europe Select Committee of Experts on the Evaluation of Money Laundering Measures,[21] the Eastern and South African Anti-Money Laundering Group,[22] the Eurasian Group,[23] the Intergovernmental Action Group Against Money Laundering in Africa[24] and the Middle Eastern and North African Financial Action Task Force.[25]

7.2.3   International Monetary Fund and the World Bank

The IMF and the World Bank play an important role in the global fight against money laundering and assist the FATF.[26] For example, in 2001 the IMF issued a statement asking all of its members to fully instigate the UN counter-terrorist resolutions.[27] Furthermore, it provides an information sharing environment, promotes the best anti-money laundering and terrorist financing practices and policy[28] and conducts financial sector assessments.[29] The assessments are referred to a Financial Sector

---

[18]   Financial Action Task Force (n/d), 'About the FATF', available at http://www.fatf-gafi.org/pages/0,3417,en_32250379_32236836_1_1_1_1_1,00.html (accessed 6 August 2010).

[19]   More information on the Asia Pacific Group on Money Laundering can be accessed from their website http://www.apgml.org/ (accessed 6 August 2010).

[20]   For more information on the work of the Caribbean Financial Action Task Force see http://www.cfatf-gafic.org/ (accessed 6 August 2010). Generally see Wilson, C. and Rattray, K. (2007), 'The Caribbean Financial Action Task Force', *Journal of Financial Crime*, **14**(3), 227–249.

[21]   See generally http://www.coe.int/t/dghl/monitoring/moneyval/ (accessed 6 August 2010).

[22]   For more information see http://www.esaamlg.org/ (accessed 6 August 2010).

[23]   See http://www.eurasiangroup.org/ (accessed 6 August 2010).

[24]   Generally see http://www.giaba.org/ (accessed 6 August 2010).

[25]   See http://www.menafatf.org/ as cited in Png, Choeng-Ann (2008b), 'International legal sources IV – the European Union and the Council of Europe', in W. Blair and R. Brent (eds), *Banks and financial crime – the international law of tainted money*, Oxford University Press, Oxford, 87–100, at 88.

[26]   Fisher, J. (2002), 'Recent international developments in the fight against money laundering', *Journal of International Banking Law*, **17**(3), 67–72, at 71.

[27]   Hopton, Doug (2009), *Money laundering – a concise guide for all businesses*, Gower, Farnham, at p. 16.

[28]   Dellinger above, n 13 at 433.

[29]   Leong, A. (2007a), 'Chasing dirty money: domestic and international

Assessment Programme, part of which involves an assessment of the country's anti-money laundering scheme.[30] The assessment also determines whether or not a country's anti-money laundering regime complies with the FATF recommendations.[31] The IMF has three functions in relation to combating money laundering and terrorist financing – promoting the anti-money laundering and counter-terrorist financing regime; providing technical assistance; and surveillance.[32] It is important to note that the IMF does not play an active part in the enforcement of the international money laundering initiatives.[33] Indeed, it wasn't until the terrorist attacks of September 2001 that the IMF became more involved in these types of financial crime.[34] Leong noted that the purpose of the IMF in relation to financial crime is the 'development and promotion of policies, both at national and international levels, to combat money laundering and terrorist financing and to preserve the integrity of the financial system'.[35] The World Bank Group, established in 1944, performs an identical function to that of the IMF.[36] In conjunction with the IMF it recognized the 40 Recommendations and the Nine Special Recommendations of the FATF. The World Bank Group has three relevant functions – the Global Dialogue Series; developing a universal anti-money laundering and counter-terrorist financing assessment methodology; and building institutional capacity.[37]

7.2.4   European Union

The EU was the first international organization to tackle financial crime in the 1970s and it has implemented a number of legislative measures. For instance, it introduced the first of its three Money Laundering Directives in 1991, and the second was introduced in 2001.[38] The third Money

---

measures against money laundering', *Journal of Money Laundering Control*, *10*(2), 140–156, at 149.

[30]   Fisher above, n 26 at 71.

[31]   Dellinger above, n 13 at 433.

[32]   Zagaris, Bruce (2010), *International white collar crime – cases and materials*, Cambridge University Press, New York, at 60–63.

[33]   Bachus above, n 5 at 856–857.

[34]   Zagaris above, n 32, at 60.

[35]   Leong above, n 29 at 148. For a more detailed discussion on the role of the World Bank see Arnone, M. and Padoan, P. (2008), 'Anti-money laundering by international institutions: a preliminary assessment ', *European Journal of Law & Economics*, **26**(3), 361–386, at 363–364.

[36]   Zagaris above, n 32, at 433.

[37]   *Ibid.*, at 433–436.

[38]   Council Directive (EC) 2001/97.

Laundering Directive obliges Member States to implement a number of measures aimed at tackling money laundering and terrorist financing.[39] In 2009, the EU Commission proposed to institute a Fourth Money Laundering Directive, which was widely criticized by Member States. However, as Hopton notes, 'it is clear that a Fourth Directive is possible in a few years'.[40] Another measure was the Council of Europe Convention on Laundering, Search, Seizure and Confiscation of the Proceeds from Crime.[41] This was amended in 2005 and required Member States to implement measures designed to confiscate the proceeds of crime.[42] The EU has also implemented a number of measures designed to tackle terrorist financing. This includes for example the Council of Europe's Common Position on combating terrorism[43] and the controversial anti-terrorism sanctions regime.[44] The EU, unlike the UN and the FATF, has implemented a number of legal instruments to tackle fraud and it has also created a designated anti-fraud office, OLAF.[45] Furthermore, Europol is the EU body that manages cross-border co-operation and coordination between EU national law-enforcement agencies. Europol works in the fields of drug trafficking, illegal immigration networks, terrorism, human trafficking, forgery of money and money laundering. Finally, the EU has been instrumental in implementing a series of measures aimed at tackling insider dealing and market abuse.[46]

7.2.5   Interpol

Interpol is one of the oldest international law enforcement entities in the world. Its membership consists of 186 countries and it has three principal objectives:

---

[39]   Directive (EC) 2005/60 of 26 October 2005.
[40]   Hopton above, n 27 at 31.
[41]   Stessens, Guy (2000), *Money laundering: a new international law enforcement model*, Cambridge University Press, Cambridge, at p. 23.
[42]   For a more detailed commentary on these issues see Chapter 6.
[43]   2001/930 [2001] OJ L344/90.
[44]   This includes for example the Council Regulation 2580/2001 [2001] OJ 344/70 and Council Regulation 881/2002 [2002] OJ L139/9. For an excellent commentary of the legalities of these measures see Brent, Richard (2008), 'International legal sources IV – the European Union and the Council of Europe', in W. Blair and R. Brent (eds), *Banks and financial crime – the international law of tainted money*, Oxford University Press, Oxford, 101–150, at 125–136.
[45]   For a more detailed commentary on this see Chapter 4.
[46]   This includes for example the 1989 Insider Dealing Directive and the 2005 Market Abuse Directive.

1. to provide secure police communications;
2. to provide operational data services and databases for police; and
3. to provide operational police support services.[47]

It also plays an important role in money laundering prevention and control.[48] Interpol has an Anti-Money Laundering Unit, whose function is to improve the quality of information among financial investigators, financial intelligence units (FIUs) and law enforcement agencies.

7.2.6 Egmont Group

The Egmont Group of FIUs was created in 1995 as a response to concerns regarding the confidentiality of financial transactions.[49] It has been described as an 'informal working group of financial intelligence units that form an important network of government agencies sharing financial intelligence and analysis to fight money-laundering'.[50] The Egmont Group also acts as a 'forum for discussion and improving support to their respective national anti-money laundering programmes'.[51] Importantly, 'Egmont Group members participate in annual meetings designed to facilitate international co-operation'.[52] It is therefore a form of administrative co-operation.[53] In order to become a member of Egmont an FIU must be a 'central, national agency responsible for receiving, (and as permitted, requesting), analysing and disseminating to the competent authorities, disclosures of financial information (i) concerning suspected proceeds of crime and potential financing of terrorism, or (ii) required by national legislation or regulation, in order to combat money laundering and terrorism financing'.[54] Members of Egmont are able to be connected to its 'Secure Web' which permits the swift exchange of information relating to

---

[47] Cameron-Waller, Stuart (2008), 'International co-operation networks', in S. Brown (ed.), *Combating international crime – the longer arm of the law*, Routledge Cavendish, Abingdon, 261–272, at 261.

[48] Shehu above, n 7 at 227.

[49] Dellinger above, n 13 at 432.

[50] Springer, J. (2001), 'Obtaining foreign assistance to prosecute money laundering cases: a US perspective', *Journal of Financial Crime*, **9**(2), 153–164, at 161.

[51] Leong above, n 29 at 149.

[52] Bachus above, n 5 at 855.

[53] See He, P. (2010), 'A typological study on money laundering', *Journal of Money Laundering Control*, **13**(1), 15–32, at 23.

[54] Egmont *Statement of purpose of the Egmont Group of Financial Intelligence Units* (Egmont: Guernsey, 2004) at p. 2.

suspicious transactions.[55] Simpson concluded 'the work of Egmont has borne fruit and there has been significant progress in achieving a great level of agreement with regard to the nature and role of financial intelligence units, and the procedures for exchange of information between different financial intelligence units'.[56] The Egmont Group has 'become a genuine international forum and, though having no official status, has become an essential element in the international fight against money laundering'.[57]

7.2.7 Basel Committee

The Basel Committee was established in 1974 by the Governors of the central banks of the G10,[58] and its purpose is to 'formulate broad supervisory standards and guidelines and recommends best practices'.[59] It was established in 'recognition of the vulnerability of the financial sector to misuse by criminals'.[60] The Committee has no formal authority or law making powers; it seeks to formulate best practices. Zagaris noted that the 'Basel Committee on Banking Regulations and Supervisory Practices has been active in promulgating soft law recommendations. For example in 1988, it adopted a statement of principles entitled "Prevention of Criminal Use of the Banking System, Draft Code of Conduct". The statement requires banks to know their customers, spot suspicious transactions and fully cooperate with law enforcement authorities'.[61] In relation to financial crime, the Basel Committee has issued a number of relevant anti-money laundering and counter-terrorist financing guidelines including 'Customer Due Diligence for Banks',[62] 'Sharing in Connection with the Fight Against Terrorist Financing',[63] and 'General Guide to Account Opening and Customer Identification'.[64]

---

[55] Bachus above, n 5 at 855.

[56] Simpson, M., Smith, N. and Srivastava, A. (eds) (2010), *International guide to money laundering law and practice* (Bloomsbury Professional: Haywards Health), pp. 193–235, at 220.

[57] European Union *Second Commission report to the European Parliament and the Council on the implementation of the money laundering directive* (Brussels, 1 July 1998, COM (1998) 401).

[58] Png above, n 25 at 97.

[59] *Ibid.*

[60] Hopton above, n 27 at 11.

[61] Zagaris above, n 32 at 64.

[62] *Ibid.*

[63] Zagaris above, n 32.

[64] *Ibid.*

7.2.8 Wolfsberg Group

The Wolfsberg Group was created 'due to international concern that private banks were not adequately involved in the fight against money laundering, particularly corruption'.[65] The Wolfsberg Principles 'were drawn up in October 2000 by a group of major international private banks, and were formulated with the practical needs of that segment of the banking sector in mind'.[66] The Group has worked with financial agencies to develop rules and guidelines to prevent private banks being abused by organized criminals to launder their proceeds of crime. In particular, it has worked with Transparency International to produce these guidelines.[67]

7.3 UNITED STATES – PRIMARY AGENCIES

7.3.1 Department of Treasury

The Department of Treasury is the major government department in charge of the administration of US anti-money laundering laws and regulations.[68] Until the terrorist attacks in 2001, the Department of Treasury concentrated on money laundering.[69] Its obligations were extended to include the financing of terrorism by the Uniting and Strengthening America by Providing Appropriate Tools to Restrict, Intercept and Obstruct Terrorism Act 2001 (USA Patriot Act 2001).[70] The Act granted the Department of Treasury additional powers to tackle terrorist financing and money laundering.[71] For example, it is permitted to allocate an overseas jurisdiction, a transaction, a financial institution or a type

---

[65]   Hopton above, n 27 at 17.
[66]   Simpson above, n 56 at 219.
[67]   Hopton above, n 27 at 17.
[68]   Low, L., Tillen, J., Abendschein, K. and Fisher-Owens, D. (2004), 'Country report: the US anti-money laundering system', in M. Peith and G. Aiolfi (eds), *A comparative guide to anti-money laundering: a critical analysis of systems in Singapore, Switzerland, the UK and the USA*, Edward Elgar, Cheltenham, 346–411, at 399. Hereafter Low *et al.*
[69]   Shetterly, D. (2006), 'Starving the terrorists of funding: how the United States Treasury is fighting the war on terror', *Regent University Law Review*, **18**, 327–348, at 332.
[70]   Hereinafter USA Patriot Act 2001. Pub. L. No. 107-56, § 302(a)(1), 115 Stat. 272 (2001).
[71]   Shetterly above, n 69 at 333.

of account as a 'primary money laundering concern'.[72] The Treasury Department has previously designated the Ukraine, Nauru and Burma as primary money laundering concerns.[73] Following a designation the Department of Treasury is allowed to ban financial transactions with any person or corporation that it designates.[74] The Department of Treasury has also utilized this power against the Commercial Bank of Syria,[75] First Merchant Bank of the Turkish Republic of Northern Cyprus, Infobank in Belarus,[76] and two Latvian banks, Multibanka and VEF Bank, in 2005.[77] The President is entitled to order the Secretary of State, the Attorney General or the Secretary of the Treasury to enter into negotiations with any relevant financial regulatory agency *and* bureaucrats from overseas financial jurisdictions that have a business relationship with US financial institutions that may be exploited for the purposes of terrorist financing or money laundering.[78] The Act stipulates that the President is entitled to direct the Secretary of the Treasury to improve the levels of international co-operation to guarantee that overseas financial institutions keep records of any financial transactions that relate to a designated foreign terrorist entity, any associate or affiliate of such an entity, or any other person suspected of engaging in money laundering and to create devices so that any records can be made available to the relevant US authorities.[79] The USA Patriot Act 2001 provides the Department of Treasury with extensive powers to tackle the problems associated with terrorist financing and money laundering. The Government Accountability Office (GAO) took the view that this section 'does not constitute an express mandate – that

---

[72]   USA Patriot Act 2001, s. 11.

[73]   67 FR 78859 (26 December 2002). See Department of Treasury (2003), 'Treasury Department Designates Burma and Two Burmese Banks to be of "Primary Money Laundering Concern" and Announces Proposed Countermeasures' available at http://www.treas.gov/press/releases/js1014.htm (accessed 1 August 2010).

[74]   USA Patriot Act (2001), s. 311(5).

[75]   Department of Treasury (2004b), 'Treasury Designates Commercial Bank of Syria as Financial Institution of Primary Money Laundering Concern', available at http://www.treas.gov/press/releases/js1538.htm (accessed 30 July 2010).

[76]   Department of Treasury (2004c), 'Treasury employs USA PATRIOT Act authorities to designate two foreign banks as "Primary Money Laundering Concern"', available at http://www.treas.gov/press/releases/js1874.htm (accessed 30 July 2010).

[77]   Department of Treasury (2005b), 'Treasury Wields PATRIOT Act Powers to Isolate Two Latvian Banks: Financial Institutions Identified as "Primary Money Laundering Concerns"', available at http://www.treas.gov/press/releases/js2401.htm (accessed 16 July 2010).

[78]   USA Patriot Act 2001, s. 330.

[79]   *Ibid.*

is, section 330 does not impose an affirmative obligation on any agency or official to enter into negotiations. Nonetheless, the language of section 330 does suggest that efforts should be undertaken to engage in appropriate negotiations'.[80] Indeed, Kittrie took the view that the 'Treasury has found that its unprecedented direct outreach to a country's key private financial institutions can yield results much more quickly than an outreach to that country's government'.[81] According to the Treasury Department's Office of Terrorist Finance and Financial Crime the obligation imposed by the USA Patriot Act 2001 has resulted in the US working with other international bodies that are dedicated to tackling the problems associated with financial crime, including the FATF, its regional affiliates, the IMF and the World Bank 'to develop a global system to ensure that all countries adopt and are assessed against international standards for protecting financial systems and jurisdictions from money laundering and terrorist financing'.[82] The importance of the Department of Treasury to the global terrorist financing policy should not be underestimated. For example, it has been argued that the Department of Treasury has 'led the initiative to make the battle against terrorist financing a priority in the world'.[83]

7.3.2 Department of Justice

The Department of Justice is led by the Attorney General, a post established by the Judiciary Act (1789),[84] who is supported by the Deputy Attorney General, the Associate Attorney General and the Solicitor General.[85] The Department of Justice contains a number of agencies including the Office of Justice Programs, Executive Office for US Trustees, Office of Dispute Resolution, the Federal Bureau of Investigation (FBI), the Drug Enforcement Administration (DEA), the US Marshals Service and the Bureau of Alcohol, Tobacco, Firearms and Explosives. In relation to financial crime, the Department of Justice is

---

[80]   Government Accountability Office *International Financial Crime – Treasury's roles and responsibilities relating to selected provisions of the USA Patriot Act 2001* (US Government Accountability Office: Washington, DC, 2006) at p. 7.

[81]   Kittrie, O. (2009), 'New sanctions for a new century: Treasury's innovative use of financial sanctions', *University of Pennsylvania Journal of International Law*, **30**, 789–822, at 820.

[82]   Government Accountability Office above, n 80 at 8.

[83]   Shetterly above, n 69 at 339.

[84]   The Judiciary Act of 1789, ch. 20, sec. 35, 1 Stat. 73, 92–93 (1789).

[85]   Department of Justice (n/d), 'Department of Justice Agencies', available at http://www.justice.gov/agencies/index-org.html#NSD (accessed 4 August 2010).

responsible for undertaking investigations and pursuing prosecutions of suspected instances of money laundering, terrorist financing, fraud and insider dealing. It therefore plays an integral role in the implementation of the US financial crime policies. The importance of the Department of Justice in relation to financial crime is illustrated by the fact that it has 'disrupted the terrorist financial network by freezing $200 million in assets around the world'.[86] The Department of Justice, via the DEA, 'seeks to deny safe havens to criminal organizations involved in drug trafficking, drug-related terrorist activities, and money laundering, thus depriving drug trafficking organizations of their illicit profits'.[87] Further evidence of its involvement in the battle against money laundering is illustrated by a joint venture with the Departments of Treasury and Homeland Security that seeks to recognize and attack money laundering via a national approach that identifies particular parts of the financial system.[88] The Department of Justice also manages the US assets forfeiture provisions which seek 'to attack the economic infrastructure of criminal organizations to take the profit out of drug trafficking and deprive the criminals of the illegally-gotten gains which are used to operate and expand their enterprises'.[89] In relation to asset forfeiture and money laundering the Department of Justice stated:

> all white collar crimes are conducted for profit, and the single largest deterrent to and punishment for such activity is the forfeiture of the ill-gotten assets. Even though prosecutors only recently have had the legal tools to directly forfeit the proceeds of white collar crime, about half of the deposits to the Assets Forfeiture Fund are non-drug related, showing significant efforts toward using this tool in non-drug related crimes for profit. Likewise, money laundering cuts across all white collar crimes, and the need for these criminals to disguise the source of their ill-gotten proceeds, is a vulnerability to be exploited.[90]

Furthermore, the Department of Justice also tackles a wide range of fraudulent activities. For example, it was instrumental in the creation of the Corporate Fraud Task Force which obtained over 1000 corporate fraud convictions including Adelphia, Martha Stewart, Bernard Ebbers, Frank Quattrone, Kenneth Lay, and Jeffrey Skilling.[91]

---

[86] Department of Justice *Fiscal Years 2007–2012 Strategic Plan* (Department of Justice: Washington, DC, 2007) at p. 1.
[87] *Ibid.*, at 25.
[88] *Ibid.*, at 46.
[89] *Ibid.*
[90] *Ibid.*, at 53.
[91] *Ibid.*, at 7.

7.3.3   State Department

The State Department has a wide range of policy areas including counter-terrorism, narcotics, human trafficking and economic issues. The role of the State Department in relation to financial crime can be best described as 'international' and 'representative'. The State Department represents the US on the 'UN 1267 Sanctions and Counter-Terrorism Committees, the G-8 Roma-Lyon Group, the Dublin Group, the Organization of American States (OAS), the FATF and the FSRBs. State Department personnel also take part in multi-agency diplomatic missions relating to money laundering and terrorist financing'.[92] Furthermore, it 'also has shared policy making responsibilities with Treasury and DOJ with respect to money laundering, terrorist financing, and other financial crime, ranging from planning and implementing Presidential Decision Directives and is a lead agency and a major source of funding for the provision of foreign AML/CFT training and technical assistance'.[93]

7.4   UNITED STATES – SECONDARY AGENCIES

7.4.1   Treasury Department

Office of Terrorism and Financial Intelligence
The aim of this Office is to 'marshal the Treasury Department's policy, enforcement, regulatory, and intelligence functions in order to sever the lines of financial support to international terrorists'.[94] The Office works at both a domestic and international level to make certain that all feasible political, policy and tactical steps are undertaken to combat both money laundering and terrorist financing. Importantly, this Office is responsible for overseeing the policy trend and assimilation of the Office of Foreign Assets Control and the Department of Treasury's Executive Office for Asset Forfeiture. Furthermore, it supervises the Financial Crimes Enforcement Network (FinCEN). According to the FATF, the Office of Terrorism and Financial Intelligence is responsible for 'developing and implementing US government strategies to combat terrorist financing domestically and internationally; developing and implementing

---

[92]   Financial Action Task Force above, n 2 at 18.
[93]   *Ibid.*
[94]   Department of Treasury (n/d), 'Terrorism and financial intelligence', available at http://www.treas.gov/offices/enforcement/ (accessed 6 August 2010).

the National Money Laundering Strategy as well as other policies and programs to fight financial crimes'.[95]

Office of Intelligence and Analysis

The Office of Intelligence and Analysis, which is part of the US intelligence community, was established by the Intelligence Authorization Act 2004.[96] The Act stipulates that the Office is responsible for receiving, examining and distributing foreign intelligence and foreign counterintelligence information related to the process and obligations of the Department of Treasury.[97] Furthermore, it analyses and produces information for the Department of Treasury on the financial and support networks of terrorists. According to the FATF, it 'develops financial intelligence and conducts analysis with a view to filling gaps in intelligence targets, and adding value and expertise. Its priorities include identifying and attacking the financial infrastructure of terrorist groups; identifying and addressing vulnerabilities that may be exploited by terrorists and criminals in domestic and international financial systems; and promoting stronger relationships with Treasury's partners in the US and around the world'.[98]

Office of Terrorist Financing and Financial Crimes

The Office of Terrorist Financing and Financial Crimes liaises with other national security agencies, the private sector and other governments to 'address the threats presented by all forms of illicit finance to the international financial system'.[99] This part of the Department of Treasury develops policies that tackle a wide range of financial crime including money laundering and terrorist financing.[100] The Office also represents the US on the FATF. According to the FATF this Office 'serves as the primary point of contact for responding to international requests for information regarding particular NPOs suspected of terrorist financing or other forms

---

[95]　Financial Action Task Force above, n 2 at 16.

[96]　Pub. L. No. 108-177, §314, 1117 Stat. 2599, 2610. For a more detailed discussion about the Intelligence Authorization Act 2004 and its predecessors see Radsan, J. (2009), 'An overt turn to covert action', *Saint Louis University Law Journal*, Winter, **53**, 485–552.

[97]　Department of Treasury (n/d), 'Office of Analysis and Intelligence', available at http://www.ustreas.gov/offices/enforcement/oia/ (accessed 6 August 2010).

[98]　Financial Action Task Force above, n 2 at 16.

[99]　Department of Treasury (n/d), 'Office of Terrorist Financing and Financial Crimes', available at http://www.ustreas.gov/offices/enforcement/eotf.shtml (accessed 6 August 2010).

[100]　*Ibid.*

of terrorist support. TFFC acts as the appropriate point of contact for such requests by marshalling US intelligence and enforcement capabilities with the twin aims of combating terrorist financing in the charitable sector and promulgating policies and other initiatives to better safeguard charities from the threat of terrorist abuse'.[101]

Office of Foreign Assets Control

The origins of OFAC are to be found in the creation of the Office of Foreign Funds in 1940, which was managed by the Department of Treasury until the end of the Second World War. Its initial purpose was to thwart the Nazis' attempted 'use of the occupied countries' holdings of foreign exchange and securities and to prevent forced repatriation of funds belonging to nationals of those countries'.[102] OFAC was officially established in 1950 as a result of China's involvement in the Korean War and it now 'administers and enforces economic and trade sanctions based on US foreign policy and national security goals against targeted foreign countries and regimes, terrorists, international narcotics traffickers'.[103] Since the terrorist attacks in 2001, OFAC is permitted to freeze the assets of suspected or known terrorists and impose sanctions after being granted additional powers by President George Bush.[104] The objective of these sanctions is to 'deprive targets of the use of their assets and to deny access to the US financial system and the benefits of trade, transactions and services involving US markets, business and individuals'.[105] OFAC maintains a list of Sanctions Programs including sanctions it has imposed on Cuba, North Korea, Sudan and Zimbabwe.[106] It is important to note that OFAC's role against terrorism 'stems from the initial conception of

---

[101]   Financial Action Task Force above, n 2 at 248.

[102]   Department of Treasury (n/d), 'Office of Foreign Assets Control' available at http://www.ustreas.gov/offices/enforcement/ofac/mission.shtml (accessed 6 August 2010).

[103]   *Ibid.* Eckert took the view that 'OFAC's mission historically has been to implement sanctions against foreign governments whose policies are inimical to US foreign policy and national security interests'. Eckert, Sue (2008), 'The US regulatory approach to terrorist financing', in T. Biersteker and S. Eckert (eds) *Countering the financing of terrorism*, Routledge Cavendish, London, 209–233, at 211.

[104]   Ortblad, V. (2008), 'Criminal prosecution in sheep's clothing: the punitive effects of OFAC freezing sanctions', *Journal of Criminal Law and Criminology*, **98**, 1439–1465, at 1442.

[105]   Eckert above, n 103 at 212.

[106]   Zaring, D. and Baylis, E. (2007), 'Sending the bureaucracy to war', *Iowa Law Review*, **92**, 1359–1428, at 1399–1400.

terrorism as state-sponsored'.[107] Its role 'was to compile available evidence establishing that certain foreign entities or individuals were owned or controlled by, or acting on behalf of, a foreign government subject to an economic sanctions program'.[108] This policy altered when President Bill Clinton implemented the International Economic Emergency Powers Act 1995. The Act enabled OFAC to counter the threat presented by terrorists towards destabilizing the Middle East Peace Process by allowing it to impose sanctions on terrorists.[109] These powers were also used following the 2001 terrorist attacks via Presidential Executive Order 13224.[110] OFAC manages the Specially Designated Nationals list of individuals and corporations who are 'controlled by, or acting for or on behalf of, targeted countries'.[111] The list also contains 'individuals, groups, and entities, such as terrorists and narcotics traffickers designated under programs that are not country-specific'.[112]

The ability of OFAC to freeze the accounts of suspected terrorists is extremely controversial. The Department of Treasury claimed that the actions of OFAC were extremely successful; a point illustrated by its reference to the number of bank accounts frozen by 2004 (1500) and their value ($139m).[113] Furthermore, it has been argued that OFAC had frozen approximately $200m of suspected terrorist funds by 2004.[114] The alteration in policy from imposing sanctions on countries to imposing them on individuals is extremely controversial, yet it has been argued that it is the only way to 'keep terrorists away from their assets so that they cannot finance terrorist activities'.[115] Indeed, 'the targeted financial sanctions have thus far

---

[107]   Eckert above, n 103 at 212.

[108]   *Ibid.*

[109]   *Ibid.*

[110]   Executive Order 13224 of 23 September 2001. Federal Register, **66**(186), 25 September 2001, pp. 49079–49081.

[111]   Department of Treasury (n/d), 'OFAC frequently asked questions and answers', available at http://www.ustreas.gov/offices/enforcement/ofac/faq/answer.shtml#17 (accessed 6 August 2010).

[112]   *Ibid.*

[113]   Department of Treasury (2004a), 'Bush Administration Announces Budget Increase to help Fight Terrorist Financing and Financial Crime', available at http://www.ustreas.gov/press/releases/js1100.htm (accessed 8 May 2009). For an excellent commentary on the performance of OFAC see Fitzgerald, P. (2002), 'Managing smart sanctions against terrorism wisely', *New England Law Review*, **36**, 975–983.

[114]   Zaring and Baylis above, n 106 at 1399.

[115]   Keeney, P. (2004), 'Frozen assets of terrorists and terrorist supporters: a proposed solution to the creditor collection problem', *Emory Bankruptcy Developments Journal*, **21**, 301–341, at 340.

proven to be among the twenty-first century's most effective and important new counterterrorism and counter proliferation tools'.[116] However, the effectiveness of these measures must be questioned due to the number of sources of financing available to terrorists and their ability to become self-sufficient.[117] Furthermore, OFAC has incorrectly designated several groups who have no links to terrorists.[118] This includes for example the money remittance company Al Barakat,[119] which according to the Department of Treasury 'channelled several million dollars a year to and from al Qaida'.[120] However, it must be noted that the authorities have successfully prosecuted a number of directors of the Holy Land Foundation,[121] and OFAC's powers were upheld in *Islamic American Relief Agency v Gonzales*.[122]

Financial Crimes Enforcement Network
FinCEN is the US FIU and its objectives in relation to financial crime are to collect and distribute financial intelligence. This has been described as its 'primary law enforcement function'.[123] The idea of creating such an agency was initially discussed in 1981,[124] yet it wasn't established until 25 April 1990 with the initial aim of fighting drug trafficking.[125] Eventually, it became apparent that it had the potential to tackle a broader range of illegal activities.[126] For example, US authorities were reliant on FinCEN's database during the Gulf War, which allowed the Department of Treasury to freeze accounts and assets in excess of $3m that were suspected of

---

[116] Kittrie above, n 81 at 819.

[117] See for example Ortblad above, n 104 at 1455.

[118] *Ibid.*, at 1441.

[119] Department of Treasury (2009), 'Recent OFAC Actions', available at http://www.ustreas.gov/offices/enforcement/ofac/actions/20091103.shtml (accessed 5 June 2010).

[120] Department of Treasury *Contributions by the Department of the Treasury to the Financial War on Terrorism Fact Sheet* (Department of Treasury: Washington, DC, 2002) at p. 6.

[121] On 25 November 2008, five of the organizers of the Holy Land Foundation were convicted of providing over $12 million to Hamas. The Holy Land Foundation challenged the legality of the designation by OFAC, but was denied certiorari by the US Supreme Court. See *Holy Land Foundation for Relief & Dev. v Ashcroft*, 540 U.S. 1218, 124 S.Ct. 1506 (2004).

[122] 477 F.3d 728, 739 (D.C. Cir. 2007).

[123] Low *et al.* above, n 68 at 400.

[124] Bercu, S. (1994), 'Toward universal surveillance in an information age economy: can we handle Treasury's new police technology?', *Jurimetrics Journal*, **34**, 383–449, at 339.

[125] *Ibid.*, at 392.

[126] *Ibid.*, at 390.

having links with Saddam Hussein.[127] FinCEN's mission is to 'enhance US national security, deter and detect criminal activity, and safeguard financial systems from abuse by promoting transparency in the US and international financial systems'.[128] FinCEN manages the Bank Secrecy Act 1970 (BSA), which requires a broad range of financial institutions and other professions to submit intelligence via currency transaction reports (CTRs) and suspicious activity reports (SARs). The financial intelligence gathered from these reports is illustrated by the fact that they are utilized by law enforcement agencies in the pursuit of financial criminals.[129] Furthermore, it plays a crucial role in the fight against financial crime because it provides law enforcement agencies with detailed information that can be used in the exposure, examination and prosecution of a wide range of financial crimes.[130] FinCEN is obliged to 'analyze and disseminate the available data . . . to determine emerging trends and methods in money laundering and other financial crimes'.[131] In addition to supplying financial intelligence relating to transactions involving financial crime, FinCEN has responsibility to 'identify and discover potential forfeitable assets, and to make that information available to the law enforcement agencies'.[132] The scope of the organization's remit was extended to include terrorist financing by the USA Patriot Act 2001.[133] The FATF described this decision as 'the most important stated operational and tactical priority for FinCEN.'[134] FinCEN has assisted other countries to create financial intelligence units and supported the FATF.[135] It also has regulatory enforcement powers and it often brings administrative actions that result in civil penalties breaches of the BSA 1970.[136] It therefore plays a critical role in the international efforts to combat money laundering, terrorist financing, fraud and insider dealing.[137]

---

[127]   *Ibid.*, at 392.

[128]   FinCEN (n/d), 'Mission', available at http://www.fincen.gov/about_fincen/wwd/mission.html (accessed 5 August 2010).

[129]   Government Accountability Office *Suspicious Activity Report Use Is Increasing, but FinCEN needs to Further Develop and Document Its Form Revision Process* (US Government Accountability Office: Washington, DC, 2009) at p. 10.

[130]   General Accounting Office *Progress report on Treasury's Financial Crimes Enforcement Network* (General Accounting Office: Washington, DC, 1993) at p. 1.

[131]   31 USC § 310(b)(2)(C).

[132]   Financial Action Task Force above, n 2 at 16.

[133]   Treasury Order 180-01 dated 26 September 2002.

[134]   Financial Action Task Force above, n 2 at 61.

[135]   Jackson above, n 17 at 139.

[136]   Low *et al.* above, n 68 at 400.

[137]   Government Accountability Office above, n 80 at 33.

Treasury Executive Office for Asset Forfeiture
This Office was created in 1992 and it manages the Treasury Forfeiture Fund,[138] which involves receiving non-tax forfeitures made by the Internal Revenue Service Criminal Investigation Division, Department of the Treasury, Immigration and Customs Enforcement, Customs and Border Protection, the US Secret Service and the Coast Guard.[139]

Operation Green Quest
Operation Green Quest was launched by the Treasury Department on 25 October 2001; it is led by US Customs but it draws upon staff and the expertise of Internal Revenue Service, the Secret Service, the Bureau of Alcohol, Tobacco and Firearms, the FBI, OFAC, FinCEN and prosecutors from the Justice Department.[140] According to the Treasury Department this multiagency organization seeks to 'augment existing counter-terrorist efforts by bringing the full scope of the government's financial expertise to bear against systems, individuals, and organizations that serve as sources of terrorist funding'.[141] It is an enforcement agency that has the ability to freeze accounts, seize assets and bring criminal proceedings against people and groups who are suspected of financing terrorism.[142] MacMull took the view that Operation Green Quest concentrated upon a 'wide variety of systems that may be used by terrorists to raise and move funds'.[143] Reynolds and Papandrea took the view that '[t]he purpose of Operation Green Quest is to 'eliminate current and future terrorist funding sources, including underground financial systems, illicit charities, and corrupt financial institutions'.[144] According to one commentator, within one year of its existence Operation Green Quest resulted in the seizure of over $10m of smuggled cash and approximately $4m in assets. By October 2002, this

---

[138] It is important to note that the Department of Justice administers a separate Asset Forfeiture Program. For a more detailed commentary see Chapter 6.

[139] Department of Treasury (n/d), 'The Treasury Executive Office for Asset Forfeiture & Treasury Forfeiture Fund', available at http://www.ustreas.gov/offices/enforcement/teoaf/ (accessed 3 August 2010).

[140] Jackson above, n 17 at 140.

[141] Department of Treasury (2001), 'Deputy Secretary Dam remarks at the launch of Operation Green Quest', available at http://www.ustreas.gov/press/releases/po727.htm (accessed 21 October 2009).

[142] Jackson above, n 17 at 139.

[143] MacMull, J. (2004), 'Removing the charitable veil: an examination of US policy to combat terrorist funding charities post 9/11', *New England Journal of International and Comparative Law*, **10**, 121–136, at 132.

[144] Reynolds, J. and Papandrea, J. (2002), 'Export controls and economic sanctions', *Foreign Law Year in Review*, Fall, **36**, 1063–1079, at 1067.

total had increased to an impressive figure of $22.8 million. MacMull highlighted the success of Operation Green Quest and stated that by August 2002 'in cooperation with the Department of Justice, had led to 38 arrests, 26 indictments, the seizure of $6.8 million domestically, and the seizure of over $16 million in outbound currency at international borders, including more than $7 million in bulk cash being smuggled illegally to Middle East destinations'.[145] Jackson noted that by 2003, as a result of Operation Green Quest's work, 'nearly 200 search warrants/consent searches, 93 arrests, seizure of more than $11 million from suspected terrorist networks and another $24 million in smuggled monetary instruments' were undertaken.[146]

7.4.2   Department of Justice

Asset Forfeiture and Money Laundering Section
The Asset Forfeiture and Money Laundering Section manages the Department of Justice's asset forfeiture programme and advises its money laundering prosecuting divisions. Furthermore, it 'initiates, coordinates, and reviews legislative and policy proposals impacting on the asset forfeiture program and money laundering enforcement agencies'.[147] This division of the Department of Justice also prosecutes and directs global money laundering and asset forfeiture investigations; it provides training for law enforcement personnel and it supports policymakers by reviewing relevant financial crime policies.[148]

Counterterrorism Section
The Counterterrorism Section of the Department of Justice administers and implements strategies that seek to counter terrorism.[149] Of particular relevance is its responsibility for investigating and prosecuting terrorist financing matters, including material support cases.[150]

National Drug Intelligence Center
The National Drug Intelligence Center (NDIC) was created in 1993 with the primary objective of developing tactical domestic drug

---

[145]   MacMull above, n 143 at 133.
[146]   Jackson above, n 17 at 139.
[147]   Department of Justice (n/d), 'Asset Forfeiture and Money Laundering Section', available at http://www.justice.gov/criminal/afmls/ (accessed 17 July 2010).
[148]   Financial Action Task Force above, n 2 at 17.
[149]   Department of Justice (n/d), 'Counterterrorism section', available at http://www.justice.gov/nsd/counter_terrorism.htm (accessed 6 August 2010).
[150]   *Ibid.*

intelligence.[151] It was established to 'coordinate and consolidate drug intelligence from all national security and law enforcement agencies, and produce information regarding the structure, membership, finances, communications, and activities of drug trafficking organizations'.[152] Specifically, it constructs money laundering reports that assist the government to implement its anti-money laundering strategies.

Office of International Affairs
The Office of International Affairs plays a central role in the Department of Justice's policy towards extradition and mutual legal assistance.

7.4.3   State Department

Bureau of Economic and Business Affairs
The Bureau of Economic and Business Affairs seeks to prevent terrorist states from profiting from trading with the US and to deny them access to the international financial system.

Bureau of International Narcotics and Law Enforcement Affairs
This part of the State Department is principally concerned with money laundering and other types of financial crime.

Office of the Coordinator for Counterterrorism
The Office of the Coordinator for Counterterrorism directs the efforts of the State Department relating to the designation of Foreign Terrorist Organizations. This is an integral part of the US anti-terrorist financing measures and it has resulted in the freezing of terrorist assets. Importantly, this Office also prepares designations for Presidential Executive Order 13224.

7.5   UNITED STATES – TERTIARY AGENCIES

Federal Bureau of Investigation
The FBI was established in 1908 and its objective is to protect the US from terrorism and foreign intelligence threats, to enforce criminal laws and to

---

[151]   Department of Justice (n/d), 'National Drug Intelligence Center', available at http://www.justice.gov/ndic/about.htm#Top (accessed 6 August 2010). See the Department of Defense Appropriations Act 1993 (Public Law 102-396).
[152]   *Ibid.*

liaise with regional and international agencies.[153] The FBI is the lead agency responsible for investigating financial crime,[154] including money laundering, terrorist financing, fraud and insider dealing. It is the primary agency of the Joint Terrorism Task Force, which has the crucial role of investigating allegations of terrorist financing.[155] The FBI has established its own specialist unit, the Terrorist Financing Operations Section, within its Counterterrorism Division. The objective of the Terrorist Financing Operations Section is to provide intelligence and support to ongoing investigations. According to the GAO 'the FBI's Terrorist Financing Operations Section provides overall operational command to the interagency National Joint Terrorism Task Force at FBI headquarters and the Joint Terrorism Task Forces in the field that conduct terrorist financing investigations and operations'.[156] Furthermore, it focuses on performing a 'full financial analysis of terrorist suspects and their financial support structures in the US and abroad'.[157] The FBI has disrupted al Qaeda financing in the United Arab Emirates, Pakistan, Afghanistan and Indonesia.[158] Furthermore, it has dismantled 'a Hezbollah procurement and fund-raising network tied to cigarette smuggling and a charity that was sending money to Al Qaeda'.[159] The FBI also investigates instances of fraud, theft and embezzlement. These areas are dealt with by the Financial Crime Section whose objective is to supervise the investigation of fraud and to assist in the forfeiture of assets from those participating in the crimes. The Financial Crime Section is divided into three units – the Economic Crimes Unit I, the Economic Crimes Unit II and the Health Care Fraud Unit.[160] The remit of Economic Crime Unit I includes sizeable frauds that target individuals, business and industries. The Economic Crime Unit II deals with financial institution fraud; it promotes the tactical use of asset forfeiture and is responsible for the management of the Forfeiture Support

---

[153]   Federal Bureau of Investigation (n/d), 'About us – quick facts', available at http://www.fbi.gov/quickfacts.htm (accessed 4 August 2010).

[154]   Financial Action Task Force above, n 2 at 68.

[155]   For a more detailed discussion of the Joint Terrorism Task Force see Herman, S. (2005), 'Collapsing spheres: joint terrorism task forces, federalism, and the war on terror', *Willamette Law Review*, **41**, 941–969.

[156]   General Accounting Office *US Agencies Should Systematically Assess Terrorists' Use of Alternative Financing Mechanisms* (General Accounting Office: Washington, DC, 2003) at p. 24.

[157]   Financial Action Task Force above, n 2 at 22.

[158]   Zagaris, B. (2005), 'Brave new world: US responses to the rise in international crime', *Villanova Law Review*, **50**, 509–582, at 529.

[159]   *Ibid.*

[160]   Federal Bureau of Investigation (2007a), 'Financial crimes report to the public, fiscal year 2007', available at http://www.fbi.gov/publications/financial/fcs_report2007/financial_crime_2007.htm#corporate (accessed 5 February 2009).

Project. The Health Care Fraud Unit undertakes investigations where the fraud relates to public and private health care systems. The FBI outlined its strategy towards financial crime in its 'Strategic Plan'.[161]

Drug Enforcement Administration
The DEA was created in 1973 by President Richard Nixon as part of the US 'war on drugs'.[162] The DEA's mission is to 'enforce the controlled substances laws and regulations of the United States and bring to the criminal and civil justice system of the United States those organizations, and principal members of organizations, involved in the growing, manufacture, or distribution of controlled substances appearing in or destined for illicit traffic in the United States'.[163] Furthermore, it also manages the national drug intelligence programme, seizes and forfeits assets derived from drug trafficking, enforces the Controlled Substances Act 1970 and interacts with the UN and Interpol.[164] The DEA performs an important task in the US strategy towards money laundering due to its historical link with the illegal drugs trade. For example, it has a Financial Investigations Strategy which is spearheaded by 24 Financial Investigation Teams.[165] The importance of anti-money laundering strategies adopted by the DEA is illustrated by Operation Mallorca, Money Trail Initiative,[166] Operation Cali Exchange[167] and Operation Plata Sucia.[168]

---

[161]   Federal Bureau of Investigation *FBI Strategic Plan* (Federal Bureau of Investigation: Washington, DC, n/d).

[162]   Drug Enforcement Administration (n/d), 'DEA history', available at http://www.justice.gov/dea/history.htm (accessed 6 August 2010).

[163]   Drug Enforcement Administration (n/d), 'DEA mission statement', available at http://www.justice.gov/dea/agency/mission.htm (accessed 6 August 2010).

[164]   *Ibid.*

[165]   Drug Enforcement Administration (n/d), 'Money laundering', available at http://www.justice.gov/dea/programs/money.htm (accessed 11 July 2010).

[166]   This scheme resulted in the seizure of $28 million, 230 arrests and the confiscation of 1581 kilograms of cocaine and 37055 pounds of marijuana. See Drug Enforcement Administration (2005b), 'DEA's "Money Trail Initiative" Cuts Flow of Cash to Cartels', available at http://www.justice.gov/dea/pubs/pressrel/pr071905.html (accessed 21 June 2010).

[167]   Operation Cali Exchange resulted in 24 indictments and 18 arrests, and the seizure of over $7 million, 2107 kilograms of cocaine, and 518 pounds of marijuana. Drug Enforcement Administration (2005a), 'DEA Dismantles Large International Drug and Money Laundering Organization', available at http://www.justice.gov/dea/pubs/pressrel/pr120805.html (accessed 21 June 2010).

[168]   More than $10 million in drug proceeds and $6.5 million in cocaine, heroin, and marijuana were seized as part of the operation. Drug Enforcement Agency (n/d), '26 Arrested in International Drug Bust', available at http://www.justice.gov/dea/pubs/pressrel/pr101806.html (accessed 21 June 2010).

Securities and Exchange Commission

The SEC is the principal regulator for the securities markets and it manages the US securities laws.[169] It regulates a wide range of sectors including the securities exchanges, securities brokers and dealers, investment advisers and investment companies. Its objective is to 'protect investors, maintain fair, orderly, and efficient markets, and facilitate capital formation'.[170] Furthermore, it has a broad range of powers governing consumer protection, including the oversight of external auditors.[171] The SEC takes an active role in the US fraud and insider dealing policies. For example, it has the capability to bring civil actions but not criminal prosecutions for fraud or insider dealing.[172] Its role and enforcement powers were significantly extended following the implementation of the Sarbanes-Oxley Act (2002) as a result of the accountancy fraud that led to the collapse of Enron and WorldCom.[173] The role of the SEC in relation to fraud was illustrated during the prosecution and eventual conviction of Bernard Madoff.[174]

7.6   THE UNITED KINGDOM

The policy adopted by the UK towards financial crime agencies has been to create single entities to tackle specific types of financial crime. For example, the Serious Fraud Office (SFO) was established with the aim of tackling fraud. Conversely, the policy adopted by the Labour government since 1997 has been to provide agencies with a broader remit. For

---

[169]   This includes for example the Securities Act of 1933, the Securities Exchange Act of 1934, the Investment Company Act of 1940, the Investment Advisers Act of 1940, and the Trust Indenture Act of 1939.

[170]   Securities and Exchange Commission (n/d), 'The Investor's Advocate: How the SEC Protects Investors, Maintains Market Integrity, and Facilitates Capital Formation', available at http://www.sec.gov/about/whatwedo.shtml (accessed 2 July 2010).

[171]   Singh, Dalvinder (2007) *Banking regulation of the UK and US financial markets*, Ashgate, Aldershot, at p.173.

[172]   Rider, B. (2010), 'An abominable fraud?', *Company Lawyer*, **31**(7), 197–198, at 197. For an interesting discussion about the use of civil sanctions by the SEC see *United States Securities & Exchange Commission v Manterfield* [2009] EWCA Civ 27; [2010] 1 WLR 172 (CA (Civ Div)).

[173]   See for example Saksena, P. and Fox, M. (2004), 'Accounting fraud and the Sarbanes-Oxley Act', *International Company and Commercial Law Review*, **15**(8), 244–251.

[174]   Anon (2009), 'SEC charges key Madoff lieutenant with fraud', *Company Lawyer*, **30**(12), 371.

example, the Financial Services Authority (FSA) has a statutory objective to reduce financial crime,[175] and the Assets Recovery Agency, later to become the SOCA, to tackle money laundering and manage the confiscation of criminally obtained assets. However, toward the end of its term of office, the Labour government reverted to the policy of the former Conservative government and started to create agencies with a narrow remit. For example, to tackle fraud the National Fraud Authority (NFA) and the National Fraud Reporting Centre (NFRC) were created.

7.7   UNITED KINGDOM – PRIMARY REGULATORS

7.7.1   HM Treasury

The objective of HM Treasury is 'safeguarding the integrity of the financial system from exploitation by criminals and terrorists. It does this by deploying financial tools to deter, detect and disrupt crime and security threats. The approach taken is effective and proportionate to the risks posed as well as engaging with business, law makers and law enforcers'. This is clearly illustrated by the publication of a strategy document in 2007 that outlined how the government intended to tackle the problems associated with money laundering and the financing of terrorism.[176] HM Treasury also chairs the Money Laundering Advisory Committee which is a 'forum for all relevant stakeholders – financial institutions, trade and consumer organisations, government and law enforcement representatives'.[177] In addition to developing and implementing the anti-money laundering and terrorist financing policy, HM Treasury created an Asset Freezing Unit that is responsible for the implementation and management of international financial sanctions imposed by the UN and for licensing exemptions to financial sanctions. The Asset Freezing Unit came into existence in October 2007, and it is responsible for domestic legislation on financial sanctions; the implementation and administration of domestic financial sanctions; domestic designation; providing

---

[175]   Financial Services and Markets Act 2000, s. 6.
[176]   HM Treasury *The Financial Challenge to Crime and Terrorism* (HM Treasury: London, 2007).
[177]   Oxford Analytica Ltd (2004), 'Country report: anti-money laundering rules in the United Kingdom' in M. Pieith and G. Aiolfi (eds), *A comparative guide to anti-money laundering: a critical analysis of systems in Singapore, Switzerland, the UK and the USA*, Edward Elgar, Cheltenham, 265–345, at 271.

advice to Treasury Ministers, on the basis of operational advice, on domestic designation decisions; the implementation and administration of international financial sanctions in the UK, including those relating to terrorism, state regimes, proliferation of weapons of mass destruction; working with the Foreign and Commonwealth Office on the design of individual financial sanctions regimes and listed decisions at the UN and European Union; working with international partners to develop the international frameworks for asset freezing; and licensing exemptions to financial sanctions. In particular, the Asset Freezing Unit issues notices and notifications advising of the introduction, amendment, suspension or lifting of financial sanctions regimes with a view to making bodies and individuals likely to be affected by financial sanctions aware of their obligations. It also provides a consolidated list of financial sanctions targets which consists of the names of individuals and entities that have been listed by the UN, EU and/or the UK and processes applications for licences to release frozen funds or to make funds available to designated/ restricted persons and it responds to reports and queries from financial institutions, companies and members of the public concerning financial sanctions.

7.7.2 The Home Office

Another government department that plays an active role in the reduction of financial crime is the Home Office, which is the government department responsible for the police, drugs policy, immigration and passports and counter-terrorism. The Home Office also 'prepares legislation that relates to money laundering and related offences and is responsible for policy on confiscation and international mutual legal assistance'.[178]

7.7.3 Foreign and Commonwealth Office

The Foreign and Commonwealth Office has little involvement with the UK's anti-money laundering and counter-terrorist financing policy. However, it is important to note that it does represent the UK regarding its entry into international agreements including UN treaties and Security Council Resolutions.

---

[178] *Ibid.*, at 272.

7.8 UNITED KINGDOM – SECONDARY REGULATORS

7.8.1 Serious Organized Crime Agency

It is the UK's FIU and it also manages the assets recovering provisions under the Proceeds of Crime Act 2002.[179] SOCA came into existence on 1 April 2006 by virtue of the Serious Organized Crime and Police Act 2005. This Act imposed three functions on SOCA – serious organized crime; information relating to crime; and general considerations. In relation to serious organized crime, the Act provides that SOCA has the function of preventing and detecting serious organized crime, and contributing to the reduction of such crime in other ways and to the mitigation of its consequences.[180] Section 3 of the Act provides that in relation to information relating to crime SOCA's function is 'gathering, storing, analysing and disseminating information relevant to (a) the prevention, detection, investigation or prosecution of offences, or (b) the reduction of crime in other ways or the mitigation of its consequences'.[181] SOCA took over the role of FIU in 2006 from the National Criminal Intelligence Service (NCIS). Additionally, the government announced in 2007 that SOCA would take over the assets recovery function of the ARA.[182]

7.8.2 The Police and Special Branches

In many instances it is the police services of the UK that will encounter instances of financial crime. For example, simple instances of fraud will be reported to the police who will then pass them on to the relevant agency to deal with it. The police will only deal with relatively minor offences of financial crime, passing the more complex and larger instances on to more specialized agencies. However, it is worth noting that most small frauds will only be reported to a bank or credit card company with the police not being informed at all. Doig noted that 'by the end of the 1990s, most police forces acknowledged a decline in resourcing and prioritisation such that two surveys noted that only one police force identified fraud in their

---

[179] For a more detailed commentary on the performance of the ARA see Chapter 5.

[180] Serious Organized Crime and Police Act 2005, s. 2(1)(a) and (b).

[181] Serious Organized Crime and Police Act 2005, s. 3(1)(a) and (b).

[182] The ARA was abolished by the the Serious Crime Act 2007 (Amendment of the Proceeds of Crime Act 2002) Order 2008 (2008/949) and Serious Crime Act 2007, s. 74.

local policing plan, most fraud squads had fewer than 10 officers and that most had lost experienced senior officers'.[183] Doig took the view that 'the criminal investigation of serious fraud still falls within the responsibility of the police. In the late 1990s only one did not have a fraud squad. Today an increasing number have either abolished them or merged them into a general serious crime unit'.[184] Doig stated that the 'current City of London Police fraud squad structure was introduced in April 2004. It covers the Home Counties whose forces may or not retain their own fraud squad . . . the force collaborates with the SFO but it is not part of it'.[185] The Fraud Squad is now located within the City of London Police Economic Crime Department which is divided into seven areas including the Cheque and Credit Card Unit, the Money Laundering Investigation Unit, Financial Investigation Unit, Dedicated Cheque and Plastic Crime Unit, the Fraud Intelligence Development Team and the Overseas Anti-Corruption Unit.[186]

7.8.3   HM Revenue and Customs

HM Revenue and Customs plays an important role in the prevention of money laundering and fraud. For the purposes of money laundering it has been designated a 'supervisory authority' under the 2007 Money Laundering Regulations.[187] This means that it has an obligation to 'monitor firms that they supervise . . . and if necessary, to take measures for the purpose of securing compliance'.[188]

7.8.4   The Serious Fraud Office

The SFO is an independent government department that investigates and prosecutes serious or complex fraud cases. It has been described as 'the embodiment of the unified fraud investigations and prosecution

---

[183]   Doig, Alan (2006), *Fraud*, Willan, Collumpton, at 120–121.

[184]   *Ibid.*, at 122.

[185]   Doig above, n 183 at 132.

[186]   See City of London Police (n/d), 'Structure', available at 'http://www.cityoflondon.police.uk/CityPolice/Departments/ECD/About/structure.htm (accessed 6 August 2010). It is likely that the Coalition government will implement a series of measures aimed at reforming the structure of the police. See for example Home Office *Policing in the 21st century: reconnecting police and the people* (Home Office: London, 2010).

[187]   HMRC is responsible for high value dealers, money services businesses, auditors, bill payment service providers and telecommunications firms.

[188]   Simpson above, n 56 at p. 98.

organisation'.[189] It is part of the UK criminal justice system and commenced operation in April 1988 and has been responsible for the investigation and prosecution of some of the biggest fraud cases since its creation.[190] The impetus for creating the SFO was the Fraud Trials Committee Report, commonly known as 'the Roskill Report'. Its principal recommendation was the setting up of a unified organization responsible for the detection, investigation and prosecution of serious fraud cases. The SFO does not investigate all suspected instances of fraud, and has developed a set of 'key questions' to assist it to determine whether or not to instigate a case. The SFO investigates four types of fraud including investment fraud, bribery and corruption, corporate fraud and public sector fraud. The general effectiveness of the SFO can be questioned because of a number of high profile failed prosecutions.[191] The prosecutorial inadequacies of the SFO were highlighted in 2008 by the 'Review of the Serious Fraud Office'.[192] To improve the position, the Crown Prosecution Service announced the creation of the Fraud Prosecution Unit in 2007.[193] The Fraud Prosecution Unit limits its involvement to suspected instances of fraud exceeding £750000; cases involving the corruption of public officials; fraud on government departments; fraud on overseas governments; complicated money laundering cases; and any other matter that it feels is within its remit.[194] In October 2008, HM Crown Prosecution Service Inspectorate concluded that there 'has been a positive direction of travel in terms of successful outcomes (convictions), which stood at a creditable 85% of the defendants proceeded against in 2007–08'.[195]

7.8.5 Crown Prosecution Service

The Crown Prosecution Service (CPS) was established via the Prosecution of Offences Act 1985. The CPS is one of the prosecuting authorities in the

---

[189]   Wright, R. (2003), 'Fraud after Roskill: A view from the Serious Fraud Office', *Journal of Financial Crime*, **11**(1), 10–16, at 10.

[190]   The Serious Fraud Office was created by the Criminal Justice Act 1987.

[191]   For a more detailed discussion see Wright, R. (2006), 'Why (some) fraud prosecutions fail', *Journal of Financial Crime*, **13**(2), 177–182.

[192]   de Grazia, J. *Review of the Serious Fraud Office – Final Report* (Serious Fraud Office: London, 2008).

[193]   The Fraud Prosecution Unit has been renamed the Fraud Prosecution Service and has regional offices in York and London.

[194]   Masters, J. (2008), 'Fraud and money laundering: the evolving criminalisation of corporate non-compliance', *Journal of Money Laundering Control*, **11**(2), 103–122, at 104–105.

[195]   HM Crown Prosecution Service Inspectorate *Review of the Fraud Prosecution Service* (HM Crown Prosecution Service Inspectorate: London, 2008) at p. 5.

UK for money laundering, in conjunction with the FSA, and it initiates criminal proceedings on receiving financial intelligence from SOCA. In relation to fraud, the CPS contained a Fraud Investigation Group that was based in London, but had regional offices.[196] The Fraud Investigation Group dealt with more cases than the SFO and there was a clear overlap in their role and purposes. Therefore, the Graham Review suggested that the ambit of the SFO should be extended to include larger cases that were originally under the remit of the Fraud Investigation Group.[197] As a result of this report the Fraud Investigation Group was renamed the Fraud Division by the Davie Committee in 1995.[198] In September 2007, the CPS announced another rebranding and created the Fraud Prosecution Unit, which has also been renamed the Fraud Prosecution Division.[199]

7.8.6 National Fraud Authority

The National Fraud Authority (NFA) was launched in October 2008 as a new agency of the Attorney General's Office. The NFA aims to 'provide the leadership and national coordination needed for anti-fraud efforts to be as effective and efficient as possible. It will provide a managed programme to attack fraud through the entire pipeline of deterrence, prevention, detection, investigation, sanctions and redress for victims'.[200] However, its creation must be questioned because the NFA has joined an already very long list of law enforcement and financial regulatory agencies that aim to tackle financial crime.[201] The NFA's initial priorities include:

- the delivery of a criminal justice system that focuses on the needs of victims by bringing fraudsters to swift justice efficiently and effectively;
- stronger deterrence to fraudsters through a tough, multi-agency law enforcement and regulatory response; and
- greater public confidence in the response to fraud, and greater capability of individuals and organizations to protect themselves.[202]

---

[196] Doig above, n 183 at 126.
[197] *Ibid.*
[198] For a more detailed discussion see Sarker, R. (1993), 'The Davie Report – Anodyne for the SFO', *Journal of Financial Crime*, **3**(1), 89–91.
[199] Crown Prosecution Service Press (2009), 'DPP announces new head of Fraud Prosecution Division' available at http://www.cps.gov.uk/news/press_releases/136_09/ (accessed 6 July 2010).
[200] *Ibid.*
[201] This includes, for example, the FSA, the SFO and SOCA.
[202] National Fraud Authority (2008), 'UK toughens up on fraudsters with a new anti-fraud authority', available at http://www.attorneygeneral.gov.uk/NFSA/

Furthermore, the NFA's five strategic priorities are:

- tackling the key areas of fraud that pose the greatest threat of harm to the UK;
- acting effectively to pursue fraudsters and hold them to account and improving the support available to victims;
- reducing the UK's exposure to fraud by building the nation's capability to prevent it;
- targeting action against fraud more effectively by building, sharing and acting on knowledge; and
- securing the international collaboration necessary to protect the UK from fraud.[203]

In March 2009, the NFA published the National Fraud Strategy.[204] The objectives of the three-year strategy are:

- enhancing the exchange of information about fraud;
- challenging the threat of fraud;
- enhancing the UK's long-term ability to prevent fraud.[205]

7.8.7 National Fraud Reporting Centre

In addition to recommending the creation of the NFA, the Fraud Review also suggested the creation of a National Fraud Reporting Centre. The National Fraud Reporting Centre permits companies, financial institutions and individuals to report any suspected frauds. Its associated Intelligence Bureau is envisaged to provide satisfaction for organizations and victims and close the gap between data gathering and analysis to guide anti-fraud operations and policy. The National Fraud Reporting Centre and its associated Intelligence Bureau will be designed to address the under-reporting of fraud and lack of consolidation in managing intelligence.

7.8.8 Financial Services Authority

Three weeks after the general election victory in May 1997, the then government announced that work would begin on the reform of the

National%20Fraud%20Strategic%20Authority%20comes%20into%20being.pdf. (accessed 6 August 2010).

[203] *Ibid.*

[204] National Fraud Authority *The National Fraud Strategy – A new approach to combating fraud* (National Fraud Authority: London, 2009b).

[205] *Ibid.*

regulatory structure created under the Financial Services Act 1986.[206] The government had outlined its intention to reform the system in 1995,[207] and it implemented the Financial Services and Markets Act 2000. Under section 6, the FSA has a statutory duty to reduce financial crime by ensuring that financial institutions have systems and practices in place to protect themselves against being used as vehicles by financial criminals. Financial crime is broadly defined within FSMA 2000. It incorporates any offence including fraud or dishonesty,[208] misconduct in, or misuse of information relating to, a financial market,[209] or handling the proceeds of crime.[210] The objective requires the FSA to work with criminal law intelligence and prosecution agencies.[211] The FSA tackles three types of financial crime – money laundering, market abuse and fraud. In order to tackle them, the FSA has the power to require information or documents that may reasonably be required in connection with the discharge of its functions under the FSMA.[212] FSMA 2000 also provides that the FSA has the power to require an authorized person or a formerly authorized person to provide a report to the FSA on any matter which the FSA might specify.[213] The FSA is provided with such powers to issue public statements or impose financial penalties where the rules under the FSMA have been contravened. For example, the FSA has the power to issue a public statement concerning a breach by an authorized person of any requirement that is imposed by the 2000 Act.[214] Under FSMA 2000 the FSA has become a prosecuting authority in respect of certain financial criminal offences, such as money laundering.[215] The FSA also has the power to impose a financial penalty where it establishes that there has been a contravention by an authorized person of any requirement imposed

---

[206]   HC Debs cols. 508–511, 20 May 1997. Also see Bazley, S. (2008), 'The Financial Services Authority, risk based regulation, principles based rules and accountability', *Journal of International Banking Law and Regulation*, **23**(8), 422–440, at 422.

[207]   HC Deb 14 December 1995 cc 1184–85, Alistair Darling.

[208]   Financial Services and Markets Act 2000, s. 6(3)(a).

[209]   Financial Services and Markets Act 2000, s. 6(3)(b).

[210]   Financial Services and Markets Act 2000, s. 6(3)(c).

[211]   See for example FSA, *Partnership Agreement between the National Criminal Intelligence Service and the Financial Services Authority* (London 2001).

[212]   Financial Services and Markets Act 2000, s. 165.

[213]   Financial Services and Markets Act 2000, s. 166.

[214]   Financial Services and Markets Act 2000, s. 205.

[215]   Financial Services and Markets Act 2000, s. 402(1)(a). The FSA has the ability to prosecute for breaches of the money laundering offences under the Proceeds of Crime Act 2002, which was confirmed by the Supreme Court in *R v Rollins* [2010] UKSC 39.

under FSMA 2000.[216] The FSA has imposed a series of fines on firms who have breached their anti-money laundering and anti-fraud obligations under the FSA Handbook.[217] In addition to the ability to impose a financial penalty, the FSA also has the power to ban authorized persons and firms from undertaking any regulated activity.[218]

7.8.9 The Office of Fair Trading

The OFT is 'chiefly concerned with the protection of consumers. It also regulates competition amongst businesses but this is approached from a consumer protection perspective'.[219] The OFT has three regulatory objectives – investigation of whether markets are working well for consumers, enforcement of competition laws and enforcement of consumer protection laws. It is important to note that the OFT has its own fraud policy,[220] which requires it to inform and protect consumers from fraudulent scams.[221] Additionally, some businesses need to register with the OFT to comply with the Money Laundering Regulations (2007).[222]

7.9 UNITED KINGDOM – TERTIARY AGENCIES

7.9.1 British Bankers Association and the Joint Money Laundering Steering Group

The British Bankers Association (BBA), created in 1919, is the leading trade association for banks operating in the UK. It numbers approximately 300 members and one of its principal purposes is to combat money

---

[216] Financial Services and Markets Act 2000, s. 206(1).
[217] See for example Financial Services Authority (2002), 'FSA Fines Royal Bank of Scotland £750,000 for money laundering control failings', available at http://www.fsa.gov.uk/Pages/Library/Communication/PR/2002/123.shtml (accessed 6 January 2009).
[218] Financial Services and Markets Act 2000, s. 56.
[219] Kiernan, P. (2003), 'The regulatory bodies fraud: its enforcement in the twenty-first century', *Company Lawyer*, **24**(10), 293–299, at 295.
[220] Office of Fair Trading *Prevention of fraud policy* (Office of Fair Trading: London, n/d).
[221] See for example Office of Fair Trading *Scamnesty 2010 campaign strategy* (Office of Fair Trading, London, 2009).
[222] For a more detailed discussion of this role see Office of Fair Trading *Anti-Money Laundering: Future supervisory approach consultation* (Office of Fair Trading: London, 2010).

laundering. It has produced anti-money laundering guidelines for banks, which are published by the Joint Money Laundering Steering Group (JMLSG). The JMLSG consists of 17 of the primary leading UK trade associations in the financial services industry.[223] Its objective is to disseminate good practice amongst the financial services sector to counter the threat posed by money laundering and to provide workable and practical assistance in interpreting the 2007 Money Laundering Regulations. This is achieved by issuance of detailed guidance notes, which have been regularly amended to coincide with the publication and implementation of the new Money Laundering Regulations.[224] Leong noted that the aim of the notes is 'to provide an indication of good generic industry practice and a base from which management can develop tailored policies and procedures that are appropriate to their business'.[225] Furthermore, Hopton argued that 'they are also a good source of industry practice and provide management with advice and assistance'.[226] Importantly, the FSA has recommended that firms should 'read the JMLSG guidance notes in conjunction with the FSA's rules'.[227]

7.9.2   The Fraud Advisory Panel

The Fraud Advisory Panel is a registered charity which works to raise awareness of the immense human, social and economic damage caused by fraud and to help individuals and organizations to develop effective strategies to prevent it. It is an independent organization that was established in 1988 and has four strategic objectives:

- Advising government, business and the general public on fraud prevention, detection and reporting.
- Originating proposals to reform the law and public policy, with particular emphasis on investigation and prosecution.
- Improving education and training in business and the professions as well as amongst the general public.
- Undertaking research to establish a more accurate picture of the extent, causes and nature of fraud.

---

[223]   Joint Money Laundering Steering Group (2007a), 'Who are the members of the JMLSG?', available at http://www.jmlsg.org.uk/bba/jsp/polopoly. jsp?d=777&a=9907 (accessed 18 June 2010).

[224]   Hopton above, n 27 at 43.

[225]   Leong above, n 29 at 144–145.

[226]   Hopton above, n 27 at 43.

[227]   Oxford Analytica Ltd above, n 177 at 276.

7.10   CONCLUSION

This chapter has highlighted the important role that government departments, financial regulators and law enforcement bodies play in tackling the problems associated with financial crime. It is interesting to note that in both the US and the UK, it is the government's finance department that performs the most important role.

7.10.1   The United States of America

The Department of Treasury performs a dual role of implementing and developing the money laundering and terrorist financing policies. It is admirably supported by OFAC and FinCEN, who equally are central to the effectiveness of the broader US financial crime strategy. OFAC, in particular, has been criticized for the manner in which it has used its powers under Presidential Executive Order 13224 and how the imposition of sanctions on little more than 'rumours' and 'gossip' breaches the basic fundamental concepts of the rule of law. Nonetheless, the US judiciary has consistently upheld the actions of OFAC since the terrorist attacks of 11 September 2001. OFAC has wrongly accused several US-based Islamic charities of supporting terrorists. FinCEN also has a central role to play in the anti-money laundering and terrorist financing policy. Its primary purpose is to gather financial intelligence from financial institutions and other professions that can be distributed to law enforcement bodies in the pursuit of financial criminals. FinCEN manages the reporting requirements of the BSA 1970, a process that some commentators have described as the most traditional mechanism to prevent financial crime. The process of completing either a CTR or SAR has been described as burdensome and expensive, and it has led to a concept called defensive reporting. Nonetheless, the FATF in its 2007 Mutual Evaluation Report stated that FinCEN complies with its obligations under Recommendation 26.

The Department of Justice and in particular the FBI have adopted a very aggressive policy towards financial crime. For example, the FBI has embraced a robust stance towards mortgage fraud, a policy that has been assisted by the introduction of the Fraud Enforcement and Recovery Act 2009. The aim of this Act was threefold. Firstly, to improve the levels of responsibility and accountability for frauds that had arisen during the financial crisis. Secondly, the Act provided a substantial increase in funding for the Justice Department and other law enforcement agencies to tackle mortgage fraud. Thirdly, the Department of Justice has been given $330m to investigate any suspected instances of mortgage fraud and to pursue any potential prosecutions that arise from those investigations.

The introduction of the Fraud Enforcement and Recovery Act 2009 is a welcome addition to the extensive legislative armoury of the Justice Department. The additional funding for the FBI and other regulatory agencies authorized under the Act is as welcome as it is essential given the complexity of the fraudulent activity and the subsequent investigation and prosecution by law enforcement agencies. It is extremely difficult to determine the overall effectiveness of the policy adopted in the US to tackle mortgage fraud. Only now are we beginning to understand the extent of the sub-prime mortgage crisis and it is likely that larger instances of suspected mortgage fraud will come to light when more financial institutions collapse or seek further support from the federal agencies. However, there is one factor that has limited the effectiveness of the regulators and agencies in the US. That factor is the large number of agencies who have been given the task of tackling financial crime. Many of these regulators and agencies perform the same tasks and administer the same rules and regulations. This overcomplicates the US stance toward financial crime and muddies its operation.

7.10.2 United Kingdom

In the UK, HM Treasury plays a central role in tackling financial crime. It has for example written the policy documents for both money laundering and terrorist financing. In relation to money laundering, HM Treasury has stipulated that it sought to introduce a proportionate and cost-effective scheme. This has simply not been achieved; as this book has indicated, the compliance costs for the UK's anti-money laundering regime continue to increase on an annual basis. HM Treasury does not share the same level of consistent judicial support over the legality of its sanctions regime as OFAC does in the US. At the time of writing the entire terrorist financing policy is static and therefore largely redundant as HM Treasury awaits the decision of the Supreme Court following the Court of Appeal's decision in *A v HM Treasury*.

The FSA has a statutory objective to reduce financial crime, which is broadly defined, and it has been given the necessary enforcement and investigative powers to achieve this objective. The FSA has at times imposed a large number of financial penalties on firms that have failed to comply with their obligations under its Handbook. These figures attract significant media attention and certainly make the 'headline news'. The FSA has created a fear factor amongst these firms who will meet their financial crime requirements, not through enthusiasm or because it is the 'right thing to do', but because of the adverse publicity attracted to them if they fail to comply. However, the FSA's resources are limited and it has adopted a cyclical approach towards the types of financial crime provided for under FSMA 2000. For example, it is only recently that the FSA has attempted to tackle the problems associated with fraud. Its policy had been overly concerned with money laundering and its market abuse regime.

SOCA is the UK's FIU and it administers the confiscation regime under the PCA 2002. It is perhaps too early to determine whether or not SOCA has improved the SARs regime that it inherited from NCIS in 2006. Likewise, the effectiveness of its management of the confiscation regime is also difficult to judge at this early stage.

The SFO has come under an increased level of scrutiny since its announcement in 2009 that it is seeking permission from the Attorney General to bring corruption charges against BAE. Its performance since its creation in the 1980s has been criticized due to a number of high profile failed prosecutions. However, it is important to note that the perform-ance and effectiveness of the SFO will undoubtedly improve now that the UK has a single Fraud Act. The creation of the Fraud Prosecution Service is a welcome addition to the UK's armoury and early signs are promising in relation to its conviction rate. The creation of the NFA must be questioned, as it often duplicates the functions of both the FSA and the SFO. It is merely another level of unwanted bureaucracy, as is the ill-advised creation of the NFRC. It is strongly recommended and advisable that the function of administering suspected instances of fraud must lie with SOCA, and not another agency. In 2010, the Coalition government announced that it intends to create a new 'Economic Crime Agency' that would incorporate the SFO, FSA and some parts of the OFT. The pro-posal is very similar to that advocated by a political think tank prior to the general election. It is very unlikely that the new super agency will be created due to the costs and timescale involved. It is the author's conten-tion that this is the correct way forward.

8. Sentencing in financial crime

Karen Harrison*

8.1 INTRODUCTION

Thus far this book has been about financial crime: what it is; how it is caused; how extensive the problem of it is; and an analytical examination of national and international policy measures designed to combat it. This chapter, however, is slightly different. Rather than continuing in this line of study, it looks at what we should do with those people who have been convicted by the criminal courts of committing financial crime. To this end, the aim of this chapter is to first define what we mean by a financial criminal; discuss what the aims of sentencing should be when faced with such offenders; examine sentencing policy on a national basis; consider what sentencing options are available for financial criminals; and finally, by analysing examples of sentencing practice from both England and Wales and the US, assess whether the practice of sentencing offenders in England and Wales is satisfactory.

8.2 THE FINANCIAL CRIMINAL

As explained in Chapter 1 of this volume, despite there being 'no internationally accepted definition of financial crime',[1] in England and Wales it can be said to include 'any offence involving fraud or dishonesty; misconduct in, or misuse of information relating to, a financial market';[2] money laundering and terrorist funding. A person who has committed such offences must, therefore, be able to be described as a financial criminal. Other perhaps more common terms of parlance include that of

---

*   University of Hull, Law School.
[1]   International Monetary Fund *Financial system abuse, financial crime and money laundering – background paper* (International Monetary Fund: Washington, DC, 2001) at p. 5.
[2]   Financial Services and Markets Act 2000, s. 6(3).

the white-collar criminal and the offender who has committed corporate crime, although as acknowledged by Croall there are problems with how these terms are also defined.[3] For example, whilst we might often regard the white-collar criminal as someone who has high social status, is respectable, powerful and at management level, this is not always true; with many corporate crimes involving employees acting in the course of trade and business and with their offences relating to matters of hygiene and other health and safety issues.[4] Whilst it may therefore be true, as suggested by Croall, that the vast majority of white-collar crime is not untaken by the high status offender, this is not the type of offence or offender which this book focuses upon. Therefore, for the purpose of this book, a financial criminal will be defined as someone who has committed a financial crime (as outlined above and in Chapter 1 of this volume) and who has a certain level of standing (i.e. that of management) within a business or corporation.

8.3 THE AIMS OF SENTENCING

8.3.1 General Aims of Sentencing

The general aims of sentencing are arguably the same, irrespective of the type of offence or type of offender involved, and can largely be divided into five areas: punishment, deterrence, rehabilitation, incapacitation and reparation. These aims or purposes have recently been codified by s. 142(1) of the Criminal Justice Act 2003, although their existence significantly predates this codification. Whilst it is not the aim of this chapter to look at these aims in any great detail, they will nevertheless be briefly assessed so that a discussion focusing on the desired sentencing aims for financial criminals can follow. Whilst it is possible to divide sentencing purposes in this way, and under the Criminal Justice Act 2003 courts must have regard to these aims, there is no set hierarchy and in practice which purpose or combination of purposes is adhered to will depend on the given individual. So, for example, punishment and incapacitation will be more important when sentencing a dangerous and high-risk violent offender, whereas rehabilitation and reparation may be more suitable where the offender is someone who has stolen from a supermarket in order to curtail a sense of boredom.

---

[3]   Croall, H. (1989), 'Who is the White-Collar Criminal?', *British Journal of Criminology*, **29**(2), 157–174, at 157.
[4]   *Ibid.*

Taking the aims of sentencing in turn, punishment is the idea that if someone has committed a crime then he/she must 'pay' for this wrong-doing, with it typically involving action which when not linked to punishment would otherwise appear morally wrong (such as imprisonment or a financial penalty).[5] In modern times, it has been linked with the theory of just deserts, which is based on the premise that the seriousness of the crime should be the sole determinant of the length and type of sentence handed out by the court. This works like a weighing scale, whereby the court attempts to balance the seriousness of the offence with the gravity of the penalty. It is also inextricably linked with the idea of retribution, with the justification being that it is not only the state's right, but also its duty to punish those people who have done wrong and deserve such punishment.[6] Punishment thus has the functions of not only recognizing that an offender's rights (for example, liberty) have to be infringed but also addressing the offender as a moral agent by appealing to his/her sense of right and wrong. Examples of punishment would therefore include imprisonment, disqualification from driving or from being a company director and financial penalties.

Deterrence, on the other hand, is defined by Ashworth as a penalty which is warranted by reference to its crime preventative consequences.[7] Quintessentially, it is the use of harsher than normal penalties to deter people from either offending or reoffending. The theory comes in two forms and can thus be divided into individual deterrence (which deters a particular offender from reoffending) and general deterrence (which deters others from committing similar offences). If the aim is one of general deterrence, then the length and type of the sentence in question must be determined on the basis of what will deter others, rather than just what would deter the particular offender. It is thus general deterrence which is being used when it is said that an offender is being made an example of. One of the main reasons that people are opposed to this theory is that it is accepted that in order to create the desired fear, it is justifiable to either punish an innocent person or hand out excessive punishments. Examples

---

    5   Duff, Anthony and Garland, David (1989), 'Introduction: Thinking about Punishment', in A. Duff and D. Garland (eds), *A Reader on Punishment*, Oxford University Press, Oxford, 1–44, at 2.

    6   Moore, M. (1987), 'The moral worth of retribution', in A. von Hirsch and A. Ashworth (eds), *Principled sentencing: readings on theory and policy*, Hart Publishing, Oxford, at 150.

    7   Ashworth, A. (1987), 'Deterrence', in A. von Hirsch and A. Ashworth (eds), *Principled sentencing: readings on theory and policy*, Hart Publishing, Oxford, at 44.

of penalties, which could deter could thus include: death without trial; installing cameras on every street corner; identification cards and finger-printing everybody.

Rehabilitation is defined by von Hirsch as 'curing' an offender of his/her criminal tendencies by 'changing an offender's personality, outlook, habits, or opportunities so as to make him/her less inclined to commit crime'.[8] The model takes the view that crime is best reduced by looking at factors which directly relate to the causes of crime, whether these are economic, social or personal. For the first 60 years of the twentieth century, many considered rehabilitation to be the most important aim in criminal justice. Under this regime, the seriousness of the offence was considered to be less important, with the main concern focusing on how best the offender could be treated. Length of sentence was thus usually determined by how long this 'cure' would take, rather than on the gravity of the actual offence. Optimism about the worth of rehabilitation lasted until the early 1970s, when a number of research findings, including those by Martinson[9] and Brody,[10] concluded that 'nothing worked'. Such depressing conclusions obviously brought into question the worth of rehabilitation and more significantly whether it could serve as the primary aim of the criminal justice system. Examples of rehabilitative practices thus include offending behaviour programmes, work on victim empathy and courses centred on education, training and employment.

Incapacitation is when the offender is restrained, usually in custody, which renders him incapable of reoffending, and is usually employed because it is believed that the public need to be protected from that particular offender's future criminal behaviour. Incapacitation has existed for as long as the ideal of rehabilitation: under a traditional rehabilitative ethic, those offenders who were assessed as being treatable were 'cured', whilst those who were not were restrained. The early 1970s brought doubts about such predictive sentencing, with a growing trend of recidivist predictions being wrong, and those predicted to reoffend not doing so. In addition to the problem of false positives is the argument that by extending a person's punishment, the idea of proportionality is forgotten, therefore long-term incapacitation opposes the premise of just deserts, as discussed above. In

---

[8]   von Hirsch, A. (1987), 'Rehabilitation' in A. von Hirsch and A. Ashworth (eds) *Principled sentencing: readings on theory and policy*, Hart Publishing, Oxford, at 1.

[9]   Martinson, R. (1974), 'What Works? Questions and answers about prison reform', *The Public Interest*, **35** 22–54, at 22.

[10]   Brody, S. *The effectiveness of sentencing: a review of the literature* Home Office Research Study No. 35 (HMSO: London, 1975).

practical terms incapacitation is carried out through imprisonment, exile, house arrest and to a lesser extent through curfew orders with electronic monitoring and the removal of licences.

Finally is the notion of reparation, which whilst not a theory of sentencing as such, works on the basis that we should move away from sentences which focus largely on punishment towards those which include aspects of reparation and restitution. The aim here is to compensate the harm committed against the victim and against the community at large. Reparation hence emphasizes that it is not just the state that has been wronged, but also the victim, the wider community and the offender's family. All of those either involved in or affected by the offender's offence should therefore have a say in what the appropriate response should be and how it should be carried out. Under this aim of sentencing, reparation and compensation is more important than punishment for punishment's sake and provides the offender a means of paying back for the wrong which has been committed. Arguably, sentencing which is reparative in nature also encourages reintegration back into the community, which consequently often encourages desistance from reoffending. Examples of reparative practices include compensation payments, work in and for the community and meetings with the victims to allow them to have their say.[11]

8.3.2   Aims of Sentencing Financial Crime

As mentioned above, in general, the five sentencing aims apply to most offences and to most offenders, although of course the decision concerning which is the most suitable and thus which will be relied on the most will depend on the individual offender and his offence. To this end, what are the aims of sentencing when the sentencing process involves a financial criminal? Using the definition of a financial criminal as outlined above, it is perhaps not surprising that most of the general aims are appropriate, and depending on the actual crime, will be taken into account when the court reaches its sentencing decision. For example, where the offence in question involves an individual committing a crime of money laundering, worth hundreds of pounds, then the aim of the court may be to punish the offender for his wrongdoing; but additionally it may want to deter others from committing the same crime and encourage the offender to

---

[11]   For an interesting analysis on the use of shaming techniques against white-collar crime see Levi, M. (2002b), 'Suite justice or sweet charity? Some explorations of shaming and incapacitating business fraudsters', *Punishment & Society*, **4**(2), 147–163.

make some form of reparation to the victims involved. Where the offence concerns a vast fraud, amounting to thousands, if not millions, of pounds, whilst the court may apply the same principles as above, by applying the premise of just deserts it should also ensure that the severity of the sentence is much more heinous than that above to reflect the differences in seriousness. If the crime has been committed partly due to the offender's ignorance of business law or legislative protocols, then it is possible that rehabilitation may come into play; but in most cases it is probably not necessary to compel financial criminals to attend rehabilitative offending behaviour programmes. Likewise, unless there are extreme circumstances, it is unlikely that incapacitation will need to be taken into account as, whilst some financial crimes cause vast amounts of financial damage, the culprits can rarely be described as dangerous and classified as being at a high risk of committing further serious offending. Whilst the author has not been able to find any reliable statistics, as those concerning fraud will also include all fraud offences including low-level benefit, insurance and mortgage fraud, it is thought that the vast majority of large-scale financial criminals do not, when convicted, reoffend. Hence, it would appear that for the majority of financial criminals, the courts should pay attention to, and perhaps even concentrate on, the aims of deterrence, punishment and reparation.

8.4   SENTENCING POLICY

8.4.1   General Sentencing Policy

Sentencing policy in England and Wales over the last 20 years has seen a major policy change from that centred on rehabilitation and welfare to that premised on punishment, deterrence and just deserts.[12] Current sentencing policy, for all offences carried out within England and Wales, is contained within the Criminal Justice Act 2003, which works on the basis of seriousness and the just deserts model. As explained above, under this model a person should only receive a custodial sentence or a financial penalty if the offence is serious enough to warrant such a response. The seriousness of the offence must, therefore, be commensurate with the seriousness of the imposed penalty.

In order for this to work in practice, it is thus desirable that there is a common understanding of what the term seriousness means, which until

---

[12]   See for example the Criminal Justice Act 1991.

fairly recently was left to the discretion of the individual sentencing judge. Now, however, seriousness has been defined in both legislation and a Sentencing Guidelines Council (SGC) guideline.[13] Under s. 143(1) of the Criminal Justice Act 2003 'in considering the seriousness of any offence the court must consider the offender's culpability in committing the offence and any harm which the offence caused, was intended to cause or might foreseeably have caused'. In a similar vein, *Overarching Principles: Seriousness*[14] states that 'the seriousness of an offence is determined by two main parameters; the culpability of the offender and the harm caused or risked being caused by the offence'.[15] Whilst both definitions come from different sources, it is clear that when making a sentencing decision, the two most important notions for the sentencing judge to consider, when assessing seriousness, are those of culpability and harm. Looking at culpability first, four levels are identified: intention, recklessness, knowledge and negligence,[16] with intention being regarded as the worst or that which makes the offender most culpable. So in a practical sense, a person who intends to launder money, rather than someone who either knows that the practice is taking place or fails to check whether or not the practice is taking place, will be considered more culpable and hence his crime more serious.

Harm is defined as harm to individual victims, harm to the community and other types of harm which could include, for example, cruelty to animals (on the basis that this too could cause distress or financial loss to human victims).[17] For financial crime, harm could therefore amount to loss affecting one individual, a family, members of a group or corporation or even to entire nations and states. As with culpability, the greater the harm which is caused, and also importantly that which is risked being caused, the more serious the offence will be. Despite the level of harm caused or risked being caused being important, it is worth noting that the SGC guideline does make the culpability of the offender the initial factor in determining the seriousness of the offence.[18]

In addition to the definitions of culpability and harm, the SGC also

---

[13]   Every court is required to have regard to guidelines issued by the SGC under the Criminal Justice Act 2003, s. 172. For more information on the Council see www.sentencing-guidelines.gov.uk.

[14]   Sentencing Guidelines Council *Overarching Principles: Seriousness* (Sentencing Guidelines Secretariat: London, 2004).

[15]   *Ibid.*, at 3.

[16]   *Ibid.*, at 4.

[17]   *Ibid.*

[18]   *Ibid.*, at 5.

details factors which could increase a person's culpability and thus increase the seriousness of the crime. In terms of financial crime, these factors include: evidence of offence planning; abuse of power or a position of trust; an intention to commit more serious harm than that which was achieved; operating in a group; 'professional' offending;[19] and where there has been a high level of profit or significant consequential loss caused by the offence.[20] Conversely, lower culpability may be seen where the particular offender suffered from provocation, mental illness or a disability; was either particularly young or old and was thus vulnerable or only played a minor role in the offence.[21] If we keep to our initial definition of financial criminal as stated above, it is likely that only the latter consideration might apply in these circumstances.

Once the seriousness of the offence is determined, the next step for any sentencing judge is to match the offence to a type and level of sentence – this is the weighing scale exercise as described above. This is assisted by the existence of a number of threshold tests. For example, the custody threshold test states that:

> the court must not pass a custodial sentence unless it is of the opinion that the offence, or the combination of the offence and one or more offences associated with it, was so serious that neither a fine alone nor a community sentence can be justified for the offence.[22]

Therefore, a financial criminal can only be sentenced to imprisonment if it is considered that the offence in question is serious enough to warrant such a measure. The sentencing court should therefore ask a number of things including:

(a) Has the custody threshold been passed?
(b) If so, is it unavoidable that a custodial sentence be imposed?
(c) If so, can the sentence be suspended?
(d) If not, can the sentence be served intermittently?
(e) If not, impose a sentence which takes immediate effect for the term commensurate with the seriousness of the offence.[23]

This would therefore suggest that imprisonment is the last resort and should only be used in the most extreme of situations.

---

[19] *Ibid.*, at 6.
[20] *Ibid.*, at 7.
[21] *Ibid.*
[22] Criminal Justice Act 2003, s. 152(2).
[23] Sentencing Guidelines Council above, n 14 at 8.

Other factors which are taken into account when reaching a sentencing decision include: the presence of Court of Appeal guideline judgments or SGC guidelines; whether the particular legislation for the offence under consideration mandates maximum or minimum sentences; the presence of aggravating and/or mitigating factors; and finally the existence of a timely guilty plea. In terms of aggravating factors, those which might be relevant to a financial crime include: vulnerable victims; breach of trust; crimes which have been planned; group offending; offences committed whilst on bail; and the presence of previous convictions, especially if they are similar in nature. Relevant mitigating factors could comprise: the offender acting under duress or necessity; ignorance of the law; remorse; co-operation with law enforcement agencies;[24] where the offender has had a previous good character (that is, he has never offended before) and where the sentence may have a disproportionate effect on the offender.[25] In addition to such mitigating factors, a sentence can also be reduced if the offender has admitted guilt. The current law regarding this is contained in ss. 144 and 152 of the Criminal Justice Act 2003, which advise sentencing courts that the essential element in knowing how to take this into account is when the guilty plea is given. Traditionally a timely guilty plea amounted to a one-third discount,[26] although this has recently been modified by another SGC guideline[27] which provides a sliding scale of discounts depending on when the plea is entered into the court. For example, if the plea is entered at the first reasonable opportunity then the full one-third discount will be applied. However, if the defendant waits until the trial starts, then he can only expect to be given a one-tenth discount.[28] A guilty plea can also be used to reduce a sentence from one of custody to one carried out within the community, or from a community order to a financial penalty.[29]

---

[24]   If this is coupled with a guilty plea then the offender could expect to receive up to a 50 per cent discount.

[25]   For an example of this latter factor see *R v Richards* [1980] 2 CrAppR (S) 119 where a doctor's prison sentence of 30 months was reduced to 12 on the basis that he was 57 and would never practise again, he would lose his pension and his wife had committed suicide.

[26]   *R v Buffrey* [1993] 14 CrAppR (S) 511; although in practice this varied between a one-quarter to a one-third discount *AG's Reference* (Nos 19, 20 and 21 of 2001) [2001] EWCA Crim 1432.

[27]   Sentencing Guidelines Council *Definitive Sentencing Guideline Revised 2007 – Reduction in Sentence for a Guilty Plea* (Sentencing Guidelines Secretariat: London, 2007).

[28]   *Ibid.*, at 6.

[29]   *Ibid.*, at 4.

8.4.2 Sentencing Policy for Financial Crime

Whilst the above sub-section has been rather general in nature, this next part will concentrate on Court of Appeal guideline judgments, SGC guidelines and legislation which specifically affect financial crime and the way in which financial criminals are sentenced. Prior to the existence of the SGC, and also the Sentencing Advisory Panel,[30] the only way in which guidance on sentencing was issued was through guideline judgments which would be handed down by the Court of Appeal. Such judgments were, and still are, binding on all lower courts, but could only be issued if and when an appeal reached the higher court. This meant that the guidance was piecemeal and did not cover as many offences as would have been desirable. However, there do exist a number of judgments which are relevant to our analysis here of sentencing financial crime. For example, the case of *R v Feld*,[31] which involved offences of raising money by means of false statements relating to the financial position of a company. In such circumstances, factors which are relevant to sentencing include:

1. The amount involved and the manner in which the fraud is carried out.
2. The period over which the fraud is carried out and the degree of persistence with which it is carried out.
3. The position of the accused within the company and his measure of control over it.
4. Any abuse of trust which is revealed.
5. The consequences of the fraud.
6. The effect on public confidence in the City and the integrity of commercial life.
7. The loss to small investors, which will aggravate the fraud.
8. The personal benefit derived by a defendant.
9. The plea.
10. The age and character of the defendant.[32]

Moreover, in *R v Barrick*,[33] Lane LCJ set out a number of factors which should be taken into account when sentencing professional people for offences of fraud:

---

[30] Another sentencing advisory body which plays a complementary role in producing sentencing guidelines.

[31] [1999] 1 CrAppR (S) 1.

[32] *Ibid.*, at 4.

[33] (1985) 7 CrAppR (S) 142.

(i)   the quality and degree of trust reposed in the offender including his rank;
(ii)   the period over which the fraud or the thefts have been perpetrated;
(iii)   the use to which the money or property dishonestly taken was put;
(iv)   the effect upon the victim;
(v)   the impact of the offences on the public and public confidence;
(vi)   the effect on fellow-employees or partners;
(vii)   the effect on the offender himself;
(viii)   his own history;
(ix)   those matters of mitigation special to himself such as illness; being placed under great strain by excessive responsibility or the like; where, as sometimes happens, there has been a long delay, say over two years, between his being confronted with his dishonesty by his professional body or the police and the start of his trial; finally, any help given by him to the police.[34]

Interestingly, Lane LCJ also warned how 'professional men should expect to be punished as severely as others: in some cases, more severely'[35] and gave some recommendations as to appropriate sentencing starting points,[36] which were subsequently updated in *R v Clark*:[37]

- Where the amount is not small, but is less than £17 500, terms of imprisonment from the very short up to 21 months will be appropriate;
- Cases involving sums between £17 500 and £100 000 will merit two to three years;
- Cases involving sums between £100 000 and £250 000 will merit three to four years;
- Cases involving between £250 000 and £1m will merit between five and nine years;
- Cases involving £1m or more will merit 10 years or more.
- Where the sums involved are exceptionally large, and not stolen on a single occasion, or the dishonesty is directed at more than one victim or group of victims, consecutive sentences may be called for.[38]

Other guideline judgments relevant to fraud include *R v Palk and Smith*[39]

---

[34]   *Ibid.*, at 147.
[35]   *Ibid.*, at 143. This was also supported in the later case of *R v Stewart* [1987] 2 All ER 383.
[36]   'Where the amounts involved could not be described as small but were less than £10,000 or thereabouts, terms of imprisonment ranging from the very short up to about eighteen months were appropriate. Cases involving sums of between about £10,000 and £50,000 would merit a term of about two or three years' imprisonment. Where greater sums were involved, for example those over £100,000, then a term of three and a half to four years would be justified'. *Ibid.*, at 143–144.
[37]   [1988] 2 CrAppR (S) 95.
[38]   *Ibid.*, at 100.
[39]   [1997] 2 CrAppR (S) 167.

(fraudulent trading), *R v Stevens and others*[40] (mortgage fraud) and *R v Roach*[41] (obtaining a money transfer by deception).

Likewise for money laundering, there is the case of *R v Basra*[42] which provides general advice concerning the sentencing of money laundering offences and *R v El-Delbi*,[43] which concentrates on the proceeds of drug trafficking. For the latter case, the Court of Appeal advised that:

- Those who launder large sums that are the proceeds of drug trafficking play an essential role in enabling the drugs conspiracy to succeed and, as such, can expect severe sentences comparable to those given to others playing a significant role in the supply of drugs.
- However, it has to be borne in mind that Parliament has provided different upper limits to a judge's sentencing process for dealing in Class A drugs (life imprisonment) and money laundering (14 years).
- There will be no direct arithmetical relationship between the sums recovered by Customs or shown to be involved; nonetheless sentences very close to the maximum have to be reserved for cases where the evidence establishes laundering on a very large scale.[44]

In relation to insider dealing and market abuse, the Court of Appeal has more recently provided a list of factors which should be taken into consideration when sentencing such offences. These are stated as being:

(1) The nature of the defendant's employment or retainer, or involvement in the arrangements which enabled him to participate in the insider dealing of which he is guilty;
(2) The circumstances in which he came into possession of confidential information and the use he made of it;
(3) Whether he behaved recklessly or acted deliberately and almost inevitably therefore, dishonestly;
(4) The level of planning and sophistication involved in his activity, as well as the period of trading and the number of individual trades;
(5) Whether he acted alone or with others and, if so, his relative culpability;
(6) The amount of anticipated or intended financial benefit or (as sometimes happens) loss avoided, as well as the actual benefit (or loss avoided);

---

[40] [1993] 14 CrAppR (S) 372.
[41] [2002] 1 CrAppR (S) 12.
[42] [2002] 2 CrAppR (S) 100.
[43] [2003] EWCA Crim 1767.
[44] Taken from the Court of Appeal Guideline Judgments Case Compendium, available at: http://www.sentencing-guidelines.gov.uk/guidelines/other/courtappeal/default.asp?T=Cases&catID=10&subject=MONEY LAUNDERING&SubSubject=Proceeds of drug trafficking.

(7)　Although the absence of any identified victim is not normally a matter giving rise to mitigation, the impact (if any), where proved, on any individual victim; and

(8)　the impact of the offence on overall public confidence in the integrity of the market; because of its impact on public confidence it is likely that an offence committed jointly by more than one person trusted with confidential information will be more damaging to public confidence than an offence committed in isolation by one person acting on his own.[45]

With reference to SGC guidelines, it would appear that financial crime has not been at the top of the Council's agenda, perhaps because of the existence of the guideline judgments as detailed above, or because of other pressing matters (such as dangerous offenders, robbery and sexual offences). However, following on from a period of consultation and the publication of a draft guideline, in October 2009 a definitive guideline concerning the sentencing of fraud[46] was issued by the SGC. The guideline, in line with general sentencing policy, reiterates that the primary consideration when sentencing fraud offences is the seriousness of the offending behaviour.[47] Key considerations when assessing this in relation to fraud include 'the degree of planning, the determination with which the offender carried out the offence and the value of the money or property involved'.[48] Of importance is the assertion that in general fraud offences will involve 'the highest level of culpability',[49] with other points to be taken into consideration listed as:

(a)　The impact of the offence on the victim.
(b)　Harm to persons other than the direct victim.
(c)　Erosion of public confidence.
(d)　Any physical harm or risk of physical harm to the direct victim or another person.
(e)　Difference between loss intended and resulting.
(f)　Legitimate entitlement to part or all of the amount obtained.[50]

The Council has also identified four factors which it believes are particularly relevant when undertaking a sentencing decision for a fraud offence. These include:

---

[45]　*R v Christopher McQuoid* [2009] EWCA Crim 1301 at para. 14.

[46]　Sentencing Guidelines Council *Sentencing for Fraud – Statutory Offences Definitive Guideline* (Sentencing Guidelines Secretariat: London, 2009).

[47]　*Ibid.*, at 4.

[48]　Sentencing Guidelines Council above, n 46 at 5.

[49]　*Ibid.*

[50]　*Ibid.*, at 6–7.

(a) Number involved in the offence and role of offender.
(b) Offending carried out over a significant period of time.
(c) Use of another person's identity.
(d) Offence has a lasting effect on the victim.[51]

Finally, the guideline provides starting points and sentencing ranges for a number of fraudulent offences. For example, in the case of banking and insurance fraud and obtaining credit through fraud, where the offence was 'fraudulent from the outset, professionally planned and either fraud carried out over a significant period of time or multiple frauds',[52] the starting point,[53] whereby the amount of money obtained was £500 000 or more, is five years in custody, with the range set at four to seven years. Conversely at the other end of the spectrum, where the offence is one of a 'single fraudulent transaction, not fraudulent from the outset',[54] and involves a monetary amount of less than £5000, the starting point[55] is a financial penalty, with the range identified as being from a fine to a low-level community order. Sentencing ranges and starting points are also provided for confidence frauds; possessing, making or supplying articles for use in fraud; revenue fraud (against HM Revenue and Customs) and benefit fraud.

The final piece of guidance which a sentencing judge must adhere to, when reaching a sentencing decision, concerns the existence of maximum sentences. For example, for the offence of fraud, the maximum sentence on conviction on indictment is 10 years' imprisonment.[56] For money laundering and terrorist funding the maximum penalty is 14 years[57, 58] and for insider dealing/market abuse it is seven years.[59] It is worth noting that these are maxima and hence should only be used when the offence is deemed to be serious enough to warrant the maximum penalty. If the offence is deemed to be more serious than such penalties allow for, the only thing a sentencing judge can do, if there are a number of offences to be sentenced, is to sentence consecutively, rather than concurrently.[60] This

---

[51] *Ibid.*, at 8.
[52] *Ibid.*, at 24.
[53] Which is based on a value of £750 000.
[54] Sentencing Guidelines Council above, n 46 at 24.
[55] Which is based on a value of £2500.
[56] Fraud Act 2006, s. 1(3).
[57] Proceeds of Crime Act 2002, s. 334(1).
[58] Terrorism Act 2000, s. 22.
[59] Criminal Justice Act 1993, s. 61(1).
[60] This means that each sentence will start where a previous sentence ended, rather than all sentences running at the same time.

can be contrasted with maxima in the US,[61] where for securities fraud, mail fraud, wire fraud and money laundering the possible maximum is 20 years' imprisonment; and for spending the proceeds of crime it is 10 years.[62] Maximum financial penalties in the US for money laundering are set at $500 000 or twice the value of the property involved in the crime.[63]

8.5 SENTENCING OPTIONS FOR FINANCIAL CRIME

Thus far the main sentencing option which has been discussed is that of imprisonment, with brief mention of the possibility of using community and/or financial penalties. Whilst these responses are general sentencing options, available to all offenders and most offences, there are additionally a number of orders which have been designed specifically with financial crime in mind. These include the confiscation order, the restraint order, the financial reporting order, disqualification and the serious crime prevention order.[64] Such orders can be described as ancillary orders in that they are often given in addition to the other general sentencing penalties, rather than instead of. For the most part, they are designed either to recover the proceeds of crime (as detailed in Chapter 5 of this volume) or to monitor the offender's financial and business practices after his conviction and/or release from custody.

The confiscation order[65] is legislated for under sections 6 to 13 of the Proceeds of Crime Act 2002. It can be made against a convicted offender who is thought to have a criminal lifestyle and seeks to recover all financial benefit which the offender has accumulated from this lifestyle.[66] If the

---

[61] It is also worth noting for the interest of a comparative study that China has the death penalty for a number of white-collar crimes including fraud and money laundering.

[62] Australian Government and Australian Institute of Criminology *Charges and Offences of Money Laundering* Transnational Crime Brief No. 4 (Australian Institute of Criminology: Canberra, 2008).

[63] Van Cleef, C., Silets, H. and Motz, P. (2004), 'Does the punishment fit the crime', *Journal of Financial Crime*, **12**(1), 56–65, at 57. Hereafter Van Cleef *et al.*

[64] This is a civil order that only has to be proven on the balance of probabilities and thus is given by a civil court, although breach can lead to criminal consequences. As it is not often given as part of a criminal conviction it will not be discussed here although details of the order can be found in the Serious Crime Act 2007, s. 1.

[65] The equivalent in the US is criminal and civil forfeiture.

[66] Proceeds of Crime Act 2002, s. 6.

sentencing court believes that the offender had a criminal lifestyle (using assumptions set out in the Act[67]) and financially benefited from it, it can decide what recoverable amount it believes is appropriate in the circumstances and then make an order to ensure that such a payment is made. The amount payable is that which the offender has criminally obtained, an amount which is available to be confiscated, or a nominal amount if all financial assets have been spent.[68] Priority of available funds is given first to court-sanctioned financial penalties,[69] with confiscation expected to be achieved within six months.[70] As mentioned above, the order is ancillary to possible imprisonment with the effect of a confiscation order having no bearing on the length of a possible custodial term.[71]

In order to try and ensure that available assets exist at the time of sentencing, as soon as a defendant begins to be investigated for a crime, the court can issue a restraint order under section 41 of the Proceeds of Crime Act 2002: if there is 'reasonable cause to believe that the defendant has benefited from his criminal conduct'.[72] The main purpose of a restraint order is to prevent the disposal of criminal assets and it can be made even before the defendant has been charged with a criminal offence, provided that this is the expected course of action. If such an order is made, it can instruct a defendant to not only disclose the nature and whereabouts of his assets but also to relocate assets back within the jurisdiction of England and Wales, so that all realizable assets can be restrained. The order will apply to all realizable property held by the defendant and can additionally include any property which is transferred to him after the order has been made. When deciding which property to seize the court must take into account the cost of reasonable living and legal expenses and if appropriate allow the defendant to continue in the course of his trade, business, profession or occupation.[73]

Once a conviction for a financial crime has been secured,[74] the court

---

[67] Proceeds of Crime Act 2002, s. 10.
[68] Proceeds of Crime Act 2002, s. 7.
[69] Proceeds of Crime Act 2002, s. 9.
[70] Proceeds of Crime Act 2002, s. 11. This can be extended to 12 months if the Crown Court believes that exceptional circumstances warrant such an extension. Upon the making of a confiscation order the court should also order a period of imprisonment which will be served if the payment is not made. Maximum default periods are outlined in Powers of the Criminal Courts (Sentencing) Act 2000, s. 139(4).
[71] *R v Rogers* [2001] EWCA Crim 1680.
[72] Proceeds of Crime Act 2002, s. 40.
[73] Proceeds of Crime Act 2002, s. 41.
[74] The full list of relevant crimes can be found in Serious Organized Crime and

also has the option of ordering a financial reporting order under sections 76 to 79 of the Serious Organized Crime and Police Act 2005. The order requires the offender to make regular reports to the authorities about his financial affairs and can last up to 20 years.[75] Failure to provide the necessary reports or the inclusion of false or misleading information in a report, can lead to a separate criminal conviction and possible term of imprisonment.[76] Furthermore, if the offence was in connection with 'the promotion, formation, management, liquidation or striking off of a company, with the receivership of the company's property or with his being an administrative receiver of a company',[77] the court can disqualify the offender from acting as a director of a company for a specified period of time. The disqualification, found under the Company Directors Disqualification Act 1986, prevents the offender from acting as a company director, even if the job title is different or from instructing others to act on his behalf. Whilst the offender can work for a company (although whether a financial criminal would ever be re-employed in the sector is another matter), without the court's permission he cannot act as a receiver of a company's property; be concerned in the promotion, formation or management of the company; act as an insolvency practitioner; or take part in the promotion, formation or management of a limited liability partnership. Disqualification can last for a maximum period of 15 years and is thus a clear example of incapacitating the offender to prevent further offending behaviour. Anyone who is found to be in contravention of the order is liable for an additional criminal offence with a maximum imprisonment period of two years.[78]

8.6   SENTENCING FINANCIAL CRIME: EXAMPLES OF PRACTICE

The final section in this chapter is an analysis of sentencing practice concerning financial crime. By looking at sentencing examples not just from England and Wales, but also from the US, this examines whether sentencing practice in England and Wales is appropriate, takes into account all of the guidelines and procedures as outlined above and thus can be said

---

Police Act 2005, s. 76, and includes fraud, false accountancy, money laundering and funding arrangements with regards to terrorism.

[75]   If the person was given life imprisonment. Otherwise, the maximum period is 15 years – Serious Organized Crime and Police Act 2005, s. 76.

[76]   Serious Organized Crime and Police Act 2005, s. 79.

[77]   Company Directors Disqualification Act 1986, s. 2.

[78]   Company Directors Disqualification Act 1986, s. 13.

to be just. The sentencing examples which will be examined from England and Wales include Michael Bright; John and Anne Darwin; Ussama El-Kurd; Shell Transport and Trading Company and Christopher McQuoid; and from the US, Jeffrey Skilling, Bernard Madoff, Riggs Bank N.A. and Martha Stewart.

8.6.1 Sentencing Examples from England and Wales

Fraud

An example of fraud sentencing, which is reasonably well known, is that of Michael Bright, the founder and Chief Executive of Independent Insurance. In 2000 the company was thought to be worth £1bn, but it collapsed in 2001 with the loss of more than 1000 jobs and at a cost of £357m in compensation paid for by the Financial Services Authority (FSA).[79] Bright was charged with two counts of conspiracy to defraud by dishonestly withholding claims data and making incomplete disclosure of all actual or intended agreements between the company and its re-insurers; and with the alternative offence of fraudulent trading in relation to non-disclosure of contracts. In October 2007, Bright was sentenced to seven years in custody and disqualified from being a director for 12 years. It is worth noting that Bright received a term of seven years for each conspiracy count, with the two terms to run concurrently (that is, at the same time). As the offences in this case took place before the Fraud Act 2006 existed, the 10-year sentence, as mentioned above, was not open to the sentencing judge. However, despite this, the maximum sentence available for fraudulent trading was seven years (although this has now been increased to 10[80]) and for conspiracy to defraud was 10 years.[81] Despite the 10-year sentence being available, and the fact that the sentencing judge said that the offence committed by Bright was 'so grave' and 'altogether beyond the scope that Parliament could have had in mind when fixing such a maximum, probably by a factor of several times' and 'if any offence should attract the maximum penalty, it is this one',[82] a sentence of only seven years was given. This was because it was decided that whilst the

---

[79] For more information about the collapse of Independent Insurance see *R v Bright* [2008] 2 CrAppR (S) 102.

[80] Companies Act 2006, s. 993.

[81] Criminal Justice Act 1987, s. 12(3).

[82] Leroux, M. (2007), 'Michael Bright gets maximum seven years from Independent Insurance' available at: http://business.timesonline.co.uk/tol/business/industry_sectors/banking_and_finance/article2733660.ece (accessed 1 December 2009).

conspiracy charge was the most appropriate for trial purposes, the lesser charge of fraudulent trading fully covered the substance of the offences in question, and thus it should only be this maximum which was available. Notwithstanding receipt of the lesser sentence, Bright appealed,[83] arguing that it was unjust to use the full maximum and additionally that his mitigation of age, good character and poor health had not been taken into account. The Court of Appeal dismissed the appeal, stating that the crime had been one of 'utmost gravity'.[84] Interestingly, it also stated that the sentencing court had been wrong in limiting the sentence to seven years and that the maximum applicable sentence was 10 years. Whilst the Court of Appeal had the power to increase the sentence to 10 years the sentence remained unchanged and arguably Bright was lucky that he did not receive a longer sentence; especially when considering, as per the guidelines above, his crime included 'professional' offending; was a planned offence; was committed with a high level of culpability and caused a vast amount of harm. This leniency is further supported by the sentencing guidelines issued in *R v Clark*, mentioned above, which stated that 10 years or more would be appropriate where the case involved £1m or more. The guidelines additionally suggest that in Bright's case, the use of consecutive sentencing may have been appropriate and so perhaps a more just sentence should have been in the region of 14 or 20 years. In October 2008, Michael Bright also paid £1 258 467 pursuant to a confiscation order.[85]

The example of Bright, which is (or should have been) an example at the upper end of the tariff can be compared with other fraud cases. For example, in 2009 Jacinta Kibunyi[86] was sentenced to 12 months' imprisonment following a plea of guilty to possession of a false identity document: she had used a false passport to open a bank account. Whilst the court acknowledged that she may have been a victim of trafficking, the 12-month sentence was still upheld. Whilst using false passports is obviously serious, the sentence here would appear harsh, especially when compared to the facts and the amount of money involved in the *Bright* case. Surely in terms of seriousness and commensurability, and the mitigation involved,

---

[83]   *R v Bright* [2008] 2 CrAppR (S) 102.

[84]   *R v Bright* [2008] EWCA Crim 462, para. 33.

[85]   Lomas was ordered to pay £470 113 and Condon, £1 280 896. Serious Fraud Office (2009), 'Independent Insurance fraudsters ordered to pay over £1 million confiscation', available at http://www.sfo.gov.uk/press-room/latest-press-releases/press-releases-2009/independent-insurance-fraudsters-ordered-to-pay-over-%C2%A31-million-confiscation.aspx (accessed 5 August 2010).

[86]   *R v Jacinta Kibunyi*, Court of Appeal Criminal Division, 14 January 2009, unreported.

a community order or even a financial penalty would have been more appropriate. It also appears harsh when compared to the case of John and Anne Darwin, who were sentenced to six years three months and six years six months respectively, for convictions on six counts of fraud and nine counts of money laundering. By faking John Darwin's death, the couple received nearly £250 000 in benefits, with John Darwin also being convicted of dishonestly obtaining a passport.[87] What is interesting with this case is that whilst John Darwin pleaded guilty, his wife was convicted. Even though Anne Darwin received a higher custodial term, this was only three months more than that of her husband. Whilst it is acknowledged that John Darwin's crimes may have been viewed as more serious, it still does not suggest that a guilty plea in his case led to a full one-third discount on his sentence.[88] Also when compared to *Kibunyi* it is assumed that the sentences for fraud and money laundering were imposed to run concurrently, otherwise for 15 counts the total length of the sentence would have been expected to have been 20 years plus. When one year is given for one offence where there is no financial gain achieved or loss caused, it appears unjust that six years is given whereby the offence count is 15-fold and the financial benefit is £250 000.

Another example is the case of Guy Pound,[89] who had his initial sentence of three years' imprisonment increased to one of six years, due to the fact that the former was deemed to be unduly lenient. Pound had been involved in defrauding a charitable trust, over a period of 11 years, amounting to £2m. Bearing in mind his level of planning, breach of trust, abuse of power and high culpability, the increase in his sentence would appear to have been just. In fact if we compare this to the case involving the Darwins, whereby the financial benefit was 75 per cent less, there is an argument that the sentence should actually have been higher still, which again the guidelines in *R v Clark* would support. Other cases include Carl Cusnie (former chairman of Versailies) who was jailed for six years for a £150m fraud (although he was sentenced on the basis of a loss of £20m) and disqualified from being a director for 10 years; Fred Clough (Finance

---

[87] Bunyan, N. and Edwards, R. (2008), 'Canoe wife trial: Darwin's jailed for more than six years', available at: http://www.telegraph.co.uk/news/2448044/Canoe-wife-trial-Darwins-jailed-for-more-than-six-years.html (accessed 4 August 2010).

[88] As the case is unreported and details can only be gleaned from newspaper reports it is unknown when the sentencing judge detailed how much the discount was that John Darwin received.

[89] *R v Pound (Guy)*; Attorney General's Reference (No. 59 of 2004), [2004] EWCA 2488.

Director of Versailies) who received five years' imprisonment (he had co-operated with the authorities and pleaded guilty and had received a 50 per cent discount off his sentence) and a 15-year disqualification; Abbas Gokal (connected with the fall of BCCI) who received 14 years and Ernest Saunders (former Chief Executive of Guinness) who was sentenced to a five-year jail term.[90]

Whilst there are obviously several other sentencing examples which can be given, can any concluding remarks be made about those few illustrated here? From an analysis of the cases it would be useful for sentencing judges if a pattern had emerged and it was possible to devise a table whereby the amount of the financial benefit achieved or loss caused could be equated with the length and severity of the sentence, equating to a weighing scale notion of just deserts. Practice, displayed in these few cases does not appear to be able to offer this however. Whilst Bright received seven years for a fraud costing the FSA £357m, a sentence of one year less was given where the amounts were £250 000 (John Darwin), £2m and £20m. Whilst it is acknowledged that the harm caused, or risked being caused, is not the only factor for the sentencing judge to take into account, it is one which has been identified by the Criminal Justice Act 2003, the relevant SGC guideline and the guideline judgments of *R v Barrick* and *R v Clark*. All of these offenders showed high levels of culpability and so the length of their sentences should arguably have been more diverse to show the differences in seriousness and harm caused. It is also surprising, if not shocking, that offences involving millions of pounds do not initiate the maximum sentence of 10 years and this provides evidence that we are in desperate need of sentencing guidelines to provide for not just more consistent sentencing, but also sentencing at the higher end of the sentencing scale. Bearing in mind that current SGC sentencing guidelines on fraud only cover amounts up to £500 000 it is suggested here that not only do we need the guidelines but that they also need to be extended to include amounts ranging up to millions of pounds and sentencing ranges and starting points to include the legislative maxima. Whilst *R v Clark* includes guidelines where cases involve £1m or more, the cases above would suggest that sentencing judges are not paying much attention to these. Another consideration is that of concurrent and consecutive sentencing. Whilst this is not the place to have a full discussion about the merits of each, is it fair that one person can commit 10 or 20 offences and effectively be sentenced to the same length of imprisonment as someone who has only committed one? Again, *R v Clark* briefly mentions this issue but much more in-depth advice is still desperately needed.

---

90   Although this was later reduced due to his poor health.

Money laundering

An example involving money laundering is that of Ussama El-Kurd,[91] who in 1999 was sentenced to the maximum penalty of 14 years' imprisonment and fined £1m for being involved in a £70m laundering operation, which took place over a period of two and a half years at his bureau de change. At the time, the operation was described as the largest in Europe, with El-Kurd being the first person in England and Wales to be convicted on sole money laundering charges (that is, his offence was not additionally connected to other drug or terrorist offences).[92] This would appear to suggest that the courts and also the legislature regard money laundering as a more serious crime, not just because the maximum imprisonment length is four years longer than for fraud, but also importantly, the fact that such maxima are being used. Whilst it is acknowledged that there can be far-reaching effects caused by the offence of money laundering, when comparing the *Bright* and *El-Kurd* cases does it equate to double the seriousness? This would suggest once again that those being sentenced for fraud may have received lenient sentences.

At the other end of the spectrum is the case of Philip Griffiths,[93] a solicitor, who received a term of six months' imprisonment for failing to tell the authorities about a transaction where he had reasonable grounds for knowing or suspecting that it involved money laundering. Whilst the judge acknowledged that Griffiths had lost his practice, he had not made any money out of the transaction (apart from his usual conveyancing fee) and it had had a dramatic impact on his health and life, it was still felt that a custodial sentence was proportionate and thus justified. Leveson J argued 'organizing the cover-up or laundering the proceeds of crime is always particularly serious, especially if organised or set up as an operation. Custodial sentences are absolutely inevitable in almost every case, if not every case'.[94] This was also shown in *R v Duff*[95] where the Court of Appeal upheld a six-month custodial sentence against a solicitor who had failed to report the fact that he had received £70 000 to invest in a joint business from a client, who was later charged with a drugs offence. Even though he took advice from another solicitor as to his duty to notify and consulted the Law Society's guidance notes, the Court still held that the

---

[91] *R v Ussama El-Kurd* [2001] CrimLR 234 (CA).

[92] BBC (1999), 'UK maximum sentence for money launder', available at http://news.bbc.co.uk/1/hi/uk/285759.stm (accessed 4 August 2010).

[93] *R v Griffiths (Philip)* [2006] EWCA Crim 2155.

[94] *Ibid.*, at para. 11.

[95] [2003] 1 CrAppR (S) 88.

sentence was not 'in any way excessive'.[96] What is interesting here is the penalizing of someone who fails to act, rather than penalizing someone for committing a positive act. In English criminal law, there are very few situations where a failure to act will initiate criminal proceedings, although being under a duty to act is obviously one such exception. The fact that the government has created such a duty and that failure is being penalized and arguably severely punished shows how serious the government is in tackling this crime.[97] Whilst terms of imprisonment for solicitors and other professionals in these circumstances act as individual and general deterrence, there is a question mark over whether they are commensurate with the seriousness of the actual offence. However, despite this, perhaps sentencing judges and through them the government need to make examples of a few such professionals to warn others and subsequently deter them from turning a blind eye to such behaviour.

Other cases regarding money laundering include that of Jacovos Iannou,[98] who received a custodial term of 18 months having pleaded guilty to one count of laundering money amounting to £1m. The money had been fraudulently obtained from a large financial service provider and put into a number of third party bank accounts, with £91 240 going into the offender's. Taking the guilty plea into account the trial judge said that the starting point would otherwise have been two and a half years, amounting to a 12-month discount for the plea. Bearing in mind that the largest discount is meant to be one-third, the discount applied here should have been 10 months rather than that of 12 months. There would, therefore, appear to be a certain amount of leniency being shown here. Conversely, Tarsemwal Lal Sabharwal[99] received 12 years' imprisonment for the laundering of over £53m of drug trafficking proceeds. Whilst the Court of Appeal acknowledged that this was at the top end of sentencing, it stated that the offence was also at the top end in terms of seriousness,[100] and thus it felt that the model of just deserts had been properly applied. Similarly, David Simpson[101] received 11 years' imprisonment for the laundering of money worth £2.5m. Whilst the Court of Appeal acknowledged that he was not the most seriously involved in the scam, his role was still

---

96 *Ibid.*, at 471.
97 For more information on this see Chapter 2.
98 *R v Iannou (Jacovos)* [2009] EWCA Crim 1755.
99 *R v Tarsemwal Lal Sabharwal* [2001] 2 CrAppR (S) 81.
100 *Ibid.*, at 375.
101 *R v Simpson* [1998] 2 CrAppR (S) 111.

said to be 'crucial and pivotal'.[102] Again this would suggest an application of the just deserts model.

The sentencing of money laundering, on these few examples, would thus appear to be more severe than that for fraud,[103] with sentences much closer to the maxima and failures to act being treated as particularly serious. Whilst this would appear to be a positive thing, as arguably terms of 14 years' imprisonment should be engaged when the financial benefit amounts to £70m, there would again appear to be little consistency in terms of harm caused and length of sentence. Whilst 14 years for £70m may be just, it does not follow that one and a half years would equate to £1m and 11 years to £2.5m. As previously mentioned sentencing is more complicated than this and there could have been other aggravating and mitigating factors involved; but again we see rather disparate sentencing practice, suggesting that detailed SGC guidelines need to be developed not only for fraud, but also for money laundering and all other financial crimes.

Insider dealing/market abuse

For insider dealing and market abuse, there are several examples which involve not just individuals but also major and multi-national corporations. In 2004, Shell Transport and Trading Company, Royal Dutch Petroleum and the Royal Dutch/Shell Group of Companies were fined £17m for committing market abuse offences in connection with misstatements relating to their proved reserves. When the misstatements were uncovered their share price fell from 401 pence to 371 pence, equating to a loss of approximately £2.9bn. Commenting on the fine, the Director of Enforcement at the FSA stated how, 'the size of the penalty in this case reflects the seriousness of Shell's misconduct and the impact it had on markets and shareholders'.[104] Whilst £17m is a considerable amount, the FSA also stated that if it had not been for the full co-operation of Shell then the penalty would have been significantly higher, making this co-operation almost the equivalent of a guilty plea in criminal court proceedings. Moreover, in 2006, the FSA issued the largest fine that had ever been issued against an individual, fining hedge fund manager GLG Partners LP (GLG) and Philippe Jabre (former Managing Director) £750 000 each, for

---

[102] *Ibid.*, at 114.

[103] Apart from that of *Iannou* which appears to be rather lenient both in terms of guilty plea discount and the amount of money involved.

[104] Financial Service Authority (2004a), 'FSA fines Shell 17,000,000 for market abuse', available at http://www.fsa.gov.uk/Pages/Library/Communication/PR/2004/074.shtml (accessed 31 March 2010).

insider dealing and market abuse. Jabre was privy to confidential share information on 11 February 2003, which he agreed not to use until it had become public. The information was announced on 17 February, but on 12 and 13 February he breached the restriction by short selling approximately $16m of ordinary shares.[105]

More recently, in 2009, the FSA fined Mark Lockwood, a trading desk manager, £20 000 for failing to prevent insider dealing. Whilst he had reason to believe that a transaction was being conducted on the basis of insider dealing he failed to either prevent the trade or alert the FSA through the submission of a Suspicious Activity Report (SAR).[106] What is interesting in this example is that Lockwood was fined for a failure to act rather than being positively involved in the offence, as with the money laundering examples involving Griffiths and Duff above; although it is acknowledged that under his job role he too was under an obligation to notify the FSA of any suspicious behaviour, which in this case he obviously failed to do. Again this exemplifies the tough role which the government and designated task force agencies are taking in the battle against financial crime; although a fine of £20 000 is arguably far less severe in terms of stigma, loss of liberty and effect on health and family than a six-month term in custody. This would therefore suggest that whilst the general deterrence issued against failing to let the authorities know about possible insider dealing transactions is severe, it is not as harsh as that for transactions involving potential money laundering activity. Again we see how sentencing for money laundering would appear to be stricter than that for other types of financial crime.

From those examples cited above, the majority of market abuse cases would thus appear to be dealt with by the FSA via a regulatory system rather than through criminal prosecution. This is generally because it has been accepted to be particularly hard to prove insider dealing cases on the criminal standard of proof,[107] meaning that the FSA has preferred to opt for civil cases where the burden of proof is obviously less strenuous. Despite this favouring of the civil courts, the FSA can still, as seen

---

[105]   Financial Services Authority (2006b), 'FSA fines GLG Partners and Philippe Jabre £750,000 each for market abuse', available at http://www.fsa.gov.uk/pages/Library/Communication/PR/2006/077.shtml (accessed 13 March 2010).

[106]   Financial Services Authority (2009a), 'FSA fines broker for failing to prevent insider dealing', available at http://www.fsa.gov.uk/pages/Library/Communication/PR/2009/115.shtml (accessed 13 March 2010).

[107]   This is because the jury have to be sure that not only did the defendant have insider information, but that he also knew that it was price sensitive and either acted using this information or encouraged someone else to act as an accomplice.

above, fine and/or ban city workers without a trial. The policy of favouring the civil route seemed to change, however, in 2007/08 when a number of criminal cases were brought for insider dealing.[108] One of the first was Christopher McQuoid[109] who was given an eight-month custodial term for using insider information to make a profit of almost £50 000. In addition to the term of imprisonment, a confiscation order was made to retrieve all of the benefit and he was ordered to pay £30 000 in prosecution costs. In his appeal against sentence, which was dismissed, the Court of Appeal confirmed that those involved in insider dealing were criminals,[110] that it was a species of fraud and hence was cheating.[111] Despite what some may have seen as a warning that insider dealing would be classed as a serious offence and commensurate with an immediate custodial term, in March 2009, Timothy Power, former executive of the Belgo Group, received an 18-month jail sentence suspended for two years, for two counts of insider trading amounting to a benefit of £9.8m.[112] Whilst it is accepted that Power had served 163 days in imprisonment awaiting trial, had pleaded guilty and his offences were old in nature (committed in 1997–1998), his suspended sentence would still appear to be lenient, especially when the sentencing judge described the offences as 'serious because they are a grave breach of trust by someone at the centre of a company which is going to cause sensitive movement on the Stock Exchange and upon which other people are relying for honesty and transparency'.[113] Furthermore, by suspending the sentence, arguably the sentencing judge went against the principle set out in *R v Barrick* that 'it would not usually be appropriate in cases of serious breach of trust to suspend any part of the sentence'.[114]

Prior to this policy change, the last criminal conviction for insider dealing in the UK was Asif Butt,[115] who was initially sentenced to five

---

[108]   Others include Neel and Mathew Uberoi; Malcolm Calvert, a former partner of Cazenove; and Neil Rollins. Herman, M., 'Former Belgo executive faces insider-dealing trial as wave of prosecutions reaches court', *The Times*, 16 February 2009, p. 40.
[109]   *R v Christopher McQuoid* above, n 45.
[110]   *Ibid.*, at para. 8.
[111]   *Ibid.*, at para. 9.
[112]   Cheston, P. (2009), 'Former Belgo chief spared prison for insider trading deal' available at: http://www.thisislondon.co.uk/standard/article-23656323-former-belgo-chief-is-spared-prison-for-insider-trading-deal.do;jsessionid=A890 C0DFCC53652272A3B0EA79225CFE (accessed 26 November 2009).
[113]   *Ibid.*
[114]   *Barrick* above, n 33 at 144.
[115]   *R v Butt (Asif Nazir)* [2006] 2 CrAppR (S) 44.

years' imprisonment for conspiracy to commit insider dealing. Using confidential information, over a period of three years and through 19 criminal transactions, Butt made £388 488 profit for his investment bank (Credit Suisse), equating to £237 000 in personal benefit. Whilst describing his offence as serious, 'flagrant, calculated and deliberate',[116] the Court of Appeal did reduce the sentence to one of four years. Prior to this was the case involving Michael Smith, Catherine Spearman, Norman Payne and Richard Spearman. The four defendants were involved in using insider information in connection with a number of takeover and merger transactions, with profits amounting to £336 000. The first three defendants pleaded guilty and were sentenced to custodial terms of 18 months, 18 months and 21 months respectively. Richard Spearman was convicted at trial and sentenced to 30 months. Unfortunately the cases are unreported, so it is unclear what level of involvement each offender had; but presuming that it was equal, we can see how a guilty plea has worked to reduce the sentence in this case, by up to 12 months or 40 per cent. Additional confiscation orders amounted to £36 012 against Smith, £107 935 against Catherine Spearman and £169 000 against Richard Spearman.[117] When compared to the case of Power, these examples would again suggest that his sentence was lenient; especially as there were guilty pleas also involved in the cases of Smith, Catherine Spearman and Payne.

Shifts in FSA prosecution procedures and rhetoric from the Court of Appeal would thus suggest that the FSA and the courts are trying to project the deterrent image that insider dealing is just as serious as other financial crimes and thus will be dealt with in a similar way. However, this is arguably not being mirrored in practice, with serious and dishonest offences being met with suspended sentences. Whilst it is accepted that further offences will initiate immediate custody, as mentioned above, it is thought that large-scale financial criminals rarely reoffend and so arguably apart from the 163 days awaiting trial Power has been given a let-off. It is acknowledged, though, that criminal enforcement procedures for insider dealing are still in their infancy and so conclusions regarding sentencing practice concerning it cannot, as of yet, be made. It will thus be interesting to monitor how sentencing practice emerges over the next few years; whether it does live up to the threat of equalling other serious financial offences and gets any closer to imposing its maximum of seven years.

116   *Ibid.*, at para. 25.
117   Serious Fraud Office (2004), 'Fourth conviction in insider dealing conspiracy', available at: http://www.sfo.gov.uk/news/prout/pr_269.asp?id=269 (accessed 1 December 2009).

8.6.2 Sentencing Examples from the US

Fraud

Perhaps one of the most famous financial scandals from the US is that involving Enron and its former Chief Executive Officer, Jeffrey Skilling. For a period of three years and with the help of several other key people within Enron, Skilling was accused of being involved in a number of irregular practices which inflated the share price of the company. In 2001, the company declared bankruptcy: 4000 people lost their jobs; $60bn was lost in Enron stock value and $2bn in pension funds disappeared. In 2004, Skilling was charged with 10 counts of insider trading, 15 counts of securities fraud, four counts of wire fraud, six counts of making false statements to auditors, and one count of conspiracy to commit wire and securities fraud. In all he was tried on 28 counts (the majority involving securities fraud) and found guilty on 19 of them,[118] being sentenced to 24 years and four months' imprisonment and ordered to pay $26m towards restoring the Enron pension fund. Bearing in mind, as noted above, the maximum penalty for securities fraud is 20 years' imprisonment, the sentencing judge obviously ordered that some of the sentences were to run consecutively; although, mirroring practice in England and Wales, it would appear that the vast majority were ordered to run concurrently. As there were 12 counts of securities fraud, five counts of making false statements to auditors, one count of insider trading and one count of conspiracy, the maximum possible sentence would have been nearer to 300 years if all sentences ran consecutively. Despite this, Skilling appealed against his sentence, arguing that sentencing guidelines were not appropriately followed and that his sentence was too harsh. In 2009 the 5th US Circuit Court of Appeals in New Orleans agreed and have thus vacated the original sentence and remanded him for resentence, although this matter has now been postponed until the matter goes before the Supreme Court.[119]

Another, and perhaps even more famous, case is that of Bernard Madoff, who in 2008 was charged with 11 offences[120] in relation to a massive Ponzi scheme which he had been operating through his company

---

[118] *US v Jeffrey K Skilling* verdict slip. Available at: www.docstoc.com/ . . . /U-S-vs.-Jeffrey-K-Skilling-Verdict-Slip.

[119] *US v Jeffrey K Skilling* No. 06-20885, 6 January 2009.

[120] Including one count of securities fraud; one count of investment adviser fraud; one count of mail fraud; one count of wire fraud; three counts of money laundering; one count of false statements; one count of perjury; one count of false filings with the US Securities and Exchange Commission; and theft from an employee benefit plan.

Bernard L. Madoff Investment Securities LLC. The maximum penalty for all offences, if they were to run consecutively, was 150 years in prison; and despite pleading guilty, this was the sentence which Madoff received in March 2009. In addition to this custodial term there was also a forfeiture order covering property amounting to $100m.[121] Whilst the scale of the crime was vast, approximating $65bn, involved both individuals and corporations and was described by the sentencing judge as extraordinary evil, it is questionable whether the 150 years of custody, bearing in mind the offender's age (71), was necessary or even practical. Despite the seriousness of the crime, no allowance was given for the guilty plea, the defendant's poor health or age. Bearing in mind the sentencing aims discussed above, whilst this is a clear example of punishment and deterrence (both individual and general) it arguably exceeds that which is required for incapacitation and just deserts. The seriousness of Madoff's offence cannot be disputed, but was it serious enough to warrant an effective death penalty, which would have been operative even if he had been in his late teens? Also it is questionable why the court decided to issue the maxima for all offences and to order that all terms be served consecutively when, as seen in Skilling, this was not the usual practice of the courts in the US. This would therefore suggest that the sentencing decision here was based too heavily on punishment, incapacitation and making an example of Madoff rather than on justice and just deserts.

Notwithstanding such comments, Madoff, whilst arguably being responsible for the largest investment fraud of all time, did not receive the longest-ever sentence. In 2000, Shalom Weiss was sentenced to 845 years for racketeering, fraud, money laundering and transportation of stolen property and his accomplice Keith Pound received 740 years. With release dates set at 2845 and 2740 respectively, this is an example of even more ludicrous and fantastical sentencing. Other cases include Norman Schmidt, who in 2008 was sentenced to 330 years for offences of fraud and money laundering amounting to a benefit of $56m; and Will Hoover who received 100 years for offences of fraud and theft. Whilst the gravity of these crimes is not disputed, it is still questionable whether such custodial terms are useful, practical, necessary and above all justified. Other severe examples, although not in comparison with those described above, include: Bernard Ebbers (WorldCom) 25 years' imprisonment; Scott Sullivan (WorldCom) five years' imprisonment (pleaded guilty and testified against Ebbers); Conrad Black (Hollinger International) six years and

---

[121]   For full details of the realizable property involved see: news.bbc.co.uk/2/shared/bsp/hi/pdfs/16_03_09_madoff_assets.pdf.

six months' imprisonment and David Radler (Hollinger International) two years and five months (pleaded guilty and testified against Black). Significant discounts in sentence length would appear to be evident where the defendant has not only pleaded guilty but has helped to secure the conviction of other more serious offenders involved in the case and would suggest discounts of between 62 and 80 per cent.[122]

Comparing these cases with examples from England and Wales, the US is without doubt much harsher when it comes to sentencing fraud cases. With the maximum penalty available in England and Wales being 10 years, this is likely to be the maximum length of time which an offender will serve in prison even if there are a number of counts against him, as the use of consecutive sentencing would appear to be rare. In the US, however, not only is the maximum penalty double that found in England and Wales, but there are also examples where the courts have used consecutive sentencing to produce bizarre, unjust and seemingly pointless terms of imprisonment. Whilst the US has clear sentencing guidelines,[123] which would appear to be useful, the inconsistency in sentence between the cases of Skilling and Madoff would suggest either that they are not working effectively or that clearer guidance needs to be issued on when the use of concurrent and consecutive sentencing is appropriate.

Money laundering

The US, like England and Wales, deals with some aspects of financial crime through civil regulatory systems rather than by using the criminal prosecution route and money laundering is one instance of where these are used. One example is the case of Riggs Bank N.A. which in 2004 agreed to pay a civil fine of $25m for violating anti-money laundering requirements.[124] Furthermore, in 2005, it pleaded guilty to failing to make SARs relating to transactions worth hundreds of millions of dollars in connection with the Chilean dictator Augusto Pinochet. Taking a guilty plea into account it was fined an additional $16m and put on corporate probation for a period of five years.[125] Other cases where the US Financial Crimes

---

[122]   Although it is acknowledged that these offenders were probably less seriously involved than their counterparts and so it would have been unlikely that they would have received as severe sentences as those whom they had informed on.

[123]   US Sentencing Commission *Guidelines Manual* (US Sentencing Commission: Washington, DC, 2008).

[124]   FinCEN (2004), 'Assessment of civil money penalty', available at www.fincen.gov/riggsassessment3.pdf (accessed 4 August 2010).

[125]   Red Flags (n/d), 'Handling questionable assets', available at http://www.redflags.info/index.php?topic=illicitassets (accessed 6 June 2010).

Enforcement Network has issued fines include Great Eastern Bank, which was fined $100 000 for wilfully violating SAR requirements, and Western Union, which was fined £3m for failing to file SARs and establishing a SAR procedure.[126]

Cases of money laundering which have gone through criminal prosecution include that of Joshua Macke who received five years' imprisonment for money laundering (amounting to $600 000) and conspiracy to distribute marijuana. Macke laundered the proceeds of drugs by investing in property, with the lawyer involved in the conveyancing of his property also imprisoned for 18 months, for failing to notify the authorities about the suspicious transactions. This can be compared with Dheadry Lloyd Powell who was given life in a federal prison for laundering approximately $99 673 of drug trafficking proceeds, and with Richard Lizitte, who received a five-year custodial sentence for drug distribution and the laundering of money amounting to $123 295. Lizitte also received a forfeiture order[127] for $500 000. Other examples include Sean Bucci who was given a 12-year and seven-month imprisonment term for possession with intent to distribute marijuana and laundering hundreds of thousands of dollars through various bank accounts and Joel Manalang, a conveyancing lawyer, who received an 18-month sentence and a $6000 fine for helping people to exchange drug profits for property. At trial Manalang admitted that he knew that the money in question was suspicious and failed to tell the authorities about it. As seen in the sentencing examples from England and Wales, failing to act when there is a duty to do so can initiate harsh criminal penalties.[128] Another more recent case involved the indictment of 39 individuals and one business for charges relating to money laundering and concealing terrorist financing. One of the men involved, Saifullah Ranjha, pleaded guilty to counts of money laundering and terrorist financing, involving $2.2m. In 2008, he was sentenced to nine years two months' imprisonment.[129, 130] Another example at the upper end of the tariff is that involving Hoang Nguyen and Terri Nguyen. Hoang Nguyen was given 19 years and seven months' imprisonment and Terri Nguyen three years and

---

[126]   Van Cleef *et al.* above, n 63.

[127]   This is the equivalent of a confiscation order in England and Wales.

[128]   IRS (n/d), 'Criminal enforcement', available at http://www.irs.gov/compliance/enforcement/article/0,,id=174640,00.html (accessed 4 August 2010).

[129]   The NEFA Foundation (n/d), 'US legal cases', available at http://www.nefafoundation.org/documents-legal-N_Z.html#ranjha (accessed 1 August 2010).

[130]   A motion to vacate this, however, was filed in May 2009, so what the sentence will actually be is currently unclear: http://dockets.justia.com/docket/court-mddce/case_no-1:2009cv01379/case_id-168880/.

five months, for being convicted of a number of counts of laundering the profits of drugs in excess of $15m.[131] Bearing in mind that 20 years is the maximum penalty available, this is an example of where that maximum was almost reached; but interestingly it also shows how sentences were given to run concurrently rather than consecutively.

Comparing these examples to those from England and Wales, it would appear that whilst, as noted above, the maximum available punishment is higher in the US than in England and Wales (by six years), there appears to be some consistency in sentencing practice. For example in *Ranjha* nine years was given for $2.2m which can be compared with the 11 years given to Simpson for laundering money worth £2.5m. However, in relation to conveyancing lawyers failing to report suspicious transactions, it would seem from the few examples considered that the US is more punitive against professionals failing in their duty to act, with 18-month sentences appearing to be the norm, compared to six-month terms expected in England and Wales. The only case which seems to be totally out of sync is that of Powell. Whilst this is a serious case it is unclear how sentencing was broken down into the offences of money laundering and drug trafficking, so it is impossible to say that life imprisonment would have been given had the offence been solely that of money laundering. Indeed, as mentioned above, it is very rare for charges against an offender to be just for money laundering and in all of these examples it is probable that the drugs aspects of the cases were considered to be more serious than the money laundering. Caution therefore needs to be exercised when conclusions are drawn regarding money laundering sentencing practice in the US and in England and Wales.

Insider dealing/market abuse

As with money laundering, it would appear that the majority of insider dealing/market abuse cases which are dealt with by the Securities and Exchange Commission (SEC) are done so through civil prosecution routes. For example, in September 2009 Reza Saleh, an employee of Perot Systems, had a civil lawsuit filed against him for using information about the firm's buyout by Dell before the official announcement was made. By buying call options, Saleh is said to have made approximately $8.6m.[132] Likewise, in 2008, the SEC filed a civil complaint against Mark Cuban, the owner of the Dallas Mavericks,[133] accusing him of selling 600 000 shares

---

[131] Assets of $2.5 million were also seized.

[132] Steele, F. (2009), 'Perot employee charged with insider dealing', available at http://business.timesonline.co.uk/tol/business/law/article6847523.ece (accessed 11 November 2009).

[133] A professional basketball team.

due to insider information and thus avoiding more than $750000 in losses. The matter is yet unresolved,[134] but currently Cuban is facing a potential $2.3m civil fine.[135] Other well-known cases include that of Robert Slattery (Vice President of Reebok International Ltd) who had a civil injunctive action taken against him by the SEC for using insider information to avoid losses of $9209 and make a profit of $1920. The case was settled, without Slattery admitting guilt, but agreeing to pay back the money he had gained and an additional fine of $11 129.[136]

Also similar to action against money laundering, some cases are prosecuted again using the criminal courts. One example is that of Roger Blackwell, who in 2007 was convicted for illegal trading in the stock of Worthington Foods Inc. based on insider knowledge that the Kellogg Company were interested in a buyout. Blackwell was fined $240 879 (plus interest of $129 802), banned from being a company director for life and sentenced to six years' imprisonment.[137] Criminal prosecution was also used against Martha Stewart, a famous television presenter, who was charged with insider dealing in 2004, after a share deal in 2001 saved her approximately $51 000.[138] Facing several years in custody, Stewart pleaded guilty to lying to a federal investigator and received a five-month sentence in prison, followed by two years of probation and a $30 000 fine. Peter Bacanovic, Stewart's former broker at Merrill Lynch, also received five months in prison, a two years' probation order and a fine of $4000.[139] In 2006, after being released from prison, Stewart also agreed a settlement

---

[134] As of October 2009, the SEC was appealing a federal judge's decision to dismiss the case. The appeal is waiting to be decided by the US Court of Appeals – Whitehouse, K. (2009), 'Full Court Press – SEC Appeals Cuban Insider Trading Decision', available at http://www.allbusiness.com/legal/trial-procedure-appeals/13164328-1.html (accessed 10 November 2010).

[135] Older, S. and Goldsamt, S. (2009), 'Does it Pay to be a Maverick When Trading Securities?', available at http://www.mondaq.com/article.asp?articleid=72360 (accessed 14 December 2009).

[136] US Securities and Exchange Commission (1988), 'SEC News Digest', available at http://www.404.gov/news/digest/1988/dig090288.pdf (accessed 2 September 2009).

[137] US Securities and Exchange Commission (2007), 'Litigation Release No. 20245', available at http://www.sec.gov/litigation/litreleases/2007/lr20245.htm (accessed 13 August 2009).

[138] *Times Online* (2004), 'Martha Stewart faces jurors at insider dealing trial', available at http://www.timesonline.co.uk/tol/news/article999303.ece (accessed 14 August 2009).

[139] Crawford, K. (2004), 'Martha: I cheated no one', available at http://money.cnn.com/2004/07/16/news/newsmakers/martha_sentencing/ (accessed 30 August 2009).

with the SEC, paying $195 000[140] and accepting a five-year ban from being a company director.[141]

When comparing sentencing practice between England and Wales and the US it is apparent that there is a tradition of dealing with insider dealing/market abuse through civil regulatory procedures rather than initiating criminal prosecution. As mentioned above, this may be because of the less burdensome standard of proof required in the civil courts, but could also be based on the fact that civil cases, in instances of companies, can still result in hefty financial penalties, which also work to serve the criminal sentencing aims of punishment, deterrence and reparation to the community. Comparing actual sentencing examples, it would appear that practice is fairly consistent, in that companies are issued with large fines, sometimes in the millions of pounds/dollars and individuals can expect not just financial penalties but also periods of time in custody; although lengths would appear to be less severe than those for the other financial crimes of money laundering and fraud.

8.7 CONCLUSIONS

The main aims when sentencing financial criminals would appear to be deterrence, punishment (using the just deserts model) and reparation and in the main these would appear to be being used in sentencing practice in England and Wales. The punishment of imprisonment seems to be a popular sentence and one which is now not exceptional for 'professional' offending. However, it is worth noting that the punishment of imprisonment may have significantly more negative effects for the financial criminal (and his family) due to the fact that he is unlikely to have been imprisoned before and arguably will suffer more in terms of change in lifestyle, social stigma, loss of status and loss of finances.[142] Perhaps, therefore, sentencing

---

[140]   This included disgorgement of $45 673, representing losses avoided from her insider trading, plus prejudgment interest of $12 389, for a total of $58 062 and a maximum civil penalty of $137 019, representing three times the amount of losses avoided.

[141]   US Securities and Exchange Commission (2006), 'Martha Stewart and Peter Bacanovic settle SEC's Insider Trading Charges', available at http://www.sec.gov/news/press/2006/2006-134.htm (accessed 10 September 2009).

[142]   Although of course this might mean that imprisonment for such offenders is far more effective than with other types of criminals. Weisburd, David (2001), *White Collar Crime & Criminal Careers*, Cambridge University Press, Port Chester, NY, USA, at p. 92. See Chapter 5 of Weisburd for more detail concerning the effect of prison sentences on white-collar criminals.

courts need to be aware of this when making a decision regarding sentence and sentence length; although on the other hand there is also the argument that if a person commits a crime he should be prepared to serve the time, regardless of status or background.

Despite the use of imprisonment and high-level fines, it still doesn't appear that the deterrent effect of these penalties is working, with serious cases continuing to appear. For example, at the time of writing, the corruption case against BAE Systems is just beginning to unfold, with financial penalties, ordered by the Serious Fraud Office, being estimated to be between £500m and £1bn.[143] If it is true that deterrence is not working as a legitimate aim of sentencing with regard to financial crime, then perhaps it is more understandable that the courts are resorting to longer and more severe sentencing; to not only punish those involved but to additionally give out the message that such behaviour will not be tolerated and echoing Lane LCJ in *R v Barrick* that 'professional men should expect to be punished as severely as others: in some cases, more severely'.[144]

As this chapter has attempted to outline, the sentencing of any offender is not an easy task; but perhaps it is even more complicated regarding financial crime, as it involves not just individuals who have committed criminal offences but also companies, and professionals who have failed in their duty to act. General sentencing principles will nevertheless still apply and there are a number of guidelines judgments and SGC guidelines which aid sentencing judges in this difficult task. However, it is suggested here that more guidelines and guidance are still needed. Whilst judgments such as *R v Barrick* and *R v Clark* exist, the cases cited above would suggest that in some instances these are not being followed. Sentencing judges are suspending sentences of imprisonment when it would not appear just to do so, do not appear to be using legislative maxima to their full in cases of fraud and also appear to be showing some leniency in insider dealing cases; although severe fines exist if the case is dealt with through the civil enforcement route. The only financial crime for which judges appear to be using the full range of the sentencing tariff is that of money laundering.[145] Whilst the reasons for this are unclear, it is suggested here that it is because the government has perhaps singled this crime out in terms of enforcement

---

143 BBC (2009), 'BAE Systems faces bribery charges', available at http://news.bbc.co.uk/1/hi/business/8284073.stm (accessed 3 March 2010).

144 (1985) 7 CrAppR (S) 143.

145 Although it is accepted that this view has been gained from an analysis of the sentencing examples contained within this chapter and that the use of other cases may have produced a different viewpoint.

and criminal prosecutions and because it is also often intertwined with other more serious drug offences.

Determining what these guidelines should be is not easy. The SGC has started to produce sentencing starting points for fraud, but arguably these do not go far enough in terms of starting amounts of loss involved and range of penalties, including the legislative maximum. There is no reason that serious cases of fraud such as that of *Bright* should not be attracting the maximum penalty and no reason that the maximum should not be used as often as it is with money laundering. Whilst this is not advocating for the use of fantastical sentences which have been seen in the US, sentences at the upper end of the tariff with clear guidance on when consecutive sentencing should be used would be most useful. This also applies to other financial crimes including money laundering, terrorist funding and insider dealing/market abuse. When there is a plethora of national and international policy measures to try to combat financial crime, the same level of interest, care and precision also needs to be employed regarding the sentencing of financial offenders, if the battle against financial crime is ever to stand a chance of being won.

9. Conclusions and recommendations

Financial crime is a global problem that demands a co-ordinated global response. This book has reviewed the financial crime policies adopted by the international community, the United States of America (US) and the United Kingdom (UK) towards four types of financial crime:

1. Money laundering;
2. Terrorist financing;
3. Fraud; and
4. Insider dealing.

The book has highlighted the importance of the mechanisms used by the international community, the US and the UK to forfeit and confiscate the proceeds of crime. Furthermore, this research has uniquely categorized the financial crime agencies and regulators in both countries into three categories:

1. Primary;
2. Secondary; and
3. Tertiary.

Finally, comparisons have been drawn between the sentencing practices in the US and the UK in relation to the financial crimes outlined above. Holistically, the international community's financial crime policies are led by the United Nations (UN) and the European Union (EU), who have implemented a number of legal instruments designed to tackle financial crime. The UN has clearly prioritized implementing policies designed to tackle money laundering and terrorist financing. This is illustrated by the fact that many nation states have instigated the integration of the Vienna Convention, the Palermo Convention and the UN Security Council Resolutions following the terrorist attacks in 2001. The UN has been assisted by the Financial Action Task Force (FATF) who have implemented the '40 Recommendations' and the 'Special Recommendations' to combat money laundering and terrorist financing. However, it must be noted that a majority of the UN measures have been implemented due to the influence of the US government. This is partly due to its inspired 'War on Drugs' in the 1980s and the declaration of the 'Financial War on Terrorism' in 2001. The UN policy towards fraud can be contrasted with its anti-money laundering and counter-terrorist financing policies. Its fraud strategy has concentrated on the alleged fraudulent activities of its employees and fraud committed against its own finances. The EU has adopted an equally impressive policy towards financial crime. This is clearly illustrated by the number of measures it has introduced to tackle money laundering, terrorist financing and insider dealing. In fact, the EU was the first international institution to recognize the threat posed by money laundering in the 1970s and, as a result, the EU has implemented three Money Laundering Directives that apply in 27 Member States. Similarly, the EU has adopted a tough stance towards insider dealing which includes a market abuse regime. Its terrorist financing policy has been influenced by the terrorist attacks in 2001 and it has followed the legislative measures introduced by the UN. The EU policy towards fraud is similar to that of the UN, a point illustrated by the fact that it has prioritized tackling fraud committed against its own finances. These measures have influenced the financial crime policies of the US and the UK, which are summarized below:

UNITED STATES OF AMERICA

Money Laundering

1. Criminalization
2. Financial intelligence

Terrorist Financing

1. Criminalization
2. Freezing terrorist assets
3. Financial intelligence

Fraud

1. Criminalization
2. Regulatory agencies
3. Financial intelligence

Insider Trading

1. Criminalization
2. Financial intelligence

UNITED KINGDOM

Money Laundering

1. Criminalization of money laundering
2. Regulated financial institutions anti-money laundering systems
3. Financial intelligence

Terrorist Financing

1. Criminalization
2. Freezing terrorist assets
3. Financial intelligence

Fraud

1. Criminalization
2. Regulatory agencies
3. Financial intelligence

Insider Dealing

1. Criminalization
2. Market abuse regime
3. Enforcement
4. Financial intelligence

Therefore, this book proposes the following model of financial crime policy:

1. Criminalization
2. Financial intelligence
3. Confiscation and forfeiture of the proceeds of crime
4. Financial crime regulators and agencies
5. Enforcement

Criminalization

The first part of the policy is evident in the four types of financial crime discussed in this book. Both the US and the UK criminalized money laundering in 1986, two years prior to the signing of the Vienna Convention and five years before the first EU Money Laundering Directive. Both jurisdictions have also criminalized terrorist financing. However, it is important to note that the UK has a longer history of tackling terrorist financing than the US, who only criminalized terrorist financing following the terrorist attacks in 2001. Both countries have criminalized fraud, the US in the late nineteenth century, while the UK codified and updated its fraud statutes via the Fraud Act in 2006. Likewise, the US criminalized insider trading in 1934, while the UK criminalized insider dealing in the 1980s.

Financial Intelligence

What becomes apparent from reviewing the policies adopted by the US and the UK is that they are heavily reliant on the use of financial intelligence for money laundering, terrorist financing, fraud and insider trading/dealing. Both countries have financial intelligence units, the Financial Crimes Enforcement Network (FinCEN) and the Serious Organized Crime Agency (SOCA) respectively, that use the submission of suspicious activity reports by a wide range of deposit-taking institutions. The US has relied on the financial intelligence extracted from the reports since 1970, whilst the UK introduced similar measures in 1986. Clearly, the use of financial intelligence is of the utmost importance in the global efforts against financial crime.

Confiscation and Forfeiture of the Proceeds of Crime

The third part of the model policy is the confiscation and forfeiture of the proceeds of crime. The use of these measures to tackle the proceeds of crime has long been recognized by the international community as illustrated by the provisions of the Vienna Convention and the Recommendations of the FATF. These measures are extremely contentious and their use by US law enforcement agencies has been categorized as 'legalized theft' and the ability to confiscate the proceeds of crime in the UK has faced numerous challenges under human rights law. Nonetheless, these powers are a central tenant of a country's fight against financial crime.

Financial Crime Regulators and Agencies

The fourth part of the model financial crime policy is the role of financial crime regulators and agencies. These can be divided into three categories – primary, secondary and tertiary. The primary agencies in the US are the Department of Treasury, Department of Justice and the State Department. In the UK the functions are performed by HM Treasury, the Home Office and the Foreign and Commonwealth Office. These institutions are generally responsible for developing the countries' financial crime strategy. The secondary agencies tend to be specialized criminal justice entities that investigate and initiate criminal proceedings where deemed necessary. The tertiary agencies are financial regulatory bodies and trade associations.

Enforcement

The final part of the policy is the effective enforcement of laws and regulations for breaches of the law discussed in this book. It is essential that a country seeks to maximize the use of the criminal and civil sanctions against those who commit financial crime.

Bibliography

Abarca, M. (2004), 'The need for substantive regulation on investor protection and corporate governance in Europe: does Europe need a Sarbanes-Oxley?', *Journal of International Banking Law and Regulation*, **19**(11), 419–431.

Acharya, U. (2009), 'The war on terror and its implications for international law and policy – war on terror or terror wars: the problem in defining terrorism', *Denver Journal of International Law and Policy*, **37**, 653–679.

Action Fraud (n/d), 'Action Fraud', available at http://www.actionfraud.org.uk/ (accessed 13 March 2010).

Alcock, A. (2001), 'Market abuse – the new witchcraft', *New Law Journal*, **151**, 1398.

Alcock, A. (2002), 'Market abuse', *Company Lawyer*, **23**(5), 142–150.

Alcock, A. (2007), 'Five years of market abuse', *Company Lawyer*, **28**(6), 163–171.

Alexander, K. (2000), 'Multi-national efforts to combat financial crime and the Financial Action Task Force', *Journal of International Financial Markets*, **2**(5) 178–192.

Alexander, K. (2001), 'The international anti-money laundering regime: the role of the Financial Action Task Force', *Journal of Money Laundering Control*, **4**(3), 231–248.

Alexander, Richard (2007), *Insider dealing and money laundering in the EU: Law and Regulation*, Ashgate, Aldershot.

Alexander, R. (2009a), 'Corporate crimes: are the gloves coming off?', *Company Lawyer*, **30**(11), 321–322.

Alexander, R. (2009b), 'Money laundering and terrorist financing: time for a combined offence', *Company Lawyer*, **30**(7), 200–204.

Alford, D. (1994), 'Anti-money laundering regulations: a burden on financial institutions', *The North Carolina Journal of International Law and Commercial Regulation*, **19**, 437–468.

Alldridge, B. (2002), 'Smuggling, confiscation and forfeiture', *Modern Law Review*, **65**(5), 781–791.

Alldridge, Peter (2003), *Money Laundering Law*, Hart, Oxford.

Alldridge, P. (2008), 'Money laundering and globalisation', *Journal of Law and Society*, **35**(4), 437–463.

Amann, D. (2000), 'Spotting money launderers: a better way to fight organised crime?', *Syracuse Journal of International Law and Commerce*, **27**, 199–231.

American Bankers Association *A new framework for partnership – Recommendations for Bank Secrecy Act/Anti-money laundering reform* (American Bankers Association: Washington, DC, 2007).

Anabtawi, I. (1989), 'Toward a definition of insider trading', *Stanford Law Review*, **41**, 377–399.

Anderson, T., Lane, H. and Fox, M. (2009), 'Consequences and responses to the Madoff fraud', *Journal of International Banking and Regulation*, **24**(11), 548–555.

Anon (2009), 'SEC charges key Madoff lieutenant with fraud', *Company Lawyer*, **30**(12), 371.

Arnone, M. and Padoan, P. (2008), 'Anti-money laundering by international institutions: a preliminary assessment', *European Journal of Law & Economics*, **26**(3), 361–386.

Arogeti, J. (2006), 'How much co-operation between government agencies is too much? Reconciling *United States v Scrushy*, the Corporate Fraud Task Force, and the nature of parallel proceedings', *Georgia State University Law Review*, **23**, 427–453.

Arora, A. (2006), 'The statutory system of the bank supervision and the failure of BCCI', *Journal of Business Law*, August, 487–510.

Ashe, M. (1992), 'The directive on insider dealing', *Company Lawyer*, **13**(1), 15–19.

Ashe, M. (2009), 'The long arm of the SEC', *Company Lawyer*, **30**(7), 193–194.

Ashworth, A. (1987), 'Deterrence', in A. von Hirsch and A. Ashworth (eds), *Principled sentencing: readings on theory and policy*, Hart Publishing, Oxford.

Assets Recovery Agency *Annual Report 2003/2004* (Assets Recovery Agency: London, 2004).

Assets Recovery Agency *Annual Report 2004/2005* (Assets Recovery Agency: London, 2005)

Assets Recovery Agency *Annual Report 2005/2006* (Assets Recovery Agency: London, 2006).

Assets Recovery Agency *Annual Report 2006/2007* (Assets Recovery Agency: London, 2007).

Attorney General's Office *Fraud Review – Final Report* (Attorney General's Office: London, 2006).

Attorney General's Office *Extending the powers of the Crown Court to prevent fraud and compensate victims: a consultation* (Attorney General's Office: London, 2008).

Australian Government and Australian Institute of Criminology *Charges and Offences of Money Laundering* Transnational Crime Brief No. 4 (Australian Institute of Criminology: Canberra, 2008).

Bachus, A. (2004), 'From drugs to terrorism: the focus shifts in the international fight against money laundering after September 11, 2001', *Arizona Journal of International and Comparative Law*, **21**, 835–872.

Bainbridge, S. (1985), 'A critique of the Insider Trading Sanctions Act of 1984', *Virginia Law Review*, **71**, 455–498.

Bainbridge, S. (1986), 'The insider trading prohibition: a legal and economic enigma', *University of Florida Law Review*, **38**, 35–68.

Bainbridge, S. (2004), *An Overview of US Insider Trading Law: Lessons for the EU*, Research Paper No. 05-5, UCLA, School of Law, Law and Economic Research Paper Series, available from http://ssrn.com/abstract=654703 (accessed 1 June 2010).

Baker, G. (1994), 'Your worst nightmare: an accountant with a gun! The Criminal Investigation Division of the Internal Revenue Service: its past, present, and future', *Georgia State University Law Review*, **11**, 331–379.

Baker, R. (1999), 'Money Laundering and Flight Capital: The Impact on Private Banking', testimony before the Permanent Subcommittee on Investigations, Committee on Governmental Affairs, US Senate, 10 November 1999, available at http://www.brookings.edu/testimony/1999/1110financialservices_baker.aspx (accessed 2 August 2010).

Baldwin, F. (2004), 'The financing of terror in the age of the internet: wilful blindness, greed or a political statement?', *Journal of Money Laundering Control*, **8**(2), 127–158.

Bantekas, I. (2003), 'The international law of terrorist financing', *American Journal of International Law*, **97**, 315–333.

Barnett, W. (1996), 'Fraud enforcement in the Financial Services Act 1986: an analysis and discussion of s. 47', *Company Lawyer*, **17**(7), 203–210.

Baron, B. (2005), 'The Treasury guidelines have had little impact overall on US international philanthropy, but they have had a chilling impact on US based Muslim charities', *Pace Law Review*, **25**, 307–320.

Bassiouni, M. (1989), 'Critical reflections on international and national control of drugs', *Denver Journal of International Law and Policy*, **18**(3), 311–337.

Bauman, T. (1984), 'Insider trading at common law', *University of Chicago Law Review*, **51**, 838–867.

Bay, N. (2005), 'Executive power and the war on terror', *Denver University Law Review*, **83**, 335–386.

Bazley, S. (2008), 'The Financial Services Authority, risk based regulation, principles based rules and accountability', *Journal of International Banking Law and Regulation*, **23**(8), 422–440.

BBC (1999), 'UK maximum sentence for money launder', available at http://news.bbc.co.uk/1/hi/uk/285759.stm (accessed 4 August 2010).

BBC (2005), 'New laws target criminal's case', available at http://news.bbc.co.uk/1/hi/uk/4294581.stm (accessed 8 March 2005).

BBC (2009), 'BAE Systems faces bribery charges', available at http://news.bbc.co.uk/1/hi/business/8284073.stm (accessed 3 March 2010).

BBC (2010a), 'Car bomb found in New York's Times Square', 2 May 2010, available at http://news.bbc.co.uk/1/hi/world/americas/8656651.stm (accessed 14 July 2010).

BBC (2010b), '"Somali link" as 74 World Cup fans die in Uganda blasts', 12 July 2010, available at http://news.bbc.co.uk/1/hi/world/africa/10593771.stm (accessed 3 August 2010).

BBC (2010c), 'US to access Europeans' bank data in new deal', 8 July 2010, available at http://www.bbc.co.uk/news/10552630 (accessed 14 July 2010).

Bell, R. (2003a), 'The confiscation, forfeiture and disruption of terrorist finances', *Journal of Money Laundering Control*, **7**(2), 105–125.

Bell, R. (2003b), 'The seizure, detention and forfeiture of cash in the UK', *Journal of Financial Crime*, **11**(2), 134–149.

Benning, J. (2002), 'Following dirty money: does bank reporting of suspicious activity pose a threat to drug dealers?', *Criminal Justice Policy Review*, **13**(4), 337–355.

Bentley, D. and Fisher, R. (2009), 'Criminal property under POCA 2002 – time to clean up the law?', *Archbold News*, **2**, 7–9.

Bercu, S. (1994), 'Toward universal surveillance in an information age economy: can we handle Treasury's new police technology?', *Jurimetrics Journal*, **34**, 383–449.

Binning, P. (2002), 'In safe hands? Striking the balance between privacy and security – anti-terrorist finance measures', *European Human Rights Law Review*, **6**, 737–749.

Blair, W. (1998), 'The reform of financial regulation in the UK', *Journal of International Banking Law*, **13**(2), 43–49.

Blanchard, A. (2006), 'The next step in interpreting criminal forfeiture', *Cardozo Law Review*, **28**, 1415–1445.

Blank, S., Kasprisin, J. and White, A. (2009), 'Health Care Fraud', *American Criminal Law Review*, **46**, 701–759.

Blanque, B. (2002), 'Crisis and fraud', *Journal of Financial Regulation and Compliance*, **11**(1), 60–70.

Blumel, R. (2005), 'Mail and wire fraud', *American Criminal Law Review*, **42**, 677–698.

Blumenson, E. and Nilsen, E. (1998), 'Policing for profit: the drug war's hidden economic agenda', *University of Chicago Law Review*, **65**, 35–114.

Borgers, M. and Moors, J. (2007), 'Targeting the proceeds of crime: bottle-necks in international cooperation', *European Journal of Crime*, **15**(1), 1–22.

Bosworth-Davies, R. (2006), 'Money laundering: towards an alternative interpretation – chapter two', *Journal of Money Laundering Control*, **9**(4), 346–364.

Bosworth-Davies, R. (2007a), 'Money laundering – chapter four', *Journal of Money Laundering Control*, **10**(1), 66–90.

Bosworth-Davies, R. (2007b), 'Money laundering – chapter five: the implications of global money laundering laws', *Journal of Money Laundering Control*, **10**(2), 189–208.

Bosworth-Davies, R. (2009), 'Investigating financial crime: the continuing evolution of the public fraud investigation role – a personal perspective', *Company Lawyer*, **30**(7), 195–199.

Bowling, B. and Ross, J. (2006), 'The Serious Organised Crime Agency – should we be afraid?', *Criminal Law Review*, December, 1019–1034.

Boyer, S. (2009), 'Computer Fraud and Abuse Act: abusing federal juris-diction?', *Rutgers Journal of Law and Public Policy*, **6**(3), 661–702.

Brent, Richard (2008), 'International legal sources IV – the European Union and the Council of Europe', in W. Blair and R. Brent (eds), *Banks and financial crime – the international law of tainted money*, Oxford University Press, Oxford, 101–150.

Brickey, K. (2003), 'From Enron to WorldCom and beyond: life and crime after Sarbanes-Oxley', *Washington University Law Review*, **81**, 357–382.

Brickey, K. (2004), 'White collar criminal law in comparative perspec-tive: the Sarbanes-Oxley Act of 2002', *Buffalo Criminal Law Review*, **8**, 221–276.

Briggs, J. (2006), 'Criminal confiscation, civil recovery and insolvency under the Proceeds of Crime Act 2002', *Insolvency Intelligence*, **19**(10), 145–150.

British Bankers Association (2008), 'Financial services sector tops UK growth tables', Press Release, 18 January 2008, available at http://www.bba. org.uk/bba/jsp/polopoly.jsp?d=1569&a=12022 (accessed 9 June 2009).

British Institute of International and Comparative Law *Comparative implementation of EU directives (1) – insider dealing and market abuse* (British Institute of International and Comparative Law: Corporation of London, 2005).

Brody, S. *The effectiveness of sentencing: a review of the literature* Home Office Research Study No. 35 (HMSO: London, 1975).

Brown, G. and Evans, T. (2008), 'The impact: the breadth and depth of the anti-money laundering provisions requiring reporting of suspicious activi-ties', *Journal of International Banking Law and Regulation*, **23**(5), 274–277.

Brown, M. (2008), 'Prosecutorial discretion and federal mail fraud prosecutions for honest services fraud', *Georgetown Journal of Legal Ethics*, **21**, 667–682.

Bublick, E. (2008), 'Upside down? Terrorists, proprietors, and civil responsibility for crime prevention in the post-9/11 tort reform world', *Loyola of Los Angeles Law Review*, **31**, 1483–1543.

Buchanan, B. (2004), 'Money laundering – a global obstacle', *Research in International Business and Finance*, **18**, 120–122.

Bunyan, N. and Edwards, R. (2008), 'Canoe wife trial: Darwin's jailed for more than six years', available at http://www.telegraph.co.uk/news/2448044/Canoe-wife-trial-Darwins-jailed-for-more-than-six-years.html (accessed 4 August 2010).

Burger, R. (2007), 'A principled front in the war against market abuse', *Journal of Financial Regulation and Compliance*, **15**(3), 331–336.

Burger, R. and Davies, G. (2005a), 'The most valuable commodity I know of is information', *Journal of Financial Regulation and Compliance*, **13**(4), 324–332.

Burger, R. and Davies, G. (2005b), 'What's new in market abuse – Part 2', *New Law Journal*, **155**, 964.

Burnett, A. (1986), 'Money laundering – recent judicial decisions and legislative developments', *Federal Bar News Journal*, **33**, 372.

Byrne, J., Densmore, D. and Sharp, J. (1995), 'Examining the increase in federal regulatory requirements and penalties: is banking facing another troubled decade?', *Capital University Law Review*, **24**, 1–66.

Cabinet Office *Recovering the Proceeds of Crime – A Performance and Innovation Unit Report* (Cabinet Office: London, 2000).

Cabinet Office *The UK and the Campaign against International Terrorism – Progress Report* (Cabinet Office: London, 2002).

Cameron-Waller, Stuart (2008), 'International co-operation networks', in S. Brown (ed.), *Combating international crime – the longer arm of the law*, Routledge Cavendish, Abingdon, 261–272.

Cantos, F. (1989), 'EEC draft directive on insider dealing', *Journal of International Banking Law*, **4**(4), N174–176.

Cardwell, P., French, D. and White, N. (2009), 'Kadi v Council of the European Union (C-402/05 P) (Case Comment)', *International Comparative Legal Quarterly*, **58**(1), 229–240.

Carlton, D. and Fischel, D. (1983), 'The regulation of insider trading', *Stanford Law Review*, **35**, 857–895.

Cassella, S. (2001), 'The Civil Asset Forfeiture Reform Act of 2000: expanded government forfeiture authority and strict deadlines imposed on all parties', *Journal of Legislation*, **27**, 97–151.

Cassella, S. (2002), 'Forfeiture of terrorist assets under the USA Patriot Act of 2001', *Law and Policy in International Business*, **34**, 7–15.

Cassella, S. (2003), 'Reverse money laundering', *Journal of Money Laundering Control*, **7**(1), 92–94.

Cassella, S. (2004a), 'Criminal forfeiture procedure: an analysis of developments in the law regarding the inclusion of a forfeiture judgment in the sentence imposed in a criminal case', *American Journal of Criminal Law*, **32**, 55–103.

Cassella, S. (2004b), 'Overview of asset forfeiture law in the United States', *South African Journal of Criminal Justice*, **17**(3), 347–367.

Cassella, S. (2004c), 'The forfeiture of property involved in money laundering offences', *Buffalo Criminal Law Review*, **7**, 583–660.

Cassella, S. (2008), 'The case for civil recovery: why in rem proceedings are an essential tool for recovering the proceeds of crime', *Journal of Money Laundering Control*, **11**(1), 8–14.

Cassella, S. (2009), 'An overview of asset forfeiture in the United States', in S. Young (ed.), *Civil forfeiture of criminal property – legal measures for targeting the proceeds of crime*, Edward Elgar, Cheltenham, 23–51.

Chase, A. (2004), 'Legal mechanisms of the international community and the United States concerning the state sponsorship of terrorism', *Virginia Journal of International Law*, **45**, 41–137.

Cheston, P. (2009), 'Former Belgo chief spared prison for insider trading deal', available at http://www.thisislondon.co.uk/standard/article-23656323-former-belgo-chief-is-spared-prison-for-insider-trading-deal.do;jsessionid=A890C0DFCC53652272A3B0EA79225CFE (accessed 26 November 2009).

Chi, K. (2002), 'Follow the money: getting to the root of the problem with civil asset forfeiture in California', *California Law Review*, **90**, 1635–1673.

City of London Police (n/d), 'Structure', available at http://www.cityoflondon.police.uk/CityPolice/Departments/ECD/About/structure.htm (accessed 6 August 2010).

CNN (2010), 'U.S. to share terror finance info with E.U.', 8 July 2010, available at http://news.blogs.cnn.com/2010/07/08/u-s-to-share-terror-finance-info-with-e-u/?iref=allsearch (accessed 14 July 2010).

Collins, R. (2005), 'The unknown unknowns – risks to the banking sector from the dark side of the shadow economy', *The Company Lawyer*, **26**(3), 84–87.

Colvin, O. (1991), 'A dynamic definition of and prohibition against insider trading', *Santa Clara Law Review*, **31**, 603–640.

Commonwealth Secretariat *Combating money laundering and terrorist financing – a model of best practice for the financial sector, the professions and other designated businesses* (Commonwealth Secretariat: London, 2006).

Conceicao, C. (2007), 'The FSA's approach to taking action against market abuse', *Company Lawyer*, **29**(2), 43–45.

Congressional Research Service *Saudi Arabia: Terrorist Financing Issues* (Congressional Research Service: Washington, DC, 2005).

Connorton, P. (2007), 'Tracking terrorist financing through SWIFT: when US subpoenas and foreign privacy law collide', *Fordham Law Review*, **76**, 283–322.

Corbett, P. (2007), 'Prosecuting the internet fraud case without going for broke', *Mississippi Law Journal*, **76**, 841–873.

Corporate Fraud Task Force *First year report to the President* (Department of Justice: Washington, DC, 2003).

Corporate Fraud Task Force *Second year report to the President* (Department of Justice: Washington, DC, 2003).

Corporate Fraud Task Force *Report to the President* (Department of Justice: Washington, DC, 2008).

Cox, C. and Fogarty, K. (1988), 'Basis of insider trading law', *Ohio State Law Journal*, **49**, 353–372.

Crawford, K. (2004), 'Martha: I cheated no one', available at http://money.cnn.com/2004/07/16/news/newsmakers/martha_sentencing/ (accessed 30 August 2009).

Crimm, N. (2004), 'High alert: the Government's war on the financing of terrorism and its implications for donors, domestic charitable organizations and global philanthropy', *William & Mary Law Review*, **45**, 1369–1451.

Croall, H. (1989), 'Who is the White-Collar Criminal?', *British Journal of Criminology*, **29**(2), 157–174.

Crona, S. and Richardson, N. (1996), 'Justice for war criminals of invisible armies: a new legal and military approach to terrorism', *Oklahoma City University Law Review*, **21**, 349–407.

Crown Prosecution Service *Financial Reporting Orders Sections 76 & 79–81 SOCPA 2005* (Crown Prosecution Service: London, n/d).

Crown Prosecution Service (2009), 'DPP announces new head of Fraud Prosecution Division', available at http://www.cps.gov.uk/news/press_releases/136_09/ (accessed 22 January 2010).

Darroch, F. (2003), 'The Lesotho corruption trials – a case study', *Commonwealth Law Bulletin*, **29**(2), 901–975.

Davies, Glyn (2002), *A history of money from ancient times to the present day*, University of Wales Press, Cardiff.

Davies, P. (2008), *Gower and Davies Principles of Modern Company Law*, Sweet & Maxwell, London.

de Grazia *Review of the Serious Fraud Office – Final Report* (Serious Fraud Office: London, 2008).

Dean, J. and Green Jr, D. (1988), 'McNally v United States and its effect on the federal mail fraud statute: will white collar criminals get a break?', *Mercer Law Review*, **39**, 697–716.

Defeo, M. (1989), 'Depriving international narcotics traffickers and other organized criminals of illegal proceeds and combating money laundering', *Denver Journal of International Law and Policy*, **18**(3), 405–415.

Dellinger, L. (2008), 'From dollars to pesos: a comparison of the US and Colombian anti-money laundering initiatives from an international perspective', *California Western International Law Journal*, **38**, 419–454.

Delone, C. and Gwartney, S. (2009), 'Financial institutions fraud', *American Criminal Law Review*, **46**, 621–670.

Dennis, I. (2007), 'Fraud Act 2006', *Criminal Law Review*, January, 1–2.

Dent, R. (2008), 'The role of banking regulation in data theft and security', *Review of Banking and Financial Law*, **27**, 381–392.

Department of Justice (n/d), 'Asset Forfeiture and Money Laundering Section', available at http://www.justice.gov/criminal/afmls/ (accessed 17 July 2010).

Department of Justice (n/d), 'Counterterrorism Section', available at http://www.justice.gov/nsd/counter_terrorism.htm (accessed 6 August 2010).

Department of Justice (n/d), 'Department of Justice Agencies', available at http://www.justice.gov/agencies/index-org.html#NSD (accessed 4 August 2010).

Department of Justice (n/d), 'Fraud Section', available at http://www.justice.gov/criminal/fraud (accessed 19 March 2010).

Department of Justice (n/d), 'National Drug Intelligence Center', available at http://www.justice.gov/ndic/about.htm#Top (accessed 6 August 2010).

Department of Justice (n/d), 'Identity theft and identity fraud', available at http://www.justice.gov/criminal/fraud/websites/idtheft.html (accessed 19 March 2010).

Department of Justice *United States Attorney's Bulletin: Terrorist Financing Issues* (Department of Justice: Washington, DC, 2003).

Department of Justice *Fiscal Years 2007–2012 Strategic Plan* (Department of Justice: Washington, DC, 2007).

Department of Justice *Fraud Section Activities Report Fiscal Year 2008* (Department of Justice: Washington, DC, 2008a).

Department of Justice *National Asset Forfeiture Strategic Plan 2008–2012* (Department of Justice: Washington, DC, 2008b).

Department of Justice (2009), 'Mortgage Fraud Surge Investigation Nets More Than 100 Individuals Throughout Middle District of Florida',

Press Release, 4 November 2009, available at http://tampa.fbi.gov/doj-pressrel/2009/ta110409.htm (accessed 15 March 2010).

Department of Treasury (n/d), 'Fighting illicit finance', available at http://www.ustreas.gov/topics/law-enforcement/index.shtml (accessed 16 April 2010).

Department of Treasury (n/d), 'OFAC frequently asked questions and answers', available at http://www.ustreas.gov/offices/enforcement/ofac/faq/answer.shtml#17 (accessed 6 August 2010).

Department of Treasury (n/d), 'Office of Analysis and Intelligence', available at http://www.ustreas.gov/offices/enforcement/oia/ (accessed 6 August 2010).

Department of Treasury (n/d), 'Office of Foreign Assets Control', available at http://www.ustreas.gov/offices/enforcement/ofac/mission.shtml (accessed 6 August 2010).

Department of Treasury (n/d), 'Office of Terrorist Financing and Financial Crimes,' available at http://www.ustreas.gov/offices/enforcement/eotf.shtml (accessed 6 August 2010).

Department of Treasury (n/d), 'Terrorism and financial intelligence', available at http://www.ustreas.gov/offices/enforcement/ (accessed 6 August 2010).

Department of Treasury (n/d), 'The Treasury Executive Office for Asset Forfeiture & Treasury Forfeiture Fund', available at http://www.ustreas.gov/offices/enforcement/teoaf/ (accessed 3 August 2010).

Department of Treasury *The National Money Laundering Strategy 1999* (Department of Treasury: Washington, DC, 1999).

Department of Treasury *The National Money Laundering Strategy 2000* (Department of Treasury: Washington, DC, 2000).

Department of Treasury (2001), 'Deputy Secretary Dam remarks at the launch of Operation Green Quest', available at http://www.treas.gov/press/releases/po727.htm (accessed 21 October 2009).

Department of Treasury *The National Money Laundering Strategy 2002* (Department of Treasury: Washington, DC, 2002a).

Department of Treasury *Contributions by the Department of the Treasury to the Financial War on Terrorism* (Department of Treasury: Washington, DC, 2002b).

Department of Treasury (2003), 'Treasury Department Designates Burma and Two Burmese Banks to be of "Primary Money Laundering Concern" and Announces Proposed Countermeasures', available at http://www.ustreas.gov/press/releases/js1014.htm (accessed 1 August 2010).

Department of Treasury (2004a), 'Bush Administration Announces Budget Increase to help Fight Terrorist Financing and Financial Crime', available at http://www.ustreas.gov/press/releases/js1100.htm (accessed 8 May 2009).

Department of Treasury (2004b), 'Treasury Designates Commercial Bank of Syria as Financial Institution of Primary Money Laundering Concern', available at http://www.ustreas.gov/press/releases/js1538.htm (accessed 30 July 2010).

Department of Treasury (2004c), 'Treasury employs USA PATRIOT Act authorities to designate two foreign banks as "Primary Money Laundering Concern"', available at http://www.ustreas.gov/press/releases/js1874.htm (accessed 30 July 2010).

Department of Treasury *US Money Laundering Threat Assessment* (Department of Treasury: Washington, DC, 2005a).

Department of Treasury (2005b), 'Treasury Wields PATRIOT Act Powers to Isolate Two Latvian Banks: Financial Institutions Identified as "Primary Money Laundering Concerns"', available at http://www.ustreas.gov/press/releases/js2401.htm (accessed 16 July 2010).

Department of Treasury *Office of Terrorism and Financial Intelligence – US Department of Treasury Fact Sheet* (Department of Treasury: Washington, DC, 2006).

Department of Treasury *The National Money Laundering Strategy 2007* (Department of Treasury: Washington, DC, 2007).

Department of Treasury (2009), 'Recent OFAC Actions', available at http://www.ustreas.gov/offices/enforcement/ofac/actions/20091103. shtml (accessed 5 June 2010).

Department of Treasury (2010a), 'Statement of Secretary Geithner on the Signing of the Iran Sanctions Act', 1 July 2010, available at http://www.ustreas.gov/press/releases/tg767.htm (accessed 10 July 2010).

Department of Treasury *Terrorist financing tracking program questions and answers* (Department of Treasury: Washington, DC, 2010b).

Diamong, E. (1992), 'Outside investors: a new breed of insider traders?', *Fordham Law Review*, **60**, 316–347.

Doig, A. (1996), 'A fragmented organizational approach to fraud in a European context', *European Journal on Criminal Policy and Research*, **3**(2), 48–73.

Doig, A. (2006), *Fraud*, Willan Publishing, Cullompton.

Donohue, Laura (2008), *The cost of counterterrorism – power, politics and liberty*, Cambridge University Press, Cambridge.

Doyle, T. (2002), 'Cleaning up anti-money laundering strategies: current FATF tactics needlessly violate international law', *Houston Journal of International Law*, **24,** 279–313.

Drage, John (1993), 'Countering money laundering: the response of the financial sector', in H. Macqueen (ed.), *Money laundering*, Edinburgh University Press, Edinburgh, 60–70.

Drug Enforcement Administration (n/d), 'DEA history', available at http://www.justice.gov/dea/history.htm (accessed 6 August 2010).

Drug Enforcement Administration (n/d), 'DEA mission statement', available at http://www.justice.gov/dea/agency/mission.htm (accessed 6 August 2010).

Drug Enforcement Administration (n/d), 'Money laundering', available at http://www.justice.gov/dea/programs/money.htm (accessed 11 July 2010).

Drug Enforcement Administration (n/d), '26 Arrested in International Drug Bust', available at http://www.justice.gov/dea/pubs/pressrel/pr101806.html (accessed 21 June 2010).

Drug Enforcement Administration (2005a), 'DEA Dismantles Large International Drug and Money Laundering Organization', available at http://www.justice.gov/dea/pubs/pressrel/pr120805.html (accessed 21 June 2010).

Drug Enforcement Administration (2005b)', 'DEA's "Money Trail Initiative" Cuts Flow of Cash to Cartels', available at http://www.justice.gov/dea/pubs/pressrel/pr071905.html (accessed 21 June 2010).

Duff, Anthony and Garland, David (1989), 'Introduction: thinking about punishment', in A. Duff and D. Garland (eds), *A reader on punishment*, Oxford University Press, Oxford, 1–44.

Durkin, C. (1990), 'Civil forfeiture under federal narcotics law: the impact of the shifting burden of proof upon the Fifth Amendment privilege against self-incrimination', *Suffolk University Law Review*, **24**, 679–705.

Eckert, Sue (2008), 'The US regulatory approach to terrorist financing', in T. Biersteker and S. Eckert (eds), *Countering the financing of terrorism*, Routledge Cavendish, London, 209–233.

Ed. (1993), 'Insiders beware!', *Company Lawyer*, **14**(11), 202.

Ed. (2009), 'Commission seeks evidence in review of Market Abuse Directive', *Company Law Newsletter*, **252**.

Eddy, A. (2000), 'The effect of the Health Insurance Portability and Accountability Act of 1996 on health care fraud in Montana', *Montana Law Review*, **61**, 175–221.

Egmont *Statement of purpose of the Egmont Group of Financial Intelligence Units* (Egmont: Guernsey, 2004).

Elder, J. (1998), 'Federal mail fraud unleashed: revisiting the criminal catch-all', *Oregon Law Review*, **77**, 707–733.

Engel, M. (2004), 'Donating "bloody money": fundraising for international terrorism by United States charities and the government's efforts to constrict the flow', *Cardozo Journal of International and Company Law*, **12**, 251–296.

European Commission (2009), 'Call for evidence review of Directive 2003/6/EC on insider dealing and market manipulation (Market Abuse Directive)', available at http://ec.europa.eu/internal_market/consultations/docs/2009/market_abuse/call_for_evidence.pdf (accessed 12 August 2010).

European Court of Auditors (n/d), 'About us', available at http://eca.europa.eu/portal/page/portal/aboutus (accessed 3 August 2010).

European Union *Second Commission report to the European Parliament and the Council on the implementation of the Money Laundering Directive* (Brussels, 1 July 1998, COM (1998)).

Evans, J. (1996), 'International money laundering: enforcement challenges and opportunities', *Southwestern Journal of Law and Trade in the Americas*, **2**, 195–221.

Farah, D. (2002), 'Al-Qaeda's road paved with gold', *Washington Post*, 17 February 2002, available at http://www.washingtonpost.com/ac2/wp-dyn/A22303-2002Feb16?language=printer (accessed 7 July 2009).

Faro, E. (1990), 'Telemarketing fraud: is RICO one answer?', *University of Illinois Law Review*, 675–710.

Federal Bureau of Investigation (n/d), 'About us – quick facts', available at http://www.fbi.gov/quickfacts.htm (accessed 4 August 2010).

Federal Bureau of Investigation (n/d), 'Mortgage fraud', available at http://www.fbi.gov/hq/mortgage_fraud.htm (accessed 22 April 2010).

Federal Bureau of Investigation (n/d), 'White collar crime', available at http://www.fbi.gov/whitecollarcrime.htm (accessed 1 March 2009).

Federal Bureau of Investigation *FBI Strategic Plan* (Federal Bureau of Investigation: Washington, DC, n/d).

Federal Bureau of Investigation (2007a), 'Financial crimes report to the public, fiscal year 2007', available at http://www.fbi.gov/publications/financial/fcs_report2007/financial_crime_2007.htm#corporate (accessed 5 February 2009).

Federal Bureau of Investigation *White-Collar Crime: Strategic Plan* (Federal Bureau of Investigation: Washington, DC, 2007b).

Federal Bureau of Investigation (2009), 'President Obama Establishes Interagency Financial Fraud Enforcement Task Force', available at http://www.fbi.gov/pressrel/pressrel09/taskforce_111709.htm (accessed 29 November 2009).

Federal Trade Commission (n/d), 'Fighting back against identity theft', available at http://www.ftc.gov/bcp/edu/microsites/idtheft// (accessed 26 March 2010).

Federal Trade Commission *Consumer fraud and identity theft complaint data: January–December 2005* (Federal Trade Commission: Washington, DC, 2006).

Ferguson, Niall (2008), *The ascent of money*, Allen Lane, London.

Filby, M. (2004), 'Part VIII Financial Services and Markets Act: filling insider dealing's regulatory gaps', *Company Lawyer*, **23**(12), 363–370.

Financial Action Task Force (n/d), '9 Special Recommendations (SR) on Terrorist Financing (TF)', available at http://www.fatf-gafi.org/doc ument/9/0,3343,en_32250379_32236920_34032073_1_1_1_1,00.html (accessed 3 August 2010).

Financial Action Task Force (n/d), 'About the FATF', available at http:// www.fatf-gafi.org/pages/0,3417,en_32250379_32236836_1_1_1_1_1,00. html (accessed 6 August 2010).

Financial Action Task Force (n/d), 'Mandate' available at http://www. fatf-gafi.org/pages/0,3417,en_32250379_32236846_1_1_1_1_1,00.html (accessed 4 August 2010).

Financial Action Task Force (n/d), 'Money laundering FAQ', available at http://www.fatf-gafi.org/document/29/0,3343,en_32250379_ 32235720_33659613_1_1_1_1,00.html (accessed 13 January 2010).

Financial Action Task Force (n/d), 'Forty recommendations', available at www.fatf-gafi.org/document/28/0,3343,en_32250379_32236920_ 33658140_1_1_1_1,00.html (accessed 6 August 2010).

Financial Action Task Force (2001), 'FATF cracks down on terrorist financing', Press Release, 31 October 2001, available at http:// www.fatf-gafi.org/dataoecd/45/48/34269864.pdf (accessed 3 January 2009).

Financial Action Task Force *Interpretative Note to Special Recommendation II: Criminalising the financing of terrorism and associated money laundering* (Financial Action Task Force: Paris, 2001).

Financial Action Task Force *Report on Money Laundering and Terrorist Financing Typologies 2003–2004* (Financial Action Task Force, Paris: 2004).

Financial Action Task Force *Third mutual evaluation report: anti-money laundering and combating the financing of terrorism – United States of America* (Financial Action Task Force, Paris: 2006).

Financial Action Task Force *The third mutual evaluation report: anti-money laundering and combating the financing of terrorism – the United Kingdom of Great Britain and Northern Ireland* (Financial Action Task Force: Paris, 2007).

Financial Action Task Force *Financial Action Task Force Annual Report 2007–2008* (Financial Action Task Force: Paris, 2008).

Financial Action Task Force (2009), 'FATF Statement', 25 February 2009, available at http://www.fatf-gafi.org/dataoecd/18/28/42242615.pdf (accessed 3 August 2010).

Financial Action Task Force *Best Practices: Confiscation (Recommendations 3 and 38)* (Financial Action Task Force: Paris, 2010).

Financial Crimes Enforcement Network (n/d), 'Mission', available at http://www.fincen.gov/about_fincen/wwd/mission.html (accessed 5 August 2010).

Financial Crimes Enforcement Network (2004), 'Assessment of civil money penalty', available at www.fincen.gov/riggsassessment3.pdf (accessed 4 August 2010).

Financial Crimes Enforcement Network *The SAR Activity Review – By the Numbers* (FinCEN: Washington, DC, 2006).

Financial Crimes Enforcement Network *Strategic Plan Financial Crimes Enforcement Network Fiscal Years 2008–2012* (FinCEN: Washington, DC, 2007).

Financial Crimes Enforcement Network *Suspicious activity review – trends, tips and issues*, issue 15 (FinCEN: Washington, DC, 2009a).

Financial Crimes Enforcement Network *Mortgage loan fraud connections with other financial crime: an evaluation of suspicious activity reports filed by money service businesses, securities and futures firms, insurance companies and casinos* (FinCEN: Washington, DC, 2009b).

Financial Crimes Enforcement Network *Mortgage loan fraud update – suspicious activity report filings from July–September 30, 2009* (FinCEN: Washington, DC, 2009c).

Financial Crimes Enforcement Network *SAR Activity Review – By the Numbers* (FinCEN: Washington, DC, 2009d).

Financial Crimes Enforcement Network *SAR Activity Review – By the Numbers Issue 14* (FinCEN: Washington, DC, 2010).

Financial Services Authority (n/d), 'Enforcement Notices, Financial Services Authority', available from http://www.fsa.gov.uk/pages/About/What/financial_crime/market_abuse/library/notices/index.shtml (accessed 1 July 2010).

Financial Services Authority (n/d), 'Fraud', available at http://www.fsa.gov.uk/Pages/About/What/financial_crime/fraud/index.shtml (accessed 22 April 2010).

Financial Services Authority (1998), 'Consultation Paper 10: Market Abuse Part 1: Consultation on a draft Code of Market Conduct', available at http://www.fsa.gov.uk/pubs/cp/cp10.pdf (accessed 5 July 2010).

Financial Services Authority (1999), 'Feedback statement on responses to Consultation Paper 10: Market Abuse', available at http://www.fsa.gov.uk/pubs/cp/cp10_response.pdf (accessed 5 July 2010).

Financial Services Authority *Consultation Paper 46 Money Laundering – The FSA's new role* (Financial Services Authority: London, 2000).

Financial Services Authority *Partnership Agreement between the National Criminal Intelligence Service and the Financial Services Authority* (Financial Services Authority: London, 2001).

Financial Services Authority (2002), 'FSA Fines Royal Bank of Scotland £750,000 for money laundering control failings', available at http://www.fsa.gov.uk/Pages/Library/Communication/PR/2002/123.shtml (accessed 6 January 2009).

Financial Services Authority *Developing our policy on fraud and dishonesty – discussion paper 26* (Financial Services Authority: London, 2003).

Financial Services Authority (2004a), 'FSA fines Shell 17,000,000 for market abuse', available at http://www.fsa.gov.uk/Pages/Library/Communication/PR/2004/074.shtml (accessed 31 March 2010).

Financial Services Authority (2004b), 'UK Implementation of EU Market Abuse Directive', available from http://www.fsa.gov.uk/pubs/other/eu_mad.pdf (accessed 5 July 2010).

Financial Services Authority (2004c), 'The FSA's new approach to fraud – fighting fraud in partnership', speech by Philip Robinson, 26 October 2004, available at http://www.fsa.gov.uk/Pages/Library/Communication/Speeches/2004/SP208.shtml (accessed 3 August 2010).

Financial Services Authority (2006a), 'FSA fines Capita Financial Administrators Limited £300,000 in first anti-fraud controls case', available at http://www.fsa.gov.uk/pages/Library/Communication/PR/2006/019.shtml (accessed 16 March 2006).

Financial Services Authority (2006b), 'FSA fines GLG Partners and Philippe Jabre £750,000 each for market abuse', available at http://www.fsa.gov.uk/pages/Library/Communication/PR/2006/077.shtml (accessed 13 March 2010).

Financial Services Authority (2007a), 'Market Watch. Market Division: Newsletter on market conduct and transaction reporting issues', available at http://www.fsa.gov.uk/pubs/newsletters/mw_newsletter21.pdf (accessed 30 June 2010).

Financial Services Authority (2007b), 'FSA fines Nationwide £980,000 for information security lapses', available at http://www.fsa.gov.uk/pages/Library/Communication/PR/2007/021.shtml (accessed 14 February 2007).

Financial Services Authority (2007c), 'FSA fines Norwich Union Life £1.26m', available at http://www.fsa.gov.uk/pages/Library/Communication/PR/2007/130.shtml (accessed 4 November 2009).

Financial Services Authority (2007d), 'Insider dealing in the city', speech by Margaret Cole at the London School of Economics, 17 March 2007, available at http://www.fsa.gov.uk/pages/Library/Communication/ Speeches/2007/0317_mc.shtml (accessed 10 June 2009).

Financial Services Authority *Financial Services Authority Annual Report 2007/2008* (Financial Services Authority: London, 2008a).

Financial Services Authority *FSA Handbook – SUP (Supervision)* (Financial Services Authority: London, 2008b).

Financial Services Authority (2008c), 'FSA fines firm and MLRO for money laundering controls failings', 29 October 2008, available at http://www.fsa.gov.uk/pages/Library/Communication/PR/2008/125.shtml (accessed 29 October 2008).

Financial Services Authority (2008d), 'After dinner remarks at Cambridge Symposium on economic crime', available at http://www.fsa.gov.uk/pages/Library/Communication/Speeches/2008/0901_mc.shtml (accessed 1 July 2010).

Financial Services Authority (2008e), 'FSA and enforcing the Market Abuse Regime', available at http://www.fsa.gov.uk/pages/Library/Communication/Speeches/2008/1106_js.shtml (accessed 16 July 2010).

Financial Services Authority (2008f), 'Why market abuse could cost you money – The revised Code of Market Conduct is here to help protect you', available at http://www.fsa.gov.uk/pubs/public/market_abuse.pdf (accessed 29 June 2010).

Financial Services Authority (2009a), 'FSA fines broker for failing to prevent insider dealing', available at http://www.fsa.gov.uk/pages/Library/Communication/PR/2009/115.shtml (accessed 13 March 2010).

Financial Services Authority (2009b), 'Solicitor and his father-in-law found guilty in FSA insider dealing case', available at http://www.fsa.gov.uk/pages/Library/Communication/PR/2009/042.shtml (accessed 4 July 2010).

Financial Services Authority (2010a), 'FSA fines Alpari and its former money laundering reporting officer, Sudipto Chattopadhyay for anti-money laundering failings', 5 May 2010, available at http://www.fsa.gov.uk/pages/Library/Communication/PR/2010/077.shtml (accessed 6 May 2010).

Financial Services Authority (2010b), 'FSA returns £270,000 to victims of share fraud', available at http://www.fsa.gov.uk/pages/Library/Communication/PR/2010/032.shtml (accessed 21 March 2010).

Fisch, J. (1991), 'Start making sense: an analysis and proposal for insider trading', *Georgia Law Review*, **26**, 179–251.

Fischer, A. and Sheppard, J. (2008), 'Financial institutions fraud', *American Criminal Law Review*, **45**, 531–578.

Fisher, J. (2002), 'Recent international developments in the fight against money laundering', *Journal of International Banking Law*, **17**(3), 67–72.

Fisher, J. (2003), 'A review of the new investigation powers under the Proceeds of Crime Act 2002', *Journal of International Banking Law*, **18**(1), 15–23.

Fisher, J. *Fighting Fraud and Financial Crime: A new architecture for the investigation and prosecution of serious fraud, corruption and financial market crimes* (Policy Exchange: London, 2010).

Fitzgerald, P. (2002), 'Managing smart sanctions against terrorism wisely', *New England Law Review*, **36**, 975–983.

Fleming, M. *UK Law Enforcement Agency Use and Management of Suspicious Activity Reports: Towards Determining the Value of the Regime* (University College London: London, 2005).

Fleming, M. *FSA's Scale & Impact of Financial Crime Project (Phase One): Critical Analysis Occasional Paper Series 37* (Financial Services Authority: London, 2009).

Flynn, E. (2007), 'The Security Council's Counter-terrorism Committee and human rights', *Human Rights Law Review*, **7**, 371–384.

Forston, Rudi (2008), 'Money laundering offences under POCA 2002', in W. Blair and R. Brent (eds), *Banks and Financial Crime – The International Law of Tainted Money*, Oxford University Press, Oxford, 155–202.

Fraud Advisory Panel *Roskill Revisited: Is there a case for a unified fraud prosecution office?* (Fraud Advisory Panel: London, 2010).

Fraud Trials Committee Report (1986) HMSO.

Gagliardi, J. (1993), 'Back to the future: federal mail and wire fraud under 18 U.S.C. § 1343', *Washington Law Review*, **68**, 901–921.

Gallagher, J., Lauchlan, J. and Steven, M. (1996), 'Polly Peck: the breaking of an entrepreneur?', *Journal of Small Business and Enterprise Development*, **3**(1), 3–12.

Gallant, Michelle (2005), *Money laundering and the proceeds of crime*, Edward Elgar, Cheltenham.

Garretson, H. (2008), 'Federal criminal forfeiture: a royal pain in the assets', *Southern California Review of Law & Social Justice*, **18**, 45–77.

Geiger, H. and Wuensch, O. (2007), 'The fight against money laundering: an economic analysis of a cost–benefit paradoxon', *Journal of Money Laundering Control*, **10**(1), 91–105.

General Accounting Office *Money laundering – the US government is responding to the problem* (General Accounting Office: Washington, DC, 1991).

General Accounting Office *Progress report on Treasury's Financial Crimes Enforcement Network* (General Accounting Office: Washington, DC, 1993).

General Accounting Office *Money laundering – needed improvements for reporting suspicious transactions are planned* (General Accounting Office: Washington, DC, 1995).

General Accounting Office *Combating money laundering – opportunities exist to improve the national strategy* (General Accounting Office: Washington, DC, 2003a).

General Accounting Office *Terrorist Financing – US Agencies should systematically assess terrorists' use of alternative financing mechanisms* (General Accounting Office: Washington, DC, 2003b).

General Accounting Office *Investigating money laundering and terrorist financing – federal law enforcement agencies face continuing challenges* (General Accounting Office: Washington, DC, 2004).

Gill, M. and Taylor, G. (2003), 'The risk-based approach to tackling money laundering: matching risk to products', *Company Lawyer*, **24**(7), 210–213.

Gill, M. and Taylor, G. (2004), 'Preventing money laundering or obstructing business? Financial companies' perspectives on "know your customer" procedures', *British Journal of Criminology*, **44**(4), 582–594.

Gilmore, William *Dirty money – the evaluation of international measures to counter money laundering and the financing of terrorism* (Council of Europe: Brussels, 2004).

Girard, V. (2009), 'Punishing pharmaceutical companies for unlawful promotion of approved drugs: why the False Claims Act is the wrong rx', *Journal of Health Care Law and Policy*, **12**, 119–158.

Goldberg, H., Dale, K., Lee, D., Shyr, P. and Thakker, D. (2003), *The NASD Securities Observation, News Analysis & Regulation System (SONAR)*, available from http://www.aaai.org/Papers/IAAI/2003/IAAI03-002.pdf (accessed 12 August 2010).

Goldby, M. (2010), 'The Impact of Schedule 7 of the Counter-Terrorism Act 2008 on Banks and their Customers', *Journal of Money Laundering Control*, **13**(4), 351–371.

Government Accountability Office *Better Strategic Planning Needed to Coordinate U.S. Efforts to Deliver Counter-Terrorism Financing Training and Technical Assistance Abroad* (Government Accountability Office: Washington, DC, 2005).

Government Accountability Office *International Financial Crime – Treasury's roles and responsibilities relating to selected provisions of the USA Patriot Act 2001* (Government Accountability Office: Washington, DC, 2006).

Government Accountability Office *Suspicious Activity Report Use is Increasing, but FinCEN needs to Further Develop and Document its Form Revision Process* (Government Accountability Office: Washington, DC, 2009).

Greenberg, M., Wechsler, W. and Wolosky, L. (2002), *Terrorist financing*, Council on Foreign Relations, New York.

Greenwood, L. (2008), 'Mail and wire fraud', *American Criminal Law Review*, **45**, 717–740.

Griffin, L. (2007), 'Compelled co-operation and the new corporate criminal procedure', *New York University Law Review*, **82**, 311–382.

Gurule, J. (2009a), 'Does "proceeds" really mean "net profits"? The Supreme Court's efforts to diminish the utility of the Federal Money Laundering Statute', *Ave Maria Law Review*, **7**, 339–390.

Gurule, J. (2009b), 'The demise of the UN economic sanctions regime to deprive terrorists of funding', *Case Western Reserve Journal of International Law*, **41**, 19–63.

Haines, J. (2008), 'FSA determined to improve the cleanliness of markets: custodial sentences continue to be a real threat', *Company Lawyer*, **29**(12), 370.

Haines, J. (2009), 'The National Fraud Strategy: new rules to crackdown on fraud', *Company Lawyer*, **30**(7), 213.

Hall, M. (1995–96), 'An emerging duty to report criminal conduct: banks, money laundering, and the suspicious activity report', *Kentucky Law Journal*, **84**, 643–683.

Halverson, A. and Olson, E. (2009), 'False statements and false claims', *American Criminal Law Review*, **46**, 555–587.

Hanneman, J. (1997), 'The evolution of co-operation between authorities in the United States of America and Switzerland in the enforcement of insider trading law', *Wisconsin International Law Journal*, **16**, 247–270.

Hannigan, Brenda (1994), *Insider Dealing*, Longman, London.

Hannigan, Brenda (2009), *Company Law*, Oxford University Press, Oxford.

Hanning, P. (1993), 'Testing the limits of investigating and prosecuting white collar crime: how far will the courts allow prosecutors to go? *University of Pittsburgh Law Review*, **54**, 405–476.

Hansen, J. (2002), 'The new proposal for a European Union directive on market abuse', *University of Pennsylvania Journal of International Economic Law*, **23**, 241–268.

Hansen, J. (2007), 'MAD in a hurry: the swift and promising adoption of the EU Market Abuse Directive', *European Business Law Review*, **15**(2), 183–221.

Hansen, L. (2009), 'Corporate financial crime: social diagnosis and treatment', *Journal of Financial Crime*, **16**(1), 28–40.

Hardister, A. (2003), '"Can we buy peace on earth?": The price of freezing terrorist assets in a post-September 11 world', *North Carolina Journal of International Law and Commercial Regulation*, **28**, 606–661.

Harfield, C. (2006), 'SOCA: a paradigm shift in British policing', *British Journal of Criminology*, **46**(4), 743–761.

Harris, D. and Herzel, L. (1989), 'USA: do we need insider trading laws?', *Company Lawyer*, **10**(1), 34–35.

Harris, J. (2010), 'Getting over Madoff: how the SEC must restore its credibility', *Company Lawyer*, **31**(2), 33–34.

Harvey, J. (2004), 'Compliance and reporting issues arising for financial institutions from money laundering regulations: a preliminary cost benefit study', *Journal of Money Laundering Control*, **7**(4), 333–346.

Harvey, J. (2005), 'An evaluation of money laundering policies', *Journal of Money Laundering Control*, **8**(4), 339–345.

Hatch, J. (1987), 'Logical inconsistencies in the SEC's enforcement of insider trading: guidelines for a definition', *Washington and Lee Law Review*, **44**, 935–954.

Haynes, A. (2007), 'Market abuse: an analysis of its nature and regulation', *Company Lawyer*, **28**(11), 323–335, at 323.

Hayrynen, J. (2008), 'The precise definition of inside information?', *Journal of International Banking Law and Regulation*, **23**(2), 64–70.

He, P. (2010), 'A typological study on money laundering', *Journal of Money Laundering Control*, **13**(1), 15–32.

Henning, P. (1995), 'Maybe it should be called federal fraud: the changing nature of the Mail Fraud Statute', *Boston College Law Review*, May, 435–477.

Herman, S. (2005), 'Collapsing spheres: joint terrorism task forces, federalism, and the war on terror', *Willamette Law Review*, **41**, 941–969.

Hernandez, B. (1993), 'RIP to IRP – money laundering and the drug trafficking controls score a knockout victory over bank secrecy', *North Carolina Journal of International Law and Commercial Regulation*, **18**, 235–304.

HM Crown Prosecution Service Inspectorate *Review of the Fraud Prosecution Service* (HM Crown Prosecution Service Inspectorate: London, 2008).

HM Customs and Excise *Oils Fraud Strategy: Summary of Consultation Responses; Regulatory Impact Assessment* (HM Customs and Excise: London, 2002).

HM Government *The Coalition: our programme for government* (HM Government: London, 2010).

HM Revenue and Customs *Renewal of the 'Tackling Alcohol Fraud' Strategy* (HM Revenue and Customs: London, 2009).

HM Treasury (n/d), 'Counter illicit finance', available at http://www.hm-treasury.gov.uk/fin_money_index.htm (accessed 16 April 2010).

HM Treasury *Combating the financing of terrorism – a report on UK Action* (HM Treasury: London, 2002).

HM Treasury *Anti-Money Laundering Strategy* (HM Treasury: London, 2004).

HM Treasury *The UK financial services sector: rising to the challenges and opportunities of globalisation* (HM Treasury: London, 2005).

HM Treasury *The financial challenge to crime and terrorism* (HM Treasury: London, 2007).

HM Treasury (2009), 'HM Treasury warns businesses of serious threats posed to the international financial system', 11 March 2009, available at http://webarchive.nationalarchives.gov.uk/+/http://www.hm-treasury.gov.uk/press_26_09.htm (accessed 3 August 2010).

HM Treasury *Public consultation: draft terrorist asset-freezing bill* (HM Treasury: London, 2010).

Holder, W. (2003), 'The International Monetary Fund's involvement in combating money laundering and the financing of terrorism', *Journal of Money Laundering Control*, **6**(4), 383–387.

Home Office (n/d), 'Fraud', available at http://www.crimereduction.home-office.gov.uk/fraud/fraud17.htm (accessed 7 December 2009).

Home Office *Home Office Working Group on Confiscation* (Home Office: London, 1998a).

Home Office *Legislation against terrorism – a consultation paper* (Home Office: London, 1998b).

Home Office *Working Group on Confiscation Third Report: Criminal Assets* (Home Office: London, 1998c).

Home Office *Home Office circular 47/2004: Priorities for the investigation of fraud cases* (Home Office, London, 2004a).

Home Office *One Step Ahead – A 21st century strategy to defeat organised crime* (Home Office: London, 2004b).

Home Office *Report on the Operation in 2004 of the Terrorism Act 2000* (Home Office: London, 2004c).

Home Office *Rebalancing the criminal justice system in favour of the law-abiding majority: Cutting crime, reducing reoffending and protecting the public* (Home Office: London, 2006).

Home Office *Asset recovery action plan – a consultation document* (Home Office: London, 2007).

Home Office *Lord Carlile Report on the operation in 2008 of the Terrorism Act 2000 and of Part 1 of the Terrorism Act 2006* (Home Office: London, 2009).

Home Office *Policing in the 21st century: reconnecting police and the people* (Home Office: London, 2010).

Hopton, Doug (2009), *Money laundering – a concise guide for all businesses*, Gower, Farnham.

House of Commons *Report of the Official Account of the Bombings in London on 7th July 2005* (House of Commons: London, 2005).

House of Commons Committee of Public Accounts *Assets Recovery Agency – 5th Report of Session 2006/2007* (House of Commons Committee of Public Accounts: London, 2007).

House of Lords European Union Committee *Strengthening OLAF, the European Anti-Fraud Office* (House of Lords European Union Committee: London, 2004).

Hudson, Alistair (2009), *The Law of Finance*, Sweet and Maxwell, London.

Hulsse, R. (2007), 'Creating demand for global governance: the making of a global money-laundering problem', *Global Society*, **21**(2), 155–178.

Hulsse, R. (2008), 'Even clubs can't do without legitimacy: Why the anti-money laundering blacklist was suspended', *Regulation & Governance*, **2**(4), 459–479.

Hulsse, R. and Kerwer, D. (2007), 'Global standards in action: insights from anti-money laundering regulation', *Organization*, **14**(5), 625–642.

Hurst, T. (2006), 'A post-Enron examination of corporate governance problems in the investment company industry', *The Company Lawyer*, **27**(2), 41–49.

Hurt, C. (2008), 'The under civilization of corporate law', *Journal of Corporation Law*, **33**, 361–445.

Hutman, A., Herrington, M. and Krauland, E. (2005), 'Money laundering enforcement and policy', *The International Lawyer*, **39**(2), 649–661.

Identity Theft Task Force *Combating identity theft: a strategic plan* (Identity Theft Task Force: Washington, DC, 2007).

Identity Theft Task Force *The President's Identity Theft Task Force Report* (Identity Theft Task Force: Washington, DC, 2008).

International Monetary Fund (1998), 'Michael Camdessus, Address to the FATF at the Plenary Meeting of the Financial Action Task Force on Money Laundering, 10 February 1998', available at www.imf.org/external/np/speeches/1998/021098.htm (accessed 6 September 2009).

International Monetary Fund *Financial system abuse, financial crime and money laundering – background paper* (International Monetary Fund, Washington, DC, 2001).

International Monetary Fund and World Bank *Enhancing contributions to combating money laundering: policy paper* (International Monetary Fund and World Bank, Washington, DC, 2001).

IRS (n/d), 'Criminal enforcement', available at http://www.irs.gov/compliance/enforcement/article/0,,id=174640,00.html (accessed 4 August 2010).

Jackson, C. (2004), 'Combating the new generation of money laundering: regulations and agencies in the battle of compliance, avoidance, and prosecution in a post-September 11 world', *Journal of High Technology Law*, **3**, 139–171.

Jain, N. (2004), 'Significance of mens rea in insider trading', *Company Lawyer*, **25**(5), 132–140.

Jamwal, N. (2000), 'Hawala – the invisible financing system of terrorism', *Strategic Analysis*, **26**(2), 181–198.

Jimenez, P. (1990), 'International Securities Enforcement Cooperation Act and Memoranda of Understanding', *Harvard International Law Journal*, **31**, 295–311.

Johnson, B. (2002), 'Restoring civility – the Civil Asset Forfeiture Reform Act 2000: baby steps towards a more civilised civil forfeiture system', *Indiana Law Review*, **35**, 1045–1085.

Johnson, J. (2008), 'Is the global financial system AML/CTF prepared?', *Journal of Financial Crime*, **15**(1), 7–21.

Johnston, A. (2009), 'Frozen in time? The ECJ finally rules on the Kadi appeal', *Cambridge Law Journal*, **68**(1), 1–4.

Johnston, A. and Nanopoulos, E. (2010), 'Case Comment: The new UK Supreme Court, the separation of powers and anti-terrorism measures', *Cambridge Law Journal*, **69**(2), 217–220.

Joint Committee on Financial Services and Markets (1999), 'First Report', available at http://www.publications.parliament.uk/pa/jt199899/jtselect/jtfinser/ 328/32809.htm (accessed 8 July 2010).

Joint Committee on Human Rights *Joint Committee on Human Rights – Third Report – The Proceeds of Crime Bill* (Joint Committee on Human Rights: London, 2001).

Joint Money Laundering Steering Group (2007a), 'Who are the members of the JMLSG?', available at http://www.jmlsg.org.uk/bba/jsp/polo-poly.jsp?d=777&a=9907 (accessed 18 June 2010).

Joint Money Laundering Steering Group *Prevention of money laundering/ combating terrorist financing guidance for the UK financial sector Part 1* (Joint Money Laundering Steering Group: London, 2007b).

Joo, T. (2007), 'Legislation and legitimation: Congress and insider trading in the 1980s', *Indiana Law Journal*, **82**, 575–622.

Kamman, T. and Hood, R. (2009), 'With the spotlight on the financial crisis, regulatory loopholes, and hedge funds, how should hedge funds comply with insider trading laws?', *Columbia Business Law Review*, **2**, 357–467.

Keeney, P. (2004), 'Frozen assets of terrorists and terrorist supporters: a proposed solution to the creditor collection problem', *Emory Bankruptcy Developments Journal*, **21**, 301–340.

Kennedy, A. (2004), 'Justifying the civil recovery of criminal proceeds', *Journal of Financial Crime*, **12**(1), 8–23.

Kennedy, A. (2005), 'Justifying the civil recovery of criminal proceeds', *Company Lawyer*, **26**(5), 137–145.

Kennedy, A. (2006), 'Civil recovery proceedings under the Proceeds of Crime Act 2002: the experience so far', *Journal of Money Laundering Control*, **9**(3), 245–264.

Kennedy, A. (2007a), 'An evaluation of the recovery of criminal proceeds in the United Kingdom', *Journal of Money Laundering Control*, **10**(1), 33–46.

Kennedy, A. (2007b), 'Winning the information wars: collecting, sharing and analysing information in asset recovery investigations', *Journal of Financial Crime*, **14**(4), 372–404.

Kessimian, P. (2004), 'Business fiduciary relationships and honest services fraud: a defence of the statute', *Columbia Business Law Review*, 197–230.

Kiernan, P. (2003), 'The regulatory bodies fraud: its enforcement in the twenty-first century', *Company Lawyer*, **24**(10), 293–299.

Kiernan, P. and Scanlan, G. (2003), 'Fraud and the Law Commission: the future of dishonesty', *Journal of Financial Crime*, **10**(3) 199–208.

Kittrie, O. (2009), 'New sanctions for a new century: Treasury's innovative use of financial sanctions', *University of Pennsylvania Journal of International Law*, **30**, 789–822.

Kleiman, M. (1992), 'The right to financial privacy versus computerised law enforcement: a new fight in an old battle', *Northwestern University Law Review*, **86**, 1169–1228.

Klein, Laura (2008), *Bank Secrecy Act Anti-Money Laundering*, Nova Science, New York.

KPMG *Money Laundering: Review of the Reporting System* (KPMG: London, 2003).

KPMG *Global Anti-Money Laundering Survey 2007 – How banks are facing up to the challenge* (KPMG: London, 2008).

Kruse, A. (2005), 'Financial and economic sanctions – from a perspective of international law and human rights', *Journal of Financial Crime*, **12**(3), 217–220.

Labour Party *Labour Party manifesto – Britain forward not back* (Labour Party: London, 2005).

Lacey, K. and George, N. (2003), 'Crackdown on money laundering: a comparative analysis of the feasibility and effectiveness of domestic and multilateral policy reforms', *Northwestern Journal of International Law and Business*, Winter, **23**, 263–351.

Lafferty, I. (2007), 'Medical identity theft: the future of health care is now – lack of Federal law enforcement efforts means compliance professionals will have to lead the way', *Health Care Compliance*, **9**(1), 11–20.

Lambert, T. (2006), 'Overvalued equity and the case for an asymmetric insider trading regime', *Wake Forest Law Review*, **41**, 1045–1129.

Law Commission *Legislating the Criminal Code: Fraud and Deception – Law Commission Consultation Paper no. 155* (Law Commission: London, 1999).

Law Commission *Informal discussion paper: fraud and deception – further proposals from the criminal law team* (Law Commission: London, 2000).

Lee, I. (2002), 'Fairness and insider trading', *Columbia Business Law Review*, 119–192.

Lee, R. *Terrorist Financing: The US and International Response Report for Congress* (Congressional Research Service: Washington, DC, 2002).

Leigh, D. and Evans, R. (2010), 'Cost of new economic crime agency could prove prohibitive', available at http://www.guardian.co.uk/busi ness/2010/jun/02/economic-crime-agency-scheme-cost (accessed 12 July 2010).

Leong, A. (2006), 'Civil recovery and taxation regime: are these powers under the Proceeds of Crime Act 2002 working?', *Company Lawyer*, **27**(12), 362–368.

Leong, A. (2007a), 'Chasing dirty money: domestic and international measures against money laundering', *Journal of Money Laundering Control*, **10**(2), 140–156.

Leong, A. (2007b), 'The Assets Recovery Agency: future or no future?', *Company Lawyer*, **28**(12), 279–380.

Leong, A. (2008), 'Passing the buck!', *Journal of Money Laundering Control*, **11**(2), 101–102.

Leong, Angela (2009), 'Asset recovery under the Proceeds of Crime Act 2002: the UK experience', in S. Young (ed.), *Civil forfeiture of criminal property – legal measures for targeting the proceeds of crime*, Edward Elgar, Cheltenham, 187–227.

Leroux, M. (2007), 'Michael Bright gets maximum seven years from Independent Insurance', available at http://business.timesonline.co.uk/ tol/business/industry_sectors/banking_and_finance/article2733660.ece (accessed 1 December 2009).

Letsika, O. (2004), 'Creating a corruption-free zone through legislative instruments: some reflections on Lesotho', *Journal of Financial Crime*, **12**(2), 185–191.

Levi, M. (2002a), 'Money laundering and its regulation', *The Annals of the American Academy of Political and Social Science,* **582**(1), 181–194.

Levi, M. (2002b), 'Suite justice or sweet charity? Some explorations of shaming and incapacitating business fraudsters', *Punishment & Society*, **4**(2), 147–163.

Levi, M. (2003), 'The Roskill Fraud Commission revisited: an assessment', *Journal of Financial Crime*, **11**(1), 38–44.

Levi, M. (2010), 'Combating the financing of terrorism: a history and assessment of the control of threat finance', *British Journal of Criminology*, **50**(4), 650–669.

Levi, M. and Burrows, J. (2008), 'Measuring the impact of fraud in the UK: a conceptual and empirical journey', *British Journal of Criminology*, **48**(3), 293–318.

Levi, M. and Osofsky, L. *Investigating, seizing and confiscating the proceeds of crime* (Home Office: London, 1995).

Levi, M. and Reuter, P. (2006), 'Money laundering', *Crime & Justice*, **34**, 289–368.

Levi, M., Burrows, J., Fleming, M. and Hopkins, M. *The Nature, Extent and Economic Impact of Fraud in the UK* (ACPO: London, 2007).

Levitt, B. (2003), 'Sarbanes-Oxley insider trading prohibitions affect insiders outside the US', *International Company and Commercial Law Review*, **14**(9), 293–299.

Levitt, M. (2003), 'Stemming the flow of terrorist financing: practical and conceptual challenges', *The Fletcher Forum of World Affairs*, **27**(1), 59–70.

Linklater, L. (2001), 'The market abuse regime: setting standards in the twenty-first century', *Company Lawyer*, **22**(9), 267–272.

Linn, C. (2004), 'International asset forfeiture and the Constitution: the limits of forfeiture jurisdiction over foreign assets under 28 U.S.C. § 1355(b)(2)', *American Journal of Criminal Law*, **31**, 251–303.

Linn, C. (2005), 'How terrorists exploit gaps in US anti-money laundering laws to secrete plunder', *Journal of Money Laundering Control*, **8**(3), 200–214.

Liro, C. (2000), 'Prosecution of minor subcontractors under the Major Fraud Act of 1988', *Michigan Law Review*, **99**, 669–695.

Loke, A. (2006), 'From the fiduciary theory to information abuse: the changing fabric of insider trading law in the UK, Australia and Singapore', *The American Journal of Comparative Law*, **54**(1), 123–172.

Lomnicka, E. (1994), 'The New Insider Dealing Provisions: Criminal Justice Act 1993, Part V', *Journal of Business Law*, March, 173–188.

Low, L., Tillen, J., Abendschein, K. and Fisher-Owens, D. (2004), 'Country report: the US anti-money laundering system', in M. Peith and G. Aiolfi (eds), *A comparative guide to anti-money laundering: a critical analysis of systems in Singapore, Switzerland, the UK and the USA*, Edward Elgar, Cheltenham, 346–411.

Lowe, P. (2006), 'Counterfeiting: links to organised crime and terrorist funding', *Journal of Financial Crime*, **13**(2), 255–257.

Lunt, M. (2006), 'The extraterritorial effects of the Sarbanes-Oxley Act 2002', *Journal of Business Law*, May, 249–266.

Lusty, D. (2003), 'Taxing the untouchables who profit from organised crime', *Journal of Financial Crime*, **10**(3), 209–228.

Lyden, G. (2003), 'The International Money Laundering and Anti-terrorist Financing Act of 2001: Congress wears a blindfold while giving money laundering legislation a facelift', *Fordham Journal of Corporate & Financial Law*, **3**, 201–243.

Lyons, G. (1990), 'Taking money launderers to the cleaners: a problem solving analysis of current legislation', *Annual Review of Banking Law*, **9**, 635–675.

MacKay, S. (1992), 'Major fraud against the United States', *Army Lawyer*, September, 7–14.

MacMull, J. (2004), 'Removing the charitable veil: an examination of US policy to combat terrorist funding charities post 9/11', *New England Journal of International and Comparative Law,* **10**, 121–136.

Madia, M. (2005), 'The Bank Fraud Act: a risk of loss requirement?', *University of Chicago Law Review*, **72**, 1445–1471.

Mahendra, B. (2002), 'Fighting serious fraud', *New Law Journal*, **152**(7020), 289.

Maimbo, S. and Passas, N. (2004), 'The regulation and supervision of informal remittance systems', *Small Enterprise Development*, **15**(1), 53–61.

Malani, A. (1999), 'The scope of criminal forfeiture under RICO: the appropriate definition of "proceeds"', *University of Chicago Law Review*, **66**, 1289–1316.

Mann, M. and Barry, W. (2005), 'Developments in the internationalization of securities enforcement', *International Lawyer*, **39**, 667–696.

Manne, Henry (1966), *Insider Trading on the Stock Market*, Free Press, New York.

Marron, D. (2008), '"Alter reality": governing the risk of identity theft', *British Journal of Criminology*, **48**(1), 20–38.

Marshall, P. (2010), 'Does Shah v HSBC Private Bank Ltd make the anti-money laundering consent regime unworkable?', *Butterworths Journal of International Banking & Financial Law*, **25**(5), 287–290.

Martinson, R. (1974), 'What Works? Questions and answers about prison reform', *The Public Interest*, **35**, 22–54.

Maskaleris, S. (2007), 'Identity theft and frauds against senior citizens: "who's in your wallet?"', *Experience*, **18**, 14–32.

Masters, J. (2008), 'Fraud and money laundering: the evolving criminalisation of corporate non-compliance', *Journal of Money Laundering Control*, **11**(2), 103–122.

Maxeiner, J. (1977), 'Bane of American Forfeiture Law: Banished at Last?', *Cornell Law Review*, **62**(4), 768–802.

McCoy, K.A. and Summe, M. (1998), 'Insider trading regulation: a developing state's perspective', *Journal of Financial Crime*, **5**(4), 311–346.

McCulloch, J. and Pickering, S. (2005), 'Suppressing the financing of terrorism – proliferating state crime, eroding censure and extending neo-colonialism', *British Journal of Criminology*, **45**(4), 470–486.

McHugh, G. (2007), 'Terrorist Finance Tracking Program: illegality by the President or the press?', *Quinnipiac Law Review*, **26**, 213–256.

McKee, M. (2001), 'The proposed EU Market Abuse Directive', *Journal of International Financial Markets*, **3**(4), 137–142.

Meltzer, P. (1991), 'Keeping drug money from reaching the wash cycle: a guide to the Bank Secrecy Act', *The Banking Law Journal*, **108**(3), 230–255.

Melville-Brown, A. and Burgess, D. (2003), 'The right to be rehabilitated – can you ever escape your past?', *Entertainment Law Review*, **14**(4), 88–90.

Meyer, C. (1991), 'Zero tolerance for forfeiture: a call for reform of civil forfeiture law', *Notre Dame Journal of Law, Ethics and Public Policy*, **5**, 853–887.

Mistry, H. (2002), 'Battle of the regulators: is the US system of securities regulation better provided for than that which operates in the United Kingdom?', *Journal of International Financial Markets*, **4**(4), 137–142.

Mitchell, D. (2003), 'US Government agencies confirm that low-tax jurisdictions are not money laundering havens', *Journal of Financial Crime*, **11**(2), 127–133.

Mitsilegas, V. and Gimlore, B. (2007), 'The EU legislative framework against money laundering and terrorist finance: a critical analysis in light of evolving global standards', *International and Comparative Law Quarterly*, **56**(1), 119–140.

Mogin, P. (2002), 'Refining in the Mail Fraud Statute', *Champion*, **26**, 12–17.

Molz, T. (1997), 'The Mail Fraud Statute: an argument for repeal by implication', *University of Chicago Law Review*, **64**, 983–1007.

Moore, M. (1987), 'The moral worth of retribution', in A. von Hirsch and A. Ashworth (eds), *Principled sentencing: readings on theory and policy*, Hart Publishing, Oxford.

Moores, E. (2009), 'Reforming the Civil Asset Forfeiture Reform Act', *Arizona Law Review*, **51**, 777–803.

Morais, H. (2005), 'Fighting international crime and its financing: the importance of following a coherent global strategy based on the rule of law', *Villanova Law Review*, **50**, 583–644.

Morgan, M. (1997), 'Money laundering: the American law and its global influence', *NAFTA: Law & Business Review of the Americas*, **3**, 24–52.

Morris, P. (2004), 'The importance of being appropriate', *Journal of International Banking Law and Regulation*, **19**(7), 258–260.

Mumford, A. and Alldridge, P. (2002), 'Taxation as an adjunct to the criminal justice system: the new Assets Recovery Agency regime', *British Tax Review*, **6**, 458–469.

Murphy, S. (2000), 'US designation of foreign terrorist organisation', *American Journal of International Law*, **9**, 365–366.

Myers, J. (2003), 'Disrupting terrorist networks: the new US and international regime for halting terrorist finance', *Law and Policy in International Business*, **34**, 17–23.

National Audit Office *The Assets Recovery Agency – Report by the Comptroller and Auditor General* (National Audit Office: London, 2007).

National Fraud Authority (2008), 'UK toughens up on fraudsters with a new anti-fraud authority', available at http://www.attorneygeneral.gov.uk/NFSA/National%20Fraud%20Strategic%20Authority%20comes%20into%20being.pdf (accessed 6 August 2010).

National Fraud Authority (2009a), 'National Fraud Reporting Centre's "0300" line launches in the West Midlands', available at http://www.attorneygeneral.gov.uk/nfa/WhatAreWeSaying/NewsRelease/Documents/NFRC%20launch%2026%20Oct%202009.pdf (accessed 3 March 2010).

National Fraud Authority *The National Fraud Strategy – A new approach to combating fraud* (National Fraud Authority: London, 2009b).

National Fraud Authority *National Fraud Authority Annual Fraud Indicator* (National Fraud Authority: London, 2010).

Navias, M. (2002), 'Financial warfare as a response to international terrorism', *The Political Quarterly*, **73**(1), 57–79.

Naylor, J. (1990a), 'The use of criminal sanctions by UK and US authorities for insider trading: how can the two systems learn from each other? Part 1', *Company Lawyer*, **11**(3), 53–61.

Naylor, J. (1990b), 'The use of criminal sanctions by UK and US authorities for insider trading: how can the two systems learn from each other? Part 2', *Company Lawyer*, **11**(5), 83–91.

NEFA Foundation (n/d), 'US legal cases', available at http://www.nefafoundation.org/documents-legal-N_Z.html#ranjha (accessed 1 August 2010).

Nelen, H. (2004), 'Hit them where it hurts most? The proceeds of crime approach in the Netherlands', *Crime, Law & Social Change*, **41**(5), 517–534.

Nelson, S. (1994), 'The Supreme Court takes a weapon from the drug war arsenal: new defences to civil drug forfeiture', *Saint Mary's Law Journal*, **26**, 157–201.

Newkirk, T. (2001), 'Conflicts between public accountability and individual privacy in SEC enforcement actions', *Journal of Financial Crime*, **8**(4), 319–324.

Newkirk, T. and Robertson, M. (1998), 'Speech given at the 16th International Symposium on Economic Crime', Jesus College, Cambridge, 19 September 1998, available from http://www.sec.gov/news/speech/speecharchive/1998/spch221.htm (accessed 1 June 2010).

Nice-Petersen, N. (2005), 'Justice for the designated: the process that is due to alleged US financiers of terrorism', *Georgetown Law Journal*, **93**, 1389–1392.

Nicols, G. (2008), 'Repercussions and recourse for specially designated terrorist organisations acquitted of materially supporting terrorism', *Review of Litigation*, **28**, 263–293.

Nnona, G. (2001), 'International insider trading: reassessing the propriety and feasibility of the US regulatory approach', *North Carolina Journal of International Law and Commercial Regulation*, **27**, 185–253.

Northamptonshire Police (2009), 'Financial reporting order among the first in country', available at http://www.northants.police.uk/default.aspx?id=18341&db=old&datewant=yes (accessed 4 August 2010).

NuraKami, K. (1987), 'Mail and wire fraud', *American Criminal Law Review*, **24**, 623–637.

O'Connor, M. (1989), 'Toward a more efficient deterrence of insider trading: the repeal of section 16(b)', *Fordham Law Review*, **58**, 309–381.

O'Leary, R. (2010), 'Improving the terrorist finance sanctions process', *New York University Journal of International Law and Politics*, Winter, 549–590.

Office of Fair Trading *Prevention of fraud policy* (Office of Fair Trading: London, n/d).

Office of Fair Trading *Memorandum of understanding between the Office of Fair Trading and the Director of the Serious Fraud Office* (Office of Fair Trading: London, 2003).

Office of Fair Trading (2005), 'OFT and Nigerian financial crime squad join forces to combat spam fraud', available at http://www.oft.gov.uk/news-and-updates/press/2005/210-05 (accessed 2 August 2010).

Office of Fair Trading *Scamnesty 2010 campaign strategy* (Office of Fair Trading: London, 2009).

Office of Fair Trading *Anti-Money Laundering: Future supervisory approach consultation* (Office of Fair Trading: London, 2010).

Older, S. and Goldsamt, S. (2009), 'Does it pay to be a maverick when trading securities?', available at http://www.mondaq.com/article.asp?articleid=72360 (accessed 14 December 2009).

Ormerod, D. (2007), 'The Fraud Act 2006 – criminalising lying?', *Criminal Law Review*, March, 193–219.

Ormerod, David and Williams, David (2007), *Smith's Law of Theft*, Oxford University Press, Oxford.

Orr, K. (2006), 'Fencing in the frontier: a look into the limits of mail fraud', *Kentucky Law Journal*, **95**, 789–809.

Ortblad, V. (2008), 'Criminal prosecution in sheep's clothing: the punitive effects of OFAC freezing sanctions', *Journal of Criminal Law and Criminology*, **98**, 1439–1465.

Oxford Analytica Ltd (2004), 'Country report: anti-money laundering rules in the United Kingdom', in M. Pieith and G. Aiolfi (eds), *A comparative guide to anti-money laundering: a critical analysis of systems in Singapore, Switzerland, the UK and the USA*, Edward Elgar, Cheltenham, 265–345.

Painter, R. (1999–2000), 'Insider trading and the stock market thirty years later', *Case Western Reserve Law Review*, **50**, 305–311.

Passas, N. (2004), 'Law enforcement challenges in hawala-related investigations', *Journal of Financial Crime*, **12**(2), 112–119.

Pathak, R. (2004), 'The obstacles to regulating the hawala: a cultural norm or a terrorist hotbed?', *Fordham International Law Journal*, **27**, 2007–2061.

Pazicky, L. (2003), 'A new arrow in the quiver of federal securities fraud prosecutors: section 807 of the Sarbanes-Oxley Act of 2002', *Washington University Law Quarterly*, **81**, 801–828.

Pearson, T. (2008), 'When hedge funds betray a creditor committee's fiduciary role: new twists on insider trading in the international financial markets', *Review of Banking and Financial Law*, **28**, 165–220.

Peat, R., Mason, I. and Bazley, S. (2010), 'Market abuse in the debt markets – a new FSA case', *Company Lawyer*, **31**(2), 50.

Peddie, Jonathan (2008), 'Anti-terrorism legislation and market regulation', in W. Blair and R. Brent (eds), *Banks and financial crime – the international law of tainted money*, Oxford University Press, Oxford.

Petrou, P. (1984), 'Due process implications of shifting the burden of proof in forfeiture proceedings arising out of illegal drug transactions', *Duke Law Journal*, September, 822–843.

Ping, H. (2004), 'New trends in money laundering – from the real world to cyberspace', *Journal of Money Laundering Control*, **8**(1), 48–55.

Pitt, H. and Hardison, D. (1992), 'Games without frontiers: trends in the international response to insider trading', *Law and Contemporary Problems*, **55**, 199–229.

Png, Cheong-Ann (2008a), 'International legal sources I – the United Nations Conventions', in W. Blair and R. Brent (eds), *Banks and financial crime – the international law of tainted money*, Oxford University Press, Oxford, 41–59.

Png, Cheong-Ann (2008b), 'International legal sources IV – the European Union and the Council of Europe', in W. Blair and R. Brent (eds), *Banks and financial crime – the international law of tainted money*, Oxford University Press, Oxford, 87–100.

Podgor, E. (1998), 'Mail fraud: redefining the boundaries', *Saint Thomas Law Review*, **10**, 557–570.

Podgor, E. (1999), 'Criminal fraud', *American University Law Review*, **48**, 729–768.

Postal Services Inspectorate *2007 Annual Report of Investigations* (Postal Services Inspectorate: Washington, DC, 2008).

Prakash, S. (1999), 'Our dysfunctional insider trading regime', *Columbia Law Review*, **99**, 1491–1550.

Prentice, R. and Donelson, D. (2010), 'Insider trading as a signalling device', *American Business Law Journal*, **47**, 1–73.

PriceWaterhouseCoopers *2009 Global Economic Crime Survey* (PriceWaterhouseCoopers: London, 2009).

Proctor, L. (1997), 'The Barings collapse: a regulatory failure, or a failure of supervision?', *Brooklyn Journal of International Law*, **22**, 735–767.

Profits of Crime and their Recovery: the Report of a Committee chaired by Sir Derek Hodgson: 1984: Cambridge Studies in Criminology.

Provost, M. (2009), 'Money laundering', *American Criminal Law Review*, **46**, 837–861.

Pujas, C. (2003), 'The European Anti-Fraud Office (OLAF): a European policy to fight against economic and financial fraud?', *Journal of European Public Policy*, **10**(5), 778–797.

Quirke, B. (2007), 'Critical appraisal of the role of UCLAF', *Journal of Financial Crime*, **14**(4), 460–473.

Quirke, B. (2010), 'OLAF's role in the fight against EU fraud: do too many cooks spoil the broth?', *Crime, Law and Social Change*, **53**(1), 97–108.

Quirke, B. and Pyke, C. (2002), 'Policing European Union Expenditure: a critical appraisal of the transnational institutions', *Journal of Finance and Management in Public Services*, **2**(1), 21–32.

Radsan, J. (2009), 'An overt turn to covert action', *Saint Louis University Law Journal*, **53**, 485–552.

Rakoff, J. and Easton, J. (1996), 'How effective is US enforcement in deterring insider trading?', *Journal of Financial Crime*, **6**(3), 283–287.

Raphaeli, N. (2003), 'Financing of terrorism: sources, methods, and channels', *Terrorism and Political Violence*, **15**(4), 59–82.

Red Flags (n/d), 'Handling questionable assets', available at http://www.redflags.info/index.php?topic=illicitassets (accessed 6 June 2010).

Rees, Edward and Fisher, Richard, *Blackstone's guide to the Proceeds of Crime Act 2002*, Oxford University Press, Oxford.

Reynolds, J. and Papandrea, J. (2002), 'Export controls and economic sanctions', *Foreign Law Year in Review*, Fall, **36**, 1063–1079.

Rhodes, R. and Palastrand, S. (2004), 'A guide to money laundering legislation', *Journal of Money Laundering Control*, **8**(1), 9–18.

Richard, A. (2005), *Fighting terrorist financing: transatlantic cooperation and international institutions*, Washington, DC, Center for Transatlantic Relations.

Rider, B. (2001), 'Wrongdoers' Rights', *Company Lawyer*, **22**(3), 87.

Rider, B. (2003), 'Thinking outside the box', *Journal of Financial Crime*, **10**(2), 198.

Rider, B. (2008), 'Where angels fear!', *Company Lawyer*, **29**(9), 257–258.

Rider, B. (2009), 'A bold step?', *Company Lawyer*, **30**(1), 1–2.

Rider, B. (2010), 'An abominable fraud?', *Company Lawyer*, **31**(7), 197–198.

Robb, George (1992), *White-collar crime in modern England – Financial fraud and business morality 1845–1929*, Cambridge University Press, Cambridge.

Roberts, M. (2004), 'Big brother isn't just watching you, he's also wasting your tax payer dollars: an analysis of the anti-money laundering provisions of the USA Patriot Act', *Rutgers Law Review*, **56**(2), 573–602.

Robinson, Jeffrey (1995), *The Laundrymen*, Pocket Books, London.

Robinson, J. (2008), 'The federal Mail and Wire Fraud Statutes: correct standards for determining jurisdiction and venue', *Willamette Law Review*, **44**, 479–540.

Roth, J., Greenburg, D. and Wille, S. (2004), *Monograph on terrorist financing: staff report to the Commission*, Washington, DC, National Commission on Terrorist Attacks against the United States of America.

Rowlett, J. (1993), 'The chilling effect of the Financial Institutions Reform, Recovery, and Enforcement Act of 1989 and the Bank Fraud Prosecution Act of 1990: has Congress gone too far?', *American Journal of Criminal Law*, **20**, 239–262.

Royal Embassy of the Kingdom of Saudi Arabia, Press Release, 'Response to CFR Report', 17 October 2002.

Royal Embassy of the Kingdom of Saudi Arabia, Press Release, 'Saudi Arabia blasts CFR task force report', 15 June 2004.

Ruff, K. (2006), 'Scared to donate: an examination of the effects of designating Muslim charities as terrorist organisations on the First

Amendment rights of Muslim donors', *New York University Journal of Legislation and Public Policy*, **9**, 447–502.

Ruimschotel, D. (1994), 'The EC budget: ten percent fraud? A policy analysis approach', *Journal of Common Market Studies*, **32**(3), 320–342.

Rusch, J. (1988), 'Hue and cry in the counting-house: some observations on the Bank Secrecy Act', *Catholic University Law Review*, **37**, 465–488.

Ryder, N. (2007a), 'A false sense of security? An analysis of legislative approaches towards the prevention of terrorists finance in the United States and the United Kingdom', *Journal of Business Law*, November, 821–850.

Ryder, N. (2007b), 'Danger money', *New Law Journal*, **157**(7300) (Charities Appeals Supplement), 6, 8.

Ryder, N. (2008a), 'Hidden money', *New Law Journal*, **158**(7348) (Charities Appeal Supplement), 36–37.

Ryder, N. (2008b), 'The Financial Services Authority and money laundering: a game of cat and mouse', *Cambridge Law Journal*, **67**(3), 635–653.

Ryder, Nicholas and Chambers, C. (2010), 'The credit crunch and mortgage fraud – too little too late? A comparative analysis of the policies adopted in the United States of America and the United Kingdom', in S. Kis and I. Balogh (eds), *Housing, housing costs and mortgages: trends, impact and prediction*, Nova Science, New York, 1–22.

Sabalot, D. and Everett, R. (2004), *Financial Services and Markets Act 2000*, Butterworths New Law Guide LexisNexis.

Saksena, P. (2009), 'The Sarbanes-Oxley Act and occupational fraud: does the law effectively tackle the real problem?', *International Company and Commercial Law Review*, **20**(2), 37–43.

Saksena, P. and Fox, M. (2004), 'Accounting fraud and the Sarbanes-Oxley Act', *International Company and Commercial Law Review*, **15**(8), 244–251.

Saltzburg, D. (1992), 'Real property forfeitures as a weapon in the government's war on drugs: a failure to protect innocent ownerships', *Boston University Law Review*, **72**, 217–242.

Santolli, J. (2008), 'The terrorist finance tracking program: illuminating the shortcomings of the European Union's antiquated data privacy directive', *George Washington International Law Review*, **40**, 553–582.

Sarker, R. (1993), 'The Davie Report – Anodyne for the SFO', *Journal of Financial Crime*, **3**(1), 89–91.

Sarker, R. (1994), 'Guinness – pure genius', *Company Lawyer*, **15**(10), 310–312.

Sarker, R. (1996), 'Maxwell: fraud trial of the century', *Company Lawyer*, **17**(4), 116–117.

Sarker, R. (2006), 'Anti-money laundering requirements: too much pain for too little gain', *Company Lawyer*, **27**(8), 250–251.

Sarker, R. (2007), 'Fighting fraud – a missed opportunity?', *Company Lawyer*, **28**(8), 243–244.

Saunders, K. and Zucker, B. (1999), 'Counteracting identity fraud in the information age: the Identity Theft and Assumption Deterrence Act', *Cornell Journal of Law and Public Policy*, **8**, 661–675.

Saunders, N. and Watson, B. (2003), 'Confiscation orders under the New Proceeds of Crime Act', *New Law Journal*, **152**(7066), 183–185.

Scanlan, G. (2006), 'The enterprise of crime and terror – the implications for good business. Looking to the future – old and new threats', *Journal of Financial Crime*, **13**(2), 164–176.

Scanlan, G. (2008), 'Offences concerning directors and officers of a company: fraud and corruption in the United Kingdom – the present and the future', *Journal of Financial Crime*, **15**(1), 22–37.

Schecter, M. (1990), 'Fear and loathing and the forfeiture laws', *Cornell Law Review*, **75**, 1151–1183.

Schwartz, J. (1987), 'Liability for structured transactions under the Currency and Foreign Transactions Reporting Act: a prelude to the Money Laundering Control Act of 1986', *Annual Review of Banking Law*, **6**, 315–340.

Securities and Exchange Commission (n/d), 'The Investor's Advocate: How the SEC Protects Investors, Maintains Market Integrity, and Facilitates Capital Formation', available at http://www.sec.gov/about/whatwedo.shtml (accessed 2 July 2010).

Securities and Exchange Commission (1988), 'SEC News Digest', available at http://www.404.gov/news/digest/1988/dig090288.pdf (accessed 2 September 2009).

Securities and Exchange Commission *International co-operation in securities law enforcement* (Securities and Exchange Commission: Washington, DC, 2004).

Securities and Exchange Commission (2006), 'Martha Stewart and Peter Bacanovic settle SEC's Insider Trading Charges', available at http://www.sec.gov/news/press/2006/2006-134.htm (accessed 10 September 2009).

Securities and Exchange Commission (2007), 'Litigation Release No. 20245', available at http://www.sec.gov/litigation/litreleases/2007/lr20245.htm (accessed 13 August 2009).

Securities and Exchange Commission *Investigation of Failure of the SEC to Uncover Bernard Madoff's Ponzi Scheme – Public Version* (Securities and Exchange Commission: Washington, DC, 2009).

Seldon, R. (2003), 'The executive protection: freezing the financial assets of alleged terrorists, the Constitution, and foreign participation in US financial markets', *Fordham Journal of Corporate & Financial Law*, **3**, 491–556.

Sentencing Commission *Guidelines Manual* (US Sentencing Commission: Washington, DC, 2008).

Sentencing Guidelines Council *Definitive Sentencing Guideline Revised 2007 – Reduction in Sentence for a Guilty Plea* (Sentencing Guidelines Secretariat: London, 2007).

Sergeant, C. (2002), 'Risk-based regulation in the Financial Services Authority', *Journal of Financial Regulation and Compliance*, **10**(4), 329–335.

Serious Fraud Office (n/d), '*What is fraud?*', available at http://www.sfo.gov.uk/fraud/what-is-fraud.aspx (accessed 22 April 2010).

Serious Fraud Office (2004), 'Fourth conviction in insider dealing conspiracy', available at http://www.sfo.gov.uk/news/prout/pr_269.asp?id=269 (accessed 1 December 2009).

Serious Fraud Office (2009), 'Independent insurance fraudsters ordered to pay over £1 million confiscation', available at http://www.sfo.gov.uk/press-room/latest-press-releases/press-releases-2009/independent-insurance-fraudsters-ordered-to-pay-over-%C2%A31-million-confiscation.aspx (accessed 5 August 2010).

Serious Fraud Office *Achievements 2009–2010* (Serious Fraud Office: London, 2010).

Serious Organized Crime Agency *Review of the Suspicious Activity Reports Regime* (Serious Organized Crime Agency: London, 2006).

Serious Organized Crime Agency (2008a), 'Merger of SOCA and ARA strengthens government drive to deprive criminals of their assets', available at www.soca.gov.uk (accessed 4 August 2010).

Serious Organized Crime Agency (2008b), 'Serious Organized Crime Agency secures first conviction under new power', available at www.soca.gov.uk (accessed 4 August 2010).

Serious Organized Crime Agency *The Suspicious Activity Reports Regime Annual Report 2008* (Serious Organized Crime Agency: London, 2009).

Serious Organized Crime Agency *The Suspicious Activity Reports Regime Annual Report 2009* (Serious Organized Crime Agency: London, 2010).

Shaffer, C. (2007), 'The impact of Medicaid reforms and false claims enforcement: limiting access by discouraging provider participation in Medicaid programs', *South Carolina Law Review*, **58**, 995–1023.

Shea, C. (2008), 'A need for swift change: the struggle between the European Union's desire for privacy in international financial transactions and the United States' need for security from terrorists as evidenced by the SWIFT scandal', *Journal of High Technology Law*, **8**(1), 143–168.

Shehu, A. (2005), 'International initiatives against corruption and money laundering: an overview', *Journal of Financial Crime*, **12**(3), 221–245.

Sheikh, S. (2008), 'FSMA market abuse regime: a review of the sunset clauses', *International Company and Commercial Law Review*, **19**(7), 234–236.

Shen, H. (2008), 'A comparative study of insider trading regulation enforcement in the US and China', *Journal of Business & Securities Law*, **9**, 41.

Shetterly, D. (2006), 'Starving the terrorists of funding: how the United States Treasury is fighting the war on terror', *Regent University Law Review*, **18**, 327–348.

Shrader, J. (2007), 'Secrets hurt: how SWIFT shook up Congress, the European Union and the US banking industry', *North Carolina Banking Institute*, **11**, 397–420.

Sidak, J. (2003), 'The failure of good intentions: the WorldCom fraud and the collapse of American telecommunications after deregulation', *Yale Journal on Regulation*, **20**, 207–261.

Simser, J. (2008), 'Money laundering and asset cloaking techniques', *Journal of Money Laundering Control*, **11**(1), 15–24.

Singh, Dalvinder (2007), *Banking regulation of the UK and US financial markets*, Ashgate, Aldershot.

Skiadas, D. (1998), 'EC: the role of the European Court of Auditors in the battle against fraud and corruption in the European Communities', *Journal of Financial Crime*, **6**(2), 178–185.

Smellie, A. (2004), 'Prosecutorial challenges in freezing and forfeiting proceeds of transnational crime and the use of international asset sharing to promote international cooperation', *Journal of Money Laundering Control*, **8**(2), 104–114.

Smith, J. and Cooper, G. (2009), 'Disrupting terrorist financing with civil litigation', *Western Reserve Journal of International Law*, **41**, 65–84.

Society for Advanced Legal Studies (2003), 'Forfeiture of terrorist property and tracing: sub-group 4: impact of the initiatives on other areas of the law', *Journal of Money Laundering Control*, **6**(3), 261–268.

Solomon, P. (1994), 'Are money launderers all washed up in the western hemisphere? The OAS model regulations', *Hastings International and Comparative Law Review*, Winter, **17**, 433–455.

Soto, J. (2004), 'Show me the money: the application of the asset forfeiture provisions of the Trafficking Victims Protection Act and suggestions for the future', *Penn State International Law Review*, **23**, 365–381.

Speta, J. (1990), 'Narrowing the scope of civil drug forfeiture: section 881, substantial connection and the Eighth Amendment', *Michigan Law Review*, **89**, 165–210.

Springer, J. (2001), 'Obtaining foreign assistance to prosecute money laundering cases: a US perspective', *Journal of Financial Crime*, **9**(2), 153–164.

Sproat, P. (2007), 'The new policing of assets and the new assets of policing: a tentative financial cost–benefit analysis of the UK's anti-money laundering and asset recovery regime', *Journal of Money Laundering Control*, **10**(3), 277–299.

Sproat, P. (2009), 'To what extent is the UK's anti-money laundering and asset recovery regime used against organised crime?', *Journal of Money Laundering Control*, **12**(2), 134–150.

Stahl, M. (2009), 'Asset forfeiture, burdens of proof and the war on drugs', *Journal of Criminal Law and Criminology*, **83**, 274–337.

Stallworthy, M. (1993), 'The United Kingdom's New Regime for the Control of Insider Dealing', *International Company and Commercial Law Review*, **4**(12), 448–453.

Stanton, K. (2010), 'Money laundering: a limited remedy for clients', *Professional Negligence*, **26**(1), 56–59.

State Department *Country Reports on Terrorism 2008* (United States State Department: Washington, DC, 2009).

Steele, F. (2009), 'Perot employee charged with insider dealing', available at http://business.timesonline.co.uk/tol/business/law/article6847523.ece (accessed 11 November 2009).

Stessens, Guy (2000), *Money laundering: a new international law enforcement model*, Cambridge University Press, Cambridge.

Stevens, P. and Bogle, T. (2002), 'Patriotic acts: financial institutions, money laundering and the war against terrorism', *Annual Review of Banking Law*, **21**, 261–290.

Stewart, D. (1989), 'Internationalizing the war on drugs: the UN Convention Against Illicit Traffic in Narcotic Drugs and Psychotropic Substances', *Denver Journal of International Law and Policy*, **18**(3), 387–404.

Strader, J. (1999), 'The judicial politics of white collar crime', *Hastings Law Journal*, **50**, 1199–1273.

Stuart, C. (2009), 'Mail and wire fraud', *American Criminal Law Review*, **46**, 813–835.

Sultzer, S. (1995), 'Money laundering: the scope of the problem and attempts to combat it', *Tennessee Law Review*, **63**, 143–237.

Sussman, R. (1991), 'Protecting clients from the government's thermonuclear war on bank fraud', *American Law Institute – American Bar Association Continuing Legal Education ALI-ABA Course of Study*, **646**, 213–260.

Sutherland, Edwin (1949), *White Collar Crime*, The Dryden Press, New York.

Swan, E. (2004), 'Market abuse: A new duty of fairness', *Company Lawyer*, **25**(3), 67–68.

Sykes, A. (1999), 'Market abuse: a civil revolution', *Journal of International Financial Markets*, **1**(2), 59–67.

Takats, E. *A theory of 'crying wolf': the economics of money laundering enforcement – IMF Working Paper* (International Monetary Fund: Washington, DC, 2007).

Tarlow, B. (1983), 'RICO revisited', *Georgia Law Review*, **17**, 291–424.

Tellechea, A. (2008), 'Economic crimes in the capital markets', *Journal of Financial Crime*, **15**(2), 214–222.

The 9/11 Commission *The 9/11 Commission Report – Final Report of the National Commission on Terrorist Attacks upon the United States* (Norton & Company: London, 2004).

The Guardian (2006a), 'Solicitor's saga highlights problems facing cash recovery unit: unrealistic figure targets for agency accused of sweeping aside civil liberties', available at http://www.guardian.co.uk/uk/2006/sep/29/ukcrime.davidleigh (accessed 4 August 2010).

The Guardian (2006b), 'Turkish drug gang leader jailed for 22 years', available at http://www.guardian.co.uk/uk/2006/may/16/drugsandalcohol.drugstrade (accessed 4 August 2010).

The Guardian (2007), 'Crime boss Adams faces ruin after trial', available at http://www.guardian.co.uk/uk/2007/may/19/ukcrime.sandralaville (accessed 4 August 2010).

The Telegraph (2008), 'Naming and shaming criminal masterminds "infringes their human rights"', available at http://www.telegraph.co.uk/news/uknews/law-and-order/3439645/Naming-and-shaming-criminal-masterminds-infringes-their-human-rights.html (accessed 12 November 2008).

Thomas, C. (2003), 'Disciplining globalization: international law, illegal trade, and the case of narcotics', *Michigan Journal of International Law*, **24**, 549–574.

Thomas, J. and Roppolo, W. (2010) 'United States of America', in M. Simpson, N. Smith and A. Srivastava (eds), *International guide to money laundering law and practice*, Bloomsbury Professional, Haywards Heath, 1095–1138.

Times Online (2004), 'Martha Stewart faces jurors at insider dealing trial', available at http://www.timesonline.co.uk/tol/news/article999303.ece (accessed 14 August 2009).

Times Online (2010), 'Conservatives confirm plans for single Economic Crime Agency', available at http://timesonline.typepad.com/law/2010/04/conservatives-confirm-plans-for-single-economic-crime-agency.html (accessed 26 April 2010).

Trehan, J. (2002), 'Underground and parallel banking systems', *Journal of Financial Crime*, **10**(1), 76–84.

Tsingou, E. *Global governance and transnational financial crime opportunities and tensions in the global anti-money laundering regime* (CSGR Working Paper No. 161/05, 2005).

Tupman, B. (2000), 'The sovereignty of fraud and the fraud of sovereignty: OLAF and the wise men', *Journal of Financial Crime*, **8**(1), 32–46.

Tupman, W. (1998), 'Where has all the money gone? The IRA as a profit-making concern', *Journal of Money Laundering Control*, **1**(4), 303–311.

Tupman, W. (2009), 'Ten myths about terrorist financing', *Journal of Money Laundering Control*, **12**(2), 189–205.

Unger, Brigitte (2007), *The scale and impacts of money laundering*, Edward Elgar, Cheltenham.

United Nations Development Programme (n/d), 'Programme and Operations Policies and Procedures', available at http://content.undp.org/go/userguide/cap/procurement/fraud-corrupt-practices/?lang=en (accessed 4 August 2010).

United Nations Development Programme *Fraud policy statement* (United Nations Development Programme: New York, 2007).

United Nations Office for Project Services *UNOPS policy to address fraud* (United Nations Office for Project Services: New York, 2008).

United States Secret Service *Fiscal year 2008 – Annual Report* (United States Secret Service: Washington, DC, 2009).

Urbelis, A. (2005), 'Towards a more equitable prosecution of cybercrime: concerning hackers, criminals and the national security', *Vermont Law Review*, **29**, 975–1008.

Vaithilingam, S. and Nair, M. (2007), 'Factors affecting money laundering: lesson for developing countries', *Journal of Money Laundering Control*, **10**(3), 352–366.

Van Cleef, C., Silets, H. and Motz, P. (2004), 'Does the punishment fit the crime', *Journal of Financial Crime*, **12**(1), 56–65.

Verbruggen, F. (1997), 'Proceeds-orientated criminal justice in Belgium: backbone or wishbone of a modern approach to organised crime?', *European Journal of Crime, Criminal Law and Criminal Justice*, **5**(3), 314–341.

Villa, J. (1988), 'A Critical View of Bank Secrecy Act Enforcement and the Money Laundering Statutes', *Catholic University Law Review*, **37**, Winter, 489–509.

Vlogaret, Johan and Pesta, Michal (2008), 'OLAF fighting fraud and beyond', in S. Brown (ed.), *Combating international crime – the longer arm of the law*, Routledge, London, 77–87.

von Hirsch, A. (1987), 'Rehabilitation', in A. von Hirsch and A. Ashworth (eds), *Principled sentencing: readings on theory and policy*, Hart Publishing, Oxford.

Wachman, R. (2010), 'Suspicious share trading before takeover news at five-year high', available at http://www.guardian.co.uk/business/2010/jun/10/fsa-takeover-suspicious-trading (accessed 30 June 2010).

Wadsley, J. (2008), 'Painful perceptions and fundamental rights – anti-money laundering regulation and lawyers', *Company Lawyer*, **29**(3), 65–75.

Waszak, D. (2004), 'The obstacles to suppressing radical Islamic terrorist financing', *Case Western Reserve Journal of International Law*, **35**, 673–710.

Weaver, S. (2005), 'Modern day money laundering: does the solution exist in an expansive system of monitoring and record keeping regulations?', *Annual Review of Banking and Financial Law*, **24**, 443–465.

Webb, P. (2005), 'The United Nations Convention Against Corruption – global achievement or missed opportunity?', *Journal of International Economic Law*, **8**(1), 191–229.

Weintraub, L. (1987), 'Crime of the century: use of the Mail Fraud Statute against authors', *Boston University Law Review*, **67**, 507–549.

Weisburd, David (2001), *White Collar Crime & Criminal Careers*, Cambridge University Press, Port Chester, NY, USA.

Weiss, A. (2010), 'From the Bonannos to the Bin Ladens: the Reves operation or management test and the viability of civil RICO suits against financial supporters of terrorism', *Columbia Law Review*, May, 1123–1117.

Weiss, M. (2004), *Terrorist Finance: Current efforts and policy issues for Congress: Report for Congress*, Washington, DC, Congressional Research Service.

Weller, P. and Roth von Szepesbela, K. (2004), 'Silence is golden – or is it? FINTRAC and the suspicious transaction reporting requirements for lawyers', *Asper Review of International Business and Trade Law*, **4**, 85–130.

Welling, S. (1989), 'Smurfs, money laundering, and the federal criminal law: the crime of structuring transactions', *Florida Law Review*, **41**, 287–339.

White, S. (1999), 'Investigating EC Fraud: the metamorphosis of UCLAF', *Journal of Financial Crime*, **6**(3), 255–260.

White, S. (2010), 'EU anti-fraud enforcement: overcoming obstacles', *Journal of Financial Crime*, **17**(1), 81–99.

White House (2001a), 'The President's Leadership in Combating Corporate Fraud', available at http://georgebush_whitehouse.archives.gov/infocus/corporateresponsibility/ (accessed 10 September 2010).

White House *Fact sheet on terrorist financing executive order* (White House: Washington, DC, 2001b).

White House (2001c), 'President freezes terrorists' assets', Remarks by the President, Secretary of the Treasury O'Neill and Secretary of State Powell on Executive Order, Office of the Press Secretary, 24 September 2001, available at http://www.fas.org/terrorism/at/docs/2001/Bush-9-24-01.htm (accessed 11 October 2009).

White House *Progress Report on the Global War on Terrorism* (The White House: Washington, DC, 2003).

White House (2010), 'Statement by the President on the U.S.–European Union Agreement on the Terrorist Finance Tracking Program', 8 July 2010, available at http://www.whitehouse.gov/the-press-office/statement-president-us-european-union-agreement-terrorist-finance-tracking-prog ram (accessed 14 July 2010).

Whitehouse, K. (2009), 'Full Court Press – SEC Appeals Cuban Insider Trading Decision', available at http://www.allbusiness.com/legal/trial-procedure-appeals/13164328-1.html (accessed 10 November 2010).

Wilson, C. and Rattray, K. (2007), 'The Caribbean Financial Action Task Force', *Journal of Financial Crime*, **14**(3), 227–249.

Winn, J. and Govern, K. (2009), 'Identity theft: risks and challenges to business of data compromise', *Temple Journal of Science, Technology & Environmental Law*, **28**, 49–63.

Wolf, P. (1995), 'International securities fraud: extraterritorial subject matter jurisdiction', *New York International Law Review*, **8**, 1–22.

Wray, C. and Hur, R. (2006), 'Corporate criminal prosecution in a post-Enron world: the Thompson Memo in theory and practice', *American Criminal Law Review*, **43**, 1095–1188.

Wright, R. (2003), 'Fraud after Roskill: a view from the Serious Fraud Office', *Journal of Financial Crime*, **11**(1), 10–16.

Wright, R. (2006), 'Why (some) fraud prosecutions fail', *Journal of Financial Crime*, **13**(2), 177–182.

Wright, R. (2007), 'Developing effective tools to manage the risk of damage caused by economically motivated crime fraud', *Journal of Financial Crime*, **14**(1), 17–27.

Xanthaki, H. (2010), 'What is EU fraud? And can OLAF really combat it?', *Journal of Financial Crime*, **17**(1), 133–151.

Xiang, G. and Buckley, R. (2003), 'Comparative analysis of the standard of fraud required under the fraud rule in letter of credit law', *Duke Journal of Comparative and International Law*, **13**, 293–336.

Yeandle, M., Mainelli, M., Berendt, A. and Healy, B. *Anti-money laundering requirements: costs, benefits and perceptions* (Corporation of London: London, 2005).

Young, Simon (2009a), 'Civil forfeiture for Hong Kong: issues and prospects', in S. Young (ed.), *Civil forfeiture of criminal property – legal measures for targeting the proceeds of crime*, Edward Elgar, Cheltenham, 278–320.

Young, Simon (2009b), 'Introduction', in S. Young (ed.), *Civil forfeiture of criminal property – legal measures for targeting the proceeds of crime*, Edward Elgar, Cheltenham, 1–10.

Zagaris, B. (1989), 'Developments in international judicial assistance and related matters', *Denver Journal of International Law and Policy*, **18**(3), 339–386.

Zagaris, B. (2004), 'International money laundering: from Latin America to Asia, who pays? The merging of anti-money laundering and counter-terrorism financial regimes after September 11, 2001', *Berkeley Journal of International Law*, **22**, 123–157.

Zagaris, B. (2005), 'Brave new world: US responses to the rise in international crime', *Villanova Law Review*, **50**, 509–582.

Zagaris, Bruce (2010), *International white collar crime – cases and materials*, Cambridge University Press, New York.

Zagaris, B. and Castilla, S. (1993), 'Constructing an international financial enforcement sub regime: the implementation of anti-money laundering policy', *Brooklyn Journal of International Law*, **18**, 871–965.

Zaring, D. and Baylis, E. (2007), 'Sending the bureaucracy to war', *Iowa Law Review*, **92**, 1359–1428.

Zekos, G. (1999), 'Insider trading under the EU, USA and English laws: a well recognised necessity or a distraction?', *Managerial Law*, **41**(5), 1–35.

Ziegler, K. (2009), 'Strengthening the rule of law, but fragmenting international law: the Kadi decision of the ECJ from the perspective of human rights', *Human Rights Law Review*, **9**(2), 288–305.

Index